PROMISED LAND, CRUSADER STATE

BOOKS BY WALTER A. McDOUGALL

France's Rhineland Diplomacy:
The Last Bid for a Balance of Power in Europe

The Grenada Papers

. . . the Heavens and the Earth:
A Political History of the Space Age

Let the Sea Make a Noise . . . A History of
the North Pacific from Magellan to MacArthur

Promised Land, Crusader State:
The American Encounter with the World
Since 1776

The American
Encounter
with the World
Since 1776

A MARINER BOOK

HOUGHTON MIFFLIN COMPANY

BOSTON   NEW YORK

PROMISED LAND, CRUSADER STATE

Walter A. McDougall

For information about permission to reproduce selections from
this book, write to Permissions, Houghton Mifflin Harcourt
Publishing Company, 215 Park Avenue South, New York,
New York 10003.
www.hmhco.com
Library of Congress Cataloging-in-Publication Data
McDougall, Walter A.
    Promised land, crusader state : the American encounter
with the world since 1776 / Walter A. McDougall.
    p.   cm.
    Includes bibliographical references and index.
    ISBN 0-395-83085-0   ISBN 0-395-90132-4 (pbk.)
    1. United States — Foreign relations. I. Title.
E183.7.M4715   1997
327.73 — dc20   96-35467   CIP

Printed in the United States of America

DOH 20 19 18
4500565829
The author is grateful for permission to reproduce lines from
"Political Science" by Randy Newman. Copyright © 1969
Unichappell Music, Inc. (BMI). All rights reserved. Used by
permission. Warner Bros. Publications U.S. Inc., Miami, FL 33014.

For
Angela Robin
and
Christopher Walter

Contents

Preface

THE SEED THAT GREW into this book was planted in 1988 when I accepted the chair in International Relations at the University of Pennsylvania. My new colleagues in the history department asked at once if I would be willing to teach a course in U.S. diplomatic history, since Bruce Kuklick, whose subject it was, would be on leave that year. I agreed, and so spent my first semester at Penn toiling like a rookie assistant professor to draft and deliver three hours of new lectures per week. Early on, I had an inspiration as to how to structure the two-hundred-year-long story I had to tell. It occurred to me that over that span Americans have developed eight discrete traditions in their attitudes and policies toward the outer world. It also struck me that none of the traditions has ever really died: to this day, all command a certain amount of loyalty among a portion of the American people, while several of them coexist uneasily within individual breasts. What is more, it seemed to me that that explained, better than the old dichotomies between idealism and realism or isolationism and internationalism, the reversals and apparent confusion in U.S. diplomacy over the decades.

Two people — one my own father and the other Alan Luxenberg of the Foreign Policy Research Institute — read my lectures and urged me to work them into a book. I resisted so long as I was busy composing my history of the North Pacific Ocean, but I finally said yes, for three reasons. First, as editor of *Orbis: A Journal of World Affairs* I had followed with increasing vexation our sterile debate over what principles or doctrines ought to define U.S. foreign policy in the post–Cold War era. Perhaps a historical perspective, I thought, was needed to enrich that debate. Second, I was annoyed by the flip way that pundits and politicians tossed around terms like isolationism and Wilsonianism, often employing them as little more than dirty words. Perhaps a book that explained the real traditions of U.S. foreign policy, when and why they arose, what they meant, and how they changed over time, might help to purge some clichés from our national dialogue. Third, I thought this book would be easy to write. It was just a matter, so I fancied, of spinning out those old lecture notes and tacking on a conclusion with contemporary relevance.

What a blunder. For as soon as I scanned those lecture notes, I realized that I had written them in haste and relied on what amounted to textbook accounts of whole swaths of history. The texts I used — especially Thomas G. Paterson's and Walter LaFeber's — were excellent. But the fact remained that if I wanted this book to be credible, I would have to review the monographic literature on all the issues and periods I had never before had occasion to research myself. In the course of that reading I came to the conclusion that my own interpretation of U.S. diplomatic history was in need of radical amendment. So I put those lectures back on the shelf and have not consulted them since.

The result is a book far different in tone and argument from the one I expected to write. At times the historians I have read convinced me that I have gotten something very wrong all these years. At times I decided that the historians have gotten it wrong. At other times I affirmed what amounts to a consensus within the profession, but one that we historians have so far failed to impress on the mind of the public. At all times I found myself pleased that the book turned out to be difficult after all, since it has taught me so much. That is the joy of the generalist and empiricist who dives into a subject, not to mold it to some preconceived theory, but to be molded by it . . . and be reminded again why one fell in love with history in the first place.

For all these reasons, I readily assign Alan Luxenberg and Dugald S. McDougall the credit for goading me into doing this book. I thank Dean Rosemary Stevens and the School of Arts and Sciences of the University of Pennsylvania for granting me a sabbatical in the fall of 1995. I thank the Foreign Policy Research Institute for its encouragement and support, especially Harvey Sicherman, from whom I learned much and with whom I laughed often, and Senior Fellows Ross Munro, Alvin Z. Rubinstein, and Adam Garfinkle. I also thank Roger Donway and Shaynee Snider of *Orbis,* and Frank Plantan and Donna Shuler of Penn's International Relations program, without whose help I would have had much less time to devote to this book.

Richard Beeman, Bruce Kuklick, Marc Trachtenberg, and John Lukacs read large portions of the manuscript and made valuable suggestions. I hasten to add, however, that whatever errors of fact or interpretation remain are mine, not theirs. Tom Childers, a dear friend, Gerry McCauley, a new friend, and my faithful editor Steve Fraser helped me to place the manuscript. Houghton Mifflin's expert staff, especially Assistant Editor Lenora Todaro, Senior Manuscript Editor Larry Cooper, and indexer Ruth Cross — all great professionals — saw the book into print. Finally, I thank my wife, Jonna, and my children for leaving Daddy alone so that he could finish this book. I pray it will be of some good, or at the least do no harm, to the country they will inherit.

WALTER A. MCDOUGALL
Philadelphia

PROMISED
LAND,
CRUSADER
STATE

INTRODUCTION
The American Bible of Foreign Affairs

CLICHÉ THOUGH IT BE, director Sergio Leone's spaghetti western *The Good, the Bad, and the Ugly* is still a better Vietnam-era film than any films really about the Vietnam War. It takes place in the midst of the brief New Mexico campaign during the American Civil War. A Union army payroll has been stolen and buried in a cemetery. Three men come to learn of its existence and race one another to the loot, but with the twist that each is dependent on the other two for clues to its exact location. The first, Clint Eastwood, is a bounty hunter in cahoots with the outlaws he nabs (and then rescues from the noose so he can "capture" them again for another reward). But he takes no life except in defense of himself and those whom he chooses to protect. He also wants to get rich, which by no means disqualifies him from representing the Good. The Bad, played by Lee Van Cleef, is a sadistic U.S. Army sergeant who exploits his rank to torture, murder, and rob. Greed has devoured his conscience, and he is all the worse for being a putative agent of civilization. Eli Wallach, the third desperado, is a Mexamerican *bandito,* and thus represents a racial minority (his nickname for Eastwood is "Blondy"). He is also symbolic of man in the natural state: simple, cunning, and predictable in his short-term calculations of self-interest. He defends his banditry before his brother, a priest, by saying that their careers were the only two available paths out of poverty, and that their choices were just a matter of guts. Wallach is not evil, just Ugly.

The film ends in a triangular Mexican standoff in the cemetery, each man eyeing the others and wondering whom to shoot first. But in metaphorical terms all three are us, which is only to say that Americans are at once typically flawed human beings, unique individualists obsessed with both justice *and* money, and citizens of the most powerful, hence potentially the most corruptible, country on earth. That observation may be less than profound, but it is the beginning of wisdom about American behavior in the state of nature called world politics. At times in our history U.S. foreign policy has been wise and decent beyond hope — but America is hardly the City on a Hill dreamt of by its Puritan founders. At times American behavior has been foolish or brutal — but America is hardly a great Satan, as Islamic fundamentalists would have it. Much of the time we have simply been human, pursuing our short-term self-interest more or less skillfully, and the rest of the world be damned.

That we need to be reminded of this common sense is evident in the recent debates over what principles ought to guide American strategy in the post–Cold War world. Of course, no one suggests that our foreign policy ought to be "bad" in the sense of exploiting our military dominance to plunder or bully other nations. Yet according to radical revisionist historians, that is precisely what the United States has done over and over again. They say that we practiced "ethnic cleansing" and "genocide" on the Indians and stole a fourth of our land mass in a predatory war against Mexico.[1] We seized overseas colonies in an imperialist jag, then killed 100,000 Filipinos when they failed to appreciate our tutelage. They say that our selfish isolationism enabled Hitler to run amok and stage the Holocaust, while our anti-Japanese racism helped to provoke Pearl Harbor. Our use of atomic bombs to end that war, as we heard *ad nauseam* in 1995, was indefensible; our economic imperialism provoked the Cold War; and our militarism caused the nuclear arms race and the Vietnam War.

If one adheres to this view of America the Bad, then there is nothing in our past (save a tradition of dissent) to guide U.S. foreign policy into the twenty-first century. Rather, the proper posture for America's dominant class (and race and gender) is penitence, and its proper policy either neo-isolationism (since everything the United States touches turns to dross) or contrite reparation.

All this contrasts with the older, self-congratulatory version of America the Good. It always held that the United States, despite occasional funks and lapses, has struggled to acquit itself abroad in a more high-minded fashion than the imperial monarchies of the nineteenth century or the dictatorships of the twentieth. From Washington's Farewell Address and the Monroe Doctrine to the Open Door policy and Woodrow Wilson's Fourteen Points, from Franklin Roosevelt's Atlantic Charter to the United Nations, Marshall Plan, and ultimate collapse of the Soviet Union, the United States weighed in on the side of human dignity, progress, and liberty. In Abraham Lincoln's phrase, America is the world's last best hope.

To those who affirm this liberal American mission, our post–Cold War task is one of redefining the world around us, not our own diplomatic traditions. We must continue to stand for Wilsonian ideals, prepare to defend them with force *in extremis,* and shoulder the leadership role that uniquely belongs to the United States. That requires, of course, that we discern the major trends, threats, and opportunities likely to pop up in the new world order, but having done so, we need only adapt our principles to them.

Finally, there are those intrepid few who do not shrink from the moniker "realist." To them the history of foreign policy ought not to be discussed in moral terms at all, because every responsible government conducts its affairs according to balance of power and *raison d'état.* Some even suggest that American moralism has been a pose, since U.S. neutrality in the nineteenth century and global involvements in the twentieth can both be explained on the basis of geopolitical calculation and enlightened self-interest, however much Americans like to convince themselves of their righteousness before they drub the next enemy.

Depending on which image we choose, devising a new strategy today will require us to rethink either the fundamental meaning of America or the fundamental nature of contemporary international relations. But if we adopt the "Sergio Leone position," to the effect that the United States has always been good, bad, *and* ugly — idealistic, hypocritical, and just realistic, often at the same time — then we are obliged to rethink traditional America *and* the contemporary world *and* the relationship between the two. Maybe that is why no new George Kennan has yet appeared to give us a post–Cold War doctrine that the American people can agree on. The prophetic assignment today is more difficult, if less urgent and risky, than it was in the late 1940s. But it can be simply defined: it is to decide which American traditions we ought to reaffirm and apply to diplomacy today, and which traditions we would do well to discard as irrelevant or even repugnant. For that is what prophecy does: measure the present against past revelation and so augur possible futures.

*

We must begin by recognizing that the end of the Cold War did *not* hurl us into a state of confusion over our role in world politics. It merely revealed anew the confusion Americans have usually displayed about foreign policy except when "clear and present danger" loomed. The symptoms of our present puzzlement are obvious: the hesitancy and lack of self-confidence over issues as disparate as Bosnia, NATO expansion, free trade, human rights, and the United Nations; the metamorphosis of Cold War doves into advocates for military intervention and of former hawks into doves; the inability of liberals and conservatives to decide, even among themselves, whether our alliances and commercial ties ought to be expanded, revised, or junked. But none of these symptoms is novel, nor are today's bedfellows so strange when we recall the weird coalitions that formed to support or oppose U.S. colonial acquisitions in 1898, the Treaty of Versailles in 1919, isolationism in the 1930s, the Truman Doctrine in 1947, even the Vietnam War.

What is more, confusion and discord have been the norm in American foreign relations not because we lack principles to guide us, but because we have canonized so many diplomatic principles since 1776 that we are pulled every which way at once. And the reason for that is that Americans have from their inception been a profoundly religious people. I do not mean that all Americans have a personal faith, much less the same one. We are like the Athenians, whom the apostle Paul said must be very religious since they had temples to so many gods! And that is precisely the point. The nation or empire with only one faith, especially if its church is established, can afford to practice power politics because whatever serves the state serves its faith, and in any case dissent is repressed. A democracy of many religious and secular faiths, by contrast, is constantly at war with itself over matters of right and wrong, prudence and folly. In domestic policy its battleground is the law; in foreign policy it is the hallowed traditions — the holy writ — that ought to guide its diplomacy.

We Americans have such a bible of foreign affairs, canonized over the course of two centuries and divided into two testaments, each with four books. Our Old Testament dominated the rhetoric and, for the most part, the practice of U.S. diplomacy from 1776 to the 1890s, and preached the doctrines of Liberty at home, Unilateralism abroad, an American System of states, and Expansion. These first four traditions were all about Being and Becoming, and were designed by the Founding Fathers to deny the outside world the chance to shape America's future. Our New Testament in foreign affairs has likewise dominated the rhetoric and, for the most part, the practice of U.S.

diplomacy in the twentieth century, and preached the doctrines of Progressive Imperialism, Wilsonianism, Containment, and Global Meliorism, or the belief that America has a responsibility to nurture democracy and economic growth around the world. These last four traditions are all about Doing and Relating, and were designed to give America the chance to shape the outside world's future.

The Old Testament traditions were coherent, mutually supportive, and reflective of our original image of America as a Promised Land, a New Israel, set apart for liberty under God. But the New Testament, however much it derived from the Old, brought discord and danger as well as great promise. For its traditions were far less coherent, clashed with each other and with the received Old Testament wisdom, and reflected an image of America not only as a Promised Land, but as a Crusader State called to save the world. The fact that even today all eight traditions still command loyalty from at least a portion of the American people helps to explain why — except in times of immediate danger — we find it so hard to agree as a people on how to behave beyond our own borders. For in terms of our biblical metaphor, we have been trying for almost a century now to be good "Jews" and good "Christians" — indeed several denominations of Christian — all at once! Does our blessed heritage as a land of liberty require us to crusade abroad on behalf of others, as our New Testament in foreign policy commands? Or does giving in to the temptation to impose our will abroad, however virtuous our intent, violate the Old Testament principles that made America great in the first place? In short, can the United States be a Crusader State and still remain a Promised Land? That question hangs over our third century.

*

The one that hung over our first century was whether the newborn United States would survive at all in a dangerous world. Indeed, the United States was conceived as a creature of foreign relations. If you doubt that assertion, consider, first, that the representatives of the thirteen colonies, in Congress assembled in 1776, decided at length to declare independence from Great Britain — a risky act of treason — because that alone could persuade France to supply the arms, and in time the alliance, needed to resist the British. Second, the U.S.A. did not exist as a legal entity until the European powers recognized its independence in the treaties that comprised the Peace of Paris — hence September 3, 1783, not July 4, 1776, is our real national birthday.

Third, the authors of the Constitution were motivated to design a "more perfect union," in large part, by the inadequacies of the Articles of Confederation in matters of defense and foreign policy. "We the People" defined ourselves from the start, over against the British, French, Spaniards, Indians, Barbary pirates, and any other "damned furriners" whose insolent plots and depredations threatened what Alexander Hamilton, in *The Federalist* #1, called "an empire in many respects the most interesting in the world": the United States of America.[2]

The proof that Americans had achieved nationhood was also found in their activity on the world stage. "As a nation we have made peace and war," wrote John Jay in *The Federalist* #2, "as a nation we have vanquished our common enemies; as a nation we have formed alliances, and made treaties, and entered into various compacts and conventions with foreign states."[3] Indeed, the first 29 of the 85 *Federalist Papers* consist of an extended argument for ratification of the Constitution on foreign policy grounds. Only with #30 did the authors turn their attention to the next most pressing issue — yes, taxation — and then to other aspects of domestic governance.

Not just the birth but the growth of the United States across the continent was, by definition, a tale of how wise foreign policy made straight the way west for generations of native and immigrant farmers and merchants without provoking European hostility. We need only ask how American social, economic, and cultural history would have differed if our western boundary had remained at the Mississippi River or Rocky Mountains.

So whatever else Americans ought to do in order to know themselves through their history, they must examine with some degree of objectivity the principles, habits, and attitudes that their 220-year encounter with the world has bred in their bones. I say "with some degree" because complete objectivity about America is a characteristic only of God and Alexis de Tocqueville. And I speak of principles, habits, and attitudes in the plural because I do not believe that any one theory, not even Louis Hartz's "liberal tradition" or William Appleman Williams's "open door" thesis, can explain all the crosscurrents of American history.[4] After all, Arnold Toynbee may have been right when he quipped that "America is a large, friendly dog in a very small room — every time it wags its tail, it knocks over a chair." But no one would advance a "large, friendly dog" theory of U.S. diplomatic history.

Instead, historians invariably frame several categories in hopes of containing the mélange of words and deeds of our forebears. Thomas A. Bailey listed six "fundamental foreign policies," including isolation, freedom of the seas, the Monroe Doctrine, Pan-Americanism, the Open Door, and peaceful settlement of disputes.[5] Bradford Perkins thought material self-interest, republicanism, individualism, and popular sovereignty shaped our young nation's diplomacy.[6] To Robert Ferrell, its three basic principles were independence, free trade, and continental expansion.[7] To Cushing Strout, they were isolationism, republican expansion, and the setting of an example of freedom for others.[8] Paul Varg identified two competing frameworks, one economic and the other ideological, but observed that in practice neither impulse blinded the Founding Fathers to the need for "a hard headed pragmatic approach."[9] Felix Gilbert likewise traced the realist and idealist strains in U.S. diplomacy to the incentives that attracted colonists to America in the first place: the desire for economic betterment and the utopian dream of a better society.[10] Arthur Schlesinger, Jr., detected cycles in American history traced by the "warfare between realism and messianism, between experiment and destiny."[11] Henry Kissinger saw abiding dualities between isolationism and globalism, idealism and power politics, while Michael Kammen called us a "people of paradox" who (at least "at our best") pursue "a politics of 'utopian pragmatism.'"[12] Edward Weisbrand saw the U.S. foreign policy norms as self-determination, a feisty us-versus-them attitude toward the world, and a belief that war is justified only in self-defense.[13] Finally (but the list could go on), Michael Hunt thought that three "core ideas" shaped our foreign affairs: the quest for national greatness and liberty, belief in a strict racial hierarchy, and suspicion of revolutions in spite of our own revolutionary heritage.[14]

For an allegedly isolationist people, Americans seem to have a hearty appetite for foreign policy doctrines! As Eugene V. Rostow summed us up: "We embrace contradictory principles with equal fervor and cling to them with equal tenacity. Should our foreign policy be based on power or morality? Realism or idealism? Pragmatism or principle? Should its goal be the protection of interests or the promotion of values? Should we be nationalists or internationalists? Liberals or conservatives? We blithely answer, 'All of the above.'"[15]

Now imagine how troublesome this is for historians, not to mention their students and the intelligent public. Those who read one book about, say, Thomas Jefferson may conclude that they have gotten a feel for the statesman. But those who read two or three books can never be sure. Was Jefferson really agrarian-minded or in fact as commercial-minded as Hamilton? Was Woodrow Wilson idealistic or as realistic in his own way as Theodore Roosevelt? Were they committed to universal principles or in fact staunchly nationalist, even racist? A competent historian might build a persuasive case to the effect that they were all of the above. And that is what led me to think, inasmuch as Jefferson and Wilson were real human beings, that perhaps our dichotomies are misleading, and that none of the lists noted above, however insightful they are, can account for the sweep and subtlety of American foreign relations.

Moreover, our arguments about these abstractions (realism versus idealism, isolationism versus interventionism) seem at times to be more semantic than substantive, since they are conducted in language that is hard to pin down. When historians cite Captain A. T. Mahan's loaded confession — "I am an imperialist because I am not isolationist" — they can leave it to the reader to imagine what those terms mean, impose their own definitions, or try to explain what Mahan himself meant by those words. The last is the best historical method, but it does not do us much good if we want to grasp the ideas that moved the nation over a long stretch of time. Did "isolationism" mean the same thing in the 1890s that it meant in the 1930s, not to mention what it may mean today? That question is what led me to conclude that any attempt to categorize the traditions of U.S. foreign policy must allow for the fact that traditions are not just words: traditions live, and living things change.

Another semantic difficulty arises from the historian's need to depend on literary sources such as documents, speeches, and memoirs that are permeated with what used to be esteemed, but is now often dismissed, as rhetoric. Can we take Franklin D. Roosevelt's eloquent wartime speeches at face value, or was he hiding his real motives behind a Wilsonian smokescreen? Might such a gap between the true thinking of policy makers and the rhetoric they employ to rally the masses be a necessary feature of foreign policy in a democracy? Indeed, how else can both escalation *and* de-escalation of the Vietnam War, deployment *and* disavowal of the neutron bomb, "constructive engagement" *and* sanctions toward South Africa or China be confidently defended as "moral," sometimes within the span of a single presidential administration? They cannot be, except by a nation that is immensely powerful yet persistently afraid or ashamed of using that power; that celebrates self-reliance yet fosters big government, big technology, and big business; that by inward grace is the most religious Western nation, yet by outward signs appears decadent; that is more generous than any people in history yet obsessed with material wealth; that trumpets diversity yet imposes its values on others; that accepts global leadership yet seems often to wish that the rest of the world would just go away; that prides itself equally on its idealism and pragmatism, and *likes to believe they are identical.* And that is what led me to suspect that the tension we sense in our past and present politics is not one between idealism and realism at all, but between competing conceptions of what is both moral *and* realistic.

Finally, I asked myself what foreigners must make of all this apparent Yankee confusion. From the point of view of Europeans and Asians, Muslims, Africans, and Latin Americans, the United States seems at once too mighty to ignore, too magnanimous to mock, too arrogant to admire, too erratic to trust, and too befuddled to explain. At the same time, nothing so annoys the average American than snide, condescending criticism from overseas, be it from Charles de Gaulle, Helmut Schmidt, Shintaro Ishihara, or Lee Kuan Yew. ("And after all I've done for *you?*" says Eastwood to Wallach in *The Good, the Bad, and the Ugly.*) No one gave voice to this American disgust with an incorrigible world better than Randy Newman in his satirical song "Political Science":

> We give them money, but are they grateful?
> No, they're spiteful and they're hateful.
> They don't respect us, so let's surprise 'em!
> We'll drop the Big One and pulverize 'em.
> "Boom" goes London! "Boom" Paree!
> More room for you and more room for me. . . .
> They all hate us anyhow
> So let's drop the Big One now!

Note that Newman does not say, "Boom goes Moscow, boom Beijing." It's the contempt of our *friends* that really gets our goat. And that damn-your-eyes scorn for all who threaten, resist, or just fail to appreciate us is another trait for which room must be made in any accounting of the attitudes that have shaped American foreign relations.

These meditations on the role of foreign policy in shaping the American character, the apparent inadequacy of our familiar dichotomies, the American tendency to equate, not oppose, morality and practical politics, the notion of traditions as living and changing, the semantic distortions and myths that arise from throwing around terms like "isolationism" too loosely, the attempt to see ourselves through foreigners' eyes, and the benign scorn with which Americans see foreigners, all combined to persuade me to compile a new roster of American diplomatic traditions based on the following criteria. To qualify as a genuine tradition, a principle or strategy must have commanded solid bipartisan support, outlived the era that gave it birth, entered the permanent lexicon of our national discourse, and continued to resonate with a portion of the American public even during eras when it did not directly inspire policy. Here again are the winners:

OUR OLD TESTAMENT
1. Liberty, or Exceptionalism (so called)
2. Unilateralism, or Isolationism (so called)
3. The American System, or Monroe Doctrine (so called)
4. Expansionism, or Manifest Destiny (so called)

OUR NEW TESTAMENT
5. Progressive Imperialism
6. Wilsonianism, or Liberal Internationalism (so called)
7. Containment
8. Global Meliorism

I have tried to regard these traditions with the same skepticism I came to have toward the other lists cited earlier. And that is why the appendage "(so called)" appears several times. It is there to suggest that conventional notions about those traditions are going to be challenged in this book. For instance, did you learn in school that our Exceptionalism — the idea that America was meant to be different and better than all other countries — came to fruition in Wilsonian idealism? That, I believe, is false. Were you taught that the Monroe Doctrine was designed to secure the independence of Latin America or, conversely, to justify Yankee imperialism? I believe those interpretations are false. Do you identify American westward expansion with the idea of Manifest Destiny? I believe it is wrong to do so. Do you think that U.S. imperialism at the turn of the twentieth century was a repudiation of our progressive, idealistic tradition? I believe it *inaugurated* that very tradition. Were you taught that the global commitments of Cold

War Containment marked a revolution in U.S. diplomacy? I am no longer convinced that they did.

Finally, my use of biblical terms is not meant to suggest that theology directly inspired U.S. foreign policy, although the influence of religious ideas (especially heterodox ones) will be clear in the chapters that follow. Rather, the biblical metaphor is meant to suggest that the leaders who founded and led the United States throughout the nineteenth century imagined the nation as a sort of New Israel destined to fill a rich Promised Land and enjoy the blessings of liberty, so long as its people kept the commandments of their Old Testament canon. Chief among those commandments was "Thou shalt not have truck with foreigners *even for the purpose of converting them.*" To be sure, a strong millenarian countercurrent in American religious and secular thought challenged that reticence, but U.S. foreign policy makers never succumbed to the crusader's call . . . until 1898, whereupon they began to draft a New Testament that did admonish Americans to go forth and do good among nations. So in the twentieth century we established four more traditions all meant to succor a world convulsed by revolution and war. But the more Americans believed it their bounden duty to reform the world and boasted of their power to do so, the farther they strayed from the "true religion and virtue" embodied in their old foreign policy testament. Predictably, the Good the United States did magnified enormously, but so too did the Bad and the Ugly.

*

Assuming you come to accept my list of traditions, what use will it have for us today? Have we not been in desperate need — ever since Mikhail Gorbachev made good on his promise to deprive us of our enemy — of an entirely new grand strategy akin to Kennan's Containment, which guided our policies during the Cold War? Perhaps, but at least two writers are on record with an answer of no. I am one.[16] The other is Kennan himself, who insists that Americans did quite well for 150 years without an overarching operational doctrine, and that today they need only abide by some of their ancient principles. The particular one he had in mind was espoused by John Quincy Adams in his Fourth of July speech of 1821. "America does not go abroad in search of monsters to destroy," cautioned Adams. To do so would involve the United States "beyond the power of extrication, in all the wars and interest and intrigue, of individual avarice, envy, and ambition. . . . She might become the dictatress of the world. She would be no longer the ruler of her own spirit."[17]

Kennan thinks that Adams's principle is as valid today, when empires are again crumbling and nationalism shreds the map, as it was in the 1820s. But we as a nation cannot assess what timeless wisdom may reside in any of our traditions until someone tells us what they were, when and why they arose, how their meaning has changed over time, and what good, bad, and ugly results they achieved. That is a task, in the first instance, for historians. And that is the task I propose to take up in this book, not because I aspire to the mantle of Kennan, but because I hope to assist, in some modest way, all who do so aspire.

I
OUR OLD
TESTAMENT

. . . the Lord your God will set you high above all the nations of the earth. And all these blessings shall come unto you and overtake you, if you obey the voice of the Lord your God.

— DEUTERONOMY 28:1–2

ONE

Liberty, or Exceptionalism (so called)

> MY COUNTRY, 'tis of thee,
> Sweet land of liberty,
> Of thee we sing:
> Land where our fathers died,
> Land of the pilgrims' pride,
> From ev'ry mountainside
> Let freedom ring!

Everyone knows these words. America is, or is supposed to be, a land of liberty. But how many Americans recall the sentiments in the last verse of our patriotic hymn?

> Our fathers' God, to Thee,
> Author of liberty,
> To Thee we sing:
> Long may our land be bright
> With freedom's holy light;
> Protect us by Thy might,
> Great God, our King.

These lyrics were written in 1832,[1] but most Americans before, during, and after their War of Independence shared the assumption they express, to wit, that liberty is a gift of God. They may have disagreed sharply about theology, and whether liberty derived in the first instance from the Cross or from natural law. For instance, Thomas Jefferson preferred to speak of Nature's God, the Creator, or Divine Providence rather than the God of the Bible. But Puritans, Anglicans, Quakers, Unitarians, and deists were all prepared to name the Deity, not some human agency, as the author of freedom. Liberty's light was not only dazzling but holy, and Americans called upon God to protect them, because He — not George III — was their king.

It is axiomatic that the colonial rebels who founded the United States believed that their country was destined to be different and presumably better than others on earth. This is what historians mean when they refer (often in irony) to American messianism, sense of mission, idealism, or the ungainly but morally neutral term "exceptionalism," popularized by Max Lerner.[2] What is more, many historians take for granted the fact that this faith, conceit, or mere tendency was the taproot of U.S. foreign relations. All that one deemed good in subsequent American encounters with the world could be traced back to that fundamental idealism, and all one deemed bad could likewise be traced to the arrogance and hypocrisy implicit in Americans' holier-than-thou attitude.[3] Perhaps that peculiar claim to the status of *novus ordo seclorum* is America's oldest political tradition. But that means we must take exceptional care to identify just what that claim did and did not embrace.

One obvious way in which the thirteen colonies were special was geographical. Their lands were functionally limitless (the colonial charters allotted them, on paper, a third of a continent), magnificently fertile, and separated from Europe by an ocean. The colonies represented, not a country by Old World standards, but a virtual New World. Another obvious difference was demographic. The colonists were immigrants or children of immigrants drawn from several nations (though British predominantly) and religious denominations. Their numbers multiplied dizzily thanks to new arrivals and a fecundity that amazed Europeans. They braved the North Atlantic crossing and the North American wilderness in hopes of opportunity and a freer, more just society.[4] They included the usual run of scoundrels and misfits, to be sure, but even scoundrels crave freedom, perhaps more than the rest of us. In sum, the English, Scots, Welsh, and Irish emigrants were a self-selected cadre of brave and enterprising men and women. A third difference was political. Thanks to their charters and isolation, the colonists took for granted a measure of self-government greater than that enjoyed by any province in Europe. From New England town meetings to the Virginia House of Burgesses, Americans grew accustomed to running their own affairs.

The cynic may pooh-pooh these old saws. What nation or people is not unique? They all have their own geographies, climates, institutions, and cultural heritages. And most nations have boasted of their superiority, or claimed a special mission, at some point in time. Moreover, any special traits Americans assigned to themselves did not spring up *ex nihilo,* but were expressions of the seventeenth- and eighteenth-century European societies whence those colonists came. All that is true. But in the eyes of the Founding Fathers, clergymen, publicists, and other opinion leaders the new nation was a distillation of virtues *latent* in the civilization they left behind, but susceptible of realization only in America.

The evidence that the colonists believed that America was a holy land (that is, "set apart") is so abundant as to be trite. As early as 1630, Massachusetts Governor John Winthrop implored his people "to Consider that wee shall be as a City upon a Hill, the eies of all people are uppon us."[5] And while the Calvinist zeal of New Englanders waned (and occasionally waxed) over the next 150 years, no preacher or writer gainsaid Oliver Cromwell's dictum to the effect that religion and civil liberty were "the two greatest concernments that God hath in the world."[6] To be sure, England became relatively more hospitable to religious Nonconformists after the Glorious Revolution of 1688 expelled the Catholic Stuarts. But the vast majority of New Englanders had learned from hard experience to be suspicious of kings and bishops, and to associate religious congregationalism with representative government.

Over and over again, colonial divines invoked God's blessing on the American cause of "civil and religious liberty," for the one could not survive without the other. Congress declared days of national fasting and prayer during the Revolutionary War, again when independence was won in 1783, and again when the Constitution was finished. Preachers up and down the seaboard attributed American independence to the sure hand of Providence: "Here has our God . . . prepared an asylum for the oppressed in every part of the earth."[7] On the 300th anniversary of Columbus's discovery of America, Elhanan Winchester praised God's Providence for preparing a place for the persecuted of all nations and "causing it to be the first place upon the globe where equal civil and religious liberty has been established." Church and state, being separate, "may both subsist and flourish," nor "will God be angry with the United States for giving to the Jews, in common with other nations, the equal blessings of protection, liberty, property." Winchester even spied the fulfillment of Saint John's prophecy to the church of ancient Philadelphia: "'Behold, I have set before thee an open door and no man shall shut it' [Revelation 2:8]. This is the door of civil and religious liberty which began to be opened in Philadelphia in North America. . . . And it will spread throughout the world."[8]

The critic may rightly reply that many colonists were no more committed to freedom of religion as we understand it today than was the Britain they left behind. Most of the colonies had established churches, and some were not disestablished until well into the nineteenth century. And the first order of business of the Continental Congress was to protest Parliament's toleration act regarding Catholicism in Canada. Hence religious liberty, to American souls rooted in the Reformation rather than the Enlightenment, meant freedom from Rome and Canterbury, no more. But the fact remained that the American colonies as a whole were, by eighteenth-century standards, as diverse and hospitable to dissenters as any place in the history of the world.

In 1783 Ezra Stiles offered the definitive interpretation of American Exceptionalism in the providential idiom. His sermon celebrating independence promised that "God has still greater blessings in store for this vine which his own right hand hath planted." For "liberty, civil and religious, has sweet and attractive charms. The enjoyment of this, with property, has filled the English settlers in America with a most amazing spirit. . . . Never before has the experiment been so effectually tried, of every man's reaping the fruits of his labour and feeling his share in the aggregate system of power." Stiles imagined a nation of 50 million within a century, and if this proved out, "the Lord shall have made his American Israel 'high above all nations which he hath made.'"[9] In short, Americans were a chosen people delivered from bondage to a Promised Land, and you can't get more exceptional than that.

Secular and religious colonists also likened the United States to the Roman Republic of ancient times. John Adams employed the analogy repeatedly,[10] and the writings of Jefferson, Benjamin Franklin, Alexander Hamilton, and John Jay are filled with classical allusions and invocations of the republican virtues celebrated by Cicero, Cato, and Virgil. Americans dubbed George Washington a modern Cincinnatus, their Senate was an echo of the Roman institution, and their symbols of state, architecture, and even place names recalled the glory of Athens and Rome.[11] And like those great republics of old, the United States seemed destined to prosper and grow into what Jefferson called an "empire for liberty."[12]

American Exceptionalism surely found its loudest enunciation in Tom Paine's *Common Sense,* the inflammatory pamphlet that rallied popular support for independence. Did commercial interests oblige the colonies to stay connected to Britain? No, wrote Paine, for the colonists' prosperity was the fruit of their own labor. Britain was only a parasite. Did security require union with Britain? No, wrote Paine, for Britain's imperial ambitions were precisely what dragged the colonies into unwanted wars and spoiled their trade. Did Americans owe an emotional debt to the mother country? No, wrote Paine, because "this new world has been the asylum for the persecuted lovers of civil and religious liberty from *every part* of Europe. Hither they have fled, not from the tender embraces of the mother, but from the cruelty of the monster." If the "legal voice of the people" should declare independence, "we have every opportunity and every encouragement before us, to form the noblest, purest constitution on the face of the earth. We have it in our power to begin the world over again."[13]

What could Americans expect to gain by independence? Why was it worth the risk? Did the signers of the Declaration, the soldiers in the Continental Army, and the farmers, townsmen, and wives of the thirteen colonies dream of social revolution, redistribution of property, abolition of a feudal or capitalist class, perfect equality, a master race, world conquest, heaven on earth? No, with few exceptions they imagined none of the projects that fed the zeal of later revolutionaries in France, Russia, Germany, or China, and they persecuted no one except those who willfully denied the glorious cause — that is to say, Tories. To be sure, the Frenchman Michel Crèvecoeur did write, in his *Letter from an American Farmer* (first published in 1782), of "the most perfect society now existing in the world" and asked, "What then is the American, this new man?" But he was not thinking in the same terms as Lenin and Stalin with their "new Soviet man" or Mao with his Cultural Revolution. Rather, wrote Crèvecoeur, the American is one "who, leaving behind him all his ancient prejudices and manners, receives new ones from the new mode of life he has embraced, the new government he obeys, and the new rank he holds."[14] Americans were special because life in America had changed them: they must *already have been* new men to have made the Revolution in the first place. Or, as John Adams wrote, "The Revolution was made in the minds of the people, and this was effected from 1760 to 1775, in the course of fifteen years before a drop of blood was shed at Lexington."[15]

Now, historian Gordon Wood has made a strong case for the radicalism of the American Revolution. And in the context of the pre-1789 world it certainly was radical. The colonists abolished aristocracy and monarchy, elevated common folk to an unheard-of dignity and degree of participation in public life, and made war on all forms of dependency, which they equated with slavery. "There are but two *sorts* of men in the world, freemen and slaves," wrote John Adams, and even well-to-do Americans were like slaves so long as they were dependent on Britain.[16] But those who claim that the Revolution was conservative (Edmund Burke was the first) can point to the lack of any ideological agenda beyond the securing of "the blessings of liberty."[17] And however much the nature of liberty, not to mention how to sustain it through institutions, became a subject of controversy for years after independence was won, politics remained an end in itself, a "technology" to be employed in a design for liberty and not a weapon for some more radical war.[18] Nor did the American revolutionaries harbor a mission to other parts of the world. They hoped that Canada might join in the fight against Britain, but shook the dust off of their feet when English- and even French-speaking Canadians demurred. Some Americans thought that their bold stand for liberty might help to reform the mother country and "keep Britain herself from ruin."[19] But their example, not force of arms, would be the agency for that boon. Finally, visionaries like Stiles and Paine imagined that Providence might employ America in a global mission to spread true religion and republicanism. But once again it would lead by example: one could not force men and nations to be free.

Is it fair to say, then, that the United States had no ideology or foreign agenda, that Americans felt no impulse to reform (or dominate) a wicked world in the name of self-determination, human rights, free trade? Perhaps they did later, but to the generation that founded the United States, designed its government, and laid down its policies, the exceptional calling of the American people was not *to do* anything special in foreign affairs, but *to be* a light to lighten the world.

The evidence for this exemption of foreign policy from the requirements of idealism can be seen in Americans' responses to four challenges the Republic faced in its formative decades, challenges that gave them the option of embracing two sorts of messianic diplomacy. One was a truly "new diplomacy" that rejected power politics, balance of power, and intrigue in favor of pacifism, idealism, and reliance on moral persuasion. The other was a truly revolutionary diplomacy that committed the nation to a militant crusade against Old World monarchy and imperialism. A few prominent Americans flirted with one or the other of these radical diplomacies, but in the end the Republic shunned them and, in a remarkable display of unanimity and good judgment, agreed to limit the content of American Exceptionalism to Liberty at home, period.

★

The first challenge that forced the Founding Fathers to define what they regarded as special about their new nation was the struggle for independence itself. It began, let us not forget, in a tax revolt. For no matter how mundane the issues may seem to us now, or how trivial the sums involved, or how justified the British Parliament may have been in seeking more revenue from the colonies, the principle of representative government was at stake. The colonists made the point repeatedly, but the British just didn't get it. They seemed blind (as Franklin complained in 1765) to the possibility that "people act from any other Principle than that of Interest" and that a threepence reduction of tax on a pound's worth of tea would be "sufficient to overcome all the Patriotism of an American."[20]

Another reason to recall that the Revolution grew out of a tax revolt is that public finance is one of the most important (if boring) subjects in any age of history. This was especially true during the early modern era when monarchies fought to suppress the remnants of feudal provincialism and forge centralized states. To do this, kings needed standing armies and bureaucracies to establish a monopoly of force, regulate commerce, administer law, and above all collect taxes. Civil wars had to be fought in England, France, and Germany before various accommodations were reached. Prussia's rulers, for example, cut a deal with nobles and townsmen, granting the former the right to turn their peasants into serfs and the latter commercial liberties in return for permanent new taxes. In time this made Prussia a military power, but stifled representative government in northern Germany. The French kings crushed the aristocracy and the church, but at the price of leaving intact their privileges and tax exemptions. This made the Bourbons absolute monarchs, but over time drove them bankrupt and provoked revolution. The British crown, by contrast, finally agreed to share power with Parliament, in return for which the landed gentry and merchants could be counted on to offer up taxes when the realm was in need. The price paid by the British was the loss of their

American colonies, for they enshrined the principle of representative government only to deny it to their overseas subjects.

American colonists never liked being taxed, especially by a haughty, corrupt, and distant legislature whose votes were for sale to special interest groups that got rich off the restrictions imposed on colonial trade. But Americans put up with it so long as they were threatened by French Canada to the north, Spanish Florida and Louisiana to the south and west, French and Spanish ships at sea, and Indians in their midst. During the reign of Louis XIV, and again from 1740 to 1763, Britain and France fought a series of wars that troubled the thirteen colonies. Colonial militias were sometimes effective, but Americans would have been hard put to secure themselves and their commerce without the aid of the Redcoats and Royal Navy.

Following the Seven Years' War in 1763, Parliament decided the time had come for the colonists to pay for a larger share of the cost. Its timing could not have been worse: Britain's conquest of Canada in that war had just removed the colonies' most dangerous enemy. Moreover, the colonials reacted to each "intolerable act" of Parliament like the good Englishmen they were, demanding either representation or else a redress of grievances. Both sides were to blame for escalating the conflict: the British for stubbornly refusing to bargain, closing the port of Boston, and sending soldiers who inevitably fired on a crowd; the colonials for destroying property (Boston Tea Party), boycotting British goods, resisting taxes, and molesting officials. Once the shooting started at Lexington and Concord, however, the colonies had to decide whether — and how — to instruct the Continental Congress to pursue independence. Drafting a Declaration that justified rebellion was a theoretical exercise — just the ticket for Jefferson, who neatly invoked the same contract theory of government and natural rights doctrine used by John Locke to justify Parliament's ouster of James II in 1688. But to realize independence (and escape a British gallows) was a practical matter for the delegates in Philadelphia, a matter of war and diplomacy.

American notions on the theory and praxis of foreign policy were also British in origin. Throughout the eighteenth century English leaders, especially the Whigs, engaged in searching debate over the principles that ought to govern their policy. They recognized the wisdom of remaining aloof from the Continent so long as a balance of power existed there. Should a threat to the balance arise, Britain might have to intervene as it had in Marlborough's time, but otherwise, as Prime Minister Robert Walpole put it in 1723, "My politics are to keep free from all engagements as long as we possibly can."[21] The exception was commerical ties, and it became conventional wisdom, as a pamphleteer wrote in 1742, that "a Prince or State ought to avoid all Treaties, except such as tend toward promoting Commerce or Manufactures. . . . All other Alliances may be look'd upon as so many Incumbrances."[22] Even in the "world wars" of 1740–63 Britain sent no armies to the Continent, but instead exploited the wars to drive the French out of India and North America.

Observers like Franklin and the other agents who represented the colonies in London readily applied these principles to American circumstances. They also appreciated Britain's exemplary drive that culminated in the union of England, Scotland, and Wales, the suppression of Ireland, and the defeat of the last Scottish revolt in 1746. England clearly would have been hamstrung in its pursuit of power and wealth abroad if in its home isles it had continued to face rebellious nations in league with foreign powers. The British Board of Trade also encouraged the colonies to think in terms of unity, even recommending in 1721 a single military command for the "Empire in America."[23] Constant trouble with Indians later inspired the 1754 Albany Plan for a supergovernment set above those of the colonies and endowed with power to command militias, limit settlements, and negotiate with Indians. The jealous colonies spurned it until, ironically, they began to think and act as a unit in opposition to Britain itself.

Unity, aloofness from Europe, exploitation of the balance of power, and a stress on commercial diplomacy — the Continental Congress knew and honored these precepts. But are they all that is needed to explain the origins of an American foreign relations? Did not some of the Founding Fathers, at least, dream of a new "republican" diplomacy informed by the spirit of reason and contrasting sharply with the Machiavellian politics of Europe? Paine called for Americans "to begin the world over again." Jefferson thought that republics would not make wars except in self-defense, and that an independent America would need no diplomats other than commercial consuls. James Madison wrote that power and force may have governed international relations "in the dark ages which intervened between antient [*sic*] and modern civilization," but those ages were over: "I know but one code of morality for man whether acting singly or collectively."[24] And John Adams insisted that where European diplomacy was secret, bellicose, and riddled with intrigue, American policy would be open, peaceful, and honest. When the French foreign minister, the Count de Vergennes, asked him to get off his high horse, Adams replied that "the dignity of North America does not consist in diplomatic ceremonials or any of the subtlety of etiquette; it consists solely in reason, justice, truth, the rights of mankind."[25] Finally, the first American diplomats, like the Bolshevik ones in the 1920s, made a point of eschewing fancy dress, titles, entertainments, and all manner of protocol, so as to be walking, talking symbols of republican piety.

Perhaps that was nothing more than a momentary enthusiasm born of revolution. Or perhaps a *prima facie* case can be made that many Americans did believe in an exceptionalism that extended beyond the water's edge. The answer depends on how one interprets the allegedly idealistic initial act of U.S. foreign policy: the Model Treaty of 1776, drafted by Adams and hailed by Congress as a true expression of American principles. How did it come about, what were its motives, and above all what was its fate?

By the fall of 1775 the Continental Congress knew that any favorable outcome to its conflict with London depended on foreign assistance. The colonies' ragtag militias might win the occasional skirmish but could not prevail, once British power was seriously engaged, without access to foreign money and munitions. So Congress formed a Committee of Secret Correspondence and charged it to seek friends abroad — seven months before the Declaration of Independence. Silas Deane left for Paris in March 1776, to be followed in time by Franklin, Adams, and others. But what incentives could they offer in foreign courts? Why should France gratuitously assist the rebellion? The answer, as Paine argued in *Common Sense*, was French lust for American trade. This was a sanguine but not absurd notion. As early as 1754 the Bostonian William Clarke boasted that the colonies were of such value to Britain that "whilst she keep them entire, she will be able to maintain not only her Independency, but her Superiority as a Maritime Power. And on the other Hand, should she once lose them, and the French gain them, Great Britain herself must necessarily be reduced to an absolute Subjection to the French Crown." French foreign minister Choiseul agreed in 1759 that the "true balance of power" rested on control of commerce and America.[26]

So Congress approved a "Plan of Treaties" in June 1776, declared independence in July to persuade Paris of the colonists' good faith, and approved the Model Treaty in September. Adams hoped the treaty would win a French "alliance," by which he meant *de jure* recognition of the United States: "I am not for soliciting any political connection, or military assistance or indeed naval, from France. I wish for nothing but commerce, a mere marine treaty with them." His purpose was not to reform world politics but to secure France's assistance without the Americans becoming pawns of French imperialism, as they had previously been pawns of the British. He later confessed that "there was not sufficient temptation to France to join us,"[27] but he feared that a full political or military alliance would oblige the Americans to acquiesce in a French reconquest of Canada or the West Indies. If there was an air of unreality about American diplomacy, it stemmed from naiveté, caution, and overestimation of the allure of American trade — not from an excess of idealism. Congress, and the delegation in Paris, quietly shelved the Model Treaty.

Thenceforward the American quest for independence proceeded according to war and diplomacy as usual. Secret agents smuggled French arms to America, where they were put to good use in the victory over General Burgoyne at Saratoga. That in turn prompted British peace feelers, which Franklin used as leverage to achieve a full French alliance. What, asked Vergennes, would suffice to forestall an Anglo-American rapprochement and ensure that the colonials commit to "full and absolute independence"? Commercial *and* military alliances between France and the American Congress, answered Franklin. The advisers to Louis XVI — with the exception of the beleaguered finance minister — then made the fateful decision to throw in their lot with America.

Nor was any new or idealistic diplomacy to be found in the process of peacemaking. Franklin had solemnly promised not to negotiate independently with Britain — the "no separate peace" clause standard in alliances. But he did not hesitate to double-cross the French when, after the Franco-American victory at Yorktown, Parliament dispatched an emissary to Paris to discuss terms of peace. The American delegation hammered out a treaty that endowed the new United States with all the land east of the Mississippi River save Spanish Florida. Franklin, confessing to Vergennes a certain lack of *bienséance* in his dealings, assured him that the Franco-American Alliance would remain in force after the peace, while the congressional secretary for foreign affairs, Robert Livingston, was pained that the American commissioners had impeached "the character for candor and felicity to its engagements which should always characterize a great people."[28] But no congressman or later historian rued Franklin's methods, the only rap against him being that he had not also won for New Englanders the right to fish off Newfoundland's Grand Banks. Even John Adams, the Puritan of tender conscience and author of the Model Treaty, boasted that he and his fellow commissioners had proven "better tacticians than we imagined."[29]

Any Americans who remained attached to the idea that their diplomacy (as opposed to their nation itself) could be different and better had that illusion punctured in the years following the Peace of Paris. Britain, France, Spain, the Iroquois, and the Barbary pirates serially humiliated the sovereign states loosely bound by the Articles of Confederation. Britain refused to evacuate forts it had built on what was now the American side of the Great Lakes, made common cause with the Indians, offered commercial advantages to Vermonters in hopes of cracking Yankee unity, and closed West Indian ports to American ships. The Court of St. James's snubbed John Adams, the first U.S. minister to Britain, to the point that he ceased preaching free trade and model treaties and recommended "reciprocal prohibitions, exclusions, monopolies, and imposts."[30] Likewise, Ambassador Jefferson failed to persuade France to reciprocate in matters of trade, while Spain alternately closed the port of New Orleans or charged oppressive fees for its use, and the corsairs of North Africa captured American ships and held sailors for ransom. Meanwhile, the United States demobilized its army and navy, lacked a central executive, and permitted the thirteen states to write their own commercial codes. It is only a slight exaggeration to say that Americans have foreign insolence to thank for inspiring the incomparable areopagus known as the Constitutional Convention.

American statesmen had two great but astoundingly vague objects in mind when they called for a new constitution: to form a "more perfect union" and to provide for a central authority — be it Congress or an Executive — able to defend the states from foreigners *without endangering their liberties at home.* They were not idealists, much less ideologues, and whether they drew inspiration from the anthropology of the Bible or of Enlightenment philosophy, they were under no illusions about the corruptible nature of men and governments. That helps to explain the clashing fears and divergences of opinion that threatened more than once to explode the convention. Would not any federal government powerful enough to stare down Britain or France *ipso facto* threaten the freedom of its own constituent states and citizens? How could the requirements of an independent and free United

States be squared with the requirements of independent and free Americans?[31] In the debates at Philadelphia over representation, the military powers of the Executive, the commercial and fiscal powers of Congress, and later over the Bill of Rights we can discern the origins of the Federalist and Democratic Republican parties of the 1790s. The former tended to stress the necessity for a strong central government and downplay its risks, and the latter tended to trumpet its dangers and question its necessity.[32] So sincere, in fact, were the disputes and fears that the delegates should be praised as much for their sheer forbearance as for the brilliance of the solutions they concocted.

At length, the framers agreed to conduct their experiment in reconciling power and liberty, in making the lion lie down with the lamb, on the basis of separation of powers, checks and balances.[33] In foreign policy they endowed a presidency ("the monarchical branch," Anti-Federalists called it) with the powers of commander-in-chief and chief diplomat, the House of Representatives ("the popular branch") with the power to vote money for armies, navies, and foreign missions, the Senate ("the aristocratic branch") with the power to advise and consent to treaties and appointments, and Congress as a whole with the power to declare war and regulate commerce for all the states. Specific contentious issues involving foreign policy included the raising and quartering of armies, the enforcement of tariffs, the making and ratifying of treaties, the slave trade, and even the size of the foreign service.[34] In every case, however, the bone of contention was whether the federal government might use its foreign policy powers to harm liberties at home. Nowhere in the Constitution did the framers stipulate how the government should exercise its powers vis-à-vis foreign countries.

Nor did the authors of the *Federalist Papers* expect that the United States would behave in a more saintly fashion by virtue of being a republic. In *The Federalist* #3 John Jay wrote that of all the objects of a wise and free people, "that of providing for their *safety* seems to be the first." That meant the preservation of peace, but also protection "against dangers from *foreign arms and influence*." He went on to enumerate the many ways in which national weakness might invite foreign powers to visit humiliation or even war on the United States. Likewise, thirteen independent states, or three or four confederations of states, must inevitably quarrel among themselves, permitting foreign powers to play them off against each other.[35] Hamilton continued the argument: "A man must be far gone in Utopian speculations, who can seriously doubt that, if these States should either be wholly disunited or only united in partial confederacies, the subdivisions into which they might be thrown would have frequent and violent contests with each other." He then smashed the myth that republics do not engage in war by choice, citing the many just and unjust wars waged either in reason or in passion by Sparta, Athens, Rome, Carthage, Venice, Holland, and parliamentary Britain: "There have been, if I may so express it, almost as many popular as royal wars."[36] The purpose of the United States was not to present an idealistic face to a world ruled by power politics — that was a sure way of ruining domestic peace and freedom — but instead to allow "one great American system, superior to the control of all transatlantic force or influence, [to] dictate the terms of the connection between the old and the new world!"[37]

"'Tis done," wrote Benjamin Rush when news arrived of the final ratification of the Constitution. "America has ceased to be the only power in the world that has derived no benefit from her declaration of independence. . . . We are no longer the scoff of our enemies."[38]

The Revolutionary War and the indignities suffered under the Articles of Confederation proved that dreams of a new, moral diplomacy, far from being necessary to an American exceptionalism, were downright injurious to it. So the constitutional process, culminating in the inauguration of President George Washington, gave birth to a government capable of deterring or, if necessary, fighting threats to American liberty. The foreign policy powers of the executive branch were the shield, sword, and lawyer's brief for American Exceptionalism; they were not themselves an expression of it.

*

The second challenge that forced Americans to define the nature of their foreign policy was the French Revolution. Before 1789, the United States existed in an Atlantic world of imperial monarchies. No wonder Americans had to fight fire with fire; they were still surrounded by enemies, which they could only hope would trouble each other more than they troubled America. Then the French Revolution declared the Rights of Man and the Citizen and, in 1792, a republic at war with monarchical Europe. O miraculous times! Woodrow Wilson's delight upon hearing that Russians had toppled the tsar in 1917 did not compare with the elation Americans felt upon learning that France had chosen liberty. Did it not behoove them to make common cause with their French allies? Ought they not champion democracy abroad as well as at home?

No, and no — although Americans took some time to decide.

A majority of the American people certainly cheered the first phase of the French Revolution, 1789–91, during which the National Assembly abolished feudal privilege, sequestered Catholic Church property, and designed a constitutional monarchy. When war broke out in Europe, Americans also cheered President Washington's policy of strict neutrality. But the mere desire to remain aloof could not spare the country an internal debate so agonizing that it gave birth to the American two-party system. Agrarians, many southerners, and all who looked to Jefferson and Madison for leadership came to be known as Democratic Republicans and tended to favor the French cause (not least because they hated and feared the British). Merchants, many New Englanders, and all who looked to Hamilton and Jay for political guidance were known as Federalists and tended to favor the British cause (not least because they hated and feared the French Revolution). Hamilton stressed the danger of antagonizing Britain, which had the power to ruin U.S. trade and withhold the capital on which American economic growth relied. Jefferson and Madison saw this very dependence on Britain as the greater risk and thought U.S. independence best served by a tilt toward its allies, the French.

The passions stirred up by this feud grew so hot that one might think civil war was at hand. Hamilton accused Jefferson and his friends of "a *womanish attachment to France and a womanish resentment against Great Britain*. . . . If these Gentlemen were left to pursue their own course there would be in less than six months an *open War between the U States & Great Britain*."[39] Democratic Republicans, in turn, damned the Federalists for a pack of moneyed monkeys dancing to England's tune. When John Jay returned from London in 1794 with a trade treaty in his baggage, crowds hanged him in effigy and called for his head. "John Jay, ah! the arch traitor —" wrote one editor, "seize him, drown him, burn him, flay him alive."[40] Another protester defaced the wall of a Federalist's house: "Damn John Jay! Damn everyone who won't damn John Jay!! Damn everyone that won't put lights in his windows and sit up all night damning John Jay!!!"[41] Jefferson, too, sounded hysterical at times. He declared that the liberty of the whole world hung on the issue in France, and rather than have the Revolution fail he "would have seen half the earth desolated; were there but an Adam and Eve left in every country, and left free, it would be better than as it now is."[42] Federalists, in turn, got all the ammunition they needed from Robespierre's Reign of Terror. They called Democratic Republicans "a despicable mobocracy," "Gallic jackals," "frog-eating, man-eating, blood drinking cannibals," and warned that if the American Jacobins had their way, churches would burn and guillotines rise on town commons.[43]

What so exercised our bewigged Founding Fathers, who had shown divine patience just a few years before in Philadelphia, that they now exchanged curses and fists in the streets? Did one side or the other advocate entry into the European war? No — except for an extreme body of Federalists at the end of the 1790s, almost no leading figures wanted to abandon neutrality. What they were arguing about was really the implication that a tilt toward France or Britain seemed to have in *domestic* policy, in the two sides' contrary visions of what America ought to be like, in their very definitions of liberty. As historian Joyce Appleby writes, the French Revolution and European war "succeeded in bringing to the surface of public life opposing conceptions of society" and created "a succession of occasions on which the ardent adversaries could take one another to task on fundamental questions about human nature and social norms."[44] It was the aristocratic-versus-popular clash all over again, as Democratic Republicans saw the Federalists' pro-British stance as evidence of their favor for a hierarchical society *at home,* and Federalists saw the Democratic Republicans' pro-French stance as indicative of their favor for extreme democracy *at home.*

The danger that the European war might affect American society became evident when Edmond Charles "Citizen" Genêt, the peripatetic thirty-year-old named as minister to the United States by the French Republic, repaid the adulation with which Americans received him, in 1793, by attempting to turn public opinion against the neutrality policy. When that failed, he surreptitiously purchased ships and dispatched them to prey on British merchantmen in American coastal waters. His wilder plots — "I am arming the Canadians to throw off the yoke of England; I am arming the Kentuckians, and I am preparing an expedition by sea to support the descent on New Orleans"[45] — came to nothing, but less than a year after his arrival Washington demanded his recall.

At that point, Jefferson resigned as secretary of state and Republican opposition nearly prevented ratification of Jay's Treaty, despite the fact that Britain had agreed to abandon its forts on the Great Lakes and grant the United States "most favored nation" status in West Indian trade. But Jay had not obtained compensation for U.S. ships, cargoes, and slaves seized by the Royal Navy, and had recognized Britain's right to interdict cargoes bound for French ports. So loud was the public protest that Washington held off asking the Senate to ratify Jay's Treaty until the apparent treason of Edmund Randolph, Jefferson's successor, demoralized the opposition. Letters captured by the British suggested that Randolph had solicited French funds for the purpose of supporting the 1794 Whiskey Rebellion in Pennsylvania.

The Genêt and Randolph affairs demonstrated the theoretical point made in *The Federalist* to the effect that disunity was an invitation to foreign powers to meddle in Americans' domestic affairs and subvert their diplomacy.[46] So it is no mystery why Washington included in his Farewell Address of September 1796 the admonition that "nothing is more essential than that permanent, inveterate antipathies against particular nations and passionate attachments for others should be excluded. . . . The nation which indulges toward another an habitual hatred or an habitual fondness is in some degree a slave. . . . Against the insidious wiles of foreign influence (I conjure you to believe me, fellow-citizens) the jealousy of a free people ought to be *constantly* awake, since history and experience prove that foreign influence is one of the most baneful foes of republican government."[47]

Under President John Adams (whose election campaign had received a decisive boost from Washington's message), U.S. relations with the French Republic hit bottom. When the Jay Treaty went into effect in 1796, the French claimed the same right to seize ships bound for their enemy, Britain, and captured more than three hundred American ships in the first year alone of this "quasi-war." Adams tried to parlay, but Talleyrand, the great French foreign minister, displayed even less ideological affinity for the United States than the Americans showed to the French. America, he said, deserved no more respect than Geneva or Genoa.[48] Content to squeeze American commerce in the belief that French leverage would only increase, Talleyrand fobbed off the U.S. commissioners on a series of nonentities (Yanks called them Messieurs X, Y, and Z), who hinted that the United States might purchase peace with bribes and loans to the French government. That is what inspired the American whoop "Millions for defense, but not one cent for tribute!"

Adams persuaded Congress to vote money for an army and capital ships, and created the Navy Department. Had the president shared the eagerness some Federalists expressed for war against France, he could have had it in 1798. But he did not, any more than Jefferson wanted to fight for France. So when Talleyrand signaled his willingness to talk in earnest, Adams's delegates concluded the Treaty of Mortefontaine in 1800. The United States dropped all financial claims arising from the quasi-war in exchange for abrogation of the Franco-American Alliance of 1778. Thus, for all their internal strife, Americans resisted the intense ideological and military pressure put on them in the 1790s to succumb to the temptation to turn their foreign policy into a crusade.

*

The third test of the principle that American Exceptionalism was not intended to dictate or constrain foreign policy was in some ways a reprise of the second. After a brief peace in 1802, the European powers waged war *à outrance* for another dozen years, the French and British spurned America's "neutral rights," and their navies and blockades played havoc with American trade. But in some ways the situation was markedly different than in the 1790s. France was no longer a republic but a militaristic gangster-state masquerading as a traditional European empire. Napoleon Bonaparte had few friends in America (mostly Irish) other than those his agents could buy. And that meant Britain was now the champion of liberty, however much Americans might resent the liberties it took in that capacity. Finally, a political sea change had occurred at home: the Federalists were out and the Democratic Republicans in. Would President Jefferson now seize the chance to practice an idealistic or revolutionary foreign policy?

Here is where we must ask, once and for all, after the significance of Jefferson's philosophical musings. One finds evidence of idealism throughout his writings and table talk. One seeks it in vain in his statecraft. Even historians who focus on the debate between Jeffersonians and Hamiltonians seem to sense that fact. Jefferson, we read, was so angry at the Europeans for interfering with American trade that he wished the United States could give up commerce altogether and become as isolated as China.[49] But that was in theory: in practice he knew it was silly. Jefferson, we read, wished that the United States could become a society of virtuous republican farmers, since wage labor, industry, and finance corrupted men or made slaves of them.

But that was in theory: in practice he knew that Americans were of both sorts, and that their elected leaders had to serve the interests of both. Jefferson, we read, dreamed of a world of republics in which war would disappear and diplomacy be an affair of consulates only. But that was in theory: in practice he knew that nations had conflicting interests they must defend at sword's point in need. Jefferson, we read, wanted to practice a new diplomacy but always bowed to reality or "strangely combined idealism, even utopianism, with cynical craft."[50] Why not say instead that Jefferson was a sensible and responsible man who, in his public life, never permitted his personal fancies to compromise the national interest? To be sure, he disagreed with Hamilton over goals at home, but his methods abroad were pragmatic, whether or not they were mistaken.

If we adopt this image of Jefferson, many things fall into place: not only his acquiescence in most of the policies of the Washington administration, but the hardball policies of his own. He began, in his inaugural address, by stating that "we are all Federalists; we are all Republicans."[51] Then he proceeded to push U.S. interests as vigorously as the young nation's strength would permit. He dispatched Adams's new navy and a force of marines "to the shores of Tripoli" to beat up on (some of) the Barbary pirates. He was so fearful of the prospect of French empire in North America that he even resigned himself to the prospect of a *British* alliance before Napoleon's fortuitous decision to sell Louisiana. And no one has ever gainsaid Jefferson's zeal for expansion by any prudent means. Even his sense of American exceptionalism appears, upon inspection, to have been 90 percent a matter of what the United States should be, not what it should or should not do in the arena of warring nations.[52]

Jefferson's most intractable problem was the old one of neutral rights at sea. In 1805 the British admiralty court ruled in the *Essex* case that neutral ships with enemy cargo aboard were liable to capture even if they were being transshipped via U.S. ports. British warships and privateers took to lurking off the American coast, seizing prizes almost at will. They also seized sailors, most notoriously in the *Chesapeake* affair of 1807, impressing alleged deserters into the Royal Navy. By then, a British Order in Council and Napoleon's Berlin Decree had declared reciprocal blockades of continental Europe and the British Isles, and the Atlantic Ocean came alive with enemies of American trade. Jefferson contemplated war and requested an increase in the naval budget. But first he tried economic weapons: the Embargo and Non-Importation Acts of 1807 banned U.S. exports to nations that interfered with our trade.

It didn't work. In fact, it was the same mistake made by the authors of the Model Treaty: overestimation of American economic clout. For if Europeans were damaged by a U.S. refusal to run their respective gauntlets, American merchants were decimated and cried for Jefferson's head. In 1809 Congress replaced the embargo with a Non-Intercourse Act, banning trade only to British and French ports in hopes of inducing those powers to repeal their restrictions. That didn't work either. So Congress tried a third approach, in 1810, lifting all restrictions but authorizing the president (now James Madison) to reimpose non-intercourse on either Britain or France should the other lift its own decrees. Napoleon professed to do so, whereupon Madison banned trade with England. This at last got London's attention. After lengthy debate the British cabinet decided, in June 1812, to lift the Orders in Council and cease molesting American ships. But before the news crossed the Atlantic, the Yankees finally lost patience and chose to make a righteous war.

Why righteous? Did the War of 1812 reflect American Exceptionalism in a way that the high-minded embargoes and such had not? Conventional wisdom ridicules that notion, suggesting instead that the war was at best stupid and at worst an act of aggression inspired by War Hawks in Congress. They, not Madison, propelled the United States into war, and they seemed (at first glance) to have been mostly young men from the West and South. Representatives from northeastern and urban constituencies, by contrast, mostly voted against war. Why was that? Why did the sections of the country least affected by maritime predations cry for war, while the Yankees who were being molested oppose it? In their attempts to answer those questions, historians explored other possible causes of war, such as continued ire over alleged British collusion with Indians, and lust for land, especially Canada.

However much some Americans (like the hothead Andrew Jackson) hoped to take this occasion to conquer new territory, frontier issues did not tip the balance. And the proof for that is simply that the vote on war was not sectional, but along party lines. Nor can it be said that economics was the issue, since the Federalists representing commercial interests opposed war.[53] Madison did not even recommend war in his message: he merely called it "a solemn question which the Constitution wisely confides to the legislative department of the Government." He then went on to list "the injuries and indignities that have been heaped on our country" and concluded that "a state of war against the United States" already existed.[54] But that could have been said in 1807 or 1810. Why in June 1812 did the House (79 to 49) and Senate (19 to 13) finally vote for war?

Three commonsense explanations suggest themselves. First and most obvious is that the American people were fed up with seizures of ships, cargoes, and sailors year after year after year. When new evidence of British manipulation of Indians and a furious new bout of impressments erupted in 1811, Congress convened in a foul mood. The second explanation is that all this bad news occurred on the Republicans' watch. For eleven years Jefferson and Madison had tried one measure after another, usually making things worse for American shippers and the export sectors that relied on them. Democratic Republicans had made electoral gains, most recently in 1810, but unless they repudiated the failed policies of the past and took decisive action, the party might fracture or lose its hold on the electorate.

The third explanation is that British violations of American sovereignty had made the decision for war less a matter of material interests than national honor. American independence was made a mockery, and war was the only way left to salvage it. In January 1812, Virginia's House of Delegates resolved: "the period has now arrived when *peace, as we now have it,* is disgraceful, and war is honorable." Madison declaimed in 1813 that "to have shrunk under such circumstance from manly resistance would have . . . acknowledged that on the element which forms three-fourths of the globe we inhabit, and where all independent nations have equal and common rights, the Americans were not an independent people, but colonists and vassals." John C. Calhoun of South Carolina warned that "if we submit to the pretensions of England, now openly avowed, the independence of this nation will be lost. . . . This is the second struggle for our liberty."[55]

The War of 1812 was an unhappy byproduct of the world war launched by Napoleon. It began just after the *casus belli* had (unbeknownst to Americans) been revoked, and it ended just before its biggest battle was fought at New Orleans. The peace treaty of December 1814 simply restored the *status quo ante bellum:* no annexations, no indemnities. It was not glorious, though some glorious deeds were done in the course of it, and was "productive of evil & good" in the judgment of one peace delegate, Albert Gallatin (he neglected to include "ugly").[56] But in the minds of most Americans the war achieved its purpose, which was to duke it out with the British and remind the world that while Americans had no intention of meddling in others' affairs, they were fiercely jealous of their own freedom.

*

If the War of Independence was echoed in some ways by the War of 1812, so was the challenge posed by the French Revolution echoed in the fourth test of U.S. diplomacy: the Latin American revolutions. U.S. policy toward that great eruption in the southern lands of the hemisphere is better described in chapter 3, in the context of the Monroe Doctrine (so called). But the upshot, as in the first three tests, was that after some false starts and false hopes the United States fled from the notion of making common cause with foreign revolutionaries as it would from a temptation of Lucifer. The guiding spirit was John Quincy Adams, who, by way of refuting the heretical doctrine of a crusader America, formulated once and for all the orthodox dogma of American Exceptionalism in that July Fourth address of 1821:

> America does not go abroad in search of monsters to destroy. She is the well-wisher to the freedom and independence of all. She is the champion only of her own. She will recommend the general cause by the countenance of her voice, and the benignant sympathy of her example. She well knows that by once enlisting under other banners than her own, were they even the banners of foreign independence, she would involve herself beyond the power of extrication, in all the wars of interest and intrigue, of individual avarice, envy, and ambition, which assumed the colors and usurped the standards of freedom. . . . She might become the dictatress of the world. She would be no longer the ruler of her own spirit.[57]

So what did American Exceptionalism mean when it came to foreign policy? That the United States would make no alliances, fight no wars, spurn all intrigue? Of course not. If anything, American vulnerability from 1776 to 1820 only proved the timeless wisdom of the Roman motto *Si vis pacem pare bellum* (If you desire peace, prepare for war), and you will find that dictum in the writings of Washington, Adams, Jefferson, Hamilton, Franklin, Jay, Patrick Henry, John Marshall, James Gadsden, and Richard Henry Lee.[58] Did American Exceptionalism mean that the Founding Fathers embraced none but idealistic ends sought by scrupulous means? Jefferson might have wished it were so, but even he bowed to reality in defense of the national interest. Did it mean that the United States would take up the cause of freedom everywhere and choose its friends on the basis of republican principles? Absolutely not. If American foreign policy was different or better than that of the Old World powers, it was solely by virtue of the fact that the United States was a republic, hence its policies reflected the people's interests and not those of some dynasty.

*

American Exceptionalism as our founders conceived it was defined by what America *was,* at home. Foreign policy existed to defend, not define, what America was. In given circumstances all sorts of tactics might be expedient save only one that defeated its purpose by eroding domestic unity and liberty. That last exception was by no means trivial. It meant that the United States had to live with a tension that authoritarian states escape: tension between the demands of national defense and the liberties of the individuals being defended. That tension was evident in the public's resistance to taxes raised for military purposes. It was evident in the outcry over the Federalists' Alien and Sedition Acts, meant to suppress French (and Irish) agitators even to the detriment of freedom of speech and assembly. It was evident in merchants' protests against the embargoes, which harmed their freedom to trade even more than did the British and French. The authors of the Constitution foresaw such tensions, but trusted that national unity and the blessings of liberty could be reconciled with the needs of defense so long as the nation's foreign policy was prudent and not ideological.

But the success of the American experiment required more than wisdom in government. It required virtue among the people: the classical and biblical virtues of patriotism, sacrifice, tolerance, and self-control. The Founding Fathers recognized the sheer unlikelihood of their undertaking, the temptations of power, and the risk that in a free society every vice might flourish. John Adams even expected that sooner or later America, like Israel and Judah and Athens and Rome, would lay down the burden of freedom, succumb to decadence, hubris, even self-hatred, and enter its decline and fall.

So the flip side of the boast of Exceptionalism was a warning. Few go on to quote it, but that was the admonition of "A City on a Hill." Echoing Moses' farewell in Deuteronomy, Winthrop cautioned "that if we shall deal falsely with our God in this work we have undertaken and so cause Him to withdraw His present help from us, we shall be made a story and a byword through the world, we shall open the mouths of enemies to speak evil of the ways of God and all professors for God's sake; we shall shame the faces of many of God's worthy servants, and cause their prayers to be turned into curses upon us till we be consumed out of the good land whither we are going."[59]

Washington, too, invoked the providential character of the American experiment, and implored his soldiers and people to cultivate virtue lest liberty perish. Jefferson spoke in secular terms, but agreed that the freer people are, the more they must exercise self-discipline. John Adams believed that the Bible offered "the only system that ever did or ever will preserve a republic in the world."[60] And in times to come, Americans continued to measure their institutions against such standards of virtue and usually found them wanting. What they did *not* require was that their relations with foreigners stand up to similar scrutiny.

That is why the twin mottoes of the new nation could not have been improved upon: *E pluribus unum* and Don't tread on me. What is more, the latter was the anterior sentiment.

TWO

Unilateralism, or Isolationism (so called)

"WOE TO THE REBELLIOUS CHILDREN," says the Lord, "who carry out a plan, but not mine; and who seek a league, but a league not of my spirit . . . who set out to go down to Egypt, without asking for my counsel, to take refuge in the protection of Pharaoh, and to seek shelter in the shadow of Egypt!"[1]

Our detached and distant situation invites and enables us to pursue a different course. . . . Why forego the advantages of so peculiar a situation? Why quit our own to stand upon foreign ground? Why, by interweaving our destiny with that of any part of Europe, entangle our peace and prosperity in the toils of European ambition, rivalship, interest, humor, or caprice?[2]

Their times and places and modes of persuasion could not have differed more, but the prophet Isaiah and President Washington preached the same lesson: Put not your trust in allies, especially those who are stronger than you. At worst they will betray or disappoint you; at best they will make you a pawn in their games. Trust instead in the Lord and yourselves in your dealings with aliens, and cast not away the protection conferred by a generous Providence.

The second great tradition of U.S. foreign policy is habitually dubbed "isolationism." This, despite dogged efforts by some diplomatic historians to instruct us that no such principle ever informed American government, and that the word itself came into general use only in the 1930s. To be sure, references to America's "isolation" can be found in documents dating back to colonial times, but their authors were just stating a geographical fact. In the post–Civil War decades the word "isolation" pops up more often, but as an echo of Victorian Britain's slogan of Splendid Isolation. American historians, whose writings have been thoroughly surveyed by Jerald Combs, affirmed a policy of "manly neutrality," but made no mention of "isolation" until the 1890s.[3] What brought "isolation" to the consciousness of the American public was the propaganda of navalists like Captain A. T. Mahan, who sought to pin on their anti-imperialist critics a tag that implied they were old-fashioned curmudgeons. Thus the *Washington Post* proclaimed at the time of the Spanish-American War that "the policy of isolation is dead,"[4] and the *Oxford English Dictionary* first made reference to the concept in 1901: "Hence *Isolationist,* one who favors or advocates isolation. In U.S. politics, one who thinks the Republic ought to pursue a policy of political isolation." The example the *O.E.D.* cites is from a *Philadelphia Press* editorial of 1899, referring to the overseas peoples absorbed by the United States after the Spanish-American War: "Their consent ought to have been obtained first, according to the creed of the isolationists." The first Webster's dictionary to define "isolationist" (but still not "isolation*ism*") seems to have been the 1921 edition. The *Encyclopaedia Britannica* never made "isolationism" a rubric, and only after World War II did its articles on diplomacy refer to the phenomenon. Most telling of all, not even the "isolationists" of the 1930s had any use for the term, preferring to call themselves neutralists or nationalists. So, our vaunted tradition of "isolation*ism*" is no tradition at all, but a dirty word that interventionists, especially since Pearl Harbor, hurl at anyone who questions their policies.

Let us dispense with the term altogether and substitute for it a word that really describes the second great tradition in American foreign relations: Unilateralism. It was a natural, even inevitable corollary of the first American tradition, for if the essence of Exceptionalism was Liberty at home, the essence of Unilateralism was to be *at Liberty* to make foreign policy independent of the "toils of European ambition." Unilateralism never meant that the United States should, or for that matter could, sequester itself or pursue an ostrich-like policy toward all foreign countries. It simply meant, as Hamilton and Jefferson both underscored, that the self-evident course for the United States was to avoid permanent, entangling alliances and to remain neutral in Europe's wars except when our Liberty — the first hallowed tradition — was at risk.

★

Unilateralism emerged quite naturally from the eighteenth-century policy debates about Britain's (hence America's) proper posture toward the European continent. Robert Walpole, the great Whig prime minister, summarized British wisdom in 1723 when he wrote, "My politics are to keep free from all engagements as long as we possibly can," and the Earl of Pomfret instructed the House of Lords in 1755, "Nature has separated us from the continent . . . and as no man ought to endeavour to separate whom God Almighty has joined, so no man ought to endeavour to join what God Almighty has separated."[5] So England's true policy was to exploit the advantages of insularity, nurture the balance of power on the Continent while avoiding land wars if possible, see to its navy, and conquer the trade of the world. And if that amounted to wisdom for Britain, how much more was it so for the "insular" colonies across the sea? Franklin was a convinced unilateralist before Congress even declared independence, and the Model Treaty was to be a model insofar as it specifically proscribed *political* ties with foreign powers. In *Common Sense* Paine named it the "true interest of America to steer clear of European contentions," and John Adams insisted "we should calculate all our measures and foreign negotiations in such a manner, as to avoid a too great dependence upon any one power of Europe."[6]

What were the motives for American Unilateralism? Were they strategic, commercial, moral, or just an expression of the separatist bias of pilgrims who had quit Europe and wanted to stay quit of her? Even historians as subtle as Felix Gilbert resort to a certain tortured logic in attempting to account for American standoffishness:

> The foreign policy of the young republic, with its emphasis on commerce and on avoidance of political connections, has usually been explained as a policy of isolation. Unquestionably, the English background of the ideas which served in the formation of the American outlook on foreign policy contained an isolationist element. However, if we place the ideas . . . beside those of the European *philosophes,* it becomes clear that the isolationist interpretation is one-sided and incomplete: American foreign policy was idealistic and internationalist no less than isolationist.[7]

But the need to reconcile such apparent opposites disappears if we conceive of American Exceptionalism as a mission not on behalf of universal principles but on behalf of Liberty at home, and then jettison the concept of an isolationism that never existed in favor of Unilateralism. Suddenly the apparent tension between idealism and realism is relieved, and early American foreign policy is revealed for what it was: a coherent, internally consistent whole.

> See this glad world remote from every foe,
> From Europe's mischiefs, and from Europe's woes.[8]

The logic for such a reformulation is, I hope, compelling. First, if the United States became enmeshed in war and imperialism on the European model, it would have to raise large armies and navies, tax and conscript its people, and generally compromise domestic freedom, the Republic's *raison d'être*. Second, if it became enmeshed in Europe's conflicts, the United States would be forced to play junior partner in alliances with mighty empires, perhaps losing, or losing sight of, its own national interests. Third, if it became enmeshed in foreign conflicts, the European powers would compete for Americans' affections, corrupt their politics with propaganda and bribes, and split them into factions. Fourth, if the United States joined in Europe's rivalries, the arenas of battle would surely include America's own lands and waters, as they had for over a century.

So neutrality was the only moral *and* pragmatic course for the new nation. Entangling alliances would only invite corruption at home and danger abroad, while neutrality could not but serve Liberty and national growth. Would that political choices were always so easy, that one could always do so well by doing good. But that was the blessed state Americans found themselves in. Their geopolitical position was so favorable that only they themselves could foul it up.

Europeans perceived this. Thomas Pownall, a British politician with extensive experience in the colonies, wrote in the midst of the Revolution that the crowned heads of Europe had better prepare for the emergence of a mighty challenger across the Atlantic. He predicted that America would in time be "the Arbitress" of commerce and "the Mediatrix" of world politics if she only sat back and exploited the European balance of power to extend her own sway over the American continent.[9] In 1784 the Swedish minister in London made the same point in earthier terms to John Adams: "Sir, I take it for granted that you will have sense enough to see us in Europe cut each other's throats with a philosophical tranquillity."[10]

But complete freedom of action — Unilateralism — was as impossible for a young and still fragile nation as complete isolation was utopian. An ocean speckled with European frigates was a hazard as well as a moat, Americans needed trade and capital in order to grow, and in any case U.S. security depended on a balance of power between Britain and France, just as Britain's depended on a continental balance. But any appearance of an American tilt toward Britain or France was bound to be viewed by the other, not as the unilateral act of a neutral, but as a partisan act that favored the enemy. How could the United States therefore maneuver itself into a position of true Unilateralism? Only by growing so large, populous, prosperous, and invulnerable on its side of the ocean that it could deal with Europe from a position of strength. And that is precisely what Pownall, Washington, Jefferson, Hamilton, and the Adamses predicted would happen in short order — assuming the nation survived its formative decades intact.

The experience of the nation over its first twenty years proved the utility of Unilateralism over and over again. No sooner was the Franco-American Alliance concluded than the Continental Congress and its commissioners in Paris spied the danger of American policy's becoming dependent on France and France's other ally, Spain. Hence Franklin's bold insistence on hammering out a separate peace with Britain. But a more seductive temptation to eschew Unilateralism popped up almost at once. European neutrals during the War of American Independence banded together under Russian leadership in a League of Armed Neutrality, their purpose being to defend their own shipping from all the belligerents. The League's slogan of "free ships, free goods" seemed to echo the principles of America's Model Treaty, and in 1783 the Dutch Republic, assuming Americans would be sympathetic, urged the United States to join. Congress deliberated, then flatly refused: "The true interest of these states requires that they should be as little as possible entangled in the politics and controversies of European nations."[11]

In the following decade, as we have seen, the United States had to struggle repeatedly to limit its entanglements during the wars of the French Revolution. There was never a question of isolation, not only because of American vulnerability at sea, but because of public finance. The country was deeply in debt from its struggle for independence, and its "Continental" bonds and currency were a laughingstock. The credit of the United States would thus rise or fall on the strength of its federal revenues. But the bulk of those revenues came from the tariff on foreign imports, and upward of 90 percent of those imports came from Great Britain. To the Federalists, especially Secretary of the

Treasury Hamilton, who favored Britain in any case, the upshot was obvious. The United States would have to swallow a certain amount of British interference with neutral shipping born of Britain's war against France in order to foster what amicable commerce it could: hence the controversial Jay Treaty of 1794. This apparent tilt toward Britain was what enraged the agents of the French Revolution, most notoriously Genêt, who conspired to turn American opinion against Federalist policies.

By 1796 theory and experience pushed Americans of all persuasions to the inescapable conclusion that the United States, precisely because it *could not isolate itself* from the commerce and conflicts on the Atlantic (not to mention the neighboring European empires in North America), must strive to minimize its exposure through a policy of abstention. "I do not love to be entangled with the politics of Europe," said John Adams drily. "[America] is remote from Europe, and ought not to engage in her politics or wars," said Madison. "[I]t is a maxim with us, and I think it is a wise one, not to entangle ourselves with the affairs of Europe," wrote Jefferson. "You ought to spurn from you as the box of Pandora, the fatal heresy of a close alliance," wrote Hamilton.[12] And most striking of all were the words of Adams's brilliant twenty-five-year-old son, Quincy, writing in 1793:

> Was it worthy of the generous and heroic self-devotion, which offered the thousands of our friends and brethren, as a willing sacrifice at the holy altar of American Independence, to be made the bubbles of foreign speculation, to be blown like feathers to and fro as the varying breath of foreign influence should be directed; to be bandied about from one nation to another, subservient to the purposes of their mutual resentments, and played with as the passive instruments of their interests and passions? Perish the American! whose soul is capable of submitting to such a degrading servitude!

Americans, rather, were "a nation whose happiness consists in a real independence, disconnected from all European interests and European politics."[13]

Washington not only read Quincy's pseudonymous letters (complimenting John Adams on his son's sagacity) but appointed him U.S. minister to the Netherlands. So in the case of Unilateralism, as in the case of Exceptionalism (and two more traditions to follow), John Quincy Adams was present at the creation.

But he was not the author of Washington's Farewell Address, which established for generations the Great Rule of American Unilateralism. Washington himself conceived of a valediction near the end of his first term, put it off until the end of his second, labored over a wooden first draft, then asked Madison and Hamilton to refine it. Madison did so; Hamilton did not. Since Washington had given him leave to "throw the whole into a different form," Hamilton produced an "Original Major Draft" that expanded the president's warning against the dangers of factionalism into a "general principle of policy."[14] No alert reader of 1796 could fail to catch his text's barely veiled references to the troubles caused by the French alliance, the Genêt affair, and the fight over the Jay and Pinckney Treaties. But Hamilton transcended the politics of the day by employing phraseology that recalled to the minds of alert Americans the very words of *Common Sense*, the congressional rejection of the League of Armed Neutrality, the *Federalist Papers*, and popular broadsides such as Quincy Adams's letters. In effect, Hamilton was reminding Americans of a tradition they had already affirmed for two decades and exploiting Washington's prestige to endow that tradition with an air of timeless wisdom. We know the results:[15]

> Observe good faith and justice toward all nations. Cultivate peace and harmony with all. Religion and morality enjoin this conduct. And can it be that good policy does not equally enjoin it? It will be worthy of a free, enlightened, and at no distant period a great nation to give to mankind the magnanimous and too novel example of a people always guided by an exalted justice and benevolence. Who can doubt that in the course of time and things the fruits of such a plan would richly repay any temporary advantages which might be lost by a steady adherence to it? Can it be that Providence has not connected the permanent felicity of a nation with its virtue? The experiment, at least, is recommended by every sentiment which ennobles human nature. Alas! is it rendered impossible by its vices?

In other words, wrote Hamilton/Washington, no conflict existed between morals and self-interest so long as Americans played no favorites abroad. Nor must they allow themselves to be lured away from the long-term rewards of such conduct by the ephemeral advantages to be gained by foreign partisanship. God would reward virtue, on which the American experiment depended in any case.

> In the execution of such a plan nothing is more essential than that permanent, inveterate antipathies against particular nations and pas-

sionate attachments for others should be excluded, and that in place of them just and amicable feelings toward all should be cultivated. The nation which indulges toward another an habitual hatred or an habitual fondness is in some degree a slave. . . . The great rule of conduct for us in regard to foreign nations is, in extending our commercial relations to have with them as little *political* connection as possible. So far as we have already formed engagements let them be fulfilled with perfect good faith. Here let us stop.

But Hamilton/Washington did not stop. Having restated the point that liberty would give way to slavery if Americans whored after foreign powers and divided at home, the authors went on to beguile their compatriots with the glory that was to be, so long as they remained fixed on their own concerns:

Europe has a set of primary interests which to us have none or a very remote relation. Hence she must be engaged in frequent controversies, the causes of which are essentially foreign to our concerns. Hence, therefore, it must be unwise in us to implicate ourselves by artificial ties in the ordinary vicissitudes of her politics. . . .

Our detached and distant situation invites and enables us to pursue a different course. If we remain one people, under an efficient government, the period is not far off when we may defy material injury from external annoyance; when we may take such an attitude as will cause the neutrality we may at any time resolve upon to be scrupulously respected; when belligerent nations, under the impossibility of making acquisitions upon us, will not lightly hazard the giving us provocation; when we may choose peace or war, as our interest, guided by justice, shall counsel.

Why forego the advantages of so peculiar a situation? Why quit our own to stand upon foreign ground? Why, by interweaving our destiny with that of any part of Europe, entangle our peace and prosperity in the toils of European ambition, rivalship, interest, humor, or caprice?

And so to the Great Rule:

It is our true policy to steer clear of permanent alliances with any portion of the foreign world, so far, I mean, as we are now at liberty to do it; for let me not be understood as capable of patronizing infidelity to existing engagements. I hold the maxim no less applicable to public than to private affairs that honesty is always the best policy. I repeat, therefore, let those engagements be observed in their genuine sense. But in my opinion it is unnecessary and would be unwise to extend them.

But note: Hamilton/Washington did not say "dump the 1778 alliance with France" (however much they may have wished to do so), for then readers might dismiss the document as a Federalist tract. But "observed in the genuine sense" and "unwise to extend them" were clearly meant to suggest the wisdom of honoring the alliance with France in name only. And lest the tone of that passage lead readers to mistake the Great Rule for an unequivocal denunciation of *all* cooperation with foreign powers (that is, real isolationism), the authors immediately balanced it with this:

> Taking care always to keep ourselves by suitable establishment on a respectable defensive posture, we may safely trust to temporary alliances for extraordinary emergencies.

Thus American security might at times require short-term alliances. Of course, the danger was always that stronger allies could then reduce the United States to the status of a client state, hence the need for "suitable" military preparedness. And finally, lest readers overemphasize that anti-isolationist endorsement of temporary alliances, Hamilton/ Washington concluded with another reminder that foreigners were not to be trusted:

> Harmony, liberal intercourse with all nations are recommended by policy, humanity, and interest. But even our commercial policy should hold an equal and impartial hand . . . constantly keeping in view that it is folly in one nation to look for disinterested favors from another; that it must pay with a portion of its independence for whatever it may accept under that character. . . . There can be no greater error than to expect or calculate upon real favors from nation to nation. It is an illusion which experience must cure, which a just pride ought to discard.

Washington's farewell message is a remarkable document.[16] Its internal checks and balances demanded that it be read and absorbed as a whole, like Holy Writ, lest one phrase or passage be wrenched from its context and made the proof text of a heresy. It was a product of the mid-1790s, but looked back to the days of the Revolution and ahead to an era of U.S. expansion and power. It laid down no inflexible policy, but rather a set of principles. First, foreign policy should be the indispensable armor of the Republic, but folly, favoritism, faction, and premature ambition could turn foreign policy into a danger to independence and liberty. Next, a wise foreign policy would seek good relations with all foreign states but eschew political ties with any except in unusual emergencies. Third, the United States must marshal its strength to defend its interests against enemies and temporary allies alike, since it as yet lacked the power to deter or avenge all "annoyances." Finally, if these prudent principles were observed, the day was not distant when the country would acquire such power. All Americans needed to do was avoid unnecessary entanglements and look to their demographic, commercial, and territorial growth.

It has often been written that neutrality, isolation, or (as I prefer) Unilateralism became an "instant tradition," so great was Washington's authority among his compatriots. That was not quite the case. However admired for his military service, Washington was a staunch Federalist and his policies were widely resented. A Philadelphia journal spoke for many when it suggested that the day of his retirement be made a jubilee: "Lord now lettest Thy servant depart in peace, for mine eyes have seen Thy salvation. . . . The man who is the source of all his country's misery is this day reduced to the rank of his fellow-citizens, and has no longer the power to multiply the woes of these United States."[17] Two decades would pass before iconographers and literary sculptors like Mason Weems, Noah Webster, and John Marshall completed Washington's metamorphosis into a marble man.[18]

In another sense, Washington's Great Rule did not even require that its author be a revered icon because, as we have seen, it laid down principles that virtually all the Founding Fathers endorsed. Only some foreign observers were initially fooled as they combed Washington's text for hints of a change in U.S. policy. French minister Pierre August Adet, for example, was initially cheered by the lip service paid to "existing engagements," then replied with a bitter *au revoir* of his own when he realized the neutralist intent of the authors. But Adet was mistaken to blame Hamilton alone for what he called the message's "insolence" and "immorality." Jefferson, too, adhered to the principles Washington laid down, and the following year wrote, "Our countrymen have divided themselves by such strong affections to the French and the English that nothing will secure us internally but a divorce from both nations."[19] By the time the Franco-American Alliance was abrogated in 1800, Talleyrand was advising Napoleon to expect nothing from U.S. policy even if a Democratic Republican should capture the presidency: "Mr. Jefferson will make it his duty to unite around himself the true Americans and to resume in all its force the system of perfect equilibrium between France and England, which alone suits the United States."[20]

If there were any doubts that Unilateralism had achieved the character of a bona fide American tradition by the turn of the century, the behavior of the Democratic Republican presidents (the "Virginia dynasty") and their secretaries of state removed them. Jefferson invoked the Great Rule in his first inaugural address and bequeathed to us the phrase "no entangling alliances." He did briefly consider an alliance with Britain in 1802, but only because of an "extraordinary emergency": the prospect of a Napoleonic empire in the Mississippi Valley. In 1804, with Louisiana safely in American hands and Napoleon at war again, the U.S. minister in Paris made a secret suggestion to the effect that the United States grab empty Texas away from Napoleon's Spanish ally. Jefferson was tempted, but as Secretary of State Madison pointed out, it all depended on getting an assurance from Britain that it would bottle up the French navy — an assurance Britain would hardly extend except in exchange for U.S. belligerence.[21] Faced with a choice between easy expansion and the maintenance of a unilateral policy, Jefferson unhesitatingly chose the latter.

In 1812 the United States did go to war, but far from abandoning neutrality, it did so in defense of neutral rights and did so *unilaterally*. That is, even though France and the United States were now both at war with Britain, the Madison administration did not pronounce itself "associated" (in Woodrow Wilson's later phrase), much less "allied," with Napoleon. And after peace was restored in 1815, Jefferson iterated, "The less we have to do with the amities or enmities of Europe, the better."[22] Finally, when George Canning commended to the American minister in London the wisdom of a joint Anglo-American affirmation of the independence of Latin American republics, Secretary of State John Quincy Adams persuaded the cabinet to spurn even this ostensibly innocuous suggestion as a threat to American freedom of action. So President James Monroe acted unilaterally in 1823.

No U.S. administration even considered another foreign engagement, much less an alliance, for the rest of the century.

*

Washington's Great Rule became in time what the antebellum historian George Tucker called a "test of orthodoxy to American patriots."[23] American scholars of the 1830s, '40s, and '50s disputed the rectitude of Federalist or Democratic Republican tactics, but every one affirmed Unilateralism. They also understood, as W. H. Trescot wrote, that the Founding Fathers defined neutrality as "the perfect independence of the United States; not their isolation from the great affairs of the world."[24] For the non-isolation of the United States was simply self-evident. As historian Paul Varg has convincingly shown, nineteenth-century Americans were intimate members of the Atlantic community in every way *except* as regards their neutrality and peculiar democracy. For instance, much of the technology driving the American industrial revolution, and the woolens and cotton cloths on American backs, came from abroad. Between 1820 and 1850 American imports quadrupled to $144 million per year, over two-thirds of them from Europe. The customs receipts from that trade remained the major source of federal revenue. The capital that financed U.S. factories, mines, and railroad construction also came mostly from abroad. Nearly two-thirds of American state and municipal bonds in the 1830s were held by Europeans, and as late as 1853 Europeans still owned over a third of Americans' public debt. In that year the U.S. Treasury put the total foreign investment in America at $222 million.

As with capital, so with labor. American fertility was prodigious, but native-born Americans could never have built their canals and railroads, manned their busy docks and workbenches, and cleared the Midwest for agriculture nearly so quickly had not millions of English and Scots, Irish and Germans crossed the Atlantic before the Civil War. The 1860 census listed 4 million immigrants, and foreign-born people in midwestern states ranged from 11 percent in Ohio to 36 percent in Wisconsin. The resulting foreign influence on American popular culture was immense, but no more than on American high culture. In salons from Boston to Philadelphia and collegiate common rooms from Dartmouth to Princeton, learned Americans discussed Jeremy Bentham's utilitarianism, the moral philosophies of Immanuel Kant and Dugald Stewart, the novels and poetry of Sir Walter Scott, Samuel Coleridge, Lord Byron, and Charles Dickens, and looked to Europe for leadership in science, medicine, theology, and law. American writers and scientists, in turn, valued nothing more than recognition in Europe. As Varg concludes, the United States "remained firmly neutral regarding European conflicts. In this sense only was it outside the Atlantic community."[25]

Nor was isolationism evident in American commercial policy.

From the Model Treaty onward the U.S. government consistently promoted trade with as many foreign nations as were willing to reciprocate. Its initiatives in the Western Hemisphere and Pacific Rim are better described in the context of other traditions. For now, suffice to say that the Van Buren administration's naval expedition to the Pacific (under Charles Wilkes) from 1838 to 1842; the Tyler administration's intervention on behalf of Hawaiian independence in 1841; the Tyler, Buchanan, and Andrew Johnson administrations' vigorous (and sometimes violent) pursuit of trade treaties with China in 1844, 1858, and 1868; the Fillmore and Pierce administrations' dispatch of Commodore Perry to Japan; the Grant administration's bid for a virtual protectorate over Hawaii; and the first Cleveland administration's assertion of a U.S. protectorate over Samoa — to name just some high points — were hardly the acts of an isolationist nation.

So what we observe when we look at nineteenth-century American history is a nation convinced of the wisdom of Unilateralism. For unless the United States remained at Liberty to pick and choose its foreign involvements, it would become entwined in the alliances and alignments of the European powers, see its interests trampled by enemies or betrayed by allies, risk reopening the American continents to the play of competing empires, and bow to the necessity of maintaining an army and navy far in excess of Washington's "suitable establishment on a respectable defensive posture" — all of which would tend to compromise Americans' first and dearest tradition, their independence and commitment to Liberty, however they might choose to define it.

*

A question remains: how was it that the United States was able to cling to strict Unilateralism throughout so much of its history? How, that is, did we get away with it? The short answer is that the nation fortunately faced no more extraordinary emergencies of the sort that might require foreign assistance. But the reasons why no emergency happened are so interconnected that their relative importance is hard to sort out.

First, the United States did rapidly acquire a latent power sufficient to deter Europeans from challenging it on its own continent. This may seem to contradict the conventional wisdom according to which the United States enjoyed "free security" throughout the nineteenth century, provided in large part by the Royal Navy, that "unwitting protector of American isolationism."[26] In fact, a big reason the United States did not have to spend much on defense was that its *potential* might was so palpable. To be sure, the U.S. Army was tiny and the state militias laughably amateur, but they were no measure of what an aroused Republic-in-arms could bring to bear if its dander was up. By 1850 the U.S. population of 23 million surpassed that of England, Scotland, and Wales, and was expanding at the enormous rate of 33 percent per decade. Nor did the British forget the shocking string of defeats the Yankees handed their frigates in single-ship actions in the War of 1812. The quality of American shipbuilding and seamanship was the equal of the British and French, and the size of the U.S. merchant marine made possible rapid expansion of the navy in need. As it turned out, Americans never had to go on a serious war footing until 1861. But perceptive Europeans like Alexis de Tocqueville saw the potential in the 1830s: "The truth is as well understood in the United States as anywhere else: the Americans are already able to make their flag respected; in a few years they will make it feared."[27]

What is more, no sane European ruler would have dreamed of defying the remoteness and size of the United States. Even if an invader overcame the logistical difficulties involved in launching a sizable military expedition to North America, how could it force its will on a continental nation? The British achieved no more by burning Washington City in 1814 than the French achieved in burning Moscow in 1812. Illinois state representative Abraham Lincoln may have gotten carried away in his spread-eagle boast of 1836, but was not far off the mark, when he cried: "Shall we expect some transatlantic military giant to step the Ocean and crush us at a blow? Never! All the armies of Europe, Asia, and Africa combined, with all the treasure of the earth (our own excepted) in their military chest; with a Buonaparte for a commander, could not by force take a drink from the Ohio or make a track on the Blue Ridge, in a trial of a thousand years."[28] So long as the United States wisely confined its definition of vital interests to the Western Hemisphere, no threat was liable to arise that might oblige Americans to abandon Unilateralism in favor of foreign alliances.

Third, the European powers had neither the leisure nor means to challenge the United States on its own turf. France was serially preoccupied with revolutions (1830, 1848, 1871) and wars and crises in the Near East and Europe (1820–23, 1840–41, 1854–56, 1859, 1866, 1870), and Britain had little military force to spare after policing her home waters, the Mediterranean, the Indian Ocean and Indian frontiers, and the South China Sea, all the while fretting about Russian expansion and periodic French attempts to steal maritime supremacy.[29] So there were few occasions over the century when Britain could have seen any advantage in taking on the United States, no matter how large the stakes. Finally, the liberal ideology that dominated British policy after 1832, and especially after 1846, preached small government, free trade, and anti-colonialism (India always excepted), reducing the possible sources of friction with an essentially like-minded United States. Whatever "favors" Britain did do for the United States were only a consequence of what the Bonapartes, India, and Adam Smith did for Britain.

The fact remained that the British Empire was the only power that could, if it wished, pose a serious threat to American interests. The United States, in turn, held Canada "hostage." Those asymmetrical threats reinforced the psychological tension born of the mother-country/rebellious-colonies heritage and made for a curious relationship between the great English-speaking nations. John Adams snarled in 1816, "Britain will never be our Friend, till We are his Master."[30] But that was spite talking. The reality was that neither friendship nor mastery but a cautious, resentful coexistence was the only sensible basis for Anglo-American relations. John Quincy Adams and his counterpart, Foreign Secretary Lord Castlereagh, recognized as much and worked to liquidate issues left over from the sterile War of 1812. A new commercial treaty was concluded in 1815, the Rush-Bagot accord of 1817 effectively demilitarized the Great Lakes, and the Convention of 1818 fixed the U.S.-Canadian boundary from Lake of the Woods (now in Minnesota) to the Rocky Mountains at the 49th parallel and awarded New Englanders a certain freedom to fish the Grand Banks. In 1830 the British even agreed to open their West Indian ports to Yankee merchants for the first time since 1776.

Then Canada flared up in revolt. Or, to be more precise, a small faction of republican-minded malcontents under William Mackenzie rebelled in 1837 against British rule, recruited American freebooters, and took refuge in a saloon in Buffalo, New York. Numerous Yankees, cheered by what appeared to be a belated Canadian "war for independence," offered aid and comfort. Once again the U.S. government was given a chance to crusade on behalf of its principles. Once again it spurned the temptation. President Martin Van Buren observed strict neutrality, and was vexed when American citizens transported Mackenzie to a Canadian island on the Niagara River and ferried supplies to him in the steamship *Caroline*. When loyal Canadian soldiers then crossed the river and torched the ship, leaving one U.S. citizen dead, thousands of enraged Americans formed "Hunters' Lodges" sworn to "attack, combat, and help to destroy . . . every power or authority of Royal origin upon this continent."[31] British opinion, in turn, was inflamed in 1840 when a drunken Canadian official, Alexander McLeod, boasted in a New York tavern of having helped burn the *Caroline* and was tried by zealous locals for murder and arson. Soon, Canadian and American lumberjacks and militiamen mustered for battle in northern Maine, the boundary of which had been botched by mapmakers in 1783. No one perished in this "Aroostook War," but Congress authorized an army of 50,000 and a war chest of $10 million, and the British reinforced Canada.

These were also the years of the so-called War of the Quarterlies, in which British and American polemicists roundly excoriated each other in print. British visitors (Charles Dickens most notably) instructed their countrymen that Americans were an ignorant, muddy, tobacco-spitting, nasal-voiced mob, and a "nation of swindlers" to boot, for having defaulted on so many public bonds after the financial Panic of 1837.[32] For the Americans' part, the British were snooty, effeminate, arrogant, envious monopolists who deserved to be taken down a peg.

For more than two years war seemed likely — but only seemed so. In fact, Van Buren and President Tyler (William Henry Harrison having died after three weeks in office) had no intention of fighting Britain, and Lord Palmerston, the fiery Liberal foreign secretary, knew it. That was why he could afford to play bluff John Bull for the sake of British public opinion and vow to teach the Yankee Doodles "a good lesson."[33] When in the end the ridiculous Mr. McLeod was acquitted and Palmerston's government fell, Lord Aberdeen and Secretary of State Daniel Webster sponsored the Webster-Ashburton Treaty of 1842, which put to rest for the time being all U.S.-Canadian boundary disputes.[34]

The crises of the late 1830s and early 1840s are instructive because both governments shunned the thought of war, fearing only that the other's hotheadedness might trigger it, and because, once they sat down, they resolved their disputes in a trice. So the crises were not the result of a clash of vital interests so much as expressions of the animosity that most Americans had for Britain, and Britons for the

United States. As the observant Tocqueville remarked: "Nothing can be more virulent than the hatred that exists between the Americans of the United States and the English. But in spite of those hostile feelings the Americans derive most of their manufactured commodities from England, because England supplies them at a cheaper rate. Thus the increasing prosperity of America turns, notwithstanding the grudge of the Americans, to the advantage of British manufactures."[35] Lord Liverpool, the British prime minister, said simply, "Who wishes prosperity to England must wish prosperity to America."[36]

As in economics, so too in diplomacy. As Eugene Rostow put it, the security interests of Britain and the United States, while not identical, were largely congruent.[37] Both relied on, but hoped to stand aloof from, the European balance of power. Both resisted attempts to resuscitate imperialism in the Americas. Both wished to avoid entangling alliances. Both had a big stake in untrammeled commerce, most of all with each other. In the long run, of course, the British were uncomfortable with the prospect that the United States might someday eclipse them, while Americans loved to believe that the devious Brits were plotting to frustrate their growth even as they yearned for British respect.[38] But both governments, no matter who was in power, were careful to contain whatever conflicts erupted. Another Anglo-American war, after all, could only redound to the interests of France or Russia.

Why this lengthy excursion into the Anglo-American relationship? There are two reasons: to dispose for all time of the notion that the United States was isolationist in the nineteenth century, or was free to be so because of the gratuitous protection provided by the British fleet; and to acknowledge that the real second tradition of U.S. foreign policy — Unilateralism — was contingent on peaceful coexistence with the only power that could sensibly contemplate harming the United States. Happily, the British recognized the risks they would incur in an American war and the overlap between U.S. and British vital interests.

The secular historian calls this good luck, or an inevitable consequence of geography, economics, and demography. But many, perhaps most, Americans in the nineteenth century assumed that the freedom they enjoyed at home and their freedom from foreign entanglements were providential. Crusty John Quincy Adams, despite a crisis of faith after his loss to Andrew Jackson in the election of 1828, did not blush to confess that "the Declaration of Independence was a leading event in the progress of the gospel dispensation," and that the correct principles of American policy were discoverable in the scientific laws laid down by God in Creation and the Scriptures.[39] A century later, in 1933, Yale professor Edwin Borchard echoed this faith. After recounting the damage done, in his view, by U.S. imperialism and World War I, he said, "I regard neutrality as the greatest gift that God has put in the hands of the American people."[40]

THREE

The American System, or
Monroe Doctrine (so called)

THE AUSTRIAN MINISTER Klemens von Metternich deplored it. "These United States, whom we have seen arise and grow . . . ," he wrote, "have suddenly left a sphere too narrow for their ambition and have astonished Europe by a new act of revolt, more unprovoked, fully as audacious, and no less dangerous than the former."[1] The Russian government thought it merited "only the most profound contempt."[2] A Parisian journal, echoing the views of the French court, ridiculed it. Who was this president of a nation but forty years old that he dared to pose as "a dictator armed with a right of suzerainty over the entire New World"?[3] Otto von Bismarck later damned it for an "insolent dogma" and "a species of arrogance peculiarly American and inexcusable."[4]

They were referring, of course, to President James Monroe's 1823 message to Congress that declared the Americas off limits to new colonization. But Americans cheered almost without exception, because Monroe, no less than Washington in his Farewell Address, affirmed principles whose virtues had long since imposed themselves on the nation. Thus the chief of the British mission reported that the message "seems to have been received with acclamation throughout the United States." Its sentiments "echoed from one end of the Union to the other. It would, indeed, be difficult, in a country composed of elements so various . . . to find more perfect unanimity than has been displayed on every side."[5] A century later American enthusiasm was, if possible, even more ardent. "I believe strictly in the Monroe Doctrine, in our Constitution and in the laws of God," proclaimed Mary Baker Eddy, the guru of Christian Science, in 1923.[6] "The briefest expression of our rule of conduct is, perhaps, the Monroe Doctrine and the Golden Rule. With this simple chart we can hardly go far wrong," said Secretary of State John Hay.[7] And all American textbooks of the early 1900s agreed.

The trouble is that in between time, say from 1825 to around 1895, the Monroe Doctrine almost disappeared from politics and history books, and when it did appear, it seemed not to mean what we suppose it meant. That is because the term "Monroe Doctrine" did not come into general use until decades after the speech that inspired it, and then, in the half-century following, acquired the trappings of myth.[8] Since World War II historians have worked hard to expose the myths that obscure the Monroe Doctrine, but have had no more success in changing conventional wisdom about it than they have had in puncturing the myth of isolationism. So let us try, one more time, to set the record straight.

First, the Monroe Doctrine was not an American initiative at all, but a bold riposte to yet another British idea. Second, it was not designed to thwart an attempt on the part of the Holy Alliance to crush Latin American independence, because none of the powers capable of intervening in Latin America — Spain, France, and Britain — were even members of the Holy Alliance. Third, Monroe's anti-colonial stand did not save, or even shelter, the incipient Spanish American republics, because they were in no need of saving, and the Monroe administration had neither the will nor the means to deliver them anyway. Fourth, the United States was not acting in formal or informal cooperation with Britain when it gave notice to Europe to stay out of the Americas, for the reason that Britain was the biggest *target* of the American policy. Fifth, the Monroe Doctrine was only superficially Monroe's, did not become a "doctrine" for at least twenty years, and was so apparently inconsequential that diplomatic historians took almost no notice of it until the closing years of the nineteenth century.[9]

So what was this great foreign policy tradition we associate with the Monroe Doctrine? Was Woodrow Wilson right when he said that the doctrine was so elusive as to defy definition? That is hardly credible, for the coauthor of Monroe's address, Secretary of State John Quincy Adams, was not given to conjuring inchoate will-o'-the-wisps. Monroe's speech was in fact precise and to the point, but to discover its substance we must first purge what historian Thomas A. Bailey called the "cult of Monroeism," and try to grasp the world situation and reasoning process that gave rise to this third tradition of U.S. foreign affairs. And the best way to do that is to equate in our minds what came to be called the Monroe Doctrine with a more descriptive term: the American System.

The reasoning process of American statesmen in the 1820s is more easily grasped than the world situation, for the concept of an "American" system of hemispheric states followed from our first two traditions, Exceptionalism and Unilateralism, as the letter C follows A and B. If the United States was to nurture its independence and Liberty at home, it must steer clear of Europe's wars and ambitions and preserve its freedom of action. Hence the dicta of Washington and Jefferson against entangling alliances. But to refuse to "go over to Europe" was not enough; the United States must also see to it that European powers did not "come over to America." For if they did, they would inevitably threaten American interests, force the United States to play a role in the European balance of power, or, what was worse, create a second balance-of-power system in the Western Hemisphere itself. Hence the United States must work to fashion, as its limited means allowed, a uniquely American international system.

The logical progression from Exceptionalism to Unilateralism to an American System was implicit from Paine's pamphlet onward. Monroe simply made it explicit by way of responding to several alarming, interconnected feints toward the Americas after 1815. Our later misunderstandings emerged, therefore, not from a false understanding of what Monroe meant, but from a failure to appreciate what he did not mean to say. What follows may be considered an inquiry into what Monroe *did not mean* in his address of 1823.

*

We tend to think of the decades following the final overthrow of Napoleon as remarkably quiescent, and they were by comparison to the 1789–1815 era. But great earthquakes have aftershocks, and revolutions continued to sputter in the Mediterranean and Latin American worlds throughout the 1820s. Moreover, the fact that the European powers were now free, after a quarter-century of war, to resume their careers of expansion in Asia, the Pacific, and America posed new sorts of dangers for the United States. Finally, after 1815 the great powers were making a stab at coordinating their foreign policies and pooling their strength for the purpose of preventing or crushing new threats to Europe's repose — and a unified Europe was America's worst nightmare.

The allied powers that defeated Napoleon restored the Bourbon dynasty to the thrones of France and Spain. They then convened the Congress of Vienna to build a new and tranquil European order resting on five pillars: a compromise territorial settlement, a balance of power, the principle of monarchical legitimacy and solidarity (as opposed to popular sovereignty and republicanism), the practice of meeting in congresses to consult on incipient crises, and an informal pact among Russia, Prussia, and Austria known as the Holy Alliance. Tsar Alexander I intended the latter to promote fraternal relations among monarchs based on Christian precepts. In practice, the Holy Alliance symbolized the determination of those three most conservative monarchies to stamp out revolutionary "Jacobinism" wherever it reared its head. The linchpin of the Congress System was Britain's Tory foreign minister, Lord Castlereagh, since his willingness to engage in permanent alliances with the Continent ran counter to British tradition, to British sympathy with constitutional movements elsewhere, and to Britain's suspicion of its imperial rivals Russia and France. Not surprisingly, strains in the Congress appeared as soon as it faced its first challenges, and Castlereagh came under pressure at home to dissociate Britain from the Continent. What it all meant for the United States was uncertain. A unified, reactionary Europe could theoretically mount a powerful challenge to American interests — but at least Castlereagh, precisely because he was obsessed with stability in Europe, was prepared to conciliate the United States.

The Congress System began to crack up in 1820 when Spain's stubborn and stupid King Ferdinand VII marshaled an army for the purpose of suppressing the colonial rebellions in Latin America. His troops rebelled at the port of Cádiz, revolution spread to Madrid and then, in 1821, to Italy. At the Congress of Troppau the tsar claimed a "general right of intervention" to suppress such revolts, which Castlereagh rejected. But the Congress (absent Britain) authorized Austria to invade the insurgent Italian states and Bourbon France to restore order in Spain. Castlereagh committed suicide, and his Liberal successor in the Foreign Office, George Canning, promptly detached Britain from the European Congress. He could not, however, prevent 100,000 French soldiers from crossing the Pyrenees in April 1823 and brutally crushing Spain's revolution. Would Ferdinand now resume his project of sending armies to America, perhaps this time with French support?

If so, it would be the second challenge to the privacy of a New World inhabited by the United States and a congeries of Spanish *independentista* regimes. For Alexander I, in 1821, had thundered forth a ukase, or tsarist decree, banning all foreign commerce in the waters of the North Pacific Ocean extending more than ninety miles off-shore from the Aleutian Islands all the way down the northwest American coast to 51 degrees north latitude (just above the tip of Vancouver Island). His purpose was to scare away the British and American captains who habitually and at great profit bartered for seal and otter pelts along the Alaskan coast. The trade had begun in the decades following the Russian discovery of Alaska in 1741, and was regularized by an imperial charter granted the Russian American Trading Company in 1799. No more than three to five hundred Russians were ever resident in Alaska, but their persistent, long-suffering manager, Alexander Baranov, founded settlements at Kodiak Island and Sitka, and an advance post in California near the mouth of what is now the Russian River. Supplying these remote outposts, however, was beyond the capacity of the rickety Russian navy and merchant marine, especially during the Napoleonic Wars. So Baranov had taken to trading a portion of his furs to visiting merchants in exchange for food, drink, tools, and weapons. But now Alexander I sacked Baranov and put the Russian navy in charge of Alaska with orders to enforce a monopoly.

The British and American governments howled. Not only was the tsar threatening to stop a lucrative commerce and treat their nations' seamen as if they were pirates, he was making a bold move to extend the Russian colony deep into lands claimed simultaneously by Britain and the United States. Congressional advocates of commercial and territorial expansion considered the ukase (in the words of a Boston merchant, William Sturgis) "little short of an actual declaration of hostilities," and lobbied the administration to take firm action.[10]

The obvious course was for Britain and the United States to join forces and call the Russian bluff, but mutual suspicion prevented it. When the British minister in Washington, Stratford Canning (George Canning's cousin), learned that the United States intended to press its claims to all of the Oregon Territory (roughly, today's British Columbia, Washington, and Oregon), he demanded to know if the grasping Yankees had their eyes on Canada, too. "Keep what is yours," barked John Quincy Adams, "but leave the rest of the continent to us."[11] Turning to the Russians, Adams warned them not to molest American ships engaged in lawful commerce, snubbed the emissaries sent by the tsar, and instructed the U.S. minister in St. Petersburg to negotiate with Russia independently of Britain. He wanted nothing less than a rollback of Russian claims to 55 degrees north latitude, and full trading rights in Russian America for U.S. merchants. Then, on July 15, 1823, Adams put on paper the following, in a letter to a senator: "But what right has Russia to *any* colonial footing on the *continent* of North America? Has she any that we are bound to recognize? And is it not time for the American *Nations* to inform the sovereigns of Europe, that the American continents are no longer open to the settlement of new European colonies?"[12] Thus did Adams first enunciate the principle later proclaimed by Monroe.

A month and a day later, the U.S. minister to Britain, Richard Rush, was summoned to meet with Canning. He expected a wide-ranging consultation about the threat of a Franco-Hispanic expedition to subdue Latin America, the Russian pretensions in northwestern America, and perhaps also the savage fighting that had recently erupted when the Greeks rose against their Ottoman Turkish masters. But Canning slyly beat around the bush until Rush himself, trawling for information, raised the issue that was on the Englishman's mind. Was it not so, queried Rush, that even if France did succeed in stamping out the sparks of revolution in Spain, "Great Britain would not allow her to go farther and lay her hands upon the Spanish colonies?" Canning did not answer; instead, he asked what Rush thought his own government's reaction would be to a suggestion that the United States go "hand in hand" with Britain on that.[13]

It was a beguiling, astonishing proposal for a strategic partnership between the young United States and the world's greatest power, a power that Americans had fought twice already but that shared America's interests, at least so far as the Spanish colonies were concerned. Rush prepared to cross the Atlantic for consultation, and before his departure Canning followed up with a list of principles to which he invited the United States to subscribe. "For ourselves," proposed Canning, "we have no disguise. 1. We conceive the recovery of the Colonies by Spain to be hopeless. 2. We conceive the question of the recognition of them, as Independent States, to be one of time and circumstances. 3. We are, however, by no means disposed to throw any impediment in the way of . . . amicable negotiation. 4. We aim not at the possession of any portion of them ourselves. 5. We could not see any portion of them transferred to any other Power, with indifference."[14]

Was this offer good and true, or too good to be true, or true but by no means good? More than relations with Britain were at stake:

U.S. relations with Latin America, the notion of an "American system of states" unencumbered by ties to Europe, and, not least, the American tradition of Unilateralism, hinged on the American response.

*

The Spanish American independence movements are complex and fascinating, and bear only slight resemblance to that of the thirteen North American colonies. The precipitating event was Napoleon's 1808 coup in Spain, which had deposed the Bourbon monarch, placed Joseph Bonaparte on the throne in Madrid, and destroyed the legitimacy of royal authority in the colonies. The United States had little attention to spare for the sputtering South American revolts until the Treaty of Ghent had liquidated the War of 1812, but in 1817 President Monroe raised the issue at a solemn meeting of his cabinet. Had the chief executive constitutional authority to recognize new states in rebellion against their sovereign, and was it in the national interest to do so? In short, should the American government lend aid and comfort to peoples who seemed, at least, to be fighting for the same principles on which the United States was founded?

Now, few Yankee colonists — save smugglers and slavers — had had much experience of Spanish America, and Americans' prevailing image of that vast empire to the south was summed up best by the nineteenth-century historian Francis Parkman: "Gloomy and portentous, she chilled the world with her baneful shadow. . . . A tyranny of monks and inquisitors, with their swarms of spies and informers, their racks, their dungeons, and their fagots, crushed all freedom of thought and speech. . . . Commercial despotism was joined to political and religious despotism."[15] But now that Spain's subjects had risen up against that, Americans were eager to laud the military exploits and patriotism of a Simón Bolívar or San Martín and compare them to those of George Washington. "At the present moment," cried Henry Clay, the feisty frontiersman and Speaker of the House, "the patriots of the South are fighting for liberty and independence — for precisely what we fought for." In March 1818 he introduced a resolution calling on the United States to recognize the indigenous Latin regimes and so encourage them in the same way that France had raised American spirits by recognizing the Continental Congress in 1778.[16]

Nor was this sympathy for the Latin cause solely the product of Yankee self-gratification. The leaders and agents of the revolutionary juntas cleverly and continually couched their appeals for help in terms of republican fraternity. As early as February 1811 the leadership in Buenos Aires wrote to President Madison: "The marked proofs which your Excellency has given of your Beneficence and magnanimity towards the Province of Caracas are irrefragable testimonies of the lively Interest which your Excellency takes in the Rights of Humanity . . . [and] gives us an equal Right to hope that . . . the United States should tighten with the Provinces on the Rio Plata the common chain of Nations, by a Cordiality more firm and expressive."[17] And San Martín de Pueyrredón congratulated Monroe on his inauguration as president with this message:[18]

> The liberal and benevolent principles which distinguish your government induce me to believe that the recent triumphs of liberty in these united provinces of South America will be heard with pleasure by your Excellency and the happy citizens of your republic. The confidence and the conformity of the principles which actuate the inhabitants of this hemisphere with those that stimulated the heroic efforts of the United States of the north in the achievement of their independence encourage me to make known to your Excellency the restoration of the opulent kingdom of Chile by the patriot forces of my government.

So when Clay rose in Congress to urge the executive branch to support the revolutions, he needed only to cite the encomia of the Latins themselves.

Commercial opportunities also turned American eyes to the south. For while the once flourishing Yankee trade with Spain and Portugal never recovered from the blow dealt by the Peninsular War of 1808–14, American exports to Spanish America expanded to $8 million per year by 1821, 13 percent of all U.S. exports.[19] To be sure, the United States could not hope to beat Britain in the competition for Latin markets — British industrial goods were far better and cheaper, and Britons invested 22 million pounds sterling in the region in the first half of the 1820s alone. But friendly relations with an independent Latin America might nonetheless benefit the U.S. economy, a point Clay repeatedly made on the basis of an influential 1816 pamphlet that promised an annual market of $100 million to American manufacturers.[20] The gradual shift in the demographic and economic centers of gravity of the United States also made the lands around the Gulf of Mexico increasingly enticing. Between 1812 and 1819 the cotton states of Louisiana, Mississippi, and Alabama and the farm states of

Indiana and Illinois achieved statehood. All of them relied in large part on the gulf ports at the mouths of the Ohio/Mississippi and Tombigbee/Alabama river systems to carry their goods to distant markets. If westerners had looked with alarm on the prospect of a French- or Spanish-run New Orleans in 1803, how much more would they protest if the entire Gulf of Mexico became home to the fleets and publicans of monopolistic European powers?

Still, none of those interests bound the United States to aid and abet the Latin revolutions. Instead, Secretary of State Monroe said in 1811, "The destiny of these provinces must depend on themselves."[21] And President Madison made a secret communication to Congress eliciting a resolution that committed the United States to take up arms for Latin America in one instance only: the attempted transfer of territories from Spain to another imperial power (for example, to England or France).[22] The reasons for that official reticence are not hard to find. American Exceptionalism and Unilateralism alike proscribed gratuitous jousts abroad no matter how holy the purport, and any suggestion that the United States meant to enter the lists was bound to spoil U.S. relations with the (frightfully united) Congress of Europe. What is more, hands-on experience with the Spanish Americans gave U.S. officials reason to doubt that the Latins would replicate the successful North American revolution; instead they might follow the path to anarchy, terror, and despotism marked out by the French Revolution.

For instance, Madison responded to those first pleas for help following the outbreak of fighting in Mexico, Venezuela, and La Plata (Argentina) by appointing three "agents for seamen and commerce" to promote and protect U.S. interests. Inevitably the agents tried to manipulate the tumultuous politics of the Latin juntas, and just as inevitably burned their fingers. In 1811 Joel Poinsett, a zealous republican, Anglophobe, and plantation owner, was named consul-general to Buenos Aires, Peru, and Chile. At that time José Miguel Carrera's family was in charge in the Chilean capital of Valparaiso, and Poinsett eagerly ingratiated himself, even providing Carrera with a copy of the U.S. Constitution. Soon Poinsett was urging the Chileans to declare full independence, arranging for them to buy arms from abroad, and even taking part in their battles against royalist forces. Then the junta split up in a family quarrel, Carrera was exiled (and later killed), Poinsett became persona non grata, and the victorious Andean patriots San Martín and Bernardo O'Higgins looked for patronage to Britain, not the United States.[23] Little wonder, then, that when President Monroe asked a panel of commissioners to advise him on Latin American policy, it threw a wet blanket on the movement for recognition. Theodorick Bland, a Baltimore merchant assumed to be friendly to the Latin revolutions, reported that "unless present civil dissensions are healed, and the warring provinces are pacified and reconciled to each other, a very great proportion, if not all, the benefits and advantages of the revolution . . . will be totally destroyed, or at least, very much diminished and delayed."[24]

Latin Americans were disillusioned as well. Their agents made repeated pilgrimages to the United States, always received a warm welcome, and always went home empty-handed. The Mexican agent José Bernardo Gutiérrez de Lara, for example, was lionized by Washington society, but his petitions for American muskets and recognition elicited nothing from the Monroe administration except a veiled invitation to cede Texas to the United States in the event of Mexican independence. Gutiérrez did manage, with the help of some four hundred New Orleans freebooters and a private line of credit, to set himself up as the head of a Texan junta. But that coup d'état, too, soon collapsed, and he and his Yankee supporters parted ways, hurling curses and accounts receivable at each other.[25]

The wisest of heads urging prudence on the United States was Secretary of State John Quincy Adams. More than anyone else, he identified the perils of acting too swiftly in Latin America and the advantages to be gained by delay. Far and away the greatest danger was that the United States would offend the government of Spain itself, because far and away the greatest advantages to be gained by U.S. diplomacy were acquisition of the Spanish colony of Florida, the definition of the boundary between the Louisiana Purchase and New Spain (Mexico), and the assumption of Spain's claims to the contested Pacific Northwest.

Spain, of course, was desperate. Its American empire was slipping away, and, as we know, its own soldiers were to mutiny rather than be sent overseas. One result was that the giant, swampy spit of land called Florida was virtually a derelict province, a lawless haven for escaped slaves and hostile Indians. Under increasing pressure from the enraged representatives and state government of Georgia, Adams demanded that Spain either police the province (something all parties knew was impossible) or turn it over to the United States. The Spanish minister,

Luis de Onís, obfuscated as long as he could, and tried in return to get the United States to promise not to help or recognize the various *independentistas* in Spanish America. Then, in 1818, General Andrew Jackson forced the issue by crossing the frontier into Florida in hot pursuit of a Red Stick (Seminole) raiding party. He captured three Spanish forts and executed two British subjects whom he suspected of selling guns to the Indians. Onís protested vigorously and counted on support from Britain and France. It was not forthcoming — the British chose to stand aside, in part because one of the two alleged gun runners was undoubtedly guilty, and the French had no interest in backing a lost cause. So Madrid finally ordered Onís to cut the best deal he could. The resulting Transcontinental (or Adams-Onís) Treaty of 1819 ceded Florida to the United States and delineated the boundary between American and Spanish territory all the way to the Pacific Ocean, thereby transferring to the United States all Spanish claims to northwestern America above 42 degrees north latitude. In return, Adams dropped the American claims to Texas and $5 million in damages. He did not promise never to recognize Latin American independence.

Neither was he ready to recognize it. For the government in Madrid failed to ratify the treaty in 1819, then collapsed in revolution in 1820. So Adams had to wait and wait, keeping Spain's rebellious colonies at arm's length and ruing those "ardent spirits who are for rushing into the conflict, without looking to the consequences." He reminded them of the sound prohibition against ideological crusades, most famously in that Fourth of July, 1821, speech.[26] He also stressed the volatility of the Latin regimes, the danger of provoking the Europeans, and the imperative need to see through the treaty with Spain: "I have never doubted that the final issue of their present struggle will be their entire independence from Spain. It is equally clear that it is our true policy and duty to take no part in the contest. The principle of neutrality to *all* foreign wars is, in my opinion, fundamental to the continuance of our liberties and of our Union. So far as they are contending for independence, I wish well to their cause; but I have not yet seen and do not now see any prospect that [Latins] will establish free and liberal institutions of government."[27] "As to an American system," he wrote, "we have it; we constitute the whole of it; there is no community of interests or of principles between North and South America."[28] And to Jackson he explained: "By this policy we have lost nothing, as *by keeping the Allies out of the quarrel,* Florida must soon be ours, and the Colonies must be independent, for if they cannot beat Spain, they do not deserve to be free."[29]

Clay continued to beat on the drum of republican solidarity, but Adams's stubborn defense of a foreign policy based on the national interest bought the time he needed. In 1821 Spain at last ratified the Transcontinental Treaty, the British themselves moved toward recognition of the Latin republics, Congress contented itself with a resolution authorizing the president to recognize the new states "whenever he may deem it expedient,"[30] and the Argentines, Colombians, Peruvians, Chileans, Mexicans, and Venezuelans achieved de facto independence — barring, of course, a Franco-Hispanic counterrevolutionary campaign. Which brings us back to Canning's extraordinary offer of August 1823 for an Anglo-American strategic partnership.

*

Monroe did not know what to do with the news carried home by Richard Rush except to poll his cabinet and Virginian mentors, Jefferson and Madison. Both were inclined to accept the British proposal. Jefferson replied from Monticello:

> The question presented by the letters you have sent me is the most momentous which has been offered to my contemplation since that of Independence. *That* made us a nation; *this* sets the compass and points the course which we are to steer through the ocean of time opening to us. . . . Our first and fundamental maxim should be never to entangle ourselves in the broils of Europe; our second, never to suffer Europe to intermeddle in cisatlantic affairs. America, North and South, has a set of interests distinct from those of Europe and peculiarly her own; she should have a system of her own, separate and apart from that of Europe.

Jefferson was flattered, especially since "Great Britain is the one nation which can do us the most harm of any one, or all on earth; and with her on our side we need not fear the whole world." But he fretted over Canning's point 4, in which Britain and the United States were to renounce any territorial ambitions for themselves: "We have first to ask ourselves a question. Do we wish to acquire to our own confederacy any one or more of the Spanish provinces? I candidly confess, that I have ever looked on Cuba as the most interesting addition which could ever be made to our system of states."[31]

John Quincy Adams could not have agreed more. He had just acquired Florida and would do nothing to foreclose future gains. Indeed, he suspected the British offer of being a trap meant to contain the United States. So instead he made a suggestion at least as provocative as Canning's: that the United States issue a unilateral proclamation encompassing all the Americas and shorn of its self-restricting clause about acquisition of territories.[32]

Historians still debate whether members of Monroe's cabinet really feared a Franco-Hispanic invasion of Latin America in 1823. For if they did, they could not shrug off lightly the proffered support of the Royal Navy. Scaremongers like Senator John Calhoun, republican crusaders like Henry Clay, and just plain worriers like Monroe might well have feared the worst, particularly after the fall of Cádiz to the French counterrevolutionary army. But Adams was apparently confident that the British could be counted on to block a Franco-Hispanic fleet with or without American assistance. "I no more believe that the Holy Allies will restore the Spanish domination on the American continent than that the Chimborazo [a great Andes mountain] will sink beneath the ocean."[33] That being the case, there was no need for the United States to place itself under Britain's tutelage, and renounce its own future claims to parts of the Spanish (and Russian) empires in the Americas. And Adams's reading was right, for in October 1823 Canning succeeded in prying the Polignac Memorandum out of Paris, in which the French foreign minister "abjured any design" of colonial reconquests.

The Americans did not know that — Canning did not publish the Polignac note until the following year (in part to save face after being preempted by Monroe's address). But they did know from Rush that Canning suddenly lost all interest in a joint Anglo-American declaration in the autumn of 1823, suggesting that either the British no longer feared a Franco-Hispanic expedition to America or they were prepared to deal with it themselves. So what really mattered to the United States was not the Franco-Hispanic threat, but the danger that Britain or Russia might try to fill part of the vacuum created by the crackup of Spain's empire!

Adams fought hard in a series of tense cabinet meetings for a presidential message that would define a unilateral U.S. policy toward the Americas. "It would," he said, "be more candid as well as more dignified, to avow our principles explicitly to Russia and France, than to come in as a cock-boat in the wake of the British man-of-war."[34]

Adams then vetted Monroe's drafts, persuading the president to exclude passages such as one that championed the cause of the Greeks and another that censured French intervention in Spain.[35] As Adams patiently explained, their true purpose was to make an "earnest remonstrance against the interference of the European powers by force with South America, but to disclaim all interference on our part with Europe; to make an American cause, and adhere inflexibly to that."[36]

So it was that Monroe's famous address of December 2 opened with a reference not to Spanish America but to the Russian claims in the Pacific Northwest, by way of introducing its first general principle:[37]

> In the discussions to which this interest has given rise and in the arrangements by which they may terminate the occasion has been judged proper for asserting, as a principle in which the rights and interests of the United States are involved that the American continents, by the free and independent condition which they have assumed and maintain, are henceforth not to be considered as subjects for future colonization by any European powers.

Monroe's next reference again avoided the issue of Spanish America, referring instead to the revolutions in Spain and Portugal themselves, by way of restating the American principle of Unilateralism and inviting Europe to obey the same rule toward the Western Hemisphere:

> The citizens of the United States cherish sentiments the most friendly in favor of the liberty and happiness of their fellow-men on that side of the Atlantic. In the wars of the European powers in matters relating to themselves we have never taken any part, nor does it comport with our policy so to do. It is only when our rights are invaded or seriously menaced that we resent injuries and make preparation for our defense. With the movements in this hemisphere we are of necessity more immediately connected, and by causes which must be obvious to all enlightened and impartial observers. The political system of the allied powers is essentially different in this respect from that of America. . . . We owe it, therefore, to candor and to the amicable relations existing between the United States and those powers to declare that we should consider any attempt on their part to extend their system to any portion of this hemisphere as dangerous to our peace and safety.

Lest anyone misconstrue this as a call to arms, Monroe immediately assured the European powers that the United States did not challenge the legitimacy of existing colonial regimes. However, the United States would view any effort to transfer such colonies to third powers or reimpose colonial status on any regions that had won independence as "the manifestation of an unfriendly disposition toward the United States."

So the American System we associate with Monroe was composed of three principles: no new colonization, no transfer of existing colonies, and no reimposition of colonial rule. But in order to ensure that no one mistook these principles for some sort of republican crusade, Monroe was careful to conclude with yet another reminder of the United States' traditional neutrality:

> Our policy in regard to Europe, which was adopted at an early stage of the wars which have so long agitated that quarter of the globe, nevertheless remains the same, which is, not to interfere in the internal concerns of any of its powers; to consider the government *de facto* as the legitimate government for us; to cultivate friendly relations with it, and to preserve those relations by a frank, firm, and manly policy, meeting in all instances the just claims of every power, submitting to injuries from none.

In other words, even the most reactionary European monarchies need have no fear that the United States might provide moral or material support to revolutionary movements, no matter how deep the sympathy of American citizens for them. All Americans asked was that the Bourbon kings, the tsar, and the British display similar deference toward the political system of the Americas.

*

So what did Monroe *not* mean to say? He did not mean to promise that the United States would intervene to secure Latin American independence.[38] Nor did he mean to imply that the United States associated itself with the republican cause. For not only did the United States turn its back on the revolutions in Europe, it even recognized Brazil, which set itself up as an empire under the émigré Portuguese dynasty. Nor did Monroe promise to fight to preserve the newly independent Latin states. He said only that the United States would view assaults upon them as "dangerous" and "evidence of an unfriendly disposition." Indeed, when the Colombian government expressed its "greatest pleasure" over Monroe's message and asked "in what manner the Government of the United States intends to resist on its part any interference of the Holy Alliance for the purpose of subjugating the new Republics," Adams replied coolly that such interference appeared far from likely, that matters of war and peace lay with the U.S. Congress, and that even in the case of concerted attack by European allies, "the United States could not undertake resistance to them by force of arms, without a prior understanding with those European Powers, whose interests and principles would secure from them an active and efficient cooperation in the cause [read: Britain]."[39]

Thus the United States did not expect to have to put teeth into its hemispheric doctrine for the simple reason that a serious challenge to U.S. interests in the Americas might force the United States, against its will, into an alliance with Britain. And that was precisely the warning U.S. minister Albert Gallatin delivered to the French foreign minister upon his departure from Paris.[40] Should Britain itself challenge American interests, the United States could back down if the affair was not worth a war — or rely on its size, potential military power, and threat to Canada to deter Britain if the affair did touch on vital U.S. interests. And that is why Adams and his successors were careful to measure the interests and limit the commitments they made to hemispheric defense. After all, the American System could no more be allowed to contradict Unilateralism (upon which it was layered) than Unilateralism could be allowed to compromise American independence and Liberty (upon which *it* was built).

The Monrovian principles were conceived narrowly and in terms of vital, nearby American interests. That they were not meant to throw a protective blanket over all Latin America is obvious from what the United States did *not* do in the years that followed. When Britain annexed the Falkland Islands in 1833 and extended the boundary of British Honduras, the United States looked the other way. When the British threw their weight around in Central America in the 1850s, especially over the issue of an isthmian canal, the United States (grudgingly, to be sure) accorded Britain equal influence there. When Spanish troops did turn up in South America for the purpose of keeping the peace within and among the new states, the United States did not protest. When, at the time of the Panama Congress of 1826, Colombia, Central America, and Mexico invited the United States to join a league for mutual defense and settlement of disputes, the United States was reluctant even to send delegates. (In the end, the delegates never even made it to Panama: one died on the way and the other went home when the meeting adjourned early, on account of Panama's feverish climate.) But Adams's purpose in sending them was strictly commercial — entangling alliances and defensive commitments were out of the question.

Nor should that surprise anyone, because a real ideological and military commitment to independence and liberty for all the peoples of the hemisphere would have been a curious departure indeed. New York, after all, is farther from Buenos Aires than it is from London; India was a nearer destination by sea than Peru. The idea that the United States ought to claim and enforce a sphere of influence over the whole of Latin America would have been absurd, not least because at times in the nineteenth century the U.S. Navy was incapable of beating up on Chile, much less on an imperial power that chose to meddle there. The American System declared by Monroe is better understood, therefore, as a purposely vague proclamation of U.S. determination to defend whatever vital national interests it had, or might in the future identify, in the Western Hemisphere.

So this time there is no need to ask how the United States got away with it, since it never tried to get away with anything especially arrogant. Should France or Russia bid for an American empire, the United States could count on British support. Should Britain be the offender, the U.S. government could bluster and bluff and ultimately cut a deal based on the merits of the case and their relative power *in North America*. Finally, it must be said that Monroe's principles did not offend the continental powers of Europe nearly so much as their quotations at the start of this chapter would suggest. For the European cabinets were as pleased to disengage themselves from the republican Americas as Americans were to disengage from monarchical Europe. As historian Paul Schroeder writes, "The Continental powers accepted Anglo-American domination of the western hemisphere, and preferred to fence Europe off from the quarrels, troubles, and dangerous ideologies of North and South America."[41] Russia and France also noted approvingly the implied anti-British twist to U.S. policy.

When situations arose that were of vital interest to the United States, of course, Americans reflexively adopted their spread-eagle posture. That is why the Monroe Doctrine, so called, became a venerated tradition of U.S. foreign policy only in the 1840s, when the struggle over Mexico's northern provinces — Texas, New Mexico, and California — reached a climax. And that, in turn, is why some historians read backward into the Monroe Doctrine an American lust for expansion. They suggest that John Quincy Adams inspired the Monroe Doctrine for the purpose of clearing North America and the Caribbean of the only competitors that might be able to thwart his own continental ambitions. As historian Thomas Paterson summarized it: "The traditional interpretation holds that the Monroe Doctrine represented a defense of American ideals, security, and commerce — an affirmation of the national interest. Others have placed the Monroe Doctrine within the American expansionist tradition and have pointed out that the declaration may have meant 'hands off' for the Europeans, but it permitted 'hands on' for the United States."[42] As we shall soon see, however, this seeming contradiction exists only in the minds of historians who insist that American foreign policy always be viewed as a battleground between idealism and realism. Keeping the imperial powers out, preventing them from extending their balance-of-power system to North America's waters and rimlands, was a vital U.S. interest *whether or not* it also led to U.S. expansion. And expansionism, when it did occur, was not identical to the policy of the Monroe Doctrine but a corollary of it. It was, in fact, the fourth and final entry in the logical, consistent, and well-proportioned set of traditions that guided early American statecraft.

*

Meanwhile, the Russian threat to the Northwest Coast dissolved into farce. The new naval governors at Sitka quickly learned that Baranov had been right: the Russian colonists would starve if they were not permitted to barter with the maritime Americans and British. The result was the Russo-American Treaty of 1824, in which Russia fixed its territorial claims at 54°40′ north latitude, granted Americans full trading rights for a period of ten years, and promised never to transfer Alaska to any third power. The treaty was not a direct consequence of Monroe's address, but was the first successful application of its principles.

There remained the fighting in Greece, which reached a ferocious peak when a Turco-Egyptian fleet and army descended on the Morea. The eloquent Daniel Webster took up the cause of the suffering Greeks and asked Congress to appoint a U.S. commissioner — in effect, to intervene in a civil war out of sentimental attachment to one side's apparent ideals. It was the final nineteenth-century temptation to expand the meaning of American Exceptionalism from Liberty at home to Liberty in general, and to abandon neutrality. John Randolph argued against it, and so gave his countrymen one of the most prophetic but little-known refutations of the notion of an American global mission:[43]

> We are absolutely combatting shadows. The gentleman would have us to believe his resolution is all but nothing; yet again it is to prove omnipotent, and fills the whole globe with its influence. Either it is nothing, or it is something. If it is nothing, let us lay it on the table, and have done with it at once; but if it is that something which it has been on the other hand represented to be, let us beware how we touch it. For my part, I would sooner put the shirt of Nessus on my back, than sanction these doctrines — doctrines such as I never heard from my boyhood till now. They go the whole length. If they prevail, there are no longer any Pyrenees — every bulwark and barrier of the Constitution is broken down; it is become a *tabula rasa* — a *carte blanche,* for every one to scribble on it what he pleases.

Webster's resolution died. And so far from placing itself at the head of a crusade against distant tyranny, the United States government eschewed ideologically driven foreign policies for another seventy-five years.

FOUR

Expansionism, or
Manifest Destiny (so called)

SINCE THE DAYS when the fleet of Columbus sailed into the waters
of the New World, America has been another name for opportunity,
and the people of the United States have taken their tone from the
incessant expansion which has not only been open but has even been
forced upon them. He would be a rash prophet who should assert
that the expansive character of American life has now entirely ceased.
Movement has been its dominant fact, and, unless this training has
no effect upon a people, the American energy will continually demand a wider field for its exercise.[1]

However much historians have disputed aspects of Frederick Jackson
Turner's "frontier thesis," his passage above is sure. Of all the traditions
of American foreign policy, the one least in need of some presidential
doctrine was expansion, for it was *sui generis*, as much a spontaneous
urge of the people as it was a government policy. Expansion*ism*, by
contrast — the ideology of national growth — is forever associated in
our minds with the peculiar doctrine of Manifest Destiny:

> The American people having derived their origin from many other
> nations, and the Declaration of Independence being entirely based
> on the great principle of human equality, these facts demonstrate at
> once our disconnected position as regards any other nation; that we
> have, in reality, but little connection with the past history of any of
> them, and still less with all antiquity, its glories, or its crimes. On the
> contrary, our national birth was the beginning of a new history . . .
> and so far as regards the entire development of the natural rights of
> man, in moral, political, and national life, we may confidently assume
> that our country is destined to be the great nation of futurity. . . .
>
> We are the nation of human progress, and who will, what can, set
> limits to our onward march? We point to the everlasting truth on the
> first page of our national declaration, and we proclaim to the millions

of other lands, that "the gates of hell" — the powers of aristocracy and monarchy — "shall not prevail against it."

The far-reaching, the boundless future will be an era of American greatness. In its magnificent domain of space and time, the nation of many nations is *destined* to *manifest* to mankind the excellence of divine principles; to establish on earth the noblest temple ever dedicated to the worship of the Most High — the Sacred and the True. Its floor shall be a hemisphere — its roof the firmament of the star-studded heavens, and its congregation an Union of many Republics, comprising hundreds of happy millions.[2]

Powerful stuff, not least for its economy. In these brief passages of 1839 the editor of the *Democratic Review*, John O'Sullivan, recalled the principles of the Puritans, Paine, and Jefferson, likened America to the "true church," accorded to it a progressive, temporal mission to mankind, alluded to Exceptionalism, Unilateralism, and the hemispherism of Monroe's American System, and capped it all by predicting that this Solomon's temple was destined to encompass a continent. Given the fact that the decade to follow proved to be the most expansionist in American history, it is little wonder that O'Sullivan is held in honor (or calumny) as the definitive interpreter of a foreign policy tradition, even as Washington and Monroe came to be honored.

He does not deserve the mantle. American expansion in all its forms long predated the Manifest Destiny craze and continued long after it died. O'Sullivan's rhetoric, and that of his imitators, was more a symptom than a cause of the expansionist fever caught by Americans in the late Jacksonian period. Moreover, he offered no motives or explanations for the expansion he prophesied, ignored the relationship of means to ends, and thus expressed a mood more than a foreign policy strategy. What he did do, however, was to suggest to his countrymen that expansion was a natural consequence of what America was: a people dedicated to liberty based on faith, who had begun history over again in a New World and might "confidently assume" a future free of limits imposed by man.

In this sense, O'Sullivan's instincts were right: expansion was a logical corollary of the first three U.S. foreign policy traditions. For if the United States was to remain free and independent — the first tradition — then it must pursue a unilateral foreign policy — the second tradition. If Unilateralism was to survive, then it must promote an American System of states — the third tradition. But it was not enough that the United States remain aloof from Europe. It must preempt European bids for influence over the vast unsettled lands that remained in North America — hence the fourth tradition.

Expansion was implicit in U.S. doctrine and explicit in its behavior from the moment in 1781 when Benjamin Franklin demanded of Britain all the lands east of the Mississippi. After all, what independence or liberty would Americans enjoy if their boundary were fixed along the Alleghenies, hemmed in by Britain, Spain, or France and their Indian allies? In 1787 the otherwise dysfunctional Congress under the Articles of Confederation passed the Northwest Ordinance to organize the vast wilderness north of the Ohio River. In 1791 Vermont entered the Union as the fourteenth state, and Kentucky, the first western state, in 1792, thereby setting the precedent under which all residents of U.S. territories were expected to become equal partners in the democratic experiment. Jefferson stretched (some said violated) the Constitution in 1803 in order to secure the Louisiana Territory. The United States annexed "West Florida" between 1810 and 1813, and the rest of Florida in the 1819 treaty with Spain that also extended America's northwestern claims to the Pacific Ocean.

Early American statesmen believed in a continental destiny. Jefferson imagined a time when "our rapid multiplication will . . . cover the whole northern if not southern continent, with people speaking the same language, governed by similar forms, and by similar laws."[3] John Quincy Adams thought that "North America appears to be destined by Divine Providence to be peopled by one *nation,* speaking one language, professing one general system of religious and political principles, and accustomed to one general tenor of social usages and customs. For the common happiness of them all, for their peace and prosperity, I believe it is indispensable that they should be associated in one federal Union."[4]

One might chalk up such sentiments to sheer ambition, or interpret them as objective extrapolations from the fact that Americans inhabited an undeveloped continent devoid of serious rivals. But there was more to it than that: expansion derived from the primordial, exceptional American commitment to liberty. Without freedom to grow, the nation would not be free at all. Or, to put it the other way around, U.S. citizens saw barriers and restraints on expansion as intolerable assaults on their liberty. Imagine Indian tribes, British lords, Mexican juntas, or U.S. federal authorities themselves telling farmers, trappers, ranchers, merchants, and missionaries: "No, you cannot settle here, or do business there. Go back where you came from!" At times all four did, and Americans screamed, for an America without opportunity would not be America at all.

So what is required is not a long explanation of U.S. expansion, but rather a short explanation of why U.S. expansion needs no explanation. Geography invited it; demography compelled it. "This is a young and growing nation," Stephen A. Douglas reminded the Senate. "It swarms as often as a hive of bees, and . . . there must be hives in which they can gather and make their honey. . . . I tell you, increase, and multiply, and expand, is the law of the nation's existence."[5] Commerce gave expansion an irresistible momentum as the U.S. population, exports, and agriculture tripled between 1815 and 1848, and Britain's Opium War with China (1839–42) opened new markets in Asia. Meanwhile, new technologies and public works — canals, levees, steamboats, clipper ships, steam-assisted ships, turnpikes, the telegraph, railroads — made revolutions in communication and transport.

So volatile and expansive was American society in the 1830s and 1840s that some historians even speak of a "second revolution" in politics, economics, and culture. The first party system had disintegrated in the wake of the War of 1812 as the Federalists metamorphosed into National Republicans, then merged into the new Whig Party, which rose to challenge the Democrats and their fearsome leader, Andrew Jackson. The rustic Tennessean knitted a coalition that included southerners (because of Jackson's commitment to states' rights and lower tariffs on foreign goods), westerners (because of his opposition to eastern moneyed interests and support for expansion), and working-class people and immigrants (especially Irish) in the eastern cities. Jackson's brain trust forged the tools of the modern national party, including patronage, political clubs in every city and town, and newspaper chains to propagate the party's message and coordinate local machines.[6] As the *Democratic Review* crowed in 1840: "Democracy in its true sense is the last best revelation of human thought. We speak, of course, of that true and genuine Democracy which breathes the air and lives in the light of Christianity — whose essence is justice, and whose object is human progress."[7]

That the new generation viewed progress as the ultimate blessing of liberty is clear from Michael Kammen's study of American iconography. By the 1830s the goddess of liberty, defiant eagles, classical allusions, and symbols of the Enlightenment (like the pyramid and all-seeing eye on the dollar bill) gave way in magazines and posters to pictures of rich fields of grain, factories, and merchant ships — the fruits of liberty rather than liberty itself.[8] Expansion, both internal and external, was among those fruits, and was an indispensable nourishment to the increasingly formless, aggressively democratic society we associate with the Jacksonian era. In contrast with the "structured republicanism" that gentrified philosophers like Jefferson had imagined and briefly knew, America by the 1830s and 1840s made what historian Robert Wiebe terms "a revolution in choices."[9] What is more, the Whigs — a loose congeries of manufacturers in favor of protective tariffs, free-soil farmers and abolitionists, and advocates of federal support for roads, canals, levees, and railroads ("internal improvements") — shared the Democrats' vision of a prosperous, expansive America, however much they may have hated "King Andrew" and balked at the extension of slavery.

Still a nation comprised mostly of farmers, Americans had a stake in an expanding frontier. Children from large families pressed westward, looking for land of their own. Latecomers stuck on small plots or on marginal soil in the Ohio and Mississippi valleys yearned for a second chance in Oregon, Texas, or on Indian lands. Farmers wiped out in the Panics of 1819 and 1837 sought to start over where land was still cheap. Even prosperous farmers might sell their acres in order to purchase larger spreads out west. As Tocqueville observed, Americans moved west for the same reason they gambled, "not only for the sake of the profit it holds out to them, but for the love of the constant excitement occasioned by that pursuit."[10]

Jacksonian Americans also drank, for reasons both vicious and innocent. In the early 1830s Americans consumed more than five gallons of distilled spirits per capita per year, the highest rate in their history. One reason was that nineteenth-century folks in town and country thought water a contemptible beverage and a carrier of disease. Tea was expensive and unpatriotic, since most of it came from Britain. Beer was not popular until German immigrants began to pour in around 1850. That left rum and, after the repeal of the hated tax on it in 1802, frontier whiskey, which grew so cheap that a lowly wage earner could drink his fill every day. In 1810 Louisville sent 250,000 gallons of whiskey up the Ohio River; by 1822 the figure was 2,250,000.[11] Upon learning that most crime in America was traced to abuse of alcohol, Tocqueville asked a Philadelphian why Congress did not put a stiff tax on it. Because, he was told, that would lose the legislators their seats, if not provoke a rebellion: "whence I am to infer that drunkards are the majority in your country."[12]

The national binge ended around 1840. The proximate cause was a religious crusade against spirits — the American Society for the Promotion of Temperance numbered more than 4 million people — but at least as important was the arrival of a cheap, stimulating substitute: coffee from Latin America.[13] From that time on, American men ceased to drink punches and toddies at breakfast and noon, on the job or in the fields, and waited until evening to punish the jug. Still, James Russell Lowell held to the opinion that all the braying about Manifest Destiny was "one half ignorance an' t'other half rum."[14]

The temperance movement was one manifestation of the Second Great Awakening, a frenetic revolt against the latitudinarianism, Unitarianism, and tired Calvinist dogma that had enervated American Protestantism over the preceding forty years. The importance of such revivals as occur periodically in American history often goes unappreciated, since their effect on secular events is hard to measure. But Robert Fogel believes that great political trends are "to a large extent spawned by changes in American religiosity," and that the anti-slavery movement, as well as the temperance movement, was born of the revival of the 1830s and 1840s.[15] It was the first religious movement to erupt in the West (especially Rochester, New York, and Oberlin, Ohio) rather than in New England. It stressed the regeneration of the soul in the fire of the Holy Spirit, the freedom of the human will to say yes to God, and the regeneration of American society as a whole in preparation for the Millennium. In staid schools and frenzied, torch-lit camp meetings Methodist, Presbyterian, and Congregationalist preachers reconsecrated America the New Israel and ascribed to it the power to inaugurate Christ's thousand-year reign on earth. "The civil religion of the American people thus came to rest not on the faith the Enlightenment had awakened in man's moral powers . . . but on revivalistic, reform-minded, and millennial Christianity."[16]

It would be risky even for an expert on the era's social history to draw bold lines of cause and effect between these phenomena and foreign policy. But there is no doubt that the United States in the 1840s was a boiling cauldron of booze, gambling, political passion, restless migration, disruptive but exciting technologies, and millenarian expectations. Such an anxious society could hardly be expected to meet with patience and equanimity the crises over Oregon and Texas that were to determine the future of North America. Rather, Americans had motive, means, and opportunity to expand their institutions and culture to the limits of their own territory and beyond.

Only if they had *not* done so would historians today be faced with a perplexing problem.

*

But if American expansion seems overdetermined, American Expansion*ism* is a matter of controversy. Given that the United States grew at the expense of people with prior claims to the land (Indians, then British and Mexicans), how did Americans justify their impositions? Historian Albert K. Weinberg identified eight elements that fed the ideology of expansion. First was natural right, as invoked by the *New York Evening Post* just before the Louisiana Purchase: "It belongs *of right* to the United States to regulate the future destiny of *North America*. The country is *ours;* ours is the right to its rivers and to all the sources of future opulence, power and happiness, which lay scattered at our feet."[17] Natural rights, of course, are derived from natural law, the author of which is Nature's God. Americans might well have believed that God had staked out North America as their Promised Land, but it was a dangerous claim because it implied a responsibility to obey all of God's *other* laws. No wonder that ardent expansionists like Jefferson, John Quincy Adams, William Henry Seward, and Theodore Roosevelt held that territorial expansion was contingent on reform at home. Otherwise, as Weinberg wrote, to invoke natural law to justify expansion would be akin to making "such a creature as Frankenstein fashioned."[18]

A second element was geographical predestination. "The Floridas may be considered as naturally belonging to the United States — or, in other words, as rightfully to be possessed by the power holding the adjacent countries of Georgia, Alabama, and Mississippi, for they are *without value* to any other."[19] This, too, might seem presumptuous, but far less so than the notion that Florida was destined to remain a vacant object of Spanish neglect. So far from apologizing for expansion, John Quincy Adams believed that "until Europe shall find it a settled geographical element that the United States and North America are identical, any effort on our part to reason the world out of a belief that we are ambitious will have no other effect than to convince them that we add to our ambition hypocrisy."[20]

Natural growth was a third excuse for expansion. As a congressman asked regarding Oregon, "What are those *natural limits* of the United States, where the impulse of *annexation* will cease of itself? Is not growth the normal state, also, of the Federal Union?" And a Senate report of 1859: "The law of our national existence is growth. We cannot, if we would, disobey it. While we should do nothing to stimulate it unnaturally, we should be careful not to impose upon ourselves a regimen so strict as to prevent its healthful development."[21] Fourth, just as Americans would gradually take over such lands as Nature assigned them, but no more, so would some foreign lands fall into the American sphere. Adams held that "there are laws of political as well as physical gravitation," and predicted that a Cuba free of Spain could "gravitate only toward the North American Union." The *Democratic Review*, employing a more trendy scientific metaphor, wrote in the 1840s of "a powerful magnet" attracting Texas to the United States.[22]

What gave the United States this attracting power? What did Americans do that won them favor with Nature and God? The answer, the fifth element in American Expansionism, was the argument from virtuous industry. As John Winthrop told his Massachusetts Bay Colony: "The whole earth is the lords garden & he hath given it to the sonnes of men, with a generall Condicion, Gen: 1.28. Increase & multiply, replenish the earth & subdue it. . . . Why then should we stand hear striveing for places of habitation . . . and in ye mean tyme suffer a whole Continent, as fruitfull & convenient for the use of man to lie waste without any improvement."[23] Indiana's governor invoked the same principle during the War of 1812: "Is one of the fairest portions of the globe to remain in a state of nature, the haunt of a few wretched savages, when it seems destined by the Creator to give support to a large population and to be the seat of civilization, of science, and of true religion?"[24] No conviction was held more deeply by nineteenth-century Americans than that virgin land was there for man to improve that he might marry, raise children, and give thanks to a bountiful God. Indians could not be allowed to halt progress, nor could the Hudson's Bay Company, which also hunted animal skins and drove away tillers of the soil, nor could torpid Mexicans, whose empire remained a desert after centuries. All those who frustrated the aspirations of free men were rightly swept aside, their lands made forfeit.

Another justification, a sixth element in Expansionism, was that American growth *ipso facto* meant an increase of liberty. Needless to say, the institution of chattel slavery made many antebellum Americans choke on this argument. But from Jefferson's Empire for Liberty to Andrew Jackson's "extending the area of freedom," republicanism was an excuse for expansion. "And it is from such materials —," wrote

Walt Whitman, "from the democracy with its manly heart and its lion strength, spurning the ligatures wherewith drivellers would bind it — that we are to expect the great FUTURE of this western world! a scope involving such unparalleled human happiness and rational freedom, to such unnumbered myriads, that the heart of a true *man* leaps with a mighty joy only to think of it!"[25]

And so we arrive at Manifest Destiny, the seventh expansionist argument. The "true title" to Oregon, O'Sullivan wrote, lay in "the right of our manifest destiny to overspread and to possess the whole of the continent which Providence has given us for the development of the great experiment of Liberty and federated self-government entrusted to us."[26] He called for no war, and did not expect it. It was enough that farmers occupy vacant land, for in time they would increase, establish self-government, and petition to enter the American temple of freedom. As historian Frederick Merk explained: "Any hurried admission to the temple of freedom would be unwise, any forced admission would be a contradiction in terms, unthinkable, revolting. But a duty lay on the people of the United States to admit all qualified applicants freely."[27] This was Manifest Destiny in its pure form: peaceful, automatic, gradual, and governed by self-determination.

But a second school of Manifest Destiny sprang up that was belligerent, insatiable, and impatient. Led by journalists and politicians from Indiana, Michigan, and Illinois, these expansionists did not reject an American mission, but were ready to force the pace and opposed any compromise with foreigners. Some radical Manifest Destinarians even contemplated "liberating" densely populated foreign countries to bring them the blessings of American civilization. Such "regeneration of other cultures," Weinberg's eighth expansionist argument, won over the *Democratic Review.* There was great danger in conquering only to enslave, but "a free nation, which shows equal toleration and protection to all religions, and conquers only to bestow freedom, has no such danger to fear."[28]

Let us stop for a moment and think. A twentieth-century American, perhaps ashamed to reflect on our despoliation of Indians and Mexicans but supportive of an American mission to help poor countries and support human rights and democracy, might sympathize with none of these justifications for expansion except the last one. But nineteenth-century Americans, true to the first three traditions of U.S. foreign policy, would have been inclined to accept the first seven of the justifications and reject only the last, which smacked of precisely the sort of crusading spirit that John Quincy Adams warned would corrupt the nation and impeach its freedom at home.

Indeed, the few nineteenth-century voices that did fret about national expansion were concerned only with its impact on freedom at home. Some feared that the Union might outgrow the limited powers of the federal government and so fly apart. Fisher Ames denounced the Louisiana Purchase as a flight into infinite space, and Josiah Quincy thought that "the destruction of the balance which it is so important to maintain between the Eastern and Western States, threatens, at no very distant day, the subversion of our Union." Others feared that a vastly empowered central government might trample on states' rights. Still others feared for the freedom of people back east. As John Randolph said in 1813: "We are the first people that ever acquired provinces . . . not for us to govern, but that they might *govern us* — that we might be ruled to our ruin by people bound to us by no common tie of interest or sentiment."[29]

By 1830 or so it was clear that these fears were exaggerated. Everyone quotes Senator Thomas Hart Benton's declaration that the ridge of the Rocky Mountains ought to be America's limit, "and the statue of the fabled god, Terminus, should be raised upon its highest peak, never to be thrown down."[30] But in 1825 that was an echo of the past, and in any case even those who feared the effects of stretching American *government* too thin never doubted that the American *people* would go on expanding. That is why the historians' debate over whether U.S. expansion was Manifest Destiny or Manifest Design is based on a false distinction.[31] Americans were going to sow their seed and commerce whether government led or followed, a fact that Theodore Roosevelt celebrated:[32]

> The warlike borderers who thronged across the Alleghanies, the restless and reckless hunters, the hard, dogged frontier farmers . . . were led by no one commander; they acted under orders from neither king nor congress; they were not carrying out the plans of any far-sighted leader. In obedience to their instincts working half-blindly within their breasts, spurred ever onwards by the fierce desires of their eager hearts, they made in the wilderness homes for their children, and by so doing wrought out the destinies of a continental nation.

What the federal government did need to do was to harness its unruly citizens and try to lower the risks associated with their spillage over international boundaries into Louisiana, Florida, Oregon, Texas, and California.[33] But before discussing those episodes, we must review the experience the U.S. government already had in wrestling with the predicaments created by people on the move, especially those that raised touchy questions of race.

★

The real moral quandary posed by expansion arose from the conflict between American liberty, which enabled and justified national expansion, and the fact that expansion occurred at the expense of dispossessed Indians, Mexicans, and (to the extent slavery spread) Africans. Now, Indian policy and slavery were not foreign policy issues, but to duck them would be a mistake. For the federal government's agonized and futile efforts to deal with those issues gave rise to patterns of thought and behavior toward alien peoples that would carry over into U.S. foreign policy. Some angry authors even argue that American history is one long story of "Indian hating and empire building" from Plymouth Rock to the "Injun country" of Vietnam; or that settlers' conflicts with Indians spawned an American "victory culture" that validated mass slaughter of peoples of other races; or that elites in Jacksonian America "constructed" a racist paradigm toward nonwhites in order to justify their removal and to dampen class conflict among whites.[34]

That white Americans held racist views — that everyone holds some racist views — is a given. But to hang all of American history on that peg is to ignore the dilemmas that the existence of Indians and slavery posed for a nation conceived in liberty. In the case of Indian policy, the federal government began with high hopes. Enlightenment philosophy taught the unity of mankind and the concept of the noble savage. Everyone took for granted that the Indians' primitive way of life was doomed; the question was whether the Indians would die with it or gradually take their place as individuals within the dominant culture. Jefferson believed that the "proofs of genius given by the Indians of N. America, place them on a level with Whites in the same uncultivated state," implying that they needed only to be educated to share in the blessings of liberty.[35] The Northwest Ordinance declared that "the utmost good faith shall always be observed toward the Indians; their lands and property shall never be taken from them without their consent." And President Washington and Secretary of War Henry Knox embraced a humane program based on restriction of white settlement, recognition of Indian lands, funding of religious and agricultural missions, regulation of trade with the Indians, and the conclusion of treaties with tribes as if they were foreign nations.[36]

Soon enough it was clear that these hopes were unwarranted. Settlers inevitably encroached on tribal lands and dragged the federal government into wars. Some Indians resisted assimilation; others were spurned in spite (or because) of their success in adapting to white men's ways. Swindlers and crooked agents preyed on them. In the War of 1812, the British again drew some Indian nations into alliance, making all Native Americans suspect as a threat to U.S. security. By the 1820s the expansion of plantations and farms in the Deep South forced everyone to recognize that time had run out on assimilation. In 1828 Georgia's state government challenged the federal government's Indian treaties, and Alabama and Mississippi followed suit, imposing state jurisdiction on all people within their borders and criminalizing any exercise of public functions by tribal authorities. The Cherokees sued, but John Marshall's Supreme Court found "after mature deliberation" that "an Indian tribe or nation within the United States is not a foreign state in the sense of the constitution, and cannot maintain an action in the courts of the United States."[37]

If Indians could not be assimilated and the federal government lacked the authority to override state law, then only two options remained: either the Indians were left to the unlikely mercy of state and local governments or they were moved to federal land beyond the Mississippi River. That both "solutions" were unjust and cruel goes without saying, but the latter seemed the lesser of evils. Jefferson had thought it might come to this as early as 1803, but no president dared bite the bullet until Andrew Jackson. According to the greatest of his biographers, Jackson's Indian Removal Act of 1830 was motivated by concern for national security, devotion to states' rights, and a genuine belief that "he had followed the 'dictates of humanity' and saved the Indians from certain death."[38]

Perhaps he had (not counting the three to four thousand who perished in camps or on the Trail of Tears). But Jackson also placed a federal imprimatur on the sheer removal of peoples who stood in the way of American expansion. As one textbook puts it, "Inevitably, racism betrayed Manifest Destiny."[39] That is a generous formulation. In truth, racial discrimination was a *sine qua non* if expansion was to be reconciled with liberty. Indians had to be understood as not possessing the rights of citizens, or else how could their lands be taken at all? What is more, most Americans believed that the Indians' inferiority was not a construct of their own making, but an obvious, empirical fact.

Were American law, agriculture and commerce, technology, religion, and culture superior to those of primitive aborigines? To suggest the opposite in the mid-nineteenth century would have certified someone as mad. Was the United States superior to Mexico? The question itself would have been met with hilarity. The question that obsessed scholars and statesmen was not whether but why Anglo-Saxons displayed a genius for self-government and industry that other peoples seemed to lack. Jefferson had pondered the question: he studied the ancient Anglo-Saxon tongue, and asked whether it was their institutions that had made the Saxons lovers of liberty, or whether some innate trait of the people inspired their self-governing institutions. By the third decade of the nineteenth century, English and American philosophers thought they were close to an answer. Whereas Christian and Enlightenment doctrines preached human uniformity and the prevalence of nurture over nature, the first evolutionary theories, the science of animal breeding, and the Romantics' notion of national genius all suggested the prevalence of nature over nurture. The free, enterprising spirit and urge to cover the earth were apparently inherent in Anglo-Saxons. That explained America, the British Empire, and why other races — not only Indians and Negroes but Latins and Slavs — seemed unable to seize or hold on to freedom.[40]

Scientists thought they had evidence for a hierarchy of races. An influential phrenologist, Charles Caldwell, examined skulls in Ohio Valley burial grounds and pronounced the Indian race genetically inferior. "The only efficient scheme to civilize the Indians," he concluded, "is to *cross the breed*. Attempt any other and *you will extinguish the race*."[41] Southern opinion embraced the hypothesis of biological inequality. William Gilmore Sims wrote, "He, only, is the slave, who is forced into a position in society which is below the claim of his intellect and moral [sic]," and Henry Clay believed it was "impossible to civilize Indians."[42] When Mexico was at issue, Americans understandably asked why British colonies flourished and ex-Spanish ones languished. The earlier, nurture-based theory stressed the leaden impress of Catholicism, feudalism, Spanish tyranny, and French-style revolutionary militarism. But the new genetic paradigm suggested that

Mexicans were (in the words of Lansford Hastings, author of a best-selling guide to California) scarcely superior in intelligence to "the barbarous tribes by whom they are surrounded." And that was no mystery, "as most of the lower order of Mexicans are Indians in fact." The *New York Evening Post* agreed: "The Mexicans are aboriginal Indians, and they must share the destiny of their race."[43]

That Americans used racial arguments to justify their claim to eminent domain over whatever lands they fancied is undeniable, but racial aggression was never their *motive* for expansion. Their motives were freedom and opportunity, as Andrew Jackson told the Congress: "What good man would prefer a country covered with forests and ranged by a few thousand savages to our extensive Republic, studded with cities, towns, and prosperous farms, embellished with all the improvements which art can devise or industry execute, occupied by more than 12,000,000 happy people, and filled with all the blessings of liberty, civilization, and religion?"[44] Another motive was security. In 1794 Tennessee's assembly begged Congress to declare war on the Creeks and Cherokees, because there was hardly "a man of this body, but can recount a dear wife or child, an aged parent or near relation, massacred by the hands of these blood-thirsty nations, in their houses or fields." It was easy enough for smug, secure easterners to weep for the Indians — they had long since killed or expelled the natives in their neck of the woods. Nor, if one's family was threatened, did it matter that the Indians might have been repeatedly molested and cheated themselves. The frontier author Hugh Henry Brackenridge, who watched a friend die of torture at the hands of "animals vulgarly called Indians," mocked the philosopher who "thinks to find perfect virtue in the simplicity of the unimproved state."[45]

The strongest argument against an interpretation of U.S. history based solely on racial aggression is that white Americans were just as eager to target other whites as they were Indians and Mexicans. The wars and war scares with Britain from 1775 to 1900 approach a dozen, and the worst bloodletting in U.S. history, the Civil War, was a case of whites killing each other. None of this justifies the brutality and hypocrisy that accompanied Americans' westward march, but it does put the racial element in perspective. If the West Coast or Texas had been claimed by Frenchmen or Britons determined to check U.S. expansion, rowdy Americans would have been just as eager to have at them. In fact, the British did measure their prospects on the West Coast and in Texas and entertain thoughts of a "containment policy." And that, too, helps to explain why Manifest Destiny became the rage in the 1840s, and not before or after.

★

The story is too familiar to need a detailed retelling. By 1844 two long-simmering issues were coming to boil. The first was the Oregon Territory, that huge no man's land between the Pacific Ocean and the Continental Divide, which the Convention of 1818 had opened to American and British settlers alike. First in were the Hudson's Bay Company agents, who built forts, monopolized the fur trade, and blazed trails for some seven hundred British subjects north of the Columbia River. Then American farmers began to settle in the Willamette Valley south of the Columbia. By 1844 they numbered two thousand, and three thousand more arrived in 1845. Oregon conventions met across the Midwest to petition the federal government to end joint occupation and press its claim to Oregon, if necessary by the sword.

Meanwhile, spontaneous American immigration to that portion of the Mexican state of Coahuila known as Texas created a second danger of war. Stephen F. Austin led the first three hundred families across the Sabine River in 1821, promising that they would become Catholics and loyal Mexican citizens. There was never a chance of that, even if the Mexican government had not been paralyzed by civil unrest. By 1836, when General Santa Anna set aside the liberal Mexican constitution and Texas declared independence, Anglos outnumbered Mexican residents there by seven or eight to one. It was a classic American filibuster, but also a clear case of self-determination. After defeating Santa Anna in the Battle of San Jacinto, Texans asked the United States to annex them.

At that moment two American traditions collided for the first time. Expansion dictated annexation. Americans had eyed Texas ever since the Louisiana Purchase made it a neighbor, and Jackson had tried twice to persuade Mexico to sell it. Now Americans had occupied the land and defended it with their blood. But Liberty at home, the first American tradition and the one the others were meant to serve, dictated abstinence in the minds of Whigs and some northern Democrats because Texas chose to permit slavery. Congress deadlocked, and every effort to annex Texas failed until the election of 1844.

There is no telling what might have happened had James K. Polk not won that election by a razor-thin margin. When the Democrats triumphed on a platform demanding all of Oregon (pleasing to free-soil northerners) and Texas too (pleasing to southerners), lame-duck President John Tyler called it a mandate for expansion and maneuvered annexation of Texas through Congress in March 1845 by joint resolution (which required only a simple majority in both houses). Still, the debate over Texas was ominous. Expansionists like Chesselden Ellis (D., N.Y.) asked, "Why wing the eagle in his bold ascent towards the sun . . . ? No, sir, to arrest our peaceful and onward march would be treason to the cause of human liberty."[46] But opponents cried that to extend slavery was the real treason to liberty. Sixteen years later Americans warred with each other over those contrasting definitions. But Polk held the nation together long enough to make it a continental republic.

First, Polk appealed in his inaugural address to America's existing foreign policy traditions, and drew the logical conclusion (sometimes called Polk's Corollary to the Monroe Doctrine) with regard to Texas:[47]

> In the existing circumstances of the world the present is deemed a proper occasion to reiterate and reaffirm the principle avowed by Mr. Monroe and to state my cordial concurrence in its wisdom and sound policy. . . . We must ever maintain the principle that the people of this continent alone have the right to decide their own destiny. Should any portion of them, constituting an independent state, propose to unite themselves with our Confederacy, this will be a question for them and us to determine without any foreign interposition.

Second, Polk's cabinet and supporters publicized, exaggerated, and when necessary provoked foreign threats so that Americans would set aside their internal conflicts in the name of patriotism. The principal bogeyman was Britain, which not only denied American claims to all of Oregon but was said to conspire with Mexico in hopes of blocking U.S. expansion. There was some truth to it. The British tried repeatedly to persuade Mexico to accept the loss of Texas and direct its energies to internal reform lest the Yankees grab Texas and California, too. But the proud and stubborn Mexicans refused to accept the loss of Texas, or put their finances in order, or strengthen their army. "The self conceit and weakness of the government here," reported the British minister in Mexico City, "preclude the possibility of giving them any advice."[48] The British also talked trade and loans with the envoys of the Republic of Texas, and suggested that the French join them in support of Texan independence. To be sure, the Tory cabinet of Robert Peel was not prepared to fight for Mexico or Texas, but if war with the United States should erupt over Oregon, then all bets were off.

Third, Polk managed at three crucial times to position himself as a moderate and deflect responsibility for his most divisive decisions onto the Congress. In the case of Oregon, Polk is famous for his spread-eagle screech that "the only way to treat John Bull is to look him straight in the eye,"[49] and for loudly restating the slogan "Fifty-Four Forty or Fight!" But he in fact was prepared to accept the same terms that John Quincy Adams had thrice offered Britain: a partition of Oregon at the 49th parallel (thereby extending the existing U.S.-Canadian boundary to Puget Sound) with navigation rights for Britain on the Columbia River. It meant giving up what is now British Columbia, but as Secretary of State James Buchanan reported, that region was almost "wholly unfit for agriculture & incapable of sustaining any considerable population." So he suggested that Polk offer partition a fourth time. If the British refused, the onus of war would fall on them and the president could feel "perfectly free to insist upon our rights to their full extent up to the Russian line."[50]

American opinion was by no means united. Business rued the prospect of war with Britain, while Whigs opposed Polk on political grounds. Many southerners, now that Texas was in the fold, went lukewarm on Oregon, leading to grumbles about "the ungrateful South." But Manifest Destinarians, especially in the Midwest, said "Oregon — every foot or not an inch!"[51] and expected Polk to stand firm. He did not. In June 1846, when the British finally proposed a treaty based on the American compromise, Polk sent it straight to the Senate, forcing it to embrace moderation or opt for war. Thus trapped, the Senate ratified the treaty, 41 to 14, prompting Edward A. Hannegan (D., Ind.) to bellow: "In the name of the past, in the name of the unborn millions whose proud future it will be to direct the destinies of free America — I protest here, in the face of Heaven and all men, against any dismemberment of our territory — the surrender of our principle — the sacrifice of our honor."[52] Hannegan's was the true voice of Manifest Destiny. It was not the policy of the Polk administration.

What Polk's intentions were regarding Mexico — and whether he even had any clear notion of what he wanted and how to get it — are a bit of a mystery even today. Texas was already a state, and while its southern boundary was a matter of dispute, no one but the Texans themselves thought it worth a war. That is why most historians believe that Polk really aimed from the start at the richest prize left in North America: the derelict province of Alta California.

It had not figured prominently in the literature of Manifest Destiny, but American elite opinion, Democrat and Whig alike, spied California's potential. Naval explorer Charles Wilkes publicized the fact that "Upper California may boast one of the finest, if not the very best harbour in the world — that of San Francisco. . . . It is very probable that this country will become united with Oregon, with which it will perhaps form a state that is destined to control the destinies of the Pacific." [53] Daniel Webster thought that "the port of San Francisco would be twenty times as valuable to us as all Texas," and the official Whig journal justified U.S. ambitions on the familiar grounds that after three centuries of Spanish rule California still had virtually no commerce or agriculture. "While California remains in possession of its present inhabitants, and under control of its present government, there is no hope of its regeneration." It must "pass into the hands of another race. . . . This point, then, being conceded, it remains only to inquire, into whose hands shall California pass?" [54] The *New York Herald* echoed business interests ready to "surrender a slice of Oregon, if we could secure a slice of California." And Polk himself confessed that "in reasserting Mr. Monroe's doctrine I had California and the fine bay of San Francisco as much in view as Oregon." [55]

American emigrants had begun to trickle in over the high Sierra Nevada, and their numbers would doubtless have grown to the point that they might overawe California's seven thousand easygoing Mexican residents in a repetition of the "Texas solution." But Polk did not think time was on the Americans' side. There was evidence of British, French, and even Prussian interest in California, and some members of the British cabinet were eager to send the Royal Navy to San Francisco in order to preempt a Yankee initiative. [56] So Polk's first move was to dispatch a personal emissary, John Slidell of Louisiana, to Mexico City in hopes of persuading Mexico to accept the Rio Grande boundary and sell California. But Mexico had broken diplomatic relations with the United States, and no Mexican leader could appease the hated *yanquis* and survive in power at home. So Polk ordered General Zachary Taylor to send an advance guard to the Rio Grande. The inevitable skirmish with Mexican troops occurred on April 25, 1846, the news reached Washington on May 9, and two days later

Congress almost unanimously endorsed Polk's request for a declaration of war. His justification was self-defense, since in his view the Mexicans had spurned his olive branch and "shed American blood on American soil."[57]

No American war has been more roundly damned than the Mexican. Within months after its outbreak Whigs and abolitionists accused Polk of plotting the ambush on the Rio Grande and misrepresenting the facts in order to stampede the nation into a war of conquest and, what was worse, a war to extend slavery. As James Russell Lowell quipped: "They jest want this Californy / So's to lug new slave-states in."[58] Years later, after secession and defeat had discredited the southern appeal to states' rights, northern historians uniformly interpreted "Jimmy Polk's War" as a slaveholders' plot.[59] Modern historians, however, have found no evidence of a slavers' conspiracy, or even that Polk believed a war would be necessary until the failure of Slidell's mission. After all, the Mexicans had been incapable of mounting a serious attack on the Republic of Texas alone — only madness would incline them to take on the entire United States. But Polk was bent on securing California before the British could meddle, so if Mexico would not deal, the United States would have to fight.

In the event, Americans seized California by filibuster after all, in the Bear Flag Revolt of American settlers supported by U.S. Army Captain John C. Frémont. But twenty-one months of military campaigns and botched diplomacy had to pass before Polk's erstwhile peacemaker, Nicholas Trist, managed to come to terms with Mexican authorities. As those frustrating months dragged on, two new perspectives on the war swept the United States. The original exponents of Manifest Destiny felt shame and disgust: U.S. expansion was supposed to be natural, peaceful, and validated by self-determination, not by the principle of might makes right. At the same time, aggressive Manifest Destinarians went to the other extreme. As American armies drove deep into Mexico and Mexicans refused to talk peace, a sizable fraction of the expansionist press launched an All-Mexico Movement, based on the supposition that the United States might, indeed should, annex the whole country and make of it what God intended. "I would not force the adoption of our form of Government upon any people by the sword," said Senator Herschel V. Johnson (D., Ga.). "But if war is forced upon us, as this has been, and the increase of our territory, and consequently the extension of the area of human liberty and happiness, shall be one of the incidents of such a contest, I believe we should be recreant to our noble mission, if we refused acquiescence in the high purposes of a wise Providence."[60]

Many midwesterners and even some easterners were converted. "The 'conquest' which carries peace into a land where the sword has always been the sole arbiter . . . ," wrote a Boston journal, "must necessarily be a great blessing to the conquered. It is a work worthy of . . . a people who are about to regenerate the world by asserting the supremacy of humanity over the accidents of birth and fortune."[61] Walt Whitman wanted to station sixty thousand American troops in Mexico and establish a reformed government there "whose efficiency and permanency shall be guaranteed by the United States. This will bring out enterprise, open the way for manufacturers and commerce, into which the immense dead capital of the country will find its way." Agriculture, books, and education would follow. "To accomplish this will cost millions, but it will abundantly pay. This is the best kind of conquest." Admiral Robert F. Stockton got thunderous applause in Philadelphia when he cried: "If I were now the sovereign authority . . . I would prosecute this war for the express purpose of redeeming Mexico from misrule and civil strife. . . . I would with a magnanimous and kindly hand gather these wretched people within the fold of republicanism. This I would accomplish at any cost."[62]

Imagine: an All-Mexico Movement for the purpose of regenerating a suffering, incompetent nation that cried out for the blessings of liberty! Was this not the most arrogant variant of U.S. Expansionism? Yes . . . and no. It was certainly imperialist in the sense that it advocated, not the absorption of sparsely populated provinces, but direct rule over millions of foreigners. Yet it also assumed that Mexicans *could* be regenerated, and thus contradicted the Anglo-Saxon view of their intractable racial inferiority. And far from appealing to Americans' greed, it played to their most humane and altruistic qualities and asked of them great sacrifice. That, too, was the voice of Manifest Destiny: a haunting, dangerous temptation to conquer and spend and preach and reform without limits. But once again, that was not the policy of the Polk administration.

Polk shrewdly exploited the All-Mexico Movement to put more pressure on the Mexicans to lay down their arms. Otherwise, he rejected the siren song of the regenerationists. They preached a crusade that would have made Henry Clay blush: Clay had merely asked that the United States stand by Latin peoples fighting for liberty, while the All-Mexico zealots wanted to fight *against* those same people for the purpose of *teaching* them liberty. When Trist brought home the Treaty of Guadalupe Hidalgo in February 1848, ceding Texas, New Mexico, and California to the United States in exchange for $18.2 million, Polk rammed it through the Senate, as he had the Oregon Treaty, before those who wanted all Mexico and those who opposed the war altogether had time to marshal their forces.

*

Historians habitually say that Manifest Destiny triumphed in the 1840s. In fact, the ideologues of Manifest Destiny were everywhere frustrated. And Polk, far from riding their rhetoric to glory, had to fight them every step of the way. It was they who dug in their heels over "Fifty-Four Forty," thereby risking war with Britain. It was they who preached a continental destiny, but balked at the tough war and diplomacy needed to realize it, and then decided that the war would be just only if Americans played sentry and schoolmaster to the entire Mexican nation. Polk, on the other hand, not only realized expansion but reconciled it with the traditions of Liberty at home (as a Tennessean understood it), Unilateralism, and the American System. That he made some false starts, improvised constantly, and lied occasionally goes without saying. But he held American policy within limits, settled the question of the Pacific Coast before more belligerent British statesmen like Lord Palmerston were in a position to stop him, annexed only the lands that Spain and Mexico had allowed to lie fallow, and unquestionably served the national interest — for no critic then or since ever suggested retrocession of the American Southwest.

Historians also say that Manifest Destiny, supposedly triumphant in the 1840s, was frustrated in the 1850s.[63] It is a fact that the United States acquired no new territories, with the exception of the Gadsden Purchase (southern Arizona and New Mexico, acquired for a Pacific railroad route). But it is also true that no other expansion was *pursued* in the decade, with the exception of William Walker's absurd filibusters in Central America and the feints made by Presidents Pierce and Buchanan toward Cuba. (There was little chance, at that date, that Congress would annex a densely populated, slaveholding Hispanic island.) It is a fact that sectional conflict stymied plans for a transcontinental railroad. But that conflict did not prevent the rapid expansion of American interests in the Panama isthmus, Hawaii, China, and Japan, or the expansion of trade with Canada through the 1854 reciprocity treaty (an early version of the present-day NAFTA). Indeed, the United States enjoyed the greatest economic boom in its history in the 1850s, thanks in part to the influx of capital stemming from the California Gold Rush.

Then the Civil War came, the great test of all four U.S. foreign policy traditions for the reason that it was born of an insoluble dispute over the meaning of Liberty at home. In their struggle to save the Union, Abraham Lincoln and Secretary of State Seward invoked independence and a "new birth of freedom," Unilateralism, and the American System (warning Europeans not to intervene in the Civil War and opposing Louis Napoleon's imperial adventure in Mexico), and gave added momentum to Expansionism through a transcontinental railroad, land-grant colleges, and the Homestead Act. The Confederacy, on the other hand, not only betrayed freedom at home insofar as it fought to preserve slavery, but threw Unilateralism and the Monroe Doctrine overboard in its quest for British and French support. If its quest for independence had succeeded, it would also have jeopardized American expansion. For in that event two jealous nations would inhabit North America, dividing and diverting their strength to the advantage of Britain, France, Russia, and Mexico.

Whatever the rights and wrongs on each side of the War Between the States, the defeat of the Confederacy removed the last impediment to the maturation of a continental superstate with a booming population, industry, agriculture, and trade. Only in retrospect can we see that two events of the post–Civil War years were bound to challenge Americans' notions of the natural laws governing their place in the world: the Meiji Restoration of 1868, which began the modernization of Japan, and the unification of Germany in 1871. But it did not occur to contemporary Americans that anything threatening might loom over their horizons of space and time. They were far more likely to laugh at the following joke of the 1880s, and conclude that their horizons were infinite.

It seems that three American travelers were toasting their nation in the presence of their foreign hosts. "Here's to the United States," said the first, "bounded on the north by British America, on the south by the Gulf of Mexico, on the east by the Atlantic, and on the west by the Pacific Ocean." No, said the second, "Here's to the United States — bounded on the north by the North Pole, on the south by the South Pole, on the east by the rising, and on the west by the setting

sun." But the third carried the day: "I give you the United States —
bounded on the north by the Aurora Borealis, on the south by the
precession of the equinoxes, on the east by the primeval chaos, and
on the west by the Day of Judgment!"[64]

All three prophets were proven right in the end, although the last
two not until deep into the twentieth century.

II

OUR NEW TESTAMENT

Go ye therefore, and teach all nations .

—MATTHEW 28:19

FIVE

Progressive Imperialism

ON MARCH 4, 1885, an unseasonably warm and sunny day in Washington, D.C., Grover Cleveland was inaugurated the first Democratic president since before the Civil War. He spoke without notes, but the foreign policy themes he endorsed were so familiar that neither he nor the crowd beneath the Capitol steps required elaboration. They were independence, unilateralism, avoidance of overseas conflicts, and defense of the American state system against European encroachment. In his first message to Congress he added: "Maintaining, as I do, the tenets of a line of precedents from Washington's day, which proscribe entangling alliances with foreign states, I do not favor a policy of acquisition of new and distant territory or the incorporation of remote interests with our own."[1]

Fifteen years later, in the midst of another presidential campaign, Senator Albert J. Beveridge (R., Ind.) invoked the same "line of precedents" to *defend* annexation of "new and distant territory" — the Philippine Islands, Puerto Rico, Guam, and Hawaii — accomplished during and after the Spanish-American War:[2]

> Fellow citizens, It is a noble land that God has given us; a land that can feed and clothe the world; a land whose coast lines would enclose half the countries of Europe; a land set like a sentinel between the two imperial oceans of the globe; a greater England with a nobler destiny. . . . Have we no mission to perform, no duty to discharge to our fellowman? Has the Almighty Father endowed us with gifts beyond our deserts and marked us as the people of his peculiar favor, merely to rot in our own selfishness, as men and nations must, who take cowardice for their companion and self for their Deity . . . ?
>
> And, now, obeying the same voice that Jefferson heard and obeyed, that Jackson heard and obeyed, that Monroe heard and obeyed, that Seward heard and obeyed, that Ulysses S. Grant heard and obeyed, that Benjamin Harrison heard and obeyed, William McKinley plants the flag over the islands of the seas, outposts of

commerce, citadels of national security, and the march of the flag goes on!

Suddenly, in 1898, the United States became a colonial power. What had happened? And how could Beveridge possibly claim that imperialism was true to American traditions, much less represent a mission, a duty, a nobler destiny?

Historians have asked themselves those questions over and over again on the assumption that America's imperial episode at the turn of the twentieth century was a "great aberration," and thus something in need of a lot of explaining. The ingenious and varied theories they have offered suggest that U.S. imperialism was a spasmodic reaction to fundamental changes in American society, in the geopolitical environment, or both. And the circumstantial evidence they muster is impressive. The trouble is, the assumption is wrong. What most historians have labeled new and bad about American policy in 1898 was in fact old and good, and what most think was traditional and good about it was in fact new and dangerous. But put that riddle out of mind for now. In order to understand 1898 and all that, we first must survey those fundamental changes in America and the world, and the events they are invoked to explain.

*

Raw statistics prove that the United States became a world power in the generation after the Civil War. Its population more than doubled to 71 million by 1900, making the United States more populous than any European nation except Russia. The industrial revolution matured to the point that by 1900 Americans produced 244 million tons of coal per year (an output equal to Britain's) and 10 million tons of steel, nearly twice the total of second-place Germany. American inventors such as Edison, Bell, and the Wright brothers, and entrepreneurs such as Du Pont and Rockefeller, made the United States a leader in the second industrial revolution, based on electricity, chemicals, oil, and internal combustion. In the same decades, the homesteading of the Great Plains and the availability of cheap bulk transport by rail and steamship made the United States a breadbasket to the world. By the mid-1870s Americans achieved, for the first time in history, a positive balance of trade on the strength of exports that quadrupled between 1865 and 1900 and reached almost $250 million per year. American railroads, stretching a quarter of a million miles in 1900, had expanded eightfold since the Civil War and now connected giant, electrically lighted cities packed with people who rode trolleys to work, read one-penny newspapers thanks to the Linotype machine, and marveled at skyscrapers made possible by Otis's elevator.

Nothing better expressed America's new industrial culture than Chicago's Columbian Exposition of 1893. Its Great White City, built from scratch in the finest beaux-arts style, was "dazzling in its perfection and awesome in its conceit." Visitors gawked at the mammoth pavilions overlooking Lake Michigan and the miraculous dynamos and electrical gadgets, and foreigners were amazed that one midwestern city could purchase museums of European art and extravagant gardens just for a season's play. Americana abounded, from pioneer and Indian displays to replicas of the latest U.S. battleships, the Great White Fleet. "The new age of America, or cosmopolitan America," the historian Richard Collin has written, "arrived not in 1898 in the Philippines or Cuba, not in 1901 with Theodore Roosevelt, but in 1893 and 1894 in great White City of Chicago."[3]

A new American age implied new or different Americans. Twenty million of them were immigrants who arrived between 1870 and 1910, and included, for the first time, large numbers of Italians, Slavs, and Jews. Their presence enriched urban culture, but also sparked an ethnic backlash. Urbanization and the beginnings of suburbanization made possible by commuter railroads also meant that by 1896 town and city dwellers outnumbered rural folk for the first time. Big business and big labor accordingly gained political clout at the expense of provincial farmers, and at the cost of sharper class conflict and violent labor disputes. The frontier was thought to have served as a safety valve for American society whenever hard times or crowding threatened to cause trouble back east. Now the frontier had been swallowed: American farmers and ranchers settled more land during the three decades after 1865 than over the previous three centuries.[4] So manufacturers, financiers, and politicians spoke of the need for foreign outlets for American goods and energies, tempting historians in turn to interpret the imperial thrust of 1898 as a buoyant or anxious search for new frontiers.

Changes in the world outside also invited Americans to reexamine their foreign policy traditions. Beginning in the late 1870s, almost all the European powers rode a new wave of imperialism, partitioned Africa and much of Asia and Oceania into colonies and protectorates, and — except for Britain — jettisoned free trade in favor of protective tariffs. France and Russia and then, most ominously, Germany after 1897 spent heavily on modern steel navies, challenging Britain's supremacy. In 1894 the Japanese Empire kicked off another scramble for ports and concessions at the expense of the decrepit Chinese Empire. European engineering redesigned the earth's political geography through the Suez Canal (1869), the British trans-Indian railroad (1870), and Russian Trans-Siberian Railway (1904), while steamships, telegraphs, malaria prophylaxis (quinine), machine guns, and other technologies made imperialism cheap and easy. At the same time, the optimistic, liberal spirit that characterized Europe in the 1850s and '60s gave way to a brooding mood of impending conflict informed by Social Darwinist notions of racial competition and survival of the fittest.

The transformation of world politics wrought by imperialism could not help but impress itself upon observant Americans. One effect was the slow gestation of the modern U.S. Navy, conceived in 1882 by Secretary of the Navy William H. Hunt and realized by Secretary Benjamin Tracy, who challenged Congress in 1890 to build a two-ocean fleet of twenty battleships and sixty cruisers by the end of the century. Meanwhile, Admiral Stephen B. Luce, founder of the Naval War College, and Captain A. T. Mahan educated Americans on the facts of life in the modern world. Mahan's *The Influence of Sea Power on History* made his reputation, but he reached a mass audience in articles arguing for a fleet, bases, and coaling stations sufficient to secure American coasts, the Caribbean, and the Pacific as far out as Hawaii. In a world of fierce commercial and naval competitors, the United States could no longer take for granted its safety or access to markets. "I am an imperialist," Mahan said, "simply because I am not isolationist."[5]

Mahan was also a devout churchman, and like most Protestants of his time he believed that God had raised the United States to world power for a reason. To be sure, the millenarian movement of the Jacksonian era was long gone, but not before it seeded a later generation with its emphasis on works over faith, immanence over transcendence, and heaven on earth as well as above — the Social Gospel. The influence of Darwinian evolution and the "higher criticism" of the Bible also hit the churches full force in the last three decades of the nineteenth century. The Catholic response was to denounce modernism and elevate an infallible papacy. One Baptist response was stubborn fundamentalism, but progressive mainstream Protestants, whose church attendance soared 75 percent in the decade after 1895,[6] tended to downplay problematical theology in favor of social uplift at home and abroad. And that meant the projection of American power overseas, far from offending the keepers of the national conscience, suited their book exactly.

No one said it better than the Reverend Josiah Strong, whose rhetorical stew mixed evangelicalism, Social Gospel, Anglo-Saxonism, and Social Darwinism. His best-selling *Our Country* of 1885 identified Americans as a

> race of unequaled energy, with all the majesty of numbers and the might of wealth behind it — the representative, let us hope, of the largest liberty, the purest Christianity, the highest civilization — having developed peculiarly aggressive traits calculated to impress its institutions upon mankind, will spread itself across the earth. . . . And can any one doubt that this race, unless devitalized by alcohol and tobacco, is destined to dispossess many weaker races, assimilate others, and mold the remainder, until, in a very true and important sense, it has Anglo-Saxonized mankind?

Strong later tossed in the Turner thesis, insisting that the rigors of the frontier had been God's way of training the race for global leadership and, with the frontier now closed, "the final competition of races."[7]

Such rhetoric, coming as it did not only from bluff nationalists like Theodore Roosevelt ("Unless we keep the barbarian virtues, gaining the civilized ones will be of little avail")[8] but from religious spokesmen as well, suggested to some historians that America's fling with imperialism was a product of Social Darwinist thought. Others spied in the events of 1898 a reprise of Manifest Destiny thinking translated onto a world stage, or evidence of a "psychic crisis" brought on by the depression of 1893–96, labor unrest, rapid social change, and the closing of the frontier. Or perhaps big businessmen had steered foreign policy toward the conquest of foreign markets. Or maybe Americans were just aping the British again — that might explain why they seemed to lose interest in colonies by 1902, when the Boer War and John Hobson's liberal critique soured the British cognoscenti on imperialism.[9] Still other historians described the U.S. colonial empire as an accidental byproduct of the Spanish-American War or, quite the opposite, the work of a conspiratorial clique bent on exploiting war with Spain to realize Mahan's "large policy" of insular empire. George F. Kennan, noting the plethora of plausible theories, just shrugged that "the American people of that day, or at least many of their more influential spokesmen, simply liked the smell of empire and felt the urge . . . to bask in the sunshine of recognition as one of the great imperial powers of the world."[10]

Yet another group of historians — the Open Door school — is the only one to argue from the premise that U.S. imperialism was not an aberration but evidence of a continuous American drive for expansion and foreign markets.[11] They can point to statesmen like Seward who, as early as the 1850s, pronounced commerce the "god of boundaries" and "chief agent of [America's] advancement in civilization and enlargement of empire." He called the Pacific Ocean "the great realm of futurity," alerted Congress to the importance of sea power decades ahead of Mahan, and, as secretary of state, tried to acquire British Columbia, the Virgin Islands, and Greenland, in addition to Alaska. Seward "clearly anticipated the objectives, if not the means, of the expansionists of 1898," and hence "the Great Aberration" was really "the Great Culmination."[12] Similar precursors can be found in the post–Civil War era. In 1890 Secretary of State James G. Blaine announced: "We are not seeking annexation of territory. At the same time I think we should be unwisely content if we did not seek to engage in what the younger Pitt so well termed the annexation of trade."[13]

The theory that U.S. diplomacy was driven by a capitalistic drive for new markets does not hold up, however, because the government really did little to promote exports in the 1865–1900 period. First, it did not have to do so, since the very figures cited by the Open Door school show that American exporters were doing famously on their own. Second, the foreign sector was always a tiny fraction of the U.S. economy, and investors were far more interested in domestic development after the Civil War. Third, if capitalists had been desperate for foreign markets, they would have lobbied for sharp reductions in U.S. tariffs to encourage other nations to lower barriers to trade. In fact, they repeatedly pushed tariffs higher, while sectors of U.S. business killed reciprocity treaties with Canada (1865) and Mexico (1883), and blocked annexation of the Hawaiian Islands (1893), for fear of competition. Thus there was "a profound gap between rhetoric and results in late 19th century economic expansion."[14]

So how exactly did the United States make a new departure in foreign relations in 1898 — and why? The way to read the riddle is to measure what the government really did before, during, and after

1898 against the four traditions we have on the books. With that method in mind, let us now examine the facts.

★

The first fact is that Americans never considered the Pacific basin to lie outside their natural purview. Not only did merchants, whalers, and missionaries ply that ocean from the South Seas to the Arctic Circle before the Civil War, the government took a keen interest, too. When a British naval officer tried to make a protectorate of the Hawaiian kingdom in 1841 and 1842, President Tyler loudly claimed for the United States a preeminent interest in the fate of those islands. In 1867 Seward annexed Midway, the uninhabited northernmost isle in the Hawaiian chain, and purchased Alaska from tsarist Russia. In the 1850s the United States opened Japan, and after 1868, when the Meiji revolutionaries declared their intention to modernize, hundreds of private Americans crossed the ocean to teach science and engineering, law and medicine, business and agriculture, government and Christianity to the Japanese. Seward was equally hopeful of influencing China, and his Burlingame Treaty of 1868 endorsed the free movement of goods and people between the two countries. Unfortunately, American paranoia about the influx of coolie labor inspired the Chinese Exclusion Act of 1882. It was the first of several occasions in which racial antipathies inhibited rather than drove U.S. expansion. Seward had even less luck with Korea, the "hermit kingdom," after an American schooner and crew were destroyed there by hostile villagers. U.S. warships retaliated in 1871 at a cost of some three hundred Korean lives. The commander, Commodore Robert Shufeldt, was zealous for trade. "The Pacific is the ocean bride of America . . . ," he cried; "let us determine while yet in our power, that no commercial rival or hostile flag can float with impunity over the long swell of the Pacific sea."[15] But in the event, Japan forced open Korea in 1876, and the 1882 U.S.-Korean treaty that followed accomplished little by way of trade.

Another American target was Samoa. As early as 1872, a native king offered the U.S. Navy a base at Pago Pago in return for protection. The Senate declined the responsibility, but in 1878 ratified a treaty promising to mediate Samoan disputes in return for the harbor. Disputes came quickly as Germany and Britain bid for portions of the island group. When Secretary of State Thomas Bayard's mediation failed to settle the issue, American, German, and British warships faced one another down in Samoan waters, and Germany complained that Bayard interpreted the Monroe Doctrine "as though the Pacific Ocean were to be treated as an American lake."[16] Bismarck eventually agreed to partition the islands in 1889, and the colony of American Samoa was formalized in 1898.

On the other side of the ledger are examples of expansion spurned. Commodore Perry, on his way to open Japan, urged the United States to colonize the Lew Chew (Ryukyu) Islands. But Secretary of War William L. Marcy replied, "It is considered sounder policy not to seize the island as suggested in your dispatch."[17] In 1867, following its grudging approval of the $7.2 million to buy Alaska, Congress passed a resolution forswearing new acquisitions until the government paid off its Civil War debt. Two years later President Grant bid for Santo Domingo, but the deal — involving a crooked Dominican president and two crooked White House cronies — was so rank that the Senate rejected the gift. In any case, Americans were not interested in absorbing large numbers of dark-skinned Spanish Catholics. Finally, the government did little more than bluster when Ferdinand de Lesseps, the Frenchman who had promoted the Suez Canal, purchased a right-of-way from Colombia in hopes of digging a canal across the Panamanian isthmus.

By 1890 U.S. naval officers and their supporters in Congress knew that sooner or later the United States would have to expand its purview, if only to secure North America from the fleets of the imperial powers. "I think there are only three places that are of value enough to be taken," said Blaine: "one is Hawaii and the others are Cuba and Porto Rico."[18] Yet when the United States got the chance to take Hawaii, President Cleveland said no. The story dates back to midcentury, when the Hawaiian king abolished the Polynesian feudal system and parceled out land under clear and transferable titles. Americans, especially sons of missionaries, scarfed it up for sugar plantations, and a reciprocity treaty in 1875 made Hawaii a virtual extension of the U.S. economy. Twelve years later the planters and merchants staged a coup, transferred power to a white-dominated parliament, and approved a treaty giving the U.S. Navy rights to Pearl Harbor. Hawaii, said Blaine, "was essentially a part of the American system of states, and a key to North Pacific trade."[19]

Then Congress changed U.S. tariff laws in favor of domestic sugar producers. Hawaiian planters faced ruin and, to make matters worse,

Queen Liliuokalani threatened to restore power to native Hawaiians. So in 1893 the whites declared a republic in Honolulu with the support of the U.S. minister and a navy cruiser, and drafted a treaty of annexation. It looked a reprise of the Bear Flag Revolt in California, except this time Americans were a small minority of the population and the United States was not at war with the victimized government. Cleveland ordered an investigation, then withdrew the treaty from the Senate. Southern Democrats objected to Hawaiian annexation on economic and racial grounds, but what paralyzed the administration was scruples. As Secretary of State Walter Q. Gresham said, he was not opposed to expansion, but could not countenance "stealing territory, or annexing a people against their consent."[20]

Then everything changed — not in 1898 but in 1895, when Secretary of State Richard Olney fired what Cleveland called "a twenty inch gun" at Great Britain, heralding a new assertiveness in U.S. foreign policy. For years London had contested the boundary between British Guiana and neighboring Venezuela. Gold and the mouth of the Orinoco River were at stake, not to mention the Monroe Doctrine. If Britain was permitted to bully Venezuela, said Olney, Latin America might be the next continent partitioned by European imperialists. Senator Henry Cabot Lodge believed the "United States must either maintain the Monroe Doctrine and treat its infringement as an act of hostility or abandon it," and the chairman of the Foreign Relations Committee resolved that the Monroe Doctrine be "indelibly engraved upon the portals of the State Department."[21] So Olney pulled the trigger: "Today the United States is practically sovereign on this continent, and its fiat is law upon the subjects to which it confines its interposition."[22]

Lord Salisbury scoffed at the Yankee presumption, and the crisis lasted until the British cabinet, distracted by the first rumors of war with the South African Boers, agreed to a tribunal and ultimate compromise. But Olney's Corollary to the Monroe Doctrine fastened itself on the minds of Americans. "Much has been settled," wrote the *Philadelphia Press:* "First, the Monroe Doctrine is definitely established in the sight of the world; second, every American republic has learned both the value of our support and our readiness to face the risk of war in defense of a country which had no claim on us but the justice of its cause and the weakness of its resources; third . . . the United States is bound to see that the countries it protects and safeguards give no just occasion for foreign interference; fourth, having assumed these grave international responsibilities, the United States must be prepared to discharge them."[23]

Sounds like spread-eagle Monroe Doctrine rhetoric reflective of America's new naval and industrial might, right? In part it does — but look again at the *Press*'s second point. Were Americans really prepared to make war, not just to defend their fellow citizens' lives or property, but on behalf of foreigners in the name of abstract justice? John Quincy Adams would have scorned the thought, but as events in Cuba soon proved, the answer to that was yes.

In 1895 Cuban rebels launched their second war for independence against Spain. Americans sympathized with "Cuba libre!" and were appalled by the ferocity of the war and the Spanish tactic of removing villagers to concentration camps. One hundred thousand Cubans died from disease and famine. Cleveland could not ignore the horror, but recognizing the *independentistas* meant risking war with Spain, since the Monroe Doctrine would then come into play. Instead, Olney urged Spain to grant a measure of autonomy to Cuba and stop the fighting. When the Spaniards refused, he threw up his hands.

Republican William McKinley entered the White House in 1897. He, too, deplored the prospect of war, and did not believe the Cubans capable of self-government, but the pressures on him increased. American property was being destroyed in the fighting and, most troubling of all, Spain was canvassing Europe's chanceries in search of support.[24] Then the Spanish minister wrote a letter (intercepted and published in New York) that dismissed McKinley as a weakling. Then the U.S. battleship *Maine* mysteriously exploded and sank in Havana's harbor, and the Hearst and Pulitzer newspaper chains competed to whip the public into a mood of righteous anger. McKinley made a final try for peace, demanding an armistice, an end to concentration camps, and negotiations. The proud Spaniards dithered and equivocated, and would not discuss Cuban independence. In short, Spain behaved as pigheadedly over Cuba as Mexico had over Texas, all but inviting the Yankees to unsheath their swords.

On April 11, 1898, McKinley requested authorization to use force to protect U.S. interests and end the war in the "cause of humanity." Congress responded, significantly, not with a declaration of war per se, but with a joint resolution that declared Cuba independent, insisted that Spanish forces withdraw, authorized the president to use force to ensure these results, and renounced any intention to annex the island. "We intervene not for conquest," said Senator John C. Spooner (R., Wis.), "not for aggrandizement, not because of the Monroe Doctrine; we intervene for humanity's sake . . . to aid a people who have suffered every form of tyranny and who have made a desperate struggle to be free." Senator Shelby M. Cullom (R., Ill.) said he would support the war *only* if it was fought in the name of liberty, in which case the United States would "earn the praises of every lover of freedom and humanity the world over."[25]

★

Given their lack of military preparation, the Americans were fortunate that the war went ahead so swiftly and well. McKinley dominated strategy, being the first president to set up a war room, communicate by telegraph and telephone with commanders in the field, and stage briefings to control the spin of the news. The most glorious and ominous victory occurred in the Philippines, where Commodore George Dewey's Asiatic squadron surprised the Spanish fleet at Manila. Assistant Secretary of the Navy Roosevelt had wired him in February to make such an attack in case of war, and historians once thought this evidence of an imperialist plot. The plan had actually been drafted in 1896 by a brilliant naval staff officer and approved by the administration. The truly fateful decision was McKinley's dispatch of soldiers to occupy the island of Luzon. By destroying Spanish authority in the Philippines, he created the problem of what should replace it.

McKinley also moved quickly to settle the future of Hawaii. The war underscored the islands' strategic value, but a new factor had entered the picture since Cleveland's cold shoulder five years before. Japanese immigrants, imported to work in the sugar cane fields, numbered a quarter of the population and were the fastest-growing element. When the white-run Hawaiian republic attempted to restrict the influx in 1897, the Japanese minister warned the United States not to annex or discriminate, and a Japanese cruiser steamed to Honolulu. The crisis subsided, but the message, as the House Foreign Affairs Committee reported, was clear: sooner or later Japanese Hawaiians would demand political rights, gain power, and annul the treaty granting Pearl Harbor to the U.S. Navy. "Annexation, and that alone will securely maintain American control in Hawaii."[26] McKinley agreed: "We need Hawaii as much and a good deal more than we did

California. It is manifest destiny."[27] Adopting the same ploy Tyler used to annex Texas, McKinley asked for a joint resolution, which passed 290 to 91 in the House and 42 to 21 in the Senate, in July 1898.

The fighting ended in August, by which time U.S. forces had seized the remnants of Spain's Columbian empire. What would become of them? McKinley professed to agonize, and toured the country to take the people's pulse. He had probably made up his mind to retain Puerto Rico and Guam for naval bases, but was still surprised to learn how little the prospect of colonies troubled the voters. The only hard case was the Philippines, a primitive, populous, and virtually unknown archipelago clear across the ocean. Manila might serve as a naval base and entrepôt for the China market, but to defend it the army would need to occupy all of the surrounding islands lest rival powers move in. That Spain could not be left in control was clear, since Americans justified the war on the grounds of Spanish colonial cruelty. But independence, in the judgment of Dewey ("The natives appear unable to govern") and a British expert (the Philippines "would not remain one year peaceful under an independent native government"),[28] was sure to condemn the Filipinos to anarchy or colonization by Japan or Germany. And so, after a prayerful night, McKinley concluded: "There was nothing left for us to do but to take them all, and to educate the Filipinos, and uplift and civilize and Christianize them, and by God's grace do the very best we could by them, as our fellow-men for whom Christ also died."[29]

Hypocritical hogwash, say modern readers. But that is because they miss the point. In fact, religious sentiment was instrumental in rallying the American people, and perhaps the pious McKinley as well, to an imperial mission. During the run-up to the war Protestant journals made noises like this: "And if it be the will of Almighty God that by war the last trace of this inhumanity of man to man shall be swept away from this Western hemisphere, let it come!"[30] And this: "Should we now go to war our cause will be just. Every Methodist preacher will be a recruiting officer."[31] After Dewey's victory, Baptist preacher Robert Stuart MacArthur saw a heavenly future for the Philippines: "We will fill them with school houses and missionaries."[32] And the *Churchman* warned: "Woe to any nation . . . called to guide a weaker people's future which hesitates for fear its own interests will be entangled and its own future imperilled by the discharge of an unmistakeable duty."[33] In September 1898, the *Literary Digest* surveyed almost two hundred journals and found them three to one in favor of annexing all or part of the Philippines.[34] Rudyard Kipling was only preaching to the choir when he mailed his poem "The White Man's Burden" to Roosevelt in November.[35]

An Anti-Imperialist League arose that same month, comprised of bizarre bedfellows ranging from industrialist Andrew Carnegie and prairie populist William Jennings Bryan to labor leader Samuel Gompers and numerous college presidents. But its members mostly were mugwumps who bemoaned all the change industrialization had wrought in American life and saw in imperialism the foreign policy expression of an overall decline in the nation's moral fiber. These cultured, mostly eastern intellectuals were "men full of years, long experienced as critics and political independents, and unshakeably convinced that they were the authentic spokesmen of old-line America."[36] They made constitutional objections to colonies that were clearly not meant for statehood, they disputed the claim that colonies were of economic benefit, they warned that empire would breed foreign entanglements, they invoked the nation's legacy of anti-imperialism, and they feared that colonial rule would corrupt democracy and breed militarism. Senator George F. Hoar (R., Mass.) cried that the Founding Fathers had never dreamed that their descendants "might strut about in the cast-off clothing of pinchbeck emperors and pewter kings," and eminent German immigrant Carl Schurz mourned to see his adopted land embrace "policies and practices even worse than those which once he had to flee from." Not least, anti-imperialists abominated the raising of the Stars and Stripes over dark-skinned races. Did the United States, which already had a "black elephant" in the South, asked the *New York World*, need a "white elephant" in the Philippines, a "leper elephant" in Hawaii, a brown one in Puerto Rico, and a yellow one in Cuba? The American flag, said Schurz, should fly over "Germanic" races and no others.[37]

The peace treaty with Spain that made the United States a colonial power passed in February 1899 by a vote of 57 to 27. Two days before, shots were exchanged in Manila between American troops and Filipino nationalists. It seemed that Yanks would have to fight the very people for whom they yearned to do good works. Three years later, at the cost of 5,000 American and some 100,000 Filipino lives, and $160 million, civil governor William Howard Taft was finally able to dedicate himself to "the interests of the people over whom we assert sovereignty . . . and to give them, to the fullest possible extent, individual freedom, self-government according to their capacity, just and equal laws, an opportunity for education, for profitable industry, and for development in civilization."[38] Taft said: "The work we are doing in the Philippines rises far above the mere question of what the total of our exports and imports may be. . . . The Philippine question is, Can the dominion of a great and prosperous civilized nation in the temperate zone exercise a healthful and positively beneficial influence upon the growth and development of a tropical people?"[39]

Americans eventually redeemed themselves. At considerable public and private expense they built ports, roads, railroads, schools, and hospitals, instituted land reform and experimented with economic policies they would later try out at home. It was imperialism, but a self-consciously progressive imperialism born of Americans' sense of secular and religious mission. For from the point of view of hard national interest almost everyone, including Teddy Roosevelt, soon concluded that annexing the Philippines had been a mistake. The islands were a military Achilles heel and an economic drain, and he hoped to set them free as soon as possible.

Otherwise, few Americans cared about the little empire acquired in 1898, or if they did care, affirmed it. Bryan tried to make the 1900 election a referendum on imperialism, but gave up the issue as a loser, while the Republicans defended the empire on "traditional and distinctively American grounds."[40] After McKinley was murdered in 1901, his successors Roosevelt, William Howard Taft, and Woodrow Wilson continued to dispatch ships, soldiers, marines, and officials to suppress civil strife and anti-American violence or to forestall financial collapse in Cuba, the Dominican Republic, Haiti, Nicaragua, and Mexico. In Panama, of course, Roosevelt conspired with locals to overthrow Colombian rule in 1903 so that the United States could acquire a zone through which to build a canal. And none of these actions met serious opposition from the American people and Congress. Imperialism was already either an accepted tradition of U.S. foreign policy or a natural expression of older traditions, or perhaps a little of both.

The older tradition most clearly relevant was the American System. John Hay prepared the pitch for Roosevelt's Panama play by persuading Britain to discard the Clayton-Bulwer agreement of 1850, by which Britain was to have equal say in any isthmian canal project. The Hay-Pauncefote Treaty (1901) that replaced it granted the United States exclusive rights to dig and defend a Panama canal. The Platt Amendment of 1901 arrogated to the United States the right to intervene in Cuba in case of threats to its independence or American lives or property. That made Cuba a virtual protectorate, the purpose being to prevent European powers from exploiting unrest or anti-*yan-qui* resentment to grab a beachhead in the Caribbean. In 1902 Venezuela was torn by civil strife and defaulted on bonds to foreign investors. British and German warships blockaded the coast, and on two occasions the Germans opened bombardments. The claims were adjudicated, but Roosevelt drew what to him was an obvious conclusion. So long as Caribbean states were permitted to fall into anarchy, the navies of Europe would have an excuse to penetrate America's sphere of influence and defense perimeter. So when the Dominican Republic fell into civil war and bankruptcy in 1904, the Roosevelt Corollary to the Monroe Doctrine declared that henceforth the United States would itself serve as gendarme and bill collector in the region:[41]

> It is not true that the United States feels any land hunger or entertains any projects as regards the other nations of the Western Hemisphere save such as are for their welfare. All that this country desires is to see the neighboring countries stable, orderly, and prosperous. If a nation shows that it knows how to act with reasonable efficiency and decency in social and political matters, if it keeps order and pays its obligations, it need fear no interference from the United States. Chronic wrongdoing, or an impotence which results in a general loosening of the ties of civilized society, may in America, as elsewhere, ultimately require intervention by some civilized nation, and in the Western Hemisphere the adherence of the United States to the Monroe Doctrine may force the United States, however reluctantly, in flagrant cases of such wrongdoing or impotence, to the exercise of an international police power. . . . We would interfere with them only as a last resort, and then only if it became evident that their inability or unwillingness to do justice at home and abroad had violated the rights of the United States or had invited foreign aggression to the detriment of the entire body of American nations.

What is more, he was truthful. "I want to do nothing but what a policeman has to do in Santo Domingo," said TR. "As for annexing the island, I have about the same desire to annex it as a gorged boa constrictor might have to swallow a porcupine wrong-end-to."[42]

The same principle held in Asia. To be sure, the United States took advantage of the foreign commercial quarters and extraterritorial rights won by the Europeans (and Japanese) at the point of a gun. But it refrained from grabbing bases and ports of its own in China. Instead, Hay reacted to the other powers' Scramble for Concessions with the Open Door Note of 1899. (As usual, the American initiative was a British idea: Hay's Asian adviser heard it from a British China hand.) It called on the powers to open their Chinese concessions to the trade and investment of all nations on an equal basis. The Europeans paid it lip service only, as demonstrated in the wake of China's xenophobic Boxer Rebellion in 1900. The United States contributed 6,300 men to the international force that rescued the besieged foreign legations in Peking, but then withdrew them rather than carve out an American zone on the Chinese mainland. Hay's second Open Door Note implored the other imperial powers to do likewise, but Russia and Japan did not, and when they went to war in 1904–5 over control of Manchuria and Korea, Roosevelt quietly jettisoned the Open Door policy. The best the United States could hope for was a balance of power among the imperial rivals in East Asia, and U.S. mediation of the Russo-Japanese War helped to bring that about. TR reasoned that since Americans did not want Japanese ships, goods, or immigrants flooding the Western Hemisphere, the United States must permit Japan to pursue outlets on its own side of the ocean.

Taft and Secretary of State Philander C. Knox reversed this policy, determined to push U.S. investments into Manchuria through what they called Dollar Diplomacy. It was a variant of the progressive policy pioneered by Taft and economic adviser Charles Conant in the Philippines. "True stability," wrote Knox, "is best established not by military, but by economic and social forces. . . . The problem of good government is inextricably interwoven with that of economic prosperity and sound finance."[43] But Dollar Diplomacy flopped: Russia and Japan joined forces to restrict competing investments, while Knox discovered that U.S. banks lacked surplus capital for risky foreign ventures. In the case of China proper, American racism trumped commerce again. Congress toughened the ban on Chinese immigration in 1902 and 1904 and prohibited the 20,000 Chinese in Hawaii from immigrating to the mainland, and the U.S. military tried to persuade the 100,000 Chinese Filipinos to depart. All this provoked a spontaneous Chinese boycott of American goods. Racism, far from being a motive force for U.S. expansion, was once again a barrier to it.[44]

★

That, in bare outline, is what the United States did before and after its imperialist "binge" in 1898. How much was consonant or dissonant with American diplomatic traditions? First, imperialism violated no "isolationist" tradition, because isolationism, as we have seen, is a myth. The genuine U.S. tradition dating from Washington's time was Unilateralism, and all the presidents from 1898 to 1917 clung to it.[45] To be sure, Roosevelt hosted the peace conference that ended the Russo-Japanese War, since he understood that the United States had an acute interest in the Asian balance of power. But he never considered anything resembling an entanglement, and would have been rebuked at home if he had.

Nor did U.S. imperial initiatives violate the tradition of the American System. On the contrary, U.S. assertion in the Caribbean seemed to be mandatory for the preservation of the principles proclaimed by Monroe. From the Venezuela crisis of 1895 to the birth of Panama in 1903, the Roosevelt Corollary of 1904, and the purchase of the Virgin Islands in 1917, the United States consistently preempted European involvements. In a world brimming with blue-water navies, the United States, as Senator Lodge said, had no choice but to back up the Monroe Doctrine with steel or renounce it.

Nor, most obviously, did imperialism violate the tradition of Expansionism. Even Cleveland's refusal of Hawaii was no last gasp of isolation, because it testified to nothing more than his own conscience: the will of inhabitants had never blocked American expansion before.

But wait — had not previous acquisitions been contiguous and continental? Were not far-flung insular possessions, especially in the Pacific, a departure in American history, and one that had nothing to do with the Monroe Doctrine? Wrong: they were not a departure and they had everything to do with the Monroe Doctrine, *because the watery boundary where America stopped and Asia began was never defined.* As early as 1867 the United States possessed the non-contiguous empire of Alaska with its Aleutian Islands stretching to Siberia, as well as Midway and a faint constellation of guano reefs and atolls.[46] By 1875 Hawaii was an economic client explicitly placed under the Monroe Doctrine's umbrella, and Bayard and Blaine risked war in the 1880s lest Samoa fall to Britain or Germany. As historian Foster Rhea Dulles observed, "There was in almost every instance a half-forgotten precedent for the overseas expansion of 1898."[47]

In any case, America's empire contained no interior chunks of continents like the European ones. It consisted of a glacis of bases and ports which, if possessed by imperial rivals, might pose a threat to the Panama Canal or sea lanes plied by American ships. The overseas episodes from 1865 to 1917 demonstrate that whenever other imperial powers were involved (Alaska, Samoa 1887, Venezuela, Cuba, the Philippines, Hawaii 1898, China 1899, Santo Domingo 1904), the United States acted with vigor; in cases where other powers did not pose a threat (Santo Domingo 1869–71, Samoa 1871, Hawaii 1893), the United States backed off.

In light of Unilateralism, the American System, and Expansionism, therefore, the imperialism of 1898–1917 was no aberration, but the sum of initiatives deemed necessary to defend America's traditional posture. And that may explain why the United States seemed to turn away from imperialism after the short burst. Once the navy had the bases it needed and foreigners were prevented from grabbing the bases they wanted, American interest required no more. It also explains why the public never raised a ruckus about the insular possessions and why no president — not Woodrow Wilson himself — ever repented of them. They were just not that big a deal.

*

So what *was* new about 1898? Why even call it imperialism, another abused word (like isolationism) with a host of nasty connotations? And above all why include it among the traditions of U.S. foreign policy? To answer these questions, let us return to the start of the chain of events. For the decidedly new, problematical feature of the era was not the colonialism that everyone now condemns, but the moral progressivism that most now applaud! The United States went off the rails, in terms of its honored traditions, when it *went to war with Spain in the first place.* Imagine: the American people and government allowed themselves to be swept by a hurricane of militant righteousness into a revolutionary foreign war, determined to slay a dragon and free a damsel in distress. It was precisely the sort of temptation that Washington and Hamilton scorned, Jefferson and Madison felt but resisted, and John Quincy Adams damned with eloquence. Exceptionalism meant Liberty at home, not crusades to change the world. In terms of U.S. traditions, the only thing wrong with the imperialist era was what everyone took for granted was *right:* the war to end war in Cuba.

Having then vanquished the Spaniards, Americans found themselves in possession of several small colonies. The problem of what to do with them raised a second temptation: not retention of foreign bases — that was sound strategy — but rather the "All-Philippine Movement," which landed the nation's moral elites in the muddle Polk had avoided at the time of the All-Mexico Movement. For not only did Americans charge off on a crusade, they remained in the lands they seized in the belief that they had a mission to transplant American civilization, even though they had no intention of allowing the islanders to graduate to statehood. Alaska (1884) and Hawaii (1900) did gain the status of incorporated territories, which meant that the U.S. Constitution fully applied there. But the navy ruled Guam directly, and the Foraker Act of 1900 and Organic Act of 1902 pronounced Puerto Rico and the Philippines unincorporated dependencies. The government was challenged in court: how could it deny self-determination and equal protection to people under its flag? But the Supreme Court's Insular Decisions ruled the Foraker Act constitutional. So the United States acted both on the racial assumption that its colonies were not fit to participate fully in national life and on the nonracial assumption that they could, in time, be taught the American way. As one historian shrewdly observed: "The imperialist compromise was to allow the flag to advance *but to deny that the Constitution followed the flag.*"[48]

What did follow the flag was the same do-gooder impulse that inspired the reforms of the Progressive Era within the United States. Colonial administrators, economists, teachers, doctors, missionaries, investors, and the Army Corps of Engineers descended on Cuba, the Philippines, Puerto Rico, Guam, and Panama to whip yellow fever and malaria, build the Panama Canal (which TR dubbed a gift to humanity), develop the economies, and free the people from their Spanish Catholic legacy.[49] That they did great harm is now a truism — consider the displacement of Puerto Rico's self-sufficient farmers, the *jíbaros,* to make way for U.S.-owned sugar plantations. But it is just as true that Americans believed themselves called to pursue what the Reverend Alexander Blackburn called "the imperialism of righteousness" and Samuel Flagg Bemis "an imperialism against imperialism."[50] Listen to McKinley: "Nations do not grow in strength, and the cause of liberty and law is not advanced by the doing of easy things. . . . It is not possible that 75 millions of American freemen are unable to establish liberty and justice and good government in our new possessions. . . . Our institutions will not deteriorate by extension, and our sense of justice will not abate under tropic suns in distant seas."[51] Now read those words again, imagining them spoken in the Boston accent of John F. Kennedy, and you may feel the abiding appeal of Progressive Imperialism.

Historians stress the dynamic crosscurrents in turn-of-the-century American society. Foster Rhea Dulles thought the era "marked by many contradictions."[52] Richard Hofstadter identified "two different moods," one tending toward protest and reform, the other toward national expansion. Frederick Merk wrote of Manifest Destiny contesting with mission, and Ernest May of "cascades of imperialistic and moralistic oratory."[53] But the contradictions are only a product of our wish to cleanse the Progressive movement of its taint of imperialism abroad. For at bottom, the belief that American power, guided by a secular and religious spirit of service, could remake foreign societies came as easily to the Progressives as trust-busting, prohibition of child labor, and regulation of interstate commerce, meatpacking, and drugs. Leading imperialists like Roosevelt, Beveridge, and Willard Straight were all Progressives; leading Progressives like Jacob Riis, Gifford Pinchot, and Robert La Follette all supported the Spanish war and the insular acquisitions.[54] Even academic historians of the time applauded the war and colonies (except, in some cases, the Philippines), and elected A. T. Mahan president of the American Historical Association.[55]

Teddy Roosevelt's "rhetoric of militant decency" was the voice of the spirit of the age. "Our chief usefulness to humanity," he preached, "rests on our combining power with high purpose."[56] But its chief ideologist was Herbert Croly, brilliant founder of the Progressive organ *The New Republic*. Writing in 1909, he defined Progressive foreign policy as the pursuit of a perfected American System of states. He applauded the annexation of Puerto Rico, the protectorate in Cuba, and the Panama Canal, and did not think that they contradicted the U.S. traditions dating back to Washington. Even the Philippines, which he thought an indefensible burden, at least had the virtue of "keeping the American people alive to their interests in the great problems which will be raised in the Far East by the future development of China and Japan."[57] Croly even believed that the Spanish-American War had *launched* the whole Progressive Era because it delivered "a tremendous impulse to the work of reform."[58]

One question remains. Why did Americans give in to the temptation to remake other countries at century's end and not, say, at the time of the Mexican War? The sense of power they felt as a nation is a definite clue. Surely God had not sheltered the United States for more than a century that it might hide its lamp under a bushel. But more than Americans' material circumstances had changed; so, too, had their spirituality. In the beginning, American revolutionaries felt no compunction "to pull the Christian heaven down to earth. . . . They did not need to make a religion out of the revolution because religion was already revolutionary."[59] Over the course of the nineteenth century, however, mainstream American faith lost its savor, deluged as it was by waves of biblical criticism, geology and Darwinism, and the secular millenarianism of the Social Gospel. "As Christianity turned liberal," wrote Arthur Schlesinger, Jr., "shucking off such cardinal doctrines as original sin, one more impediment was removed to belief in national virtue and perfectibility. Experiment gave ground to destiny as the premise of national life."[60] The result in foreign policy was that a newly prideful United States began to measure its holiness by what it did, not just by what it was, and through Progressive Imperialism committed itself, for the first time, "to the pursuit of abstractions such as liberty, democracy, or justice."[61]

The Wilsonian vision of saving the world lurked just around the corner.[62]

SIX

Wilsonianism, or Liberal Internationalism (so called)

IN JUNE 1915, eleven days short of a year after the Sarajevo assassination that sparked World War I, three hundred American dignitaries met in Independence Hall to found a League to Enforce Peace. They elected former president William Howard Taft to lead them, then invited the sitting president, Woodrow Wilson, to address their second convention the following spring. The speech served as a kickoff to Wilson's reelection campaign, and his political crony Edward M. "Colonel" House advised him to make a splash and preempt the Republicans on the peace issue. Wilson needed no encouragement: he relished the bully pulpit as much as Teddy Roosevelt and had trained himself since boyhood to draft and deliver sublime orations. "I am thinking a great deal about the speech I am to make on the twenty-seventh," he told House, "because I realize that it may be one of the most important I shall ever be called upon to make."[1]

Two thousand people cheered Wilson's progress into the grand dining room of Washington's New Willard Hotel on the evening of May 27, 1916. Referring to the European war, he said he was not concerned with its causes and objects, but only to see "peace assume an aspect of permanence" in its wake. To that end, Americans must no longer be guided by Washington's Farewell Address. "We are participants, whether we would or not, in the life of the world. The interests of all nations are our own also. We are partners with the rest." But America was destined to go beyond partnership to leadership in a world where peace

> must henceforth depend upon a new and more wholesome diplomacy. . . . So sincerely do I believe in these things that I am sure that I speak the mind and wish of the people of America when I say that

the United States is willing to become a partner in any feasible association of nations formed in order to realize these objects and make them safe against violation. . . . God grant that the dawn of that day of frank dealing and of settled peace, concord, and cooperation may be near at hand!

The room erupted, Wilson beamed, and the Progressive press likened the speech to the Declaration of Independence and Gettysburg Address. A few curmudgeonly editors thought the president's "winged phrases" obscured the "fantastic" nature of his idea, but most thought he spoke with "the voice of America."[2]

None was more transfixed than George D. Herron, a leader in the Social Gospel movement who preached as fervently as his forebears of the 1840s that the purpose of America was to realize the Kingdom of God. Progressive reforms (to be capped by Prohibition) were purifying Americans to make them worthy of their calling. But now Wilson showed the whole world a better way. His speech, wrote Herron, was "perhaps the most pregnant utterance of a national chief in two thousand years," because he "stands for a universal politic so new, so revolutionary, so creative of a different world than ours, that few have begun to glimpse his vision or appreciate his purpose." Wilson, not overly humble, wrote to Herron's publisher in October 1917, praising his "singular insight . . . into my own motives and purposes."[3]

By then, Wilson had led the United States into the war, which he styled a crusade to make the world safe for democracy. Like other advanced thinkers, he blamed the Great War on Europe's alliance systems, balance of power, armaments, authoritarian governments, economic competition, and exploitative (as opposed to progressive) imperialism. As always, these "American" ideas were imported from Britain, in this case the catechism of the British Union for Democratic Control: "The theory of 'the Balance of Power' and secret diplomacy are two factors which, in combination, make for war. Two other factors intimately associated with these ensure its certainty. They are: a constant progression in expenditure upon armaments, and the toleration of a private armaments interest." According to the Union, there could be no lasting peace until transfers of territory ceased to be made without consent of the populations, and governments spurned alliances in favor of "concerted action between the Powers, and the setting up of an International Council." Wilson also shared Bertrand

Russell's belief that the interests of democracies, as opposed to those of elite ruling classes, could never conflict with those of humanity.[4] A British League of Nations Society was founded in 1915, and the British government's own Phillimore Report would heavily influence the eventual League of Nations Covenant.

Accordingly Wilson's Fourteen Points speech of January 1918 called for a peace based on open diplomacy, freedom of the seas, equal access to raw materials (the Open Door), reduction of armaments, colonial rule only in the interests of subject peoples (Progressive Imperialism), self-determination (for Europeans), and a "general association of nations" to ensure "political independence and territorial integrity to great and small states alike." We know how the rest of the story is usually told. In November 1918 the exhausted Germans agreed to an armistice on the basis of the Fourteen Points, but at the peace conference Wilson was "obliged" to compromise his irenic principles in order to satisfy demands of the victorious Allies and win their acceptance of the League of Nations. As a result, disillusioned Wilsonians attacked the Treaty of Versailles as a sellout, while Republican senators refused to ratify it without reservations to limit U.S. commitments to the League. But the piqued president refused to countenance any amendments, the treaty failed in the Senate, and the world entered what became the interwar years bereft of American leadership.

Almost all discussions of U.S. diplomacy during and after World War I focus on this tragic confrontation between Wilson and the "little group of willful men" in the Senate,[5] and to this day some historians blame American "isolationism" for the horrors of the Second World War. But as we know, the pure isolationist is a mythical beast — even the staunchest opponent of the League of Nations, Senator William Borah (R., Idaho), knew that an ostrich posture in foreign policy was impossible. Nor was Wilson the scorned prophet of a conciliatory peace: his own moralism demanded that Germany be punished for its crimes. Nor was Wilson the sole interpreter of principles such as self-determination, disarmament, and arbitration — even his erstwhile opponents shared many of his values and goals, if not his instrumentalities. And that is why the familiar dichotomies between an old and new diplomacy, isolationism and internationalism, idealism and realism, distort our image of the debate over the League of Nations.

To be sure, the United States did nothing useful to ward off the fascist challenge in the 1930s, which is why historians sympathetic to

Wilson decried the Senate's refusal to commit American power to the cause of global stability. But after Pearl Harbor and especially after the Cold War crushed the hopes placed in the United Nations, realists such as George Kennan, Hans Morgenthau, Robert Osgood, and Henry Kissinger criticized Wilsonians, not for their internationalism but for their naive belief that power politics could be trumped by world opinion or abolished by the stroke of a pen. Then in the 1960s another wave of historians rebutted that Wilson was no starry-eyed fool but "a toughminded politician of the most ruthless type who was entirely capable of executing grand political designs in the most 'realistic' manner" (Trask), whose resourceful policies represented a "higher realism" (Link) or "sublime realism" (May).[6] But the language of these debates obscures the truth of the matter, which was that neither Wilson nor his opponents were naifs or ignoramuses. They observed the trends in contemporary history with keen eyes and knew how industrialization and imperialism had changed the world and America's place in it. Nor did they dispute abstract philosophies on the stump or in the Senate; rather, they asked hard questions about how best to reconcile the needs of global stability with U.S. national interest. As Akira Iriye writes: "It was not so much idealism as internationalism that informed Wilsonian thought, an internationalism solidly grounded on shared interests of nations and on aspirations of men and women everywhere."[7]

Stated simply, the first issue in 1919 was not whether Americans would revert to the relatively passive role they played in Asia and Europe, but rather the terms under which they would engage the twentieth-century world, and whether this or that set of terms complemented or undermined the first five traditions of U.S. foreign policy. The other issue was Thomas Woodrow Wilson himself. Would Americans have come around to his way of thinking if he had never existed, or had lost the 1916 election? Or was he himself largely responsible for the Senate's defeat of the League? Can one conclude that whereas Wilsonianism was a flop (not only in 1919, but after 1945 and again after 1989), the principles of Liberal Internationalism have been a success? We will return to these questions later, but we must start by examining Wilson the man.

*

"The only place in the world where nothing has to be explained to me is the South." An extraordinary admission by a man who would tell the whole world how to arrange its affairs, but that is what Wilson said. A Virginian descended from Presbyterian ministers on both sides of his family, he took the religion of his household for granted in the cerebral and sometimes smug way of the Calvinist elect. So certain was he of his spiritual correctness that a Catholic friend called him a "Presbyterian priest."[8] And so deaf was Wilson to the aesthetics of other Christian liturgies that he pronounced the Episcopalian service "very stupid indeed . . . a ridiculous way of worshiping God, and one which must give very little pleasure to God." And yet this man who could parse a biblical text or dissect social ills with Presbyterian exactitude might also, of an evening, summon his family or friends to a naughty séance at the ouija board. He dabbled in numerology, too, his own lucky number being thirteen.[9]

Wilson believed in predestination, not only in the hereafter but in time. He knew that God had chosen him to do great things, a faith that survived his indifferent schoolwork and utter failure while a student of law. As a Princeton undergraduate, "Tommy" Wilson drafted classmates into games and clubs so that he could play the leader and indulge his love of things British. In war games he fancied himself a British squadron commander, in political clubs a British minister swaying Parliament with his rhetoric. He kept a portrait of the crusading Christian prime minister William Ewart Gladstone on his desk, and he attributed the death of American oratory to the congressional system in which decisions were made through committee rather than debate on the floor.

Wilson's political principles were slower to develop, but in time he adopted the tenets of Gladstonian liberalism. He believed that natural law decreed a self-regulating world of free individuals, hence his devotion to free trade and hostility to big corporations, labor unions, and bureaucracy. He shared his generation's condescension toward "lesser races" like the Negroes, believing it the responsibility of Anglo-Saxons to lift them up: "When properly directed, there is no people not fitted for self-government."[10] It went without saying that a Christian of talent and means ought to serve his fellow man, for (as his first wife put it) "a man who lives only for himself has not begun to live."[11] But however great his professed concern for the human race, Wilson seemed to have little compassion for human beings in the flesh. As Prime Minister David Lloyd George later sneered, he "believed in mankind . . . but distrusted all men."[12]

After quitting the law, Wilson stormed the academy. His book *Congressional Government* of 1885 was soon so highly regarded that Johns Hopkins University conferred a doctorate in political science upon him "by special dispensation." The radical journal *Nation* considered it "one of the most important books, dealing with political subjects, which has ever issued from the American press."[13] In it, Wilson chastised the authors of the U.S. Constitution for setting up a government hamstrung by the separation of powers, and singled out for scorn the Senate's power over treaties and appointments. As a result, he wrote, the president's only means of "compelling compliance on the part of the Senate lies in his initiative in negotiation, which affords him a chance to get the country into such scrapes, so pledged in the view of the world to certain courses of action, that the Senate hesitates to bring about the appearance of dishonor which would follow its refusal to ratify the rash promises." Wilson thought that the checks and balances in American government had "proven mischievous just to the extent to which they have succeeded in establishing themselves as realities."[14] All in all, he considered the Constitution a formula for what we call gridlock and favored centralized government based on an almost plebiscitary rapport between the president and the masses. Over and over again he would play out these theories in life.

Not surprisingly, Wilson embraced Progressive Imperialism. It suited his belief in the white man's calling and his notion of presidential government. So he cheered annexation of the Philippines and Puerto Rico — "They are children and we are men in these deep matters of government and justice"[15] — and the fact that foreign policy again dominated U.S. politics. Now there would be "greatly increased power and opportunity for constructive statesmanship given the President." A strong executive, he wrote, "must utter every initial judgment, take every first step of action, supply the information upon which [the country] is to act, suggest and in large measure control its conduct."[16]

In time, Wilson was named president of Princeton University — or "prime minister," as he liked to say — where he acquired a Cromwellian reputation for being a bold reformer and thorough authoritarian. Looking to Oxford and Cambridge for models, he placed junior faculty and graduate students (preceptors) in charge of the undergraduates, and tried to break up Princeton's exclusive fraternal clubs in favor of residential quadrangles. His purpose was "to attract more high school students of slender means to Princeton and to make the sons of the wealthy as unlike their fathers as possible."[17] The expensive and radical project angered alumni and faculty, but Wilson refused to budge: "As long as I am president of Princeton, I propose to dictate the architectural policy of the university."[18]

If any trait bubbles up in all one reads about Wilson, it is this: he loved, craved, and in a sense glorified power. That may seem anomalous in a pious Progressive and contemporary of Lord Acton, who warned, "Power tends to corrupt; absolute power corrupts absolutely." But Acton was a Catholic who believed in original sin; he was making a statement about the nature of man, not about the abstraction called power. Wilson, by contrast, leaned on "God's all-powerful arm," and defined power as the "capacity to make effective decisions" so as to nudge people and institutions along their appointed road toward perfection. In *Congressional Government* Wilson confessed, "I cannot imagine power as a thing negative and not positive."[19] And in a 1911 address, "The Bible and Progress," he said, "Let no man suppose that progress can be divorced from religion . . . the man whose faith is rooted in the Bible knows that reform cannot be stayed."[20]

In fact, the Old and New Testaments provide not a whit of evidence to support the assertion that "reform cannot be stayed." The story of Israel is one of repeated rebellion against the Law in defiance of righteous judges, prophets, and penitent kings, while the Christian Scriptures describe all earthly kingdoms as the devil's domain and history as a spiral toward the apocalypse. But however heterodox, the doctrine of ineluctable progress, applied to the whole human race with the United States in the vanguard, was conventional wisdom in mainstream Protestantism and peaked in the Social Gospel of Wilson's time.[21] Americans were "custodians of the spirit of righteousness, of the spirit of equal-handed justice, of the spirit of hope which believes in the perfectibility of the law with the perfectibility of human life itself."[22] The implications were that power in the hands of righteous custodians had to be good, and that all who challenged that power were unwitting tools of Satan. To the extent Wilson believed that — and his behavior and writings suggest that he did — the man could not compromise without pushing aside God's all-powerful arm and stepping on a slippery slope toward impotence. To Bismarck, who defined politics as the art of the possible, Wilson would have replied, "With God all things are possible."

In the end, his lone-crusader stance lost him the quad fight at Princeton but attracted the attention of New Jersey Democrats, who massaged Wilson's image into that of an incorruptible paladin of the common man. He was elected governor, then nominated for president in the year when Teddy Roosevelt's insurgency tore the Republican Party asunder. The campaign of 1912 thus became a three-way fight for the soul of industrial America. Taft represented stand-pat Republicanism in league with big business. Roosevelt praised corporations for their efficiency, but called for big government agencies to referee conflicts between capital and labor. Wilson blamed the ills of industrialism on simple greed, and promised a New Freedom based on competition and opportunity for all. "In other words, ours is a program of liberty, and theirs a program of regulation. . . . I don't believe there is any other man that is big enough to play Providence."[23] What the country needed was "some great orator who could go and make men drunk with the spirit of self-sacrifice."[24] Thanks to the Republican split, that is what the country got.

*

Everyone quotes Wilson's utterance that "it would be an irony of fate if my administration had to deal chiefly with foreign affairs."[25] As it happened, he succeeded in introducing most of his domestic agenda, and won his fights for tariff reduction, the Federal Reserve Act, and the income tax. The real irony in his remark was that he had more latitude to exercise power and assert moral principles in foreign than in domestic policy — a fact that Wilson the political scientist had shrewdly observed. What is more, he did not shun foreign policy but jumped into it within days of his inauguration. His "missionary diplomacy" in Asia ("we ought to help China in some better way")[26] reversed Taft's Dollar Diplomacy, and his March 1913 "Declaration of Policy in Regard to Latin America" hinted at a *more* Progressive Imperialism. America, Wilson announced, was eager to cooperate with her "sister republics" but only "when supported at every turn by the orderly processes of just government based on law." In the absence of order, he warned, the United States would exert "influence of every kind" to restore it — and did, when Wilson imposed military protectorates on Haiti and Nicaragua.

Wilson's most vexing and threatening sister was Mexico. For more than thirty years American investors had profited from the peace imposed by the dictator Porfirio Díaz, to the point where they owned some 40 percent of the country's assets. Then, in 1911, Francisco Madero led a revolution that ousted Díaz, only to be killed himself in 1913 by the bloodthirsty General Victoriano Huerta. Wilson had no sympathy for the endangered U.S. business interests and refused to treat with a "government of butchers": "Usurpations like that of General Huerta menace the peace and development of America as nothing else could. . . . It is the purpose of the United States, therefore, to discredit and defeat such usurpations whenever they occur."[27] Thus did Wilson reaffirm the Roosevelt Corollary, but strip from it any intimation that U.S. strategic or economic self-interest was involved. On the contrary, Wilson renounced all territorial ambition and, in a speech at Mobile in October 1913, called it "a very perilous thing to determine the foreign policy of a nation in terms of material interest. It not only is unfair to those with whom you are dealing, but it is degrading as regards your own actions."[28]

Let us pause for a moment to let that sink in. According to Wilson, it was dangerous, unfair, and disgraceful to pursue a foreign policy based on material self-interest. Now, we may applaud the fact that he refused to commit the nation to conflict just to pull some bankers' bonds out of the fire. But what would John Quincy Adams have said of a policy that not only renounced but denounced the government's obligation to protect American property and suggested instead that a policy was just and prudent only if it served platonic abstractions like justice? American Exceptionalism had not meant any such thing. But that is what Wilson said that it meant, and the fact that he said it made it so. Remember the speech at the top of this chapter? "So sincerely do I believe in these things that I am sure that I speak the mind and wish of the people of America. . . ." The depth of Wilson's own belief was for him evidence enough that he spoke for the nation.

The British gave Wilson a blank check to do what he liked in Mexico, but otherwise were dumbfounded. Ambassador Sir Cecil Spring Rice wrote that Wilson talked to newspapermen or members of Congress "at length in excellent language, but when they leave him they say to each other, 'What on earth did he say?'" As to Wilson's philosophy, Spring Rice could only report that "he consults no one and no one knows what he is going to do next. He believes that God had sent him here to do something and that God knows what. This may be pleasing to God but not to Congressmen or ambassadors. I am sorry I cannot penetrate this mystery."²⁹ In 1914 British emissary Sir Edward Tyrrell told Wilson, "I shall be asked to explain your Mexican policy — can you tell me what it is?" Wilson replied, "I am going to teach the South American republics to elect good men."³⁰

A mystery indeed, because promising to make the Mexican revolution somehow turn out "right" only made Wilson a prisoner of events. When intelligence arrived in April 1914 that a German merchant ship was en route to Mexico with machine guns for Huerta, Wilson requested congressional assent to use force. And just as he had written decades before, once the president made "rash" promises and got the country into a "scrape," Congress could not repudiate him without dishonoring the nation. So eight hundred marines and sailors stormed Veracruz, resulting in nineteen American and hundreds of Mexican deaths. Wilson lectured midshipmen at the Naval Academy that "the idea of America is to serve humanity,"³¹ but really the Veracruz bloodshed served no purpose at all. So instead Wilson accepted an offer by Argentina, Brazil, and Chile to mediate in Mexico. When those talks failed, he placed his hopes in Venustiano Carranza, a provincial insurgent who drove Huerta into exile in August 1914. But Carranza, too, proved to be anti-American, and he, too, faced an internal rival, Pancho Villa, who enjoyed killing *yanquis* on both sides of the border. His New Mexico raid of March 1916 forced Wilson to dispatch General John J. Pershing on a futile chase into Mexico. The fiasco finally ended in 1917 when Wilson, now embarked on a grander crusade, recognized Carranza's regime.

But Wilson and William Jennings Bryan, the evangelical populist he named secretary of state, made a second departure in Latin American diplomacy that became more famous in a different context: a league of nations. The initiative came from Andrew Carnegie, who wrote the White House in September 1914: "There is no service American Republics can render the civilized world equal to setting them such an example as proposed. Twenty-one Republics welded into a peace of brotherhood would be such an example to the rest of the world as could not fail to impress."³² So Wilson ordered the drafting of a Pan-American Treaty based on a "mutual guarantee of territorial integrity and of political independence," arbitration to settle disputes, and renunciation of all military expeditions "hostile to the established government of any of the high contracting parties."³³ The treaty was never signed, because of the Mexican mess and intramural Latin quarrels. But the fact that Wilson could not persuade the sister republics in America's own neighborhood to form such a sorority did not discourage him from attempting to impose one on all the Great Powers of the world.

*

American diplomacy during World War I is usually described in terms of Wilson's struggle to uphold neutral rights at sea, as if it were a reprise of the situation during the Napoleonic Wars. There were parallels, for again Britain and her continental rival — France then, now Germany — blockaded each other and interfered with neutral commerce in systematic and arrogant ways. U.S. trade with German-occupied Europe shrank almost to nothing within eighteen months of the outbreak of war. By contrast, the German submarine blockade did not prevent U.S. exports to Britain and France from almost quadrupling by 1916 to $2.75 billion. But submarines necessarily took lives as well as property, and were for that reason more heinous than the Royal Navy's surface blockade. What is more, most U.S. diplomatic activity from 1914 to 1917 did concern neutral rights at sea, and the timing of Wilson's ultimate decision to fight derived in part from the German decision to sink without warning all ships of any nationality bound for Britain ("unrestricted submarine warfare").

Notwithstanding all that, the damage done to U.S. commerce seems to have interested Wilson little. Nor did he cling to neutrality because it was American tradition, or because he was a pacifist (he was not), or because the American people were almost unanimously in favor of staying out of the war. He did it because he believed that remaining above the battle was the only way that he, Wilson, could exert the moral authority needed to end the war on terms that would make for a lasting peace. Within a few weeks of the outbreak of war on August 1, 1914, Wilson told his brother-in-law that the principles guiding the future must be: no more territorial gains achieved by conquest; equality of rights for small nations; government control of arms manufacture; and an "association of nations wherein all shall guarantee the territorial integrity of each."[34] Compared with this lofty quest, the material losses of American shippers were small beer indeed.

That helps to explain why Wilson's responses to violations of neutral rights were seemingly incoherent. Even as he called on Americans to be neutral in thought as well as deed (a saintly prescription), he willingly let U.S. firms and banks supply the Allies with weapons and credits that totaled $2.3 billion during the period of U.S. neutrality. The German government protested bitterly, and German American George S. Viereck excoriated Wilson for his "prattle about humanity" while German widows and orphans mourn over graves marked "Made in America."[35] And yet, when a U-boat sank the British liner *Lusitania* in May 1915, taking 128 American lives, Wilson confined himself to sending stern but innocuous notes to Berlin. "There is such a thing," he instructed the nation, "as a man being too proud to fight. There is such a thing as a nation being so right that it does not need to convince others by force that it is right."[36] Theodore Roosevelt, who wanted war, damned the president for a "Byzantine logothete" supported by "flubdubs," "mollycoddles," and "flapdoodle pacifists."[37] Secretary of State Bryan, who wanted genuine neutrality, urged Wilson to send identical protests to Britain, and resigned when Wilson refused.

Democrats in Congress took the most reasonable approach to the problem. If Wilson was unwilling to enforce neutral rights, then let him at least prohibit Americans from sailing on ships in the war zone. No, said the president, that would unravel the "whole fine fabric of international law,"[38] and he leaned heavily on Congress to defeat the resolutions. Meanwhile, the State Department continued to palaver until, after the British ship *Arabic* was torpedoed with two Americans aboard, it pried a promise out of Berlin to suspend unrestricted submarine warfare. This "*Arabic* pledge" (and subsequent "*Sussex* pledge") satisfied Congress and reassured the electorate.

To Wilson that was all politics. He made his real feelings known in February 1916, in a speech that dismissed the importance of neutral rights: "America ought to keep out of this war. She ought to keep out of this war at the sacrifice of everything except this single thing upon which her character and history are founded, her sense of humanity and justice. If she sacrifices that, she has ceased to be America; she has ceased to entertain and to love the traditions which have made us proud to be Americans." Then, in an echo of the apostle Paul's litany on love, Wilson defined true valor: "I would be just as much ashamed to be rash as I would to be a coward. Valor is self-respecting. Valor is circumspect. Valor strikes only when it is right to strike. Valor withholds itself from all small implications and entanglements and waits for the great opportunity when the sword will flash as if it carried the light of heaven upon its blade."[39]

The sword did not flash so long as Wilson had reason to hope that he could end the war and convert the world to a "new and more wholesome diplomacy" through mediation. In March 1915 and again in January 1916 he sent Colonel House to Europe to broker a truce. But the desperate and bloodied belligerents would not reveal the terms under which they would agree to talk. So on his own authority House drafted a memorandum with Sir Edward Grey stating that when the Allies thought the time was ripe, the United States would call for a peace conference and — if the Germans proved "unreasonable" — the United States would leave the conference "as a belligerent on the side of the Allies." Wilson added the word "probably" to the last phrase, but otherwise suspended peace overtures pending his reelection on the slogan "He kept us out of war."

Historians differ on the role played by foreign policy in the 1916 campaign. As we know, Wilson's speech to the League to Enforce Peace was a preemptive move designed to steal the peace issue from moderate Republicans like Elihu Root and the eventual nominee, Charles Evans Hughes, and to portray Roosevelt Republicans as warmongers. But only five of the thirty-two Democratic campaign releases involved foreign policy, and the hottest debates concerned domestic issues.[40] Still, the stakes in foreign policy could not have been higher: one need only imagine what course history might have taken if the sober and sensible Hughes had won two thousand more votes in one state — California — and so been the one to preside over peacemaking after the war (assuming he went to war at all).

Buoyed by his victory, Wilson launched a final peace offensive. He had reason for optimism, since the German chancellor had quietly but urgently asked for a new U.S. initiative. (In truth, the German high command had given him a deadline to achieve a favorable peace or else it would resume unrestricted submarine warfare.) But the belligerents dared not trim their war aims sufficiently to interest their opponents, so Wilson aimed his Peace Without Victory speech of January 22, 1917, not at the governments but at "the peoples of the countries now at war."[41] Any peace forced on the losers, he said, would be built on sand. Hence both alliances must renounce their ambitions and "with one accord adopt the doctrine of President Monroe as the doctrine of the whole world."[42]

What sounded like reason and mercy to Wilson, however, was madness and cant in European ears. London and Paris took Wilson to mean that the United States had no intention of fighting Germany no matter what outrages the latter committed. Or, at best, the Americans might join the war but in opposition to Allied war aims as well as to Germany's. Bonar Law spoke for the British cabinet when he sighed, "What Mr. Wilson is longing for we are fighting for," and historian Sir George Trevelyan called Wilson "the quintessence of a prig. What a notion that the nations of Europe, after this terrible effort, will join him in putting down international encroachments by arms, at some future time, if he is afraid to denounce such encroachments even in words now!"[43] Georges Clemenceau, soon to become French premier, said of Wilson's speech: "Never before has any political assembly heard so fine a sermon on what human beings might be capable of accomplishing if only they weren't human."[44] But the bitterest critique of Peace Without Victory was Theodore Roosevelt's. Wilson's suggestion of a moral equivalence between the two sides was "wickedly false," talk of peacekeeping after the war "premature," and the reference to the Monroe Doctrine a contradiction in terms. "If his words mean anything, they would mean that hereafter we intended to embark on a policy of violent meddling in every European quarrel, and in return to invite Old World nations violently to meddle in everything American. Of course, as a matter of fact, the words mean nothing whatever."[45]

Now, Wilson can hardly be blamed for trying to stop the Old World from committing suicide while sparing Americans the horror of the trenches. But the truth is he failed on both counts. His tortured and shifting moral stance on neutral rights, absent the use of force or threat, slowly painted him into a corner. When Germany resumed unrestricted submarine warfare on February 1, 1917, Wilson had little choice but to abandon neutral rights and peace as well. After all, if he really did consider incidents at sea to be "small entanglements," why did he not take his own party's advice and prohibit Americans from the war zone? If, on the other hand, he considered "the whole fabric of international law" to be at stake, why did he not dispatch the U.S. Navy to command *respect* for neutral rights? If he had done the latter, some historians think, he might also have succeeded in bringing the war to an early end.[46]

Even after the United States broke off diplomatic relations with Germany, Wilson prayed in his private Gethsemane (Arthur Link's apt phrase) that he would not have to drink this bitter cup. But in March 1917 the British intercepted the infamous Zimmermann telegram, in which Germany offered Mexico a military alliance, and U-boats sank three U.S. merchant ships. Wilson agonized, then found the formula he needed to justify war. First, he was not really making this choice, because "war was thrust upon us." Second, the United States could go to war with a clear conscience because it was fighting, as in Mexico, not for material interests but "to vindicate the principles of peace and justice in the life of the world."[47] Above all, since Wilson was now convinced that he could not bring about a just peace by mediation, he had no choice but to do so by fighting. "I believe that God planted in us the vision of liberty. . . . I cannot be deprived of the hope that we are chosen, and prominently chosen, to show the way to the nations of the world how they shall walk in the paths of liberty."[48]

The American people were not crying for war; there was little "Remember the *Maine*!" jingoism in 1917. So Wilson would have to persuade them to join a crusade to end war in Europe as they had done in Cuba in '98; to make the world safe for democracy as they had tried to make Haiti safe for it; to teach Germans to elect good men as he had tried to teach the Mexicans. That is why Wilson thought it "a distressing and oppressive duty" when he went before Congress on April 2:

> It is a fearful thing to lead this great peaceful people into war, into the most terrible and disastrous of all wars, civilization itself seeming to be in the balance. But the right is more precious than peace, and we shall fight for the things which we have always carried nearest our hearts — for democracy, for the right of those who submit to authority to have a voice in their own Governments, for the rights and liberties of small nations, for a universal dominion of right by such a concert of free peoples as shall bring peace and safety to all nations and make the world itself at last free. To such a task we can dedicate our lives and our fortunes, everything that we are and everything that we have, with the pride of those who know that the day has come when America is privileged to spend her blood and her might for the principles that gave her birth and happiness and the peace which she has treasured. God helping her, she can do no other.[49]

Wilson was a masterly speaker, and his sentiments, in the words of Senator Robert La Follette (R., Wis.), were "peculiarly calculated to appeal to American hearts." But La Follette, Borah, and four other senators were appalled, not just by the prospect of war, but because the president promoted it for all the wrong reasons. "I join no crusade," announced Borah. "I seek or accept no alliance; I obligate this government to no other power. I make war alone for my countrymen and their rights, for my country and its honor." Supported by Henry Cabot Lodge (R., Mass.), Roosevelt, and other opinion leaders, Borah introduced a resolution asking the Senate to reaffirm the "time-honored principles" of Washington, Jefferson, and Monroe.[50] The resolution died, but in a sense it marked the beginning of the historic debate over the League of Nations.

★

Historians have rarely asked *whether* the United States should have gone to war in 1917, but rather what Wilson's motives were for doing so. In the 1930s critics charged that U.S. policy had become a hostage of munitions makers and Wall Street bankers, and that Wilson's unneutral acts had given the United States a stake in an Allied victory. The former contention was unfounded: as we know, Wilson rejected materialist policies and was contemptuous of big business. The latter contention seems to have been obvious, since the United States had solid security reasons for preferring an Allied victory. As U.S. diplomat Lewis Einstein had written in 1913, "The European balance of power is a political necessity which can alone sanction in the Western Hemisphere the continuance of an economic development unhandicapped by the burden of extensive armaments." Any European war would damage American interests, thought Einstein, but a German victory would be a calamity. He boldly suggested that the United States "extend the Monroe Doctrine to England" and deter Germany from launching a war.[51] But few Americans were aware of their dependence on a balance of power and Anglo-American command of the seas, and however much Wilson might have appreciated that truth, he anathematized balance-of-power politics. Instead of telling the American people that they had to fight to defend the Atlantic Ocean from Germany, Wilson "managed to convert a successful national effort into a lost crusade."[52]

And as always, Wilson stood alone. He was careful to describe the United States as an "associated" not an "allied" power, by which he meant that he did not recognize the Allies' war aims as codified in their secret treaties. So even as the United States lent military assistance to the Allies, it was implicitly a political rival of them. As of November 1917, it was also a rival of the de facto government of Russia. That was when Lenin and the Bolsheviks seized power in Petrograd and Moscow and called on the workers and soldiers of all nations to stop fighting and overthrow their imperialist governments.

Echoing Wilson, Lenin called for a peace of "No Annexations, No Indemnities!" Echoing Lenin, Wilson announced his own war aims in the Fourteen Points speech of January 1918, to which he later added twenty-four principles, ends, particulars, and declarations. So it was that four, not two, contestants fought to control the world's future in 1918: the German militarists, the democratic but imperialist Allies, Wilson with his program of Liberal Internationalism, and Communists preaching social revolution.

The British and French paid lip service to the Fourteen Points, so eager were they to encourage a vigorous American war effort. But the main impact of the ideals espoused by Wilson was as a weapon of war, not as a blueprint for peace. Airplanes and balloons dropped more than 100,000 leaflets behind the German lines promising a moderate Wilsonian peace in an attempt to break the kaiser's hold over his people. It achieved nothing at first, for German morale soared in March when the Bolsheviks signed the Treaty of Brest-Litovsk, pulling Russia out of the war. That was a tremendous blow to the Allies and Wilson. All hope of bringing Germany to accept a just peace seemed dashed, while the Bolsheviks revealed themselves as traitors. It was then that Wilson surrendered fully to his righteous anger and evinced the same martial ardor he deplored in others: "Force, Force to the utmost, Force without stint or limit, the righteous and triumphant Force which shall make Right the law of the world, and cast every selfish dominion down in the dust."[53]

His sermons scorned, Wilson took up the sword with Elijah's zeal to cast out the priests of Baal. In a Fourth of July speech at Mount Vernon he proclaimed: "The Past and the Present are in deadly grapple and the peoples of the world are being done to death between them." There could be no compromise on the ends the United States was fighting for, including the "destruction of *every* arbitrary power anywhere . . . that can disturb the peace of the world"; "settlement of *every* question . . . upon the basis of the free acceptance of that settlement by the people immediately concerned"; "consent of *all* nations to be governed in their conduct towards each other by the same principles of honor and of respect for the common law of civilized society"; and "an organization of peace which shall make it *certain* that the combined power of free nations will check *every* invasion of right and serve to make peace and justice the more secure."[54]

After the German military reversals in the fall of 1918, the propaganda value of the Fourteen Points finally made itself manifest. Strikes spread among German workers and sailors, the kaiser liberalized his government, and its new civilian leaders communicated to the United States (not the Allies) their desire for an armistice based on the Fourteen Points. But Wilson needed French and British approval, and he learned at once that it would be harder to get them to accept his plan for peace than it would be to persuade the Germans. In the end the Allies accepted the armistice of November 11, but only after appending reservations to the Fourteen Points. What was worse, the American Senate and people had already shown that they, too, would be hard to win over.

Even before the war ended, Republicans began to rebel against Wilson's lone-wolf diplomacy. Roosevelt said he would support Taft's League to Enforce Peace "as an *addition to,* but not as *substitute for* our preparing our own strength for our own defense." He urged like-minded senators to alert the public against the "sorry crew" of "professional internationalists."[55] Wilson's ill-judged riposte was to make a partisan appeal to voters before the November 1918 election:

> The leaders of the minority in the present Congress have unquestionably been pro-war, but they have been anti-administration. At almost every turn since we entered the war they have sought to take the choice of policy and the conduct of the war out of my hands and put it under the control of instrumentalities of their own choosing. . . . I need not tell you, my fellow-countrymen, that I am asking your support not for my own sake or for the sake of a political party, but for the sake of the nation itself in order that its inward unity of purpose may be evident to all the world.[56]

American voters predictably recoiled from Wilson's implicit attack on the patriotism of the opposition and his assertion that peacemaking was a partisan issue. Republicans won control of both houses of Congress. Wilson's advisers accordingly urged him to send a bipartisan American team to the peace conference in Paris. Wilson refused.[57] He was also advised not to attend the conference in person, since the hurly-burly and horsetrading were bound to hurt his prestige. But Wilson believed only he could prevail over the reactionary Allied leaders, who were "too weatherwise to see the weather." With vengeance dominating Western counsels and Bolshevism haunting the

East, Wilson felt militant liberalism "the only thing that can save civilization from chaos. . . . Liberalism must be more liberal than ever before, it must even be radical, if civilization is to escape the typhoon."[58]

His advisers were right: Wilson's leverage was sharply circumscribed at the Paris Peace Conference, and not only because he was just one of five in the supreme council of the victors. Lloyd George was coming off a smashing electoral victory and Clemenceau a rousing vote of confidence, while Wilson's party had just lost at the polls. The very fact that Germany had quit erased U.S. military leverage over the Allies, and Wilson overestimated the financial clout derived from the billions of dollars in Anglo-French war debts held by American investors. He also counted on British sympathy for his new world order, whereas the conference became the scene of a muted but dogged struggle between Britain and the United States over which would emerge from the war with the largest navy and merchant marine.[59] Britain, France, Italy, and Japan also had an interest in honoring one another's war aims so despised by Wilson. Finally, Wilson was so devoted to collective security that he compromised time and again to win the powers' acceptance of the League of Nations Covenant. Once the League was up and running, he thought, it could correct whatever flaws existed in the treaties of peace. In effect, Wilson put all his eggs in one basket.

Perhaps the greatest irony of the fight over the Treaty of Versailles, which contained the League Covenant, was that most Americans and members of the Senate were not especially hostile to its terms. Few Americans objected to the harsh conditions (disarmament, demilitarization and occupation of the Rhineland, loss of territories, seizure of Germany's fleet and overseas colonies) and open-ended reparations foisted on Germany (which Wilson himself called for in the Fourteen Points). Nor did most Americans care a fig for the fate of Fiume, which exercised the Italians, or the Chinese port of Kiao-Chow, which Japan had seized and would not give up. The Senate may even have been willing to ratify the guarantee against future German aggression that Wilson and Lloyd George promised to France even though it was an entangling alliance. The harshest critics of the peace terms, in fact, were disheartened Democrats.[60]

What did disturb senators was that the League of Nations Covenant — especially the collective security obligation in Article Ten — seemed incompatible with the existing traditions of U.S. policy. They were not "isolationists" but nationalists and prudent internationalists who suggested that Wilson's League (a) would not work without force, in which case it was a league to make war, not peace; (b) was futile, since, like the Holy Alliance, it implied an attempt to freeze the global status quo; (c) was imprudent, since it would involve the United States in conflicts where its interests were not at stake; (d) violated the powers of Congress over war, immigration, and tariffs; or (e) contradicted the true meaning of Exceptionalism, Unilateralism, and the American System.

Republican Herbert Hoover, for instance, did not like Article Ten because he thought the League's purpose should be "the pacific settlement of controversies among free nations," but he was willing to accept it with reservations.[61] Roosevelt, too, wanted "to join the other civilized nations of the world in some scheme that in a time of great stress would offer a likelihood of obtaining settlements that will avert war." He insisted only that the League not be made a substitute for military preparedness and the national interest.[62] Republicans Root and Hughes feared that Article Ten might prove to be "a trouble-breeder, and not a peace-maker." But they still viewed the League as a way to continue wartime cooperation, keep Germany down, and settle disputes so long as it complemented traditional deterrents.[63] All were willing to follow Wilson's lead. They just wanted their doubts addressed before they were asked to endorse a new diplomatic tradition.

Wilson was well aware that the Senate Foreign Relations Committee, led by his implacable enemy Lodge, intended to assert itself. So the president asked Lodge to refrain from speaking out until the Covenant was drafted. Lodge agreed, only to have Wilson double-cross him by docking in his native Boston in February and making a rousing speech on behalf of the League.[64] The senator took his revenge a week later, when a delegation from Capitol Hill tormented Wilson with queries on how this League would work in practice. Frank Brandegee (R., Conn.) came away feeling "as if I had been wandering with Alice in Wonderland and had tea with the Mad Hatter."[65] Some thirty-nine senators then signed a "round robin" note declaring it "the sense of the Senate that while it is their sincere desire that the nations of the world should unite to promote peace and general disarmament, the constitution of the league of nations in the form now proposed to the peace conference should not be accepted by the United States."[66]

Upon his return to Paris, Wilson did obtain amendments to the

Covenant including a right of withdrawal, removal of immigration and tariffs from the League's purview, and recognition of the Monroe Doctrine. So he came home confident that the revised Covenant he deposed on the Senate on July 10, 1919, would win swift ratification. "The stage is set, the destiny disclosed. It has come about by no plan of our conceiving, but by the hand of God, who led us into the way." Reporters asked if he would entertain reservations to the treaty. "I shall consent to nothing," said Wilson. "The Senate must take its medicine." [67]

★

The Republican leadership refused the spoon. Lodge bought time by reading the entire Treaty of Versailles on the floor of the Senate, then called sixty witnesses to testify before the Foreign Relations Committee. On August 19 Wilson tried to move the treaty out of committee by inviting senators to the White House. But Warren G. Harding (R., Ohio) drew blood when he asked whether Article Ten really obligated the United States to resist all aggression, in which case a truly American foreign policy would cease to exist, or whether it didn't, in which case the League was a sham. "When I speak of a legal obligation," Wilson scrambled, "I mean one that specifically binds you to do a particular thing under certain sanctions. . . . Now a moral obligation is of course superior to a legal obligation, and, if I may say so, has a greater binding force; only there always remains in the moral obligation the right to exercise one's judgment as to whether it is indeed incumbent upon one in those circumstances to do that thing."[68] Senators understandably wanted more precise clarification than this. Wilson refused to countenance the least amendment and tried, for the second time, to go to the people over the heads of the Senate. Though barely recovered from his exertions at Paris, he barnstormed the West for three weeks in September until he collapsed and suffered a crippling stroke.

During his absence his cause lost ground. William Bullitt, disillusioned and bitter over Wilson's hostility to Lenin, leaked secrets about "what really happened" at Paris and read to the Senate a memorandum in which Secretary of State Robert Lansing himself described parts of the treaty as "thoroughly bad" and the League of Nations as "entirely useless."[69] Even friends of Wilson did inadvertent damage. When Senator James A. Reed (D., Mo.) asked whether the American people would really honor League decisions made in part by "delegations from colored nations," Gilbert M. Hitchcock (D., Neb.) assured him that his fear was unfounded, since "the league has very little to do." If that is so, Reed replied, then how would this "innocuous thing" be able "to save the world"?[70]

The Senate divided into four factions. Sixteen irreconcilables, led by Hiram Johnson (R., Calif.) and Borah, were opposed to the League in any form. As Borah said, "The proposition is force to destroy force, conflict to prevent conflict, militarism to destroy militarism, war to prevent war." It also meant the extinction of American nationality: "It is difficult to tell just how long the real Americans will sit still and permit the infamous propaganda to go on. I have just as much respect for the Bolshevist who would internationalize our whole system from below as I would for the broadcloth gentlemen who would internationalize it from above."[71] The second and third factions were "hard" and "soft" reservationists, numbering twenty and twelve respectively. They were not "isolationists." As Root argued, "If it is necessary for the security of western Europe that we should agree to the support of France if attacked, then let us agree to do that particular thing plainly. . . . But let us not wrap up such a purpose in a vague universal obligation." [72] All told, some fifty reservations and amendments were introduced, but Root and Lodge narrowed them down to fourteen and released them on November 19. They stated:

1. that the U.S. be the sole judge of whether it had fulfilled its obligations to the League, and retain the right to withdraw from it;
2. that the U.S. assume no obligation to go to war under Article Ten or deploy military forces without the approval of Congress;
3. that the U.S. accept no overseas mandates (colonial trusts) without congressional approval;
4. that the U.S. be the judge of what were its own internal affairs;
5. that the U.S. tolerate no interference contrary to the Monroe Doctrine;
6. that the U.S. not endorse Japanese retention of Kiao-Chow;
7. that Congress approve all U.S. officials appointed to the League;
8. that Congress retain control of laws regulating U.S.-German commerce;
9. that Congress control all appropriations of funds for the League;
10. that no League initiative preclude U.S. military preparedness;

11. that no League sanctions override U.S. economic sovereignty;
12. that the Treaty of Versailles not restrict any individual rights of U.S. citizens;
13. that Congress regulate U.S. involvement with German reparations;
14. that the U.S. not be bound by any decision in which Britain and her dominions were permitted to cast six votes against America's one.

Clearly these reservations were designed not to gut the peace that Wilson had fashioned, but to ensure that his new order did not gut the sovereignty and Constitution of the United States and the Monroe Doctrine. Had Wilson been willing to swallow them, or an even milder package promoted by some Senate Democrats, the Treaty of Versailles would have been ratified. But he was convinced that the reservations would castrate the League, and in any case he hated Lodge. "Never, never! I'll never consent to adopt any policy with which that impossible man is so prominently identified."[73] So he drafted a letter urging loyal Democrats, the fourth Senate faction, to oppose all reservations, with the perverse result that most Republicans voted *for* the League (with reservations) and almost all Democrats *against* it. The treaty with reservations failed 39 to 55, and the treaty without reservations 38 to 53.

Almost everyone wanted a compromise, but Wilson's wife permitted few visitors and no bad news to reach the invalid president. As Wilson faded deeper into debility, he conjured plans for a third partisan appeal to the public. He wrote a letter, to be read to the Democrats' Jackson Day dinner on January 8, 1920, in which he urged the party to challenge all irreconcilables and reservationists to stand for reelection so that the 1920 campaign might be made a plebiscite on the League. Once again it boomeranged, for Republicans could only react to such apparent demagogy by rallying behind their leadership. Still, about 80 percent of the Senate and a clear majority of the American people were prepared to accept the League in some form. So Lodge brought the treaty to a vote again, in March 1920. Wilson still demanded all or nothing, so twenty-three loyal Democrats joined the twelve irreconcilables to deny the treaty a two-thirds majority. At that moment Taft remarked that "Wilson's greatness is oozing out, as it ought to. He will live in history as a man with great opportunities which were not improved, but which were wrecked by his personal egotism, selfishness, vanity, and mulishness."[74]

During his last days in office, the broken man himself cried out to a visitor: "What more could I have done? I had to negotiate with my back to the wall. Men thought I had all the power. *Would to God I had had such power.*"[75] Lodge told his side of the story in 1925, the year after Wilson's death: "Mr. Wilson in dealing with every great question thought first of himself. He may have thought of the country next, but there was a long interval. . . . Mr. Wilson was devoured by the desire for power."[76]

*

Whether or not Wilsonianism was the message the world needed to hear after World War I, Woodrow Wilson was surely the wrong messenger — not because he was too religious, but because his religion was too personal, sanctimonious, gnostic. Senator Lawrence Y. Sherman (R., Ill.) put his finger on it when he called the League Covenant "a revolutionary document" inspired by the impossible dream of "a sinless world."[77] Yet Wilson never doubted that he would be vindicated: "I would rather fail in a cause that will ultimately triumph than triumph in a cause that will ultimately fail."[78]

Many historians would say that he was vindicated, since Wilson's Liberal Internationalist tenets informed the foreign policies of every administration after him. In 1920 the Republican platform endorsed an "agreement among the nations to preserve the peace of the world [but] without the compromise of national independence." Candidate Harding supported an "association of nations" in principle, while Hoover, Hughes, Root, Henry L. Stimson, and twenty-seven other prominent Republicans endorsed the League Covenant minus Article Ten.[79] Once in office, Harding let the League issue die, but his foreign policy, designed by Secretary of State Hughes, was aggressively liberal and interventionist. At the Washington Naval Conference of 1921–22 Hughes pushed through the most severe armaments reductions in history, cajoled Japan into restoring Kiao-Chow, won all parties to the Open Door in China, broke up the Anglo-Japanese alliance and substituted for it a multilateral security regime in Asia. At the London Conference of 1924 the United States bankrolled the stabilization and recovery of the German economy, creating the environment for Franco-German rapprochement and the collective security pacts signed at Locarno. In 1927 the Coolidge administration cosponsored the Kellogg-Briand Pact under which all nations purported to outlaw war as an instrument of policy. The United States would even have joined the International Court at The Hague if the court had accepted the Senate's predictable reservations.[80]

To be sure, the Republican Congresses of the 1920s violated the liberal vision of an open world in two ways: they spurned free trade in favor of lofty protective tariffs in 1921, and they severely restricted immigration in 1924. What is more, Hughes's liberal new orders in Asia and Europe came crashing down in the Great Depression. But after Pearl Harbor Franklin D. Roosevelt resurrected and expanded upon Wilson's Fourteen Points and succeeded — first in the election of 1944, then in the Senate vote on the United Nations — in making Wilsonianism the sixth and, for the time being, dominant U.S. diplomatic tradition. Of course, his dreams for a new world order also broke up on the shoals of power politics, and Asia and Europe threatened again to spin out of control in the late 1940s.

Then, during the Cold War that followed and especially during its last decade, Americans awoke to the fact that the values Wilson inscribed on their nation's escutcheon held tremendous power after all. Czechs and Poles, Balts and East Germans, Ukrainians and the Russians themselves stood up for freedom, dignity, democracy, openness, peace, and brought down a totalitarian empire. As a blueprint for world order, Wilsonianism has always been a chimera, but as an ideological weapon against "every arbitrary power anywhere," it has proved mighty indeed. And that, in the end, is how Wilson did truly imitate Jesus. He brought not peace but a sword.[81]

SEVEN

Containment

"WE ARE NOW IN THE MIDST of a war, not for conquest, not for vengeance, but for a world in which this nation, and all that this nation represents, will be safe for our children. . . . We are going to win the war and we are going to win the peace that follows." So promised Franklin D. Roosevelt on December 8, 1941. But even more telling were the words of Senator Arthur Vandenberg (R., Mich.), who had assumed Borah's mantle as the spokesman for neutralists: "In my own mind, my convictions regarding international cooperation and collective security for peace took firm hold on the afternoon of the Pearl Harbor attack. That day isolationism ended for any realist."[1] Vandenberg's willingness to brand his own prior views with the polemical term "isolationism" sums up the lurch toward global involvement that defined U.S. policy over the next fifty years (1941 to 1991), one quarter of the nation's life. What persuaded Congress and the public so radically to alter their interpretation of American traditions that a huge military establishment, permanent alliances in Europe and Asia, and all the burdens associated with leadership of the free world now appeared realistic? Perhaps part of the answer is that the globalism they embraced did not negate the first six U.S. foreign policy traditions so much as we teachers habitually tell our classes. The chapter that follows is, among other things, an attempt to make that jarring hypothesis plausible.

Woodrow Wilson declared in his second inaugural address, "We are provincials no longer."[2] His own project for perpetual peace, however, was keenly provincial, since it presumed to transcend all the clashes of interests and values and the different historical experiences of every nation on earth. Serious people like Lodge, Root, and Hughes took those facts as their starting point for devising a prudent American role in the world. By contrast, Wilson's millenarian dream could never have converted the world to a new diplomacy because it depended on the world's having already *been* converted. And yet, the United

---

States entered World War II under that same Wilsonian banner in the expectation that the defeat of fascism would usher in a new world order. When that, too, came a cropper Americans drifted, wondering how to apply the lessons of Munich and Pearl Harbor in some fashion other than Wilson's, wondering how to stop being so provincial. Between 1946 and 1950 they found their answer in a strategy that met the Communist threat without world war and promised to do what the United Nations could not. That strategy was Containment, and it won such instantaneous bipartisan support that it became the seventh tradition of U.S. foreign relations.

We associate Containment with George F. Kennan, whose Long Telegram and "X" article of 1946–47 told Americans what made the Soviets tick and called for their containment. But Kennan himself soon rued the escalation of what Walter Lippmann dubbed the Cold War, and in any case such a reinvention of America's role in the world could not have sprung *ex nihilo* from the head of one man. Rather, the seeds of Containment were sown in the decade when Americans' deepest beliefs about the nature of their country and the world were swiftly, incredibly dashed: the decade of the Great Depression.

*

The 1930s were the first protracted period of economic contraction in U.S. history, and the first time that neither an open frontier nor an open world provided a safety valve. The West Coast was already settled, and the Great Plains a Dust Bowl. The collapse of credit and the rush to protectionism choked world trade. Savings disappeared, and not just traditional hard cases — Negroes and new immigrants — but even white farmers, factory workers, tradesmen, and shopkeepers despaired of opportunity. One result was a reflexive longing for old virtues, a return to an older small-town America quarantined from a world of economic distress and political extremism. But that old civic religion of democracy and enterprise now seemed impotent, tempting intellectuals to flirt with Communism or Mussolini-style fascism, and common folk to tune in to demagogues.

For once, traditional faith had little to say about public policy. The Depression mocked the Puritan assumption that failure in life was the wages of sin when even the hardest-working, most pious husbands began to lose hope. Moreover, conflicts among modernists, fundamentalists, and evangelicals had cracked the Protestant majority, while FDR elevated Catholics and Jews, for the first time, to high office.[3] Thus, although as recently as 1898 main-line Protestants could still speak with one voice on most issues, by the 1930s the religious chorus was a cacophony. One branch of Methodists added to its baptismal vow "I surrender my life to Christ. I renounce the Capitalist system." Radio preacher Father Coughlin mixed praise for fascism with scorn for the "financial Dillingers" on Wall Street. And Catholics, liberals, and Jews combined to oppose the Ku Klux Klan.[4] That is not to say that religion ceased to influence politics, but henceforth churches tended to follow, not instigate, national trends. The New Deal was the first wholly secular reform movement in American history.

The foreign political expression of the longing for old values was the almost universal embrace of neutrality. Urban sophisticates and small-town folk alike were deeply disillusioned by the Great War, which had seemed to redound to the benefit only of Anglo-French imperialism and war profiteers. Revisionists questioned German guilt for the war and theorized that American bankers and "merchants of death" had duped Wilson into getting involved. Senator Gerald P. Nye's highly publicized hearings failed to prove a conspiracy theory, but they did help to inspire the Neutrality Acts of 1935–37, which were designed to ensure that the United States would never again provide arms and money to belligerents or send ships into harm's way. As Senator Borah proudly explained:[5]

> In matters of trade and commerce we have never been isolationist. In matters of finance, unfortunately, we have not been isolationist and never will be. When earthquake and famine, or whatever brings human suffering, visit any part of the human race, we have not been isolationists, and never will be. . . . But in all matters political, in all commitments of any nature or kind, which encroach in the slightest upon the free and unembarrassed action of our people, or which circumscribe their discretion and judgement, we have been free, we have been independent, we have been isolationist.

Who were these "isolationists," soon to be universally scorned? Contrary to myth, they were not concentrated in the Midwest or the Republican Party, but came from all regions and camps. A tiny minority were pro-fascist, but most were honest nationalists and Unilateralists.[6] They included conservatives such as Herbert Hoover, socialists such as Norman Thomas, and (after the Nazi-Soviet pact) a few card-carrying Communists, and their members came from business, labor, universities, and pacifist and women's organizations. But they all agreed on three cardinal points: no powers across the oceans posed a threat unless the United States meddled in their affairs; the world could not be reformed through war; and another great war might destroy American liberties at home. Right-wing neutralists feared that a "war to preserve democracy or otherwise would almost certainly destroy democracy in the United States,"[7] while left-wing neutralists warned that "nothing is more likely than that the United States would go fascist through the very process of organizing to defeat the fascist nations."[8] A political cartoon expressed the mood best. Uncle Sam (in the person of Roosevelt) peeks salaciously into a closet that hides a sword marked "1917," a "War to End War" banner, and a braided uniform with sash reading "Grand Exalted Savior of the World." "Samuel!" cries his wife from the next room. "You're not going to another lodge meeting!"[9]

Roosevelt came slowly to the realization that his people were living in a fool's limbo (one could hardly call it a paradise). In the 1932 campaign he said that the League of Nations contradicted "fundamental American ideals," and in 1936 he declared, "We are not isolationists except insofar as we seek to isolate ourselves completely from war."[10] But after the European war broke out in 1939, FDR leaned on Congress to revise or repeal the Neutrality Acts, imposed economic sanctions on Japan, and took executive actions to aid the Allied war effort. And devious though he was, FDR was more honest than Wilson when he said in his Arsenal of Democracy fireside chat: "Never before since Jamestown and Plymouth Rock has our American civilization been in such danger as now. . . . If Great Britain goes down, the Axis powers will control the continents of Europe, Asia, Africa, Australia, and the high seas — and they will be in a position to bring enormous military and naval resources against this hemisphere. It is no exaggeration to say that all of us, in all the Americas, would be living at the point of a gun."[11]

Neutralists smelled a rat. In September 1939 they staged an Anti-War Mobilization that shut down Washington's Mall for days. "I would sooner see our country traffic in opium than in bombs," Charles Lindbergh cried.[12] Within a year his America First Committee counted 250,000 members who believed "the security of a nation lies in the strength and character of its own people. . . . It is a policy not of isolation, but of independence; not of defeat, but of courage."[13] Thus did the marchers of 1939–41 anticipate the 1960s protests against war, armaments, presidential abuse of power, threat-mongering, and use of a domino theory ("If Great Britain goes down . . .") to suck the nation into distant conflicts.

Indeed, Pearl Harbor would not have been such a ghastly shock had the "isolationists" been fools or bigots. Instead, they stood for so much that was moral, sensible, and *American* that their discredit left a hole in the nation's soul. The hated "Japs" had stolen the most basic of freedoms: the freedom to choose war and peace. What pole star would now guide Americans through the turbulent waters of war and peacemaking?

*

The question answers itself. Theoretically, the United States could have waged a two-ocean war in a spirit of vengeance or Progressive Imperialism. But neither one had any appeal for allies or victims of aggression, or offered Americans any hope of regaining their freedom to choose war or peace in the future. So the nation clambered back to Wilson's tent with the zeal of repentant sinners.

The movement began in 1941 when a Commission to Study the Organization of Peace formed three hundred study groups, and founding member John Foster Dulles rallied religious groups to reject the "outmoded" concept of national sovereignty. Henry Luce's *Life* editorial on "The American Century" asked Americans to assume the world leadership they had spurned in 1919, and Vice President Henry A. Wallace welcomed this "second opportunity to make the world safe for democracy."[14]

Roosevelt remained cautious. The most he would concede Winston Churchill in the Atlantic Charter of August 1941 was a call for the disarmament of aggressors "pending the establishment of a wider and permanent system of general security."[15] But after Pearl Harbor the momentum for a new and better League of Nations became irresistible. On January 2, 1942, representatives of twenty-six countries (whom FDR dubbed the United Nations) agreed to fight the Axis until final victory in the name of life, liberty, independence, religious freedom, and justice. Just days before, the president endorsed an Advisory Committee on Post-War Foreign Policy, and Secretary of State Cordell Hull, the cabinet's most avid Wilsonian, threw himself into the task of designing a United Nations Organization. In 1943 notables from business (e.g., Thomas Lamont of the J. P. Morgan bank) and publishing (e.g., James Reston of the *New York Times*) formed a Citizens Council for the U.N., and Republican Wendell Willkie helped found a U.N. Association. "I am dedicating my life," he said, "to arousing the American people so that the Senate cannot prevent the United States from taking its place in world leadership."[16]

The advocates succeeded so quickly and fully that one is tempted to think that they were behind, not ahead of, public opinion. By May 1943 Gallup polls showed 74 percent of Americans favoring "an international police force" after the war. So eager was Capitol Hill to jump on the bandwagon that Tom Connolly (D., Tex.), chairman of the Senate Foreign Relations Committee, barked, "God damn it, everybody's running around here like a fellow with a tick in his navel, howling about postwar resolutions."[17] Diehards like Burton K. Wheeler (D., Mont.) denounced "these cheap small-minded internationalists who are trying to solve all the problems of the world and saying, 'To Hell with the United States.'" But Senator Joseph Ball (D., Minn.) told a convention at the Episcopal Cathedral of St. John the Divine that the drive for world organization was "the greatest crusade since Jesus sent his twelve disciples out to preach the brotherhood of man."[18] On November 5, 1943, the Senate endorsed a global security organization by a vote of 85 to 5.

Not that internationalists were all on the same page. Historians Charles Beard and Carl Becker, geopoliticians Nicholas Spykman and Robert Strausz-Hupé, and orthodox theologian Reinhold Niebuhr rejected the notion that America's failure to join the League had somehow caused World War II, and thought the neo-Wilsonians had drawn the wrong lessons from the interwar years. Becker scoffed at the idea that nations would abandon their sovereignty and predicted that nationalism would prove more powerful than ever after this war. The strategists insisted that power and geography, far from being transcended, must form the basis of a viable international system. Niebuhr denied that human nature was malleable or perfect peace possible. And Lippmann argued that to think an international body could dispense justice and peace was to repeat Wilson's "error of forgetting that we are men and of thinking that we are gods."[19]

But if Pearl Harbor had made Americans instant internationalists, it had not made them ready to accept involvement in the Old World *on the Old World's terms* — which is what the above skeptics seemed to want. Instead, the public wept over a wartime spate of books and Hollywood films that depicted Wilson as a martyred saint, and the

Democrats exploited that mood to drive stakes through the hearts of residual "isolationists." At their 1944 convention, a veritable festival to Saint Woodrow, keynote speaker Governor Robert Kerr of Oklahoma cried that "forces of isolationism" had "crucified the great-hearted Woodrow Wilson. The same forces now strive with equal fury and frenzy to inflict the same fate on Roosevelt. But where they succeeded then, they will fail now."[20] Republican candidate Thomas Dewey in fact refrained from debating foreign policy in wartime, and his own platform endorsed "responsible participation by the United States in post-war cooperative organization . . . to attain peace and organized justice in a free world."[21] But Democrats interpreted FDR's victory as the mandate denied Wilson in the election of 1918.

More important than the election was the conversion of Vandenberg. So determined was Roosevelt to avoid Wilson's mistakes that he made sure the ex-"isolationist" was consulted during the Dumbarton Oaks Conference that planned the U.N., named him a delegate to the San Francisco Conference that founded it, and assured him that the U.N. Charter would not abrogate the Monroe Doctrine or prevent "full [U.S.] control of most of the Pacific bases taken from the Japs."[22] Even so, Vandenberg's support was conditional, as explained in his oft cited, seldom read January 10, 1945, speech to the Senate:[23]

> I have always been frankly one of those who has believed in our own self-reliance. I still believe that we can never again — regardless of collaborations — allow our national defense to deteriorate to anything like a point of impotence. But I do not believe that any nation hereafter can immunize itself by its own exclusive action. Since Pearl Harbor, World War II has put the gory science of mass murder into new and sinister perspective. . . . I want maximum American cooperation, *consistent with legitimate American interest, with constitutional process and with collateral events that warrant it,* to make the basic idea of Dumbarton Oaks succeed. . . . But Mr. President, this also requires *whole-hearted reciprocity.* In honest candor, I think we should tell other nations that this glorious thing we contemplate is not and cannot be one-sided. I think we must say again that *unshared idealism is a menace* which we could not undertake to underwrite in the postwar world.

Thanks to FDR's prudence and Vandenberg's cautious support, the U.N. Charter passed the Senate, 89 to 2, on July 28, 1945. One of the naysayers said, "We in the New World cannot and will not every 20 years redress the balance of the Old by sending our sons to war."[24]

But the American people were on board, and so sturdy was the consensus forged that it survived the failure of the U.N. itself.

*

Did Roosevelt think the U.N. could succeed? Was he genuinely convinced that the Soviet Union would play the role he assigned to it in the postwar world? Conventional histories portray FDR as a "pragmatic idealist" who pursued Liberal Internationalist goals through Great Power politics. Thus, even as he preached self-determination, the Open Door, freedom of the seas, and disarmament — all echoes of the Fourteen Points — he turned Wilsonianism on its head. Where Wilson believed in open diplomacy, world opinion, democratic procedure, and arbitration, Roosevelt saw his "four policemen" — the United States, Britain, Russia, and China — ruling the postwar world by *force*. "The rest of the world would have to disarm," he told V. M. Molotov, and if the Allies found nations cheating, "they would be threatened first with a quarantine and if the quarantine did not work they would be bombed." He even told Americans by radio that everything hinged on the Allies' remaining "in complete agreement that we must be prepared to keep the peace by force."[25]

In retrospect, it is hard to believe that Roosevelt was entirely serious. To be sure, he had established diplomatic relations with Moscow back in 1933, bucking resistance from organized labor.[26] But his hopes for Soviet-American cooperation, against Japan for instance, were hollow, and his first ambassador, Bullitt, came to hate Soviet tyranny. American leftists may have taken a "see no evil" posture toward Stalin, but rumors of his purges, famines, and slave camps, suspicion of Communist influence on the New Deal, the Soviet pact with Nazi Germany and war against Finland all deepened the distrust of Moscow that prevailed in middle America. In December 1941, when the United States and the USSR became nominal allies, almost all Americans knew about Russia bred animosity and almost nothing bred amity. What is surprising is not that America and Russia fell out so quickly after V-E Day, but that their wartime relations were as correct as they were.

Hitler, of course, gets the credit for making temporary comrades of Yanks and Commies. But a flood of articles, books, and films — starting just after the Nazi invasion of Russia on June 22, 1941 — *instructed* Americans to smile on the Kremlin. Ambassador Joseph E. Davies's *Mission to Moscow* excused Stalin's purges, pact with Hitler,

Baltic and Finnish annexations as necessary to prepare Russia for war, and cooed that the Soviet regime was based "on the same principle of the 'brotherhood of man' which Jesus preached." Willkie's bestseller *One World* praised the Bolsheviks' social policies and said it was "possible for Russia and America . . . to work together for the economic freedom and peace of the world." Russia expert Walter Duranty also excused Stalin's behavior and claimed that in the "basic ways of life, Russians are not less free than we are."[27]

All this made for a temporary change in the image of Stalin. When *Time* magazine named him Man of the Year for 1939, its cover portrayed a sinister, squint-eyed Asiatic. Three years later he was again Man of the Year, only this time his rugged, visionary gaze was that of a champion and patriot.[28] But how deep did this "loyal Russian ally" stuff go? Midwar polls showed that over half of Americans believed that the Soviets would be fit partners after the war, but all they had to go on were FDR's "I got along fine with Marshal Stalin" fireside chats. And while Americans did not know that Stalin had smuggled several thousand agents into the United States under the cover of Lend-Lease, many small-town folk, Catholics, union members, and other Americans feared the Soviet monolith or held in contempt the homegrown Communists they met in their schools, unions, and military units. Dewey was premature when he tried to make an issue of Communism in the 1944 campaign, but he was right to think that a deep well of doubt was there to be tapped. When Americans did soon learn that Soviet spies had penetrated their atomic weapons program, they were justified in asking: if that supersecret project has been compromised, where else are Communists lurking?

So FDR would have had a tough time sustaining support for a pro-Soviet policy even if no clash over war aims existed. In the event, a three-way clash occurred that pitted the United States, the Soviet Union, and Britain each against the other two. Churchill defended British imperialism and warned FDR of the need to contain Soviet power. Stalin returned FDR's winks about the coming end of colonialism, but refused to participate in Anglo-American plans for economic reconstruction, demanded all the territory he had gained under the Nazi-Soviet Pact, and sought to restore the Russian spheres of influence once enjoyed by the tsars. Finally, Roosevelt's Liberal Internationalism threatened the aims of Churchill and Stalin alike, and appeared to them as a cloak for U.S. expansion. After all, the United States made no secret of its intention to control the Atlantic and

Pacific oceans, bar the Soviets from the occupation of Italy and Japan, and force the British Empire to grant American firms a larger share of the world's commodities, especially oil.

Since Roosevelt was no innocent, it is hard to escape the conclusion that by the time of Yalta he understood that the Red Army would soon make Stalin's goals *faits accomplis*. As early as September 1943 he told New York's Cardinal Spellman that he expected the Soviets to dominate Europe after the war and only hoped that their rule would not be too harsh.[29] And that is just what he asked for at Yalta: an assurance from Stalin to tread lightly in Eastern Europe and make some concessions to Polish autonomy. When Stalin obligingly lied that Poland's people would enjoy self-determination and promised in the Declaration on Liberated Europe to set up interim governments "broadly representative of all democratic elements," *Time* buried "all doubts about the Big Three's ability to co-operate, in peace as in war," and the *New York Times* cheered "a milestone on the road to victory and peace."[30] Such optimism put the U.N. over the top in Congress, but in historian Daniel Yergin's pithy summation, it also bespoke "a considerable gap between Roosevelt's *foreign* foreign policy and his *domestic* foreign policy . . . and Roosevelt, the self-styled realist, certainly knew that."[31]

The "four policemen" scenario might have worked in one of two ways: the victors might form a condominium and act as if the whole earth were their joint sphere of influence; or they might divide the world into discrete spheres of influence and cooperate only on disposition of the defeated Axis countries. Roosevelt talked as if the first would come to pass, and sometimes acted as if he believed in the second. The fact that neither proved possible (without a Cold War) was due as much to his own vague, universal war aims as it was to the specific, self-serving war aims of Churchill and Stalin.

So who was to blame for the Cold War? For the purpose of explaining how U.S. foreign policy traditions evolved, it just does not matter.[32] What is important is how most of the American leadership and public interpreted the breakdown of Allied cooperation after 1945. And to them it seemed that they had gone the extra mile only to have Moscow spurn their good will. After all, the United States accepted Stalin's retention of the lands he had grabbed while an ally of Hitler, accepted his preferred Polish boundaries, rejected Churchill's pleas for a Balkan invasion or race to Berlin to preempt the Red Army, promised to withdraw U.S. forces from Europe, pressed China's

Chiang Kai-shek to grant the Soviets privileges in Mongolia and Manchuria, insisted on Japan's unconditional surrender even though an early truce with Tokyo might have contained Soviet power in Asia, gave $18 billion in Lend-Lease aid to Russia, granted several Soviet demands regarding the U.N., and offered the USSR a veto in the Security Council.

Stalin, of course, could balance this with a list of his own concessions and grievances about U.S. policy. But Americans found it hard to believe that they were the bad guys, or to forget the fact that Russia was a brutal dictatorship. The brooding secretary of the navy James Forrestal was ahead of the curve in 1944 when he complained, "Whenever any American suggests that we act in accordance with the needs of our own security he is apt to be called a god-damned fascist or imperialist, while if Uncle Joe suggests that he needs the Baltic Provinces, half of Poland, all of Bessarabia and access to the Mediterranean, all hands agree that he is a fine, frank, candid and generally delightful fellow who is very easy to deal with because he is so explicit in what he wants."[33] By spring 1945, as Communist-led regimes appeared across Eastern Europe, FDR drafted a cable (not sent) to Stalin: "I cannot conceal from you the anxiety I feel about the course events . . . have taken since our fruitful meeting at Yalta. . . . I am frankly disturbed about the reasons for this state of affairs, and I must tell you that I do not wholly understand the apparently indifferent attitude of your Government in many respects."[34]

The coming triumph of Containment, therefore, owed a good deal to the fact that Americans did not think in terms of containing the USSR until Stalin appeared to betray their trust. Consider the Potsdam Conference of July–August 1945, which is usually depicted as a mutual baring of fangs. Stalin paraded his army and said *nyet*, while Truman whispered about the atomic bomb and returned home convinced that the Russians could not be trusted in any "joint set-up."[35] The two sides did make a remarkable pact on an important issue, however: the reparations to be extracted from occupied Germany. At Yalta, the Big Three had agreed to divide Germany into zones but treat it as a unit after the war. It soon became clear that the Soviets intended to scrape their zone clean of all industrial assets and insist as well on shipments from the Western zones. Since American and British relief was keeping West Germany alive, Secretary of State Jimmy Byrnes at first refused: "We do not intend, as we did after the last war, to provide the money for the payment of reparations." But he and

Stalin haggled, then settled. The Soviets might do what they liked in the East and still receive 10 percent of the excess capital in the Western zones, plus another 15 percent in exchange for commodities shipped from the East. Stalin grabbed this plan for a de facto partition of Germany and "spoke from his heart" when he praised Byrnes, who "brought us together in reaching so many important decisions." Historian Marc Trachtenberg refers to this as the policy of the "amicable divorce." [36]

So the Americans *were* prepared to tolerate a Soviet "security zone" in the East. For if they were not willing to stare Stalin down over Germany or Poland, they surely would not do so over Romania or Hungary. Indeed, Byrnes seemed to believe that a policy of "what's yours is yours, what's mine is mine" was the only way to avoid a serious conflict with Russia.[37] That is not to say that Truman thought relations with Stalin warm and fuzzy. He came to office believing the sweet words about Allied unity and got mad as hell when bad news arrived.[38] The atomic bomb only increased his frustration: having it, he thought, would help get "80 percent of what we want" from the Russians. But since no one but General George Patton contemplated war with the USSR — and since Truman was committed to demobilizing U.S. conventional forces as soon as Japan surrendered — the United States had no choice but to accept the status quo. To be sure, one can dig up a plethora of hostile quotations from American officials. Averell Harriman cabled in April 1945: "We must clearly recognize that the Soviet program is the establishment of totalitarianism, ending personal liberty and democracy as we know and respect it."[39] And in May, acting Secretary of State Joseph Grew wrote that World War II achieved nothing but "the transfer of totalitarian dictatorship and power from Germany and Japan to Soviet Russia. . . . As soon as the San Francisco Conference is over, our policy toward Soviet Russia should immediately stiffen, all along the line."[40] Still, Byrnes's policy remained that of the "amicable divorce," and no less a hawk than Dulles hoped "to stem the drift apart and . . . strengthen unity and fellowship for the future."[41]

*

What changed U.S. policy? What convinced Americans that the United States must relinquish its hopes for a Wilsonian world, yet still be engaged in world affairs? The answer can be as broad and abstract as one wants — innate fear and distrust of Communism, anger and confusion born of dashed hopes, an arrogant desire to have things all their own way, the tendency to see Soviet Russia as another Nazi Germany — but the timing of the change is clear: it happened in a span of six to eight weeks in early 1946. And that in turn suggests that the proximate cause was the evidence indicating that Stalin was not content with an East European glacis but was looking farther afield: to Greece where Communist insurgents bid for control, Turkey which the Soviets pressed for border rectifications and naval passage through the straits, Iran where they stationed troops in violation of Allied accords, and China, Korea, even Japan, where Stalin wanted a piece of the action. Worse yet, Britain was not up to the job of balancing Soviet power around the rim of Eurasia.

On February 9, 1946, Stalin made a customarily interminable speech in which he declared cooperation impossible between the warlike imperialist camp and the peace-loving socialist camp. Hence the Soviet people dare not let up, despite their great wartime sacrifices, but must redouble their efforts in industry and armaments. Without mentioning the United States and Britain by name, he implicitly compared them with Nazi Germany.

On February 10, Winston Churchill visited the White House. He had been turned out of office in elections the previous July, whereupon Westminster College in Truman's home state of Missouri asked him to come there to speak. Churchill accepted, thinking it a chance to plump for the big loan Britain needed to prop up its finances. By the time he arrived, however, Soviet pressure had increased on the flimsy joints of the British Empire, so he determined to bid for the unity among English-speaking peoples he had endorsed all his life: "I think I can be of some use over there," he said on the eve of his trip.[42] During their conversation, Churchill told Truman that he meant to call for military collaboration between the United States and Britain until that distant time when the U.N. would be effective. Truman was pleased to let Churchill float a trial balloon for a get-tough policy with Russia. "It's your speech, you write it," he said, and was "more than happy" about it.[43]

On February 16, Canadian authorities announced the arrest of twenty-two Soviet spies who had penetrated the Manhattan Project and sent detailed intelligence to Moscow on American and British atomic research.

On February 22, American diplomat George Kennan cabled his Long Telegram from Moscow. A veteran observer of the Soviet Union,

Kennan had been warning that Russia would spurn cooperation, cling to its conquests in central Europe, and deploy local Communists to gain power elsewhere. The boys in Washington seemed to have no idea what they were up against, to judge by their succession of equally silly purrs and growls toward Moscow. So when the State and Treasury departments finally asked Kennan for his analysis, he vowed, "By God, they would have it."[44] He explained "the Kremlin's neurotic view of world affairs" in terms of Russia's historical fear and hostility toward the outside world. The oligarchy that hid behind a mask of Marxist ideology was "committed fanatically to the belief that with US there can be no permanent modus vivendi, that it is desirable and necessary that the internal harmony of our society be disrupted, our traditional way of life be destroyed, the international authority of our state be broken, if Soviet power is to be secure." Kennan added that "Soviet power, unlike Hitlerite Germany, is neither schematic nor adventuristic." Nevertheless he warned that the Soviets would do all they could to set the Western powers against each other, promote Communism, and subvert Western institutions.[45]

On February 27, Vandenberg voiced the unease that had been building in the Congress when he pointedly asked, "What is Russia up to now?" The New York Times had warned of the danger of losing the peace and insisted that "the West did not fight one totalitarianism . . . to yield to another." Now Vandenberg demanded to know: "Where is right? Where is justice? There let America take her stand."[46]

On February 28, Byrnes answered in a major speech to the Overseas Press Club. He promised that the United States would show "patience and firmness" and resist "aggression" in unison with "other great states." The New York Times rightly interpreted it as "a warning to Russia" and a "reorientation in America's international relations."[47]

On March 4, a day Churchill and Truman spent drinking whiskey and playing poker on the train to Missouri, Byrnes drafted curt protests against Soviet actions in Eastern Europe, Manchuria, and Iran.

On March 5, Churchill spoke: "From Stettin in the Baltic to Trieste on the Adriatic, an iron curtain has descended across the Continent." Germany, he said, was also at risk, and Italy and France, given their large Communist parties, and Turkey, Persia, and the Far East. He named the Red Army and "Communist fifth columns" abroad "a growing challenge and peril to Christian civilization." The only hope of stemming this tide was "a fraternal association of the English-speaking peoples. This means a special relationship between the British

Commonwealth and the United States." And lest Americans think such an alliance inconsistent with the U.N., Churchill explained that Anglo-American unity "is probably the only means by which this organization will achieve its full stature and strength." Above all, he warned, it would be "wrong and imprudent" to hand over atomic energy to the U.N., for God had willed that this power be placed in American hands pending the day "when the essential brotherhood of man is truly embodied and expressed in a world organization."[48]

Winnie knew his audience. He paid lip service to a Wilsonianism in which he did not believe and invoked two old saws — Providence and the Anglo-Saxon mission — to sell Americans on two new departures: a peacetime alliance and a balance-of-power policy. Americans huddled and mulled. The press praised Churchill for a great spirit and agreed that Britain and the United States must act in concert, but few opinion makers and only 18 percent of the public liked the idea of an alliance. On the other hand, Churchill did not have to goad Americans into suspecting the Soviet Union. A February poll showed that only a third of Americans now trusted the Communists, and 60 percent in a March poll thought U.S. policy toward Russia "too soft"; only 3 percent thought it "too harsh."[49] Henceforth, a large majority applauded Truman's get-tough policy and a sizable minority thought it not tough enough. The Roosevelt era was quite dead, and the Cold War was on.

★

That put the United States back on square one. A mighty bipartisan consensus had affirmed global involvement, but Wilsonianism had flopped again. And the last thing Americans wanted to hear was that they were in for another long conflict with dictators. In October 1945 a hopeful Truman had announced his plan to expand the New Deal with a jobs bill, unemployment compensation, housing projects, a higher minimum wage, anti-discrimination acts, aid to education, more Social Security, even national health care. Congress resisted — the country was eager to roll back wartime controls, as proven by the Republican capture of Congress in November 1946. But the GI Bill and Social Security remained on the books and kept hundreds of thousands of young and old off the pinched employment market. Inflation also burst forth, as pent-up buying power chased after houses, cars, and appliances, and labor unions sought to catch up through a wave of strikes. Race relations were another hot item, provoking in time the Dixiecrat rebellion against Truman. So perhaps the military welcomed the Cold War, eager as it was not to see U.S. defenses erode again, but nobody else did. Throughout 1946 Truman not only continued to reduce the armed forces, from 12 to 1.5 million, he also refrained from condemning the Soviets by name in hopes of winning them to the American plan for U.N. control of atomic energy. But by early 1947 the Soviet veto of that plan, the ongoing insurgency in Greece, Communist bids for power in Paris and Rome, and the despair of West Europeans shivering in the wreckage of war combined to oblige Americans to stitch an entirely new interventionist banner.

Dulles hinted at one, in a series of articles in *Life.* The world harmony the Russians sought, he wrote, would amount to a "Pax Sovietica" and the eradication of every non-Communist society. He urged Americans to rearm, stand up to the Russians, cure social ills at home, and cultivate their religious faith. A State Department memorandum of April 1946 likewise recommended that the United States exploit its naval and air superiority and provide "all feasible political, economic, and if necessary military support" to Britain. Most shocking was Clark Clifford's report urging that the nation prepare for atomic and biological warfare and defend "all democratic countries which are in any way menaced or endangered by the U.S.S.R." Truman knew that was a bombshell. "How many copies of the report do you have?" he asked. Ten, Clifford answered. "I want them all. Go to your office and get them. They must be locked up and kept secret."[50]

Then the British ambassador, on February 21, 1947, announced that his country was broke and would stop helping Greece and Turkey in five weeks. The new secretary of state, George Marshall, considered it "tantamount to British abdication from the Middle East with obvious implications as to their successor."[51] In other words, the strategic Eastern Mediterranean was about to become a vacuum that the Soviets were certain to fill if the Americans did not. Truman summoned Vandenberg and other Republican leaders to the White House to brief them on the scary reality. But (in Dean Acheson's familiar account) Truman "flubbed his opening statement." So Acheson whispered a plea to speak. "This was my crisis. For a week I had nurtured it. These congressmen had no conception of what challenged them; it was my task to bring it home." He proceeded to shock his audience with a geopolitical horror story: the Soviets were leaning on Greece, Turkey, and Iran; if they broke through in even one of those places, the Communist infection would spread throughout the Middle East,

Africa, and southern Europe. "The Soviet Union," said Acheson, "was playing one of the greatest gambles in history at minimal cost" and the United States alone was positioned "to break up the play." After a long silence, Vandenberg spoke. "Mr. President, if you will say that to the Congress and the country, I will support you and I believe that most of the members will do the same."[52]

So on March 12, 1947, before a joint session of Congress, Truman posed the problem in the starkest possible terms:[53]

> At the present moment in world history nearly every nation must choose between alternative ways of life. The choice too often is not a free one. Our way of life is based upon the will of the majority, and is distinguished by free institutions, representative government, free elections, guarantees of individual liberty, freedom of speech and religion, and freedom from political oppression. The second way of life is based upon the will of a minority forcibly imposed upon the majority. It relies upon terror and oppression. . . . I believe it must be the policy of the United States to support free peoples who are resisting attempted subjugation by armed minorities or by outside pressures.

Truman alluded to the vague but awful consequences should Greece or Turkey lose its independence, and noted that the $400 million he asked for was but one-tenth of 1 percent of the $341 billion spent in World War II — a small price to pay to prevent another war. He concluded by saying that only the United States was up to the job:

> The free peoples of the world look to us for support in maintaining their freedoms. If we falter in our leadership, we may endanger the peace of the world — and we shall surely endanger the welfare of this Nation. Great responsibilities have been placed on us by the swift movement of events. I am confident that the Congress will face these responsibilities squarely.

Truman's ship of state took immediate hits from port and starboard. Henry Wallace, a vocal advocate of "fair play" for Russia, said that a tough policy would only force Stalin to get tough in return: "Whether we like it or not, the Russians will try to socialize their sphere of influence just as we try to democratize our sphere of influence."[54] Lippmann warned that Truman's needlessly broad commitment would oblige the United States to rely on "satellites, puppets, clients, agents about whom we know very little," and perhaps "support them at an incalculable cost on an unintended, unforeseen, and perhaps undesirable issue."[55] James Warburg charged that the Truman Doctrine was isolationism turned inside out: "We are willing to become citizens of the world, but only if the world becomes an extension of the United States."[56] Even Kennan, whose article signed "X" popularized the policy based on "long-term, patient but firm and vigilant *containment* of Russian expansive tendencies," said he regretted his failure to specify which geographical regions were strategically important.[57] On May 23 his Policy Planning Staff recommended that "immediate measures be taken to straighten out public opinion on some implications of the President's message," especially the notion that "the Truman Doctrine is a blank check."[58]

But consider, too, Truman's dilemma. He could not sell the case for aid to Greece and Turkey if it looked as if Americans were just pulling Britain's imperial chestnuts out of the fire. Nor could he pledge to help some nations while leaving others to their fate. So he based his appeal on fear and on moral universals that Americans once had shunned but by now took almost for granted. The Senate approved the aid package 67 to 23; the House by a simple voice vote.

The Marshall Plan for European economic recovery followed almost at once. Wallace denounced it, too — he called it the "Martial Plan" — while conservatives, led by Senator Robert Taft (R., Ohio), damned it for a "bold Socialist blueprint" and insisted "we cannot afford to go on lending money on a global scale."[59] But the February 1948 Communist coup in Czechoslovakia sufficed to convince the Senate and House to pass the Marshall Plan, by votes of 69 to 17 and 318 to 75.

Stalin forbade the satellites to receive Marshall aid, and he challenged the drift toward an independent West German state by blockading West Berlin. General Lucius D. Clay, commander of U.S. forces in Germany, warned: "When Berlin falls, West Germany will be next. . . . I believe the future of democracy requires us to stay."[60] The Western powers answered Clay's plea with the heroic Berlin Airlift of 1948–49, in the midst of which Americans held an election. Dewey, confident this time of victory, refused to criticize Truman's foreign policy and ordered his supporters to maintain bipartisanship. Dulles especially cautioned against "any 'break' between [Vandenberg] and Dewey."[61] So the fact that Truman pulled off an upset probably made little difference. Dewey would doubtless have gone ahead with the administration's 1949 plans for a West German republic and a North Atlantic security alliance. NATO was America's first permanent peacetime alliance and an apparent violation of George Washington's Great Rule. But it was really no more than an elaboration of the diplomat Einstein's 1913 proposal to extend the Monroe Doctrine across the Atlantic to buttress Europe's balance of power. Acheson said as much when he told Congress that "control of Europe by a single aggressive unfriendly power would constitute an intolerable threat to the national security of the United States." The Senate ratified the North Atlantic Treaty on July 21, 1949, by 82 to 13. It was, said Truman, "the collective judgment of the people."[62]

NATO's birth notwithstanding, 1949 was *annus terribilis*. The Chinese Communists drove the Nationalists off the mainland, and the Soviet Union conducted its first atomic test. Now the world's largest and most populous countries were Communist allies soon to be armed with nuclear weapons. On January 30, 1950, Truman gave the go-ahead to develop the hydrogen bomb and ordered his national security team to prepare a thorough review of policy. Kennan howled at the militarization of the Cold War, and was replaced at the State Department by Paul Nitze. As the primary author of National Security Council memorandum 68, Nitze called for an immediate buildup of nuclear and conventional forces in order to bring U.S. power in line with its commitments. The new "gospel of national security" had four sources.[63] First, the collapse of the European and Asian balances of power meant that the United States could opt out of world politics only at the risk of a Communist Eurasian hegemony. Second, Stalin's "salami tactics" resembled Hitler's, and history proved that appeasement only whetted the aggressor's appetite.[64] Third, resistance had to be backed up by superior force, which was all dictators understood. Fourth, the advent of long-range bombers and missiles meant that the next Pearl Harbor might be Chicago or Detroit, hence Americans would no longer enjoy the luxury to mobilize for war after hostilities began.

The financial implications of NSC 68, which called for quadrupling the defense budget from $12.9 to some $50 billion, appalled Truman. But the outbreak of the Korean War in June 1950 led to its swift approval. "Communism," said Truman, "was acting in Korea just as Hitler, Mussolini, and the Japanese had acted ten, fifteen, and twenty years earlier. If this was allowed to go unchallenged it would mean a third world war."[65] The granite-like Taft warned senators that if they failed to force Truman to ask their consent before making war, then future presidents "could send troops to . . . Indo-China or anywhere else in the world, without the slightest voice of Congress in the matter." [66] The public, according to polls and mail to Congress, nevertheless applauded Truman's "police action" in Korea by a measure of ten to one. In James Reston's view, it amounted to a veritable "transformation of the spirit of the United States Government."[67]

*

So the Western powers and the Kremlin, caught in a maelstrom of mutual distrust, spun dizzily downward until the Cold War was universalized, ideologized, institutionalized, and then militarized. All that is familiar stuff. But look again at the *numbers*. The Truman Doctrine passed the Senate by a margin of 3 to 1, the Marshall Plan by 4 to 1, NATO by 6 to 1, and the public approved of the Korean intervention by 10 to 1. Why such near unanimity on behalf of a new tradition that offered less in the way of rewards and far more in the way of sacrifice than any previous one? Some historians answered that Containment was really the expression of a militant American capitalism. Yet no evidence exists to show that Truman, his cabinet, military chiefs, State Department, and four-fifths of Congress and the people were dupes or shills of Bethlehem Steel and Ford Motor Company, or that the balance sheets of such firms depended on access to Eastern Europe. Nor has anyone explained why, if a U.S. government compliant to business were the aggressor in the Cold War, it never tried to crack the Soviet bloc during the years of its atomic monopoly. Nor did Americans embrace Containment out of sentimental concern for Eastern Europe. To be sure, Truman and his successors took care to bemoan the fate of the "captive nations" — no sense offending voters of East European descent. But most Americans did not give a hoot about Bulgaria or Hungary unless its fate bore witness to some grander threat to nations they did care about. And the nation Americans cared about most was the United States itself.

The birth of Containment may in fact be less complicated than historians of all stripes have made it appear. To begin with, Truman (unlike FDR) could count from the start on an internationalist consensus. He needed only to transform the hopes Americans placed in the U.N. into fury against the Soviet Union: "You mean after two world wars the Old World *still* can't see the light? You mean we have to face down *another* aggressive ideological monster?" Next, if Americans were angry, they were also afraid. The nation thought it had learned some tough geopolitical lessons in the previous decade, above all that a Eurasian balance of power was vital to U.S. security. Scarier still were the stories of Communist espionage, which hit the country like kicks to the groin. For however much the nation came later to reject the tactics of Senator Joseph McCarthy, he did not emerge from a vacuum. There *were* Communists, Communist sympathizers, and ex–Communist sympathizers (those Truman called the "Reds, phonies, and 'parlour pinks'")[68] in positions of influence, as proven by the Alger Hiss case and atomic spy rings. No one knew how many there were or how deeply they were entrenched, and what is more — one point McCarthy had right — the allegedly compromised government agencies seemed uninterested in running checks on their own people. Hence the strange spectacle of a national panic over Communist infiltration of an administration that was rallying the world to a bold anti-Communist stand!

Oh, come on, revisionists might say, the Truman crowd knowingly exaggerated the Soviet threat. Arthur M. Schlesinger, Jr., or Stanley Hoffmann might gush about "the heroic generation of American foreign policy, the new Founding Fathers, the men of 1947–48,"[69] but the truth is that Washington *used* the Communist bogeyman not just to persuade Americans to intervene in Europe, but to justify a program that included U.S. control of the Western Hemisphere, the Atlantic and Pacific oceans, "an extensive system of outlying bases . . . , access to the resources and markets of most of Eurasia, denial of those resources to a prospective enemy, and the maintenance of nuclear superiority."[70]

Why deny it? One might go so far as to say that a big reason why Containment sat so well with the American people was that its corollary policies meshed rather well with the previous six U.S. traditions. Containment called forth that spread-eagle, damn-your-eyes, us-against-them defiance never far from the surface of the American personality, and convinced the nation that its oldest and dearest tradition, Liberty, was under siege at home and abroad. Nor did Containment violate American Unilateralism so much as it might appear, for whereas the United States made commitments all over the map, it was clearly the boss of the alliances, and so retained its freedom of action.[71] Containment meshed easily with Progressive Imperialism, since it validated the projection of U.S. military power across the oceans and made parts of Asia and the Middle East into virtual protectorates. Containment did excellent duty on behalf of Expansionism, in that it opposed both colonial and Communist empires, and thus opened or kept open the markets and resources of half the world.

Containment even honored Wilsonianism insofar as it served Liberal Internationalist values, enlisted them as weapons in the Cold War, and used the U.N. whenever possible. Hence "American hegemony" — if you will — "constituted a form of anti-imperialist imperialism."[72]

Nothing conveys the American flavor of Containment better than the language of NSC 68, precisely because it was not a propaganda broadside but an internal document that remained classified until 1975. It argued that while the Soviet rulers' main concern was to shore up their power at home, "this design requires the dynamic extension of their authority and the ultimate elimination of any effective opposition to their authority." This was so because as long as freedom, "the most contagious idea in history," reigned anywhere, it threatened to infect the restless peoples under the Kremlin's thumb. And since the United States was the only force that could frustrate the Kremlin's design, the Communists were sure to target America itself with all the weapons in their arsenal, from atomic bombs to subversion of labor unions, schools, churches, and the media. What were Americans' options? The first was to continue the existing policies aimed at containing Soviet power but lacking sufficient deterrent force. The second was to launch a preventive nuclear war. The third was to retreat into "isolationism." The fourth was to bolster Containment through a rapid buildup of the strength of the free world in order "to check and to roll back the Kremlin's drive for world domination." Lest this be misconstrued, however, the authors of NSC 68 immediately stressed the "essentially defensive character" of option four. Rollback was not to be done by force but by "dynamic steps to reduce the power and influence of the Kremlin inside the Soviet Union and the areas under its control. . . . In other words, it would be the current Soviet cold war technique used against the Soviet Union."[73]

Above all, NSC 68 defined the conflict as one between the free society, which "values the individual as an end in himself," and the collective, in which individuals exist only as slaves of the ruling party. So the peoples of the Soviet bloc were not the enemy but the strongest potential allies in the struggle against the Communist apparatus. The authors specifically declined to offer any utopia, any vision of their own, to compete and contrast with that of Marxism. "For a free society there is never total victory, since freedom and democracy are never wholly attained, are always in the process of being attained."[74] Therein lay the basic morality, even humility, of NSC 68. The false idealist is precisely the one who promises ideals, while the real idealist knows that ideals are by definition unachievable. The Soviet hierarchy, measured by its own standards, was infallible — the system was God. But America's leadership, measured by *its* own standards, was subject to every creaturely foible. Its cause was to preserve those standards of decency, justice, and tolerance against which free individuals themselves always fall short.

"A bad cause never fails to betray itself," wrote Madison in *The Federalist* #41. "That it may please thee to forgive our enemies, persecutors, and slanderers, and to turn their hearts," prays the litany in *The Book of Common Prayer.* And so it was that the authors of NSC 68 rejected preventive war, placed their faith in the "existence and persistence of the idea of freedom" within the enemy camp, and asked Americans to act on the principle that their own freedom depended on the freedom of others. Truman shared Nitze's belief that the Cold War was at bottom a fight between faith and materialism. Democracy was a spiritual force, but "the danger that threatens us in the world today is utterly and totally opposed to [spiritual values]. The international Communist movement is based on a fierce and terrible fanaticism. It denies the existence of God and wherever it can it stamps out the worship of God." Then, echoing McKinley and Wilson, Truman shared his sense "that God has created us and brought us to our present position of power and strength for some great purpose."[75] It even moved the Baptist president to do what none of his predecessors dared even consider: he established diplomatic relations with the Vatican.

*

Still, we must not overstate the case. For however much Containment recalled, built upon, dovetailed with, or at least did no intolerable violence to earlier U.S. traditions, its implications were worrisome. At home, the Cold War demanded peacetime conscription, high taxes, federal intervention in science, education, business, and labor (Truman broke strikes in the name of national security), not to mention domestic surveillance and loyalty oaths — all impositions on Liberty at home. Critics promptly echoed the neutralists of the thirties by predicting that the Cold War would usher in fascism or socialism and force the United States to behave not unlike the enemy it condemned. Kennan feared this might even be counterproductive, since "the most important influence the United States can bring to bear upon internal developments in Russia will continue to be the influence of example:

the influence of what it is, and not only what it is to others but what it is to itself."[76] Eisenhower said over and over that the only way the United States could lose the Cold War was by militarizing its society, bankrupting its treasury, and exhausting Americans' will to resist: "We must not destroy what we are attempting to defend."[77]

Abroad, Containment was onerous — "an empire on which the sun would never set is one in which the rulers never sleep"[78] — dangerous, and acutely frustrating. It promised no victory anytime soon and was rife with tensions. If pursued meekly, it amounted to appeasement. If pursued too vigorously, it risked nuclear holocaust. If pursued moderately, it risked dragging the United States into limited wars in which stalemate was all it dared aim for, in faraway places that might or might not have strategic importance. Indeed, from the moment Americans soured on the Korean War to the end of the Cold War forty years later this Containment strategy that garnered almost unanimous support was at the same time so unpopular that no candidate ever ran for office endorsing it! In 1952 the Republican platform promised to "make liberty into a beacon-light of hope that will penetrate the dark places. It will mark the end of the negative, futile and immoral policy of 'containment.'"[79] In 1956 Adlai Stevenson promised arms control and summit talks to melt the Cold War. In 1960 John Kennedy denounced the tired Republicans and promised to leapfrog the Soviets in space and missile technology and win the fight for the Third World. In 1964 Barry Goldwater echoed the rollback rhetoric of 1952. In 1968 Richard Nixon offered détente. In 1972 George McGovern cried, "Come home, America." In 1976 Jimmy Carter put human rights and North-South issues above the East-West struggle with Communism. In 1980 Ronald Reagan urged Americans to "stand tall" again and consigned Communism to the dustbin of history.

No one said, "Vote for me and I will drag the nation through four more years of nervous stalemate." But once in office, everyone did it. And the nation, far from protesting, breathed sighs of relief as hawkish presidents turned more dovish or dovish ones more hawkish. Hence the many phases of Containment. The first was the original Kennanesque phase, which inspired the Truman Doctrine, Marshall Plan, and NATO. Next came the militarized Containment of NSC 68 and the Korean War. Third was the Eisenhower-Dulles New Look, which slashed defense spending and relied on nuclear deterrence and alliances ringing the Communist world. But then the Soviet achievement of intercontinental missiles and Sino-Soviet promotion of "wars of national liberation" inspired Flexible Response, under which Kennedy and Lyndon Johnson settled for nuclear stalemate and waged counterinsurgency warfare in the Third World. Fifth, Nixon and Henry Kissinger proposed to contain Soviet power through a diplomacy of carrots and sticks ("linkage") and by exploiting the Sino-Soviet split. After Gerald Ford and Carter followed suit, Reagan opened the sixth and final phase with his defense buildup, ideological offensive, and aid to "freedom fighters" such as Poland's Solidarity movement, the Nicaraguan Contras, and Afghan mujaheddin. And then, for whatever reasons, Kennan's prophecy came true: the subject peoples themselves rose up against Moscow, and the evil empire died.

But Containment did not die with the Soviet Union. Containment was so tolerated (however unloved) and so obviously successful (however tortuous and costly in practice) that it took on a life of its own, independent of the Cold War. For all his talk of a new world order, George Bush pursued a Containment strategy during and after the Persian Gulf War. Various pundits called for Containment of Japan in the 1980s and of Muslim fundamentalists and China in the 1990s. And if and when Americans perceive new threats to their vital interests abroad, they may reflexively go into Containment mode.

That prognosis will trouble readers who dispute the role of Containment in the collapse of the Soviet bloc, or ask how one can define as successful a strategy that apparently spawned the Vietnam War. Good question. But before those readers blame Containment alone for the debacle in Vietnam, I invite them to examine the role played in the origins, nature, and outcome of that war by the eighth tradition of American foreign relations — the tradition, in fact, that was the most well meaning of all.

EIGHT

Global Meliorism

ON THE EVENING OF APRIL 7, 1965, Lyndon B. Johnson addressed the nation on television from Johns Hopkins University. A month earlier the Rolling Thunder bombing campaign had begun over North Vietnam, and the first U.S. marines had landed at Danang in the South. Ever since the assassinations of South Vietnamese premier Ngo Dinh Diem and, three weeks later, of President Kennedy, LBJ had wrestled with how to handle the deteriorating situation in Southeast Asia. Now he thought he knew. The sort of world Americans sought "will never be built by bombs or bullets," he said, but since force must sometimes precede reason, he served notice to Hanoi that the United States would not be defeated or grow tired. "We must say in Southeast Asia — as we did in Europe — in the words of the Bible: 'Hitherto shalt thou come, but no further.'" Then Johnson put on his sincerest jowly face and offered an alternative future:[1]

> The first step is for the countries of Southeast Asia to associate themselves in a greatly expanded co-operative effort for development. We would hope that North Viet-Nam would take its place in the common effort. . . . For our part I will ask the Congress to join in a billion dollar American investment in this effort as soon as it is underway. . . . The task is nothing less than to enrich the hopes and existence of more than a hundred million people. And there is much to be done. The vast Mekong River can provide food and water and power on a scale to dwarf even our own [Tennessee Valley Authority]. The wonders of modern medicine can be spread through villages where thousands die every year from lack of care. Schools can be established to train people in the skills needed to manage the process of development. . . . For all existence most men have lived in poverty, threatened by hunger. But we dream of a world where all are fed and charged with hope. And we will help make it so.

Confident that his speech was a triumph, Johnson whispered to Press Secretary Bill Moyers as he descended the podium: "Old Ho can't turn me down."[2]

The speech had many authors, all trying to answer the query that Johnson had posed to his regular Tuesday group of insiders: "Where are we going in Vietnam?" Secretary of Defense Robert McNamara insisted that the "military have been going at this wrong way around" and that victory could only come through pacification programs. Moyers imagined a "Johnson Plan" doing for Southeast Asia what the Marshall Plan had done for Europe. Aides Jack Valenti and Richard Goodwin wanted to carry LBJ's War on Poverty to Asia. And Senator George S. McGovern (D., S.Dak.) dropped by to suggest "a Mekong River regional development effort, perhaps modeled on our own TVA, to promote not only economic growth, but also a sense of regional community." LBJ was enthused. "I was a hell of a long time getting into this," he told the Tuesday group. "But I like it."[3]

Americans as a whole were a long time getting into the habit of making welfare and uplift a function of government, much less of foreign policy. They always considered themselves generous, and were acutely aware of the injunction that "to whom much is given, of him will much be required."[4] But nothing in the Constitution or the Bible enjoined them to make charity obligatory where foreigners were concerned. When John Quincy Adams was dunned for a donation to the Greek independence movement he replied that it would violate the principle of non-intervention, and in any case "we had objects of distress to relieve at home more than sufficient to absorb all my capacities of contribution."[5] Almost a century would pass before the federal government heard a calling to feed the hungry and promote democracy abroad, and then another half-century passed until such Global Meliorism became the eighth tradition of U.S. foreign relations.

Global Meliorism is simply the socio-economic and politico-cultural expression of an American mission to make the world a better place. It is based on the assumption that the United States can, should, and must reach out to help other nations share in the American dream. The modal verbs "can, should, and must" in turn imply the assumptions that the American model is universally valid, that morality enjoins the United States to help others emulate it, and that the success of the American experiment itself ultimately depends on other nations escaping from dearth and oppression. These notions can be found early on in our national discourse, but they did not triumph in policy until Americans had wrestled from 1912 to 1950 with a revolutionary world and come to believe (as LBJ said) that "we have the power, and now the opportunity to make that dream come true."

The reader may ask how one can separate the Marshall Plan or Mekong River project from Containment, or why one should distinguish, say, Jimmy Carter's vision of foreign policy from that of Wilson. To the first objection I would answer that whereas Global Meliorism won its broadest bipartisan support because of its role in the fight against Communism, its assumptions and methods emerged *before* the Cold War and have persisted *after* the Cold War. To the second objection I would answer that however much Meliorism was implicit in, or overlapped with, Wilsonianism, Wilson's own vision was modest compared with that of Americans after 1945. After all, Wilson just hoped to make the world safe for democracy; Global Meliorists aim to make the world democratic. Whereas Wilsonianism was an institutional and legal response to the challenge of a revolutionary world, and Containment a strategic and military response, Global Meliorism was economic, cultural, and political.

*

When did Americans first act on the belief that they had a mission to transform foreign societies? The answer, I think, was in 1819, when the American Board of Foreign Missions decided to evangelize the Sandwich (Hawaiian) Islands. Those earnest Congregationalists instructed their young missionaries "to aim at nothing short of covering those islands with fruitful fields and pleasant dwellings, and schools and churches; of raising up the whole people to an elevated state of Christian civilization . . . ; to make them acquainted with letters; to give them the Bible with skill to read it; to turn them from their barbarous courses and habits; to introduce . . . among them, the arts and institutions and usages of civilization and society."[6] They reasoned that Christianity could hardly take root among people in thrall to illiteracy, superstition, pagan taboos, and feudal bondage; and that, once converted, the people would want to reform every aspect of their lives in any case. With steadfast determination — and with some unwanted "help" from visiting whalers — they succeeded in Americanizing Hawaii in a matter of two decades.[7]

Of course, religious missions received no state support, but by the end of the nineteenth century their scale — involving thousands of clerics, spouses, and assistants, and tens of millions of donated dollars — prefigured the governmental aid projects of the mid-twentieth century. So, too, did the missionaries' debates over strategy. Was it right or necessary to overturn foreign cultures? The Vatican's office for the propagation of the faith had always said no: "What could be more absurd than to transport France, Spain, Italy, or some other European country to China? Do not introduce all of that to them, but only the faith."[8] Protestants, however, refused to baptize anyone unable to comprehend the Bible and considered the compromises that Jesuits, for instance, made with alien cultures to be idolatrous. Still, their consciences were sufficiently troubled by what had occurred in Hawaii that in 1845 Rufus Anderson (aping, as usual, a British trend) called for a "New Mission Policy" that did not equate Christianity with "education, industry, civil liberty, family government, social order . . . *our* idea of piety." Missionaries, he preached, should set up churches under local converts, then get out and trust in the Holy Spirit to do the rest. Opposition to "exporting specific Western modes even for the purposes of social amelioration" waxed for a time, then waned when the Social Gospel kicked in.[9] By 1898, as we know, Protestants were pleased to conflate their spiritual mission with that of Progressive Imperialism, and boasted of the hospitals, schools, and farms set up by their missions in China.

The strategic quarrel — does the gospel inspire social reform, or must social reform clear the way for the gospel? — climaxed after World War I when John D. Rockefeller, Jr., shocked readers of the *Saturday Evening Post* with an open attack on American missions. Quit peddling tired dogma and morals, he urged, and adopt programs "directly attuned to human needs." Rockefeller's meliorism quickly conquered the generation of Pearl Buck, who was also "weary unto death with this incessant preaching. . . . Let us express our religion in terms of living service." Some evangelicals dissented, but by midcentury, as one professor found to his surprise, most missionaries were no longer "your stereotypic Bible-thumping soul savers" but rather "Peace Corps types before the Peace Corps."[10]

Charity entered U.S. foreign policy during those same years, thanks mostly to Herbert Hoover. Today many imagine him as the cold Quaker and self-made millionaire who presided unmoved over the Great Depression. In fact, Hoover was generous and warm, a pacifist, and an apostle of government-business cooperation, or "ordered liberty," not cutthroat capitalism. His associates loved him, and "if he is shy," one intimate said, "so is a steam shovel."[11] But above all he was an engineer who believed in the power of applied science and management to prosper the world. His direction of the Belgian relief campaign during World War I made Hoover a humanitarian hero, and when the United States entered the war Wilson appointed him director of the War Food and American Relief administrations. By 1918, with his dynamism and skill (and a dollop of self-promotion) Hoover became one of the most powerful men in the world. By 1923, he had shipped $5 billion in food to millions of hungry Europeans and, in his estimate, "saved civilization."[12]

Hoover's experiences convinced him that revolutions such as those in Mexico, China, and Russia were the products of poverty, injustice, and despair. Wilson might preach democracy, but Hoover believed, like the missionaries of his day, that food and hope of a better future were prerequisites to conversion, since "no stability of Government can be maintained in starving populations."[13] After the armistice of 1918 he pleaded with the Allies to lift the blockade lest the desperate Germans turn to extremists, and while Wilson "sweated blood" over what to do in Russia, Hoover urged him to fight Communism with bread, not guns. He even opposed a joint Allied relief effort for fear that Britain and France would use food as a political weapon, and by April 1919 grew so angry over what he deemed Anglo-French vindictiveness that he urged Wilson to bolt the peace conference: "If the Allies cannot be brought to adopt peace at the basis of the Fourteen Points, we should retire from Europe lock, stock, and barrel, and we should lend to the whole world our economic and moral strength, or the world will swim in a sea of misery and disaster worse than the Dark Ages."[14]

In 1921 Hoover did succeed in persuading Harding to request $20 million to save "millions of Christian people starving in Russia." Congress objected, since it had recently rejected a $10 million bill for unemployed Americans, while the Bolsheviks had repudiated $200 million in tsarist debt and kept 1.5 million men under arms. But Capitol Hill bowed to Hoover's argument that food would weaken, not strengthen, the Bolshevik hold over the people. "I would rather have implanted the love of the American flag in the hearts of millions," said Hoover, "than to have added to the American Navy all the battleships that the Atlantic can float." Later he confessed that his shipments of food may well "have helped to set the Soviet Government up in business."[15]

In the 1920s Hoover worked as secretary of commerce to enlarge orderly markets through cooperation among U.S. and foreign (especially British) firms.[16] As president he tried to beat the Depression with interventionist policies that anticipated the New Deal and with internationalist policies to restore foreign trade.[17] He failed, of course, but the Depression and rise of fascism gradually convinced FDR's America of Hoover's technocratic world view. Democracy might be preached, even fought for, but it could not thrive in a world sunk in despair. Hence if the United States was to do a better job of peacemaking after the Second World War, this time it must put its money — and management — where its mouth was.

★

The Roosevelt administration's planning for the postwar world was thus Global Meliorist as well as Wilsonian. The United Nations Relief and Rehabilitation Administration, a direct descendant of Hoover's American Relief Administration, spent more than $4 billion helping war-stricken nations from 1944 to 1947. Senator Vandenberg groused about paying for "whatever illimitable scheme . . . around the world our New Deal crystal gazers might desire to pursue,"[18] but Congress coughed up the money. The International Monetary Fund and the World Bank, founded at Bretton Woods in 1944, were likewise devoted to postwar reconstruction in the belief that economic distress had fed political radicalism after the First World War. Congress worried about sovereignty issues, but subscribed more than $3 billion to the international capital fund. Finally, Roosevelt's people thought deeply about how to purge Germany and Japan of militarism and turn them into sturdy democracies.

Before the German surrender, a punitive school dominated Washington's thinking, and the Joint Chiefs of Staff's blueprint for the occupation of Germany, JCS 1067, specified tough programs to "prevent Germany from ever again becoming a threat to the peace of the world." No sooner did military and civilian officials arrive in devastated Germany, however, than they began to curse the punitive plan as having been drafted by "economic idiots." Democracy could hardly be sold to a ruined nation lacking even the basics of life.[19] So what policies *did* the Americans pursue, and how much credit should they receive for the rehabilitation of Germany after 1945? The answer is far from simple, not least because all the programs specified in JCS 1067 either failed or were aborted. For instance, the Americans made

———

a stab at denazification of German institutions only to turn the effort over in March 1946 to the Germans themselves, who quietly let it lapse. Control of German industry and punishment of war profiteers gave way by late 1946 to an Anglo-American commitment to West Germany's rapid economic recovery so as to make it a healthy, anti-Communist partner. As for impressing upon Germans their collective guilt, Americans shortly lost their appetite for herding displaced, emaciated people through death camps or into theaters to watch atrocity films. So the project was abandoned in January 1946, and soon Americans were more concerned with finding "good Germans" to put in charge of a West German republic. Nonfraternization decrees never had a chance either, if only because of the GIs' prodigious appetites for girls and beer. In July 1947, JCS 1067 was replaced altogether by JCS 1779, which stressed the goal of "a stable and productive Germany."[20]

Public opinion polls also suggest that the occupation achieved little by way of reeducation. In November 1945 over half the Germans surveyed thought Nazism a "good idea badly carried out" rather than innately bad. Four years later the figures were slightly *more* apologetic toward Nazism. When asked what factors were vital for their nation's recovery, 62 percent named hard work, 33 percent religious faith, and only a quarter said "new political orientation." Germans also resented swaggering U.S. officials who boasted of "changing the course of history," and likened them to missionaries bent on "character washing."[21]

There is no way to quantify the role played by the U.S. occupation in the making of a new Germany, but recent scholars seem to be reaching a qualitative consensus. One criticizes "the naiveté implicit in the assumption that one people can 're-educate' another toward democracy." Another concludes that "the occupation, soon after it began, became largely irrelevant to its goals. It could prevent some things from happening, but it could by itself make very little happen."[22] A third writes, "Many Germans . . . were searching for ways to create a more democratic and peaceable country. They might, over time, have been able to do so themselves. Allied policies nevertheless provided them with golden opportunities."[23] In General Lucius D. Clay's modest assessment, "It probably took the Cold War and fear of the Russians to make the Germans accept the occupation so well. We began to look like angels . . . in comparison to what was going on in Eastern Europe."[24]

In Japan, General Douglas MacArthur also arrived with a bold agenda: "First, destroy the military power. Punish war criminals. Build the structure of representative government. Modernize the constitution. Hold free elections. Enfranchise the women. Release the political prisoners. Liberate the farmers. Establish a free labor movement. Encourage a free economy. Abolish police oppression. Develop a free and responsible press. Liberalize education. Decentralize political power. Separate the church from state."[25] One need only add "Christianize the Japanese" — another project MacArthur fancied — and the list would resemble that given the missionaries to Hawaii.

The prewar ambassador to Tokyo, Joseph Grew, placed little hope in such meliorism. "I am certain," he wrote in April 1945, "that we could not graft our type of democracy on Japan because I know very well they are not fitted for it and that it could not possibly work."[26] Who turned out to be right: Grew or the enthusiastic New Dealers on MacArthur's staff eager to smash the industrial *zaibatsu,* rewrite the constitution, and liberalize Japan's society and culture?[27] The answer here is even more subjective than in the German case, not only because the United States again "changed course" by late 1947 and began to think of Japan as a Cold War ally, but also because there is reason to ask in retrospect how much Japan changed at all. In areas like women's rights, land reform, and renunciation of war, the occupation's reforms seem to have held. But Japan's bureaucratic and party politics, economic structure, and culture of education display more continuity with its own pre-fascist past than with anything one might call American.

The best witness, perhaps, was Yoshida Shigeru, the great prime minister who worked closely with MacArthur. "The so-called democratic form of government," he wrote, "is still in its infancy in my country. And though its outlines may now seem to have been determined, so far we see little indication that its spirit has come to live amongst us." He judged the occupation a success, but only because its basic aim "was identical with ours . . . to reform and recast Japan into a peaceful and democratic nation." Even so, the Japanese had to fight for this goal in the teeth of a "'new-deal' idealism" that "often went to extremes, in complete ignorance of the complex realities then prevailing in our country." Yoshida was especially dismayed by the purge, the assault on the *zaibatsu,* and educational impositions that were "sapping the moral fibre of our bewildered youth."[28]

One is tempted to conclude that if Germany and Japan ceased to be troublemakers, their overwhelming defeat was more important to that result than their postwar occupations. But that is not how Americans saw things at the time, when budding Global Meliorists were quick to praise the occupations as examples of what humane American activism could achieve overseas.

*

As with politics, so with economics. For nothing appeared to prove Meliorist assumptions so much as the Marshall Plan. It was the brainchild of Containment advocates like Kennan, Acheson, and Clifford, whose goals were frankly political. But one effect of the plan was to place the momentum of the Cold War behind a Global Meliorist trend that already existed.[29] As Henry L. Stimson put it, "Our central task in dealing with the Kremlin is to demonstrate beyond the possibility of misunderstanding that freedom and prosperity, hand in hand, can be stably [sic] sustained in the western democratic world. This would be our greatest task even if no Soviet problem existed."[30] Indeed, the UNRRA, IMF, and World Bank all preceded the Cold War, as did some $9 billion in loans and credits extended to foreign countries in 1945 and 1946. Americans were also ready to believe, with the Depression fresh in their memory, that their prosperity hinged on Europe's ability to import U.S. goods.[31] So while the clash with the Soviets raised the stakes, it did not begin the game of foreign aid.

What benefits are traceable to the $13 billion advanced under the Marshall Plan? Western Europe's combined product grew by 32 percent, and its agriculture and industry soon exceeded prewar output by 11 and 40 percent. Yet it is also true that 80 percent of the capital invested in those years was itself European![32] Some economic historians even challenge the notion that the Marshall Plan was inspired by Europe's malaise, suggesting rather that its swift start in rebuilding rendered Europe so short of dollars to pay for new plant and raw materials that the United States had to supply the greenbacks. Others point out that whatever the plan's motive, the only palpable result was not an "economic miracle," which would have come sooner or later, but the integration of Western Europe.[33]

Again, our concern is less with realities than with the mythology that enveloped the Marshall Plan, as many Americans in the government and the press leapt to the conclusion that it, too, was a model that could be applied elsewhere. John J. McCloy, high commissioner for occupied Germany, did not: when asked to discuss Third World development he growled, "Hell no. It doesn't have anything to do with the Marshall Plan." And Will Clayton, Truman's "roving ambassador" to Europe, told the 1947–48 Pan-American Conference that "the Marshall Plan is wholly inapplicable to the Latin American situation." [34] But many others found the notion delicious that the United States knew how to make people rich as well as free. "The time has come," cried Henry Wallace, "for a modern Johnny Appleseed animated by the missionary spirit to go into all the world and preach the gospel . . . of investment, science, technology, and productivity to all peoples!" And the State Department's official chronicler of the Marshall Plan thought it suggested "not the limits but the infinite possibilities of influencing the policies, attitudes, and actions of other countries." [35]

Pundits called at once for another Marshall Plan, in Asia, Latin America, or depressed regions at home, and the new Central Intelligence Agency was instrumental in carrying Marshall Plan methods to Egypt and Iran, on the theory "that developing nations receiving adequate assistance from the West in the form of planning and technology would aspire to emulate Western ideas and would be less vulnerable to Communist agendas." [36] The CIA's overthrow of the leftist Mossadegh in Iran in favor of the pro-Western Shah Reza Pahlavi seemed to prove the value of proactive Meliorism.

So the Truman administration institutionalized it, first in the Economic Cooperation Administration, which spent $30 million in South Korea before (and $110 million after) the outbreak of the Korean War, $100 million in Southeast Asia, and another $180 million in Taiwan (through 1952), where American experts helped push through land reform. In light of such precedents, the State Department's Benjamin Hardy asked why not the world? He passed a blueprint for global assistance on to Clifford, who gave it to Truman, who made it "last but not least" in his inaugural address of January 20, 1949: [37]

> Fourth, we must embark on a bold new program for making the benefits of our scientific advances and industrial progress available for the improvement and growth of underdeveloped areas. . . . For the first time in history, humanity possesses the knowledge and the skill to relieve the suffering of these people. . . . The old imperialism — exploitation for foreign profit — has no place in our plans. What we envisage is a program of development based on the concepts of

democratic fair-dealing. . . . Democracy alone can supply the vitalizing force to stir the peoples of the world into triumphant action, not only against their human oppressors, but also against their ancient enemies — hunger, misery, and despair.

Truman's Point Four, though modest at the start, amounted to a promise to extend the New Deal and Fair Deal to the world. And to preempt muttering about "money down the rathole," his administration launched a publicity campaign based on the premise that "the very basis for Point Four is practicability." Ambassador Chester Bowles asked readers to think of new nations in Asia as "like America in 1783" and of Point Four as a plan to replicate an economy "almost exactly like that of the United States." Harvard economist John Kenneth Galbraith added: "Above and far beyond Point Four, *We must put ourselves on the side of truly popular government with whatever pressure we can properly employ.*"[38] Most effective was the pitch depicted by a Herblock cartoon. In it, Truman hands the price tag for Point Four to a fat, balding congressman while across the ocean huddled masses await their decision. "Nah!" says the congressman, "Let's wait till they go Communist, then spend a few *billions* fighting them."[39]

Within three years Point Four agreements were signed with thirty-four countries and the annual cost rose to $155.6 million. Critics like British economist P. T. Bauer denounced government-to-government assistance as subsidizing socialism, Hans Morgenthau cautioned that forced industrialization was "likely to disrupt the fabric of the underdeveloped nation" rather than make it more stable, and Henry Kissinger challenged the assumption that economic progress leads to democracy: "In all the traditional democratic societies, the essentials of the governmental system antedated the industrial revolution."[40] Eisenhower too was a skeptic, until the birth of the non-aligned movement in 1955 and the Suez crisis of 1956 convinced him that the United States had to pose as a champion of "backward" nations. When he reluctantly endorsed the principle that "the freedom of nations can be menaced not only by guns but by the poverty that communism can exploit,"[41] Global Meliorism secured the bipartisan support needed to sustain grants, loans, and investments that would transfer, all told, some $2 trillion (in 1980s prices) from the First to the Third World by 1990.[42]

While Eisenhower was changing his mind, the so-called Charles River School of economists from MIT and Harvard were busy devising the theory needed to guide the deployment of all that capital. Walt W. Rostow emerged as its leader, thanks to his model of how economic "take-off" had occurred historically. With Europe frozen into blocs and the nuclear arms race heading toward mutual deterrence, the Third World emerged as the only open flank in which the superpowers might wage Cold War without risking Armageddon. Rostow, moreover, thought it might be the decisive theater, since the Soviets could point to their own rapid progress, symbolized by their apparent leadership in space technology after 1957, to convince Third World rulers "that the Communist model should be adopted for modernization, even at the cost of surrendering human liberty." In short, Communists were "scavengers of the modernization process" and Communism a "disease of the transition."[43] As early as 1954, when the Geneva Conference divided Vietnam, Ike's aide C. D. Jackson asked Rostow and Max Millikan to propose means of building a stable, non-Communist South Vietnam. They replied that "a substantial new American initiative was required in the field of development."[44]

Rostow's *The Stages of Economic Growth*, provocatively subtitled *A Non-Communist Manifesto*, stressed the role of investment in triggering a country's "take-off into self-sustaining growth." Good historian that he was, Rostow carefully listed the many political and economic preconditions for takeoff.[45] But policy makers were bound to seize on his magic formula to the effect that a sudden rise in investment from 5 to over 10 percent of national income was the secret to sparking takeoff. How could poor countries raise such capital? One way was by "primitive accumulation," which in Marxist lands meant squeezing the peasants and stifling consumption to boost exports. The other way was by foreign investment. Rostow argued that "the potentialities of external assistance must be organized on an enlarged and, especially, on a more stable basis," and figured that "an increase of the order of some $4 billion in annual external aid would be required to lift all of Asia, the Middle East, Africa, and Latin America into regular growth."[46]

Rostow's colleagues sometimes suspected his voluminous works of being more facile than brilliant ("Walt can write faster than I can read," quipped the speed-reading President Kennedy). But he was tireless, headstrong, and possessed of a steely confidence.[47] He saw the need to combat insurgents such as the Vietcong and believed that "success in resisting the combination of subversion and guerrilla operations depends directly on the political, economic, and social health of the area attacked."[48] So when Kennedy won the presidency in 1960 and appointed Rostow and like-minded intellectuals to high office, Americans neared the antipodes in their historical journey. Having begun their national life determined to shun crusades, they now mobilized for Global Meliorist war halfway 'round the world.

★

The fight for the Third World began in 1917 when Lenin called for global revolution against imperialism and Wilson replied with his Fourteen Points. But where Lenin hoped to exploit colonial unrest to distract the imperialists while he consolidated his rule in Russia, Wilson thought most colonial peoples needed decades of development and reform before they would be ready for self-rule. The competition thus took an ironic twist from the start, as the Marxists (who claimed that socio-economic forces drove history) practiced power politics and the liberals (who professed to believe in the power of ideas) acted on a sort of economic determinism. Fifty years later Communists would talk about social revolution but rely on conspiracy and guns to prevail in Vietnam, and the Americans would play at limited war but rely on "revolutionary development" programs to build nations and win hearts and minds.

In retrospect, we can see that Soviet (and Chinese) promotion of anti-colonial movements was more than a tactic: it reflected the true nature of Leninism. The Bolsheviks had already stood Marx on his head when they made a revolution in the least-mature capitalist country in Europe and transformed Communism into the agency for rapid technological and social development. Lenin also theorized that the imperialists' grip on colonial labor and resources was what allowed them to ward off the final crisis of capitalism. So Communism became in effect a revolt of the backward, and would live or die by its record at home and in the Third World. When Mao Tse-tung and Khrushchev declared, "There will be wars of national liberation as long as imperialism exists," Kennedy felt compelled to reply. Everyone knows his boast that Americans would "pay any price, bear any burden," but he went on to say: "To those people in the huts and villages of half the globe struggling to break the bonds of mass misery, we pledge our best efforts to help them to help themselves, for whatever period is required — not because the Communists may be doing it, not because we seek their votes, but because it is right. If a free society cannot help the many who are poor, it cannot save the few who are rich."[49] And in the May 25, 1961, speech in which he called for a man on the moon, JFK named the Third World "the great battleground for the defense and expansion of freedom today."[50]

Kennedy's conversion to Meliorism began early in his political career. In 1951 he visited Indochina, where the French were losing their fight against the Vietminh. "To check the southern drive of Communism makes sense," he concluded, "but not only through reliance on force of arms. The task is rather to build strong native anti-Communist sentiment." In 1956 he advised, "What we must offer [the Vietnamese] is a revolution — a political, economic, and social revolution far superior to anything the Communists can offer."[51] And his 1958 Kennedy-Cooper amendment called for billions in aid to make India a non-Communist showplace. "Shall these new powerful states emerge to maturity from a totalitarian setting," he asked (quoting Rostow), or "from a democratic setting, built on human values shared with the West?"[52]

Kennedy also developed a keen interest in Latin America after Vice President Nixon was pelted by mobs on his tour in 1960 and Fidel Castro threw in his lot with the Soviet Union. So on March 13, 1961, the same day he founded the Meliorist Peace Corps, JFK offered $20 billion to fund an Alliance for Progress and warned, in an echo of the Monroe Doctrine, against "alien forces which once again seek to impose the despotisms of the Old World on the people of the New."[53] The Alliance for Progress became the centerpiece of Kennedy's global Development Decade: "There exists, in the 1960s, an historic opportunity for a major economic assistance effort by the free industrialized nations to move more than half the people of the less-developed nations into self-sustained economic growth. . . . We shall take this step not as Republicans or as Democrats but as leaders of the Free World."[54] JFK's first Foreign Assistance Act passed the House 260 to 132 and the Senate 69 to 24, and U.S. foreign aid rose from $2.7 to $3.6 billion by 1964.

In short, Kennedy took office eager to prove that "economic growth and political democracy can develop hand in hand."[55] But therein lay a conundrum. Did economic growth lead to democracy? Or must stable, representative government exist before an economic boom could occur? Kennedy's advisers did not agree. One group, whom historian Patrick Lloyd Hatcher dubs the "Whigs," stressed the need for popular government in countries like South Vietnam and looked to U.S. embassies and the CIA to promote the necessary reforms. The other group, Hatcher's "Tories," stressed economic progress, preferred to work through the U.S. Agency for International Development (USAID), and were prepared to tolerate authoritarian regimes so long as they were effective.[56] In the case of Vietnam, Whigs asked such questions as how many independent newspapers and radio stations were there, did religious minorities enjoy freedom of worship, how fair and frequent were elections, could citizens get justice in the courts, how humane were the police? But Tories thought it premature to expect a new state beset by a ruthless insurgency to pass an American civics test. They asked such questions as how many villages had sewage and clean drinking water, what was the ratio of doctors to citizens, how many telephones and motorbikes were there, how much fertilizer was needed, what was the rice yield and per capita income? Charged with providing these data, the Military Assistance Command Vietnam (MACV) became less like a comrade-in-arms to the Saigon regime than a nagging social worker.[57]

It was the missionaries' debate all over again, with democracy substituted for Christianity. Must an alien society be modernized to prepare the ground for democracy, or would the planting of popular government suffice to flower social development? The debate became more than academic when the regime of Ngo Dinh Diem, in which Americans placed such high hopes, began to unravel.

U.S. involvement in Vietnam deepened the moment the Korean War broke out. The extension of Containment to Asia not only magnified American responsibilities, but did so in a part of the world where no strong local allies existed. Unlike NATO, the Southeast Asia Treaty Organization (SEATO) was virtually a unilateral U.S. guarantee to a congeries of post-colonial peoples. As Senator Mike Mansfield (D., Mont.) chided in 1962: "We have allies under SEATO to be sure, but allies either unwilling or unable to assume but the smallest fraction of the burdens of an alliance."[58] That meant the United States had to dominate or even invent the "genuine Asian nationalism" it purported to defend. So from 1954 to 1963 the Americans told Diem to be a strong, independent leader, but to take his orders from Washington when it came to human rights, economics, and how to fend off the Vietcong. The Communists exploited that contradiction throughout the Vietnam War. Accused of being puppets, Saigon's leaders were "whipsawed between their implacable enemy in Hanoi and their importunate ally in Washington."[59]

Ngo Dinh Diem was Catholic, but he was also a mandarin of the hierarchical Confucian tradition trying to rule an artificial half-country riddled with Communist guerrillas and agents who remained in the South after the partition. So there was never a question in the minds of Diem and his brother, who headed the secret police, of risking American-style democracy. Indeed, it was their very success in rooting out Communist cadres that prompted Hanoi to abandon political action in favor of armed insurrection. In May 1959 the North Vietnamese Politburo formed a special task force to cut what became the Ho Chi Minh Trail through Laos and Cambodia in order to reinforce and supply the Southern insurgency. By 1960 the Vietcong was murdering village chiefs and Saigon officials at an alarming rate, whereupon (as Kissinger wrote) "the central dilemma became that America's political goal of introducing a stable democracy in South Vietnam could not be attained in time to head off a guerrilla victory, which was America's strategic goal. America would have to modify either its military or its political objectives."[60] That is, the United States would have to back Diem's unpopular but effective authoritarianism or else write off South Vietnam as it had North Vietnam. But Kennedy's men were wedded, not to the tactics of Korean-style Containment, but to those of Global Meliorism. So they refused to abandon either their military or their political objectives. They abandoned Diem instead.

Later critics said that in trying to be the "world's social worker" the United States practiced "welfare imperialism."[61] They said that Vietnam was not critical to U.S. national security and disputed the assumptions behind the Vietnam War, including the domino theory and a monolithic Communist bloc. They said that Ho Chi Minh was more nationalist than Communist, and no puppet of Beijing or Moscow. All those arguments had some merit — they just missed the point so far as Kennedy's advisers were concerned. Their fear was that a Communist victory in Vietnam would signal the Communist powers and entire Third World that insurgencies work and Western development strategies don't. That was why Paul Nitze argued that if the United States "acknowledged that we couldn't beat the VC, the shape of the world would change." That was why Rostow announced: "It is on this spot that we have to break the liberation war. If we don't break it here we shall have to face it again in Thailand, Venezuela, elsewhere. Vietnam is a clear testing ground for our policy in the world."[62]

Now, when the United States acted to block Communism in Greece, Turkey, or Korea, it did not demand that those countries become model democracies or make revolutionary economic reforms. But in May 1961, the National Security Council declared it U.S. policy in South Vietnam "to create in that country a viable and increasingly democratic society."[63] Given that goal, the next obvious question was whether Diem's relatively dictatorial, corrupt, unpopular regime was part of the solution or part of the problem. "Tory" Meliorists were inclined to overlook Diem's strong-arm tactics, but when protesting Buddhist monks took to immolating themselves in Saigon before world news cameras, the "Whigs" got the upper hand and Ambassador Henry Cabot Lodge told Diem to reform his government or face "unpredictable consequences." Now, whatever his faults, Diem was a true nationalist who knew more about the feuds and factions of his people than did the Americans. He warned Lodge that real power lay with the army, and that if he was removed from office his successors would be "twice as repressive as he had been."[64] But Lodge let disaffected Vietnamese generals know that the United States would not look askance at Diem's removal. So they killed the Ngo brothers in the November 1963 coup d'état, and the turnstile military juntas that followed were even less effective at winning public support and fighting the Vietcong. That in turn gave the United States no choice but to take over the war and, at the same time, make the hothouse political and economic revolutions that Whig and Tory Meliorists deemed vital to victory. What is shocking in retrospect is how confident they were that they could do so. But as one Pentagon official replied, when reminded that France had already been beaten in Vietnam, "The French also tried to build the Panama Canal."[65] It was as if state-building and guerrilla war were mere engineering problems, like landing a man on the moon.

Therein lay a second contradiction in American Third World strategy. Even if the United States gave up its pretense that the Saigon regime was a sovereign and equal ally, what logic suggested that a pre-industrial, Asian, intensely proud people wanted to follow American political and economic models? Unfortunately, in George Ball's words, "the young movers and shakers of the Kennedy Administration had, if anything, a surfeit of theories regarding the economic development of the Third World."[66] A Pentagon consultant remembered the mood of the times as "one of change, of ferment, of self-confidence — of 'knowing' what had to be done and of unquestioning 'can do.' It would all lead to a better world. It was the time of Camelot."[67] There was actually a Project Camelot, inspired by

McNamara's belief that defeating wars of national liberation "will require a comprehensive effort involving political, economic, and ideological measures as well as military." An icy Hooverian technocrat (minus the pacifism), McNamara put more than a hundred sociologists, ethnologists, and psychologists to work "modeling" South Vietnamese society and seeking data sufficient "to describe it quantitatively and simulate its behavior on a computer." Of course, the project was based on circular reasoning — how could one judge which data were relevant unless one already had a model in mind? Nevertheless, McNamara ordered the scholars to take their model "to the field" within eight months so he could compute the progress made in pacification and revolutionary development. If World War I was the chemists' war, and World War II the physicists' war, McNamara said, then the struggle for the Third World "might well have to be considered the social scientists' war."[68]

Yes. Vietnam was the first war in which the United States dispatched its military forces overseas not for the purpose of winning but just to buy time for the war to be won by civilian social programs. Had the U.S. military been assigned the job of winning, Kennedy would never have consented to the 1962 Laos accord, which left that "neutral" country open to North Vietnamese infiltration, and Johnson would not have restricted U.S. ground and air action against the real enemy, which was North Vietnam. Instead, General William Westmoreland was obliged to disperse his forces and to waste his firepower in search-and-destroy operations against the National Liberation Front, which was in fact Hanoi's cat's-paw and rival for control of the South. As Colonel Harry Summers has shown, this approach ensured tactical victories but strategic defeat, since it failed to isolate the battlefield, neglected to attack the enemy's center of gravity in North Vietnam, and indeed assigned the offensive role not to the army and air force but to CIA, USAID, and MACV pacification agencies "tasked" with building South Vietnam's economy and winning over its people. Vietnam was thus "the international version of our domestic Great Society programs where we presumed that we knew what was best for the world in terms of social, political, and economic development and saw it as our duty to force the world into the American mold — to act not so much as the World's Policeman as the World's Nanny."[69]

*

In his 1950s novel *The Quiet American* Graham Greene described the earnest young American with the "gangly legs" and "unused face" who arrives in Southeast Asia "determined . . . to do good, not to any individual person, but to a country, a continent, a world."[70] No do-gooder was more determined than Lyndon Johnson. To be sure, he damned Vietnam as "that bitch of a war" and grew to hate its military side, but he loved its Global Meliorist side. "I want to leave the footprints of America [in Vietnam]. I want them to say, 'This is what Americans left — schools and hospitals and dams.' " In 1966 he pronounced an "overriding rule": "Our foreign policy must always be an extension of our domestic policy. Our safest guide to what we do abroad is always what we do at home." Hence Vietnam "had its origins in the same presidential impulses that gave birth to the Great Society and the April 1965 offer to North Vietnam of a billion-dollar economic development program for the Mekong River."[71]

Rostow's 1965 plan for "Politics and Victory in South Vietnam" called for nothing less than "a modern revolutionary party" that would promote "a stance of independence towards all foreigners; national unity in the South; . . . an end to corruption; rapid industrial development; land reform and other measures which would ease the burden on the farmer; anti-Communism, etc." John Paul Vann, a veteran military adviser to South Vietnam, also endorsed "social revolution" and added that if the rulers in Saigon dragged their feet, then "they must be *forced* to accept U.S. judgment and direction."[72]

Countless American crusaders soon learned the frustrations of trying to build in the midst of a battlefield, and how faulty and irrelevant were the statistics on pacified villages, body counts, rice yields, and school attendance that they dutifully sent up to McNamara and Rostow.[73] But Johnson grabbed the Meliorist sword with both hands, and grew impatient so quickly that in February 1966 (just twelve months after his war escalation began) he summoned President Nguyen Van Thieu, Vice President Nguyen Cao Ky, and the South Vietnamese health and welfare ministers to a summit in Honolulu. He wanted everyone to leave "determined not only to achieve victory over aggression but to win victory over hunger, disease, and despair." He lectured Thieu and Ky that the struggle could be won only by making "a social revolution for your people" and that this was a "kind of bible that we are going to follow." He warned everyone that he would be back in their faces to ask, "How have you built democracy in the rural areas? How much of it have you built, when and where? Give us dates, times, numbers. . . . Larger outputs, more efficient production to improve credit, handicraft, light industry, rural electrification — are those just phrases, high-sounding words, or have you coonskins on the wall?"[74] A Vietnamese dared reply, "Mr. Johnson, we are a small country and we don't have pretensions to building a Great Society." But Thieu and Ky pledged to pursue the "social revolution," "free self-government," and "attack on ignorance and disease" that Johnson demanded.[75]

LBJ named Robert Komer his special assistant for all civil programs in Vietnam and in 1967 sent him over to take personal charge, as a deputy commander of MACV, of a new Civil Operations and Revolutionary Development Support (CORDS). A former CIA agent, "Blowtorch Bob" lamented the fact that the U.S. military effort did little besides feed inflation and anti-Americanism, and he shared LBJ's belief that pacification was "central to the ultimate resolution of the war — a viable South Vietnam — and a way to lessen American involvement and losses."[76] As it was, the war was a sinkhole. "The way we're squandering money here," chided a reporter, "we could probably buy off the Viet Cong at five hundred dollars a head." Komer shot back, "We've staffed it. Twenty-five hundred dollars a head." By comparison, the price paid for each enemy corpse was estimated at $60,000.[77]

However firm their resolve, good their will, and deep their pockets, Americans could not establish democracy and prosperity in the absence of peace. As Maxwell Taylor later confessed, "We should have learned from our frontier forebears that there is little use planting corn outside the stockade if there are still Indians around in the woods outside."[78] But Komer and CORDS proceeded on the Meliorist assumption that only development could bring peace: the loyalty of villagers had to be won in order to deny the guerrillas the rural "sea" in which they swam. USAID agents took as their text Willard L. Thorp's 1951 report "Land and the Future," which praised the breakup of the landlord system in Japan and Taiwan. But land reform had already been tried twice in Vietnam — Diem's "agrovilles" and the Green Berets' "strategic hamlets" — and all it accomplished was to force thousands of families to abandon the graves of their ancestors and relocate in fortified redoubts ("prisons," said VC propaganda) under the thumb of despised Saigon officials. So MACV launched a third campaign in 1965 called *Chien Thang* (Will to Victory), then a fourth called *Hop Tac* (Victory), which tried to minimize relocation, address farmers' needs, and enlarge already secure regions (like a spreading "ink blot") rather than pacify the whole country at once.[79]

But always the war and the politics and corruption of the Saigon regime queered the pitch. Even the larger crop yields and livestock herds made possible through U.S. aid benefited the Vietcong, who taxed many villages by night as heavily as Saigon did by day. Some 325,000 peasants by 1967 saw their crops destroyed through defoliation. Relocation and the ravages of war made refugees of a million more. The revolution wrought by the Americans was just as destabilizing as the Communist one, while military action by both sides destroyed much of the infrastructure that CORDS tried to build up.[80] Indeed, the very fact that landlords in an insecure province tended to flee to Saigon and thus cease collecting rents (often up to 50 percent of the harvest) gave farmers a stake in keeping the Vietcong around. What is more, every South Vietnamese leader from Diem to Thieu dragged his feet on rural reform rather than lose the support of the landlord class or confront an empowered peasantry. The Americans repeatedly urged Saigon to unify its social and economic bureaucracies, coordinate with U.S. agencies, and push real reform. But they could not force their clients to shape up without standing forth as a colonial overlord every bit as imperious as the French had been. And even if they had been imperious, it might not have worked. When a young South Vietnamese Army general in 1966 told a chief CIA analyst that only the United States could execute the necessary "social revolution," Ambassador Lodge dismissed the idea: "We couldn't possibly do that — that would be essentially playing God."[81]

McNamara and Komer soldiered on, bankrolling and trying to coordinate the 1,000 U.S. civilians, 7,000 U.S. military personnel, 1 million Vietnamese in the Regional Forces and People's Self-Defense Corps, and 100,000 national policemen, all of whom were engaged in the pacification effort. Their Project Takeoff emphasized village security, land reform, police reform, refugee relief, and the ferreting out of the Vietcong infrastructure. That last campaign hatched the controversial *Phung Hoang* (All-Seeing Bird) or Phoenix Program, directed by the CIA's William Colby. Critics later accused Phoenix of reliance on dubious informants, false arrests, torture, and execution. Colby vehemently denied such charges, but there is no doubt that in Phoenix the Americans began to resort, to a certain extent, to the same tough methods they had overthrown Diem and his brother for using just five years before.

Meanwhile, in the cities and boomtowns near American bases, U.S. assistance may even have impeded the Vietnamese economy from getting ready for takeoff. By 1966 South Vietnam was receiving 43 percent of worldwide USAID funding, but the $8.5 billion in economic aid from 1954 to 1974, $17 billion in military aid, and billions more spent by Americans in-country only fueled a black market in pilfered consumer goods and a bazaar economy that pandered to American appetites for (among other things) liquor, drugs, and prostitutes. South Vietnam's cities — like much of inner-city America — soon became corrupt and dependent welfare zones.

Nevertheless, Komer was so pleased by his algorithms and indices that in early 1967 he boasted to David Lilienthal, "We have won the war." [82] Later that year, the White House and MACV launched public relations blitzes that also promised imminent victory. What came instead was a cascade of ironies. On the one hand, the Communists' Tet Offensive of 1968 seemed to mock all talk of "light at the end of the tunnel," and turned American elite opinion against the war. On the other hand, the decimation of the Vietcong in the Tet urban attacks finally allowed Komer's Accelerated Pacification Program to make serious progress. Inasmuch as CORDS erased from the Hamlet Evaluation Survey all criteria not relevant to security (health, education, and the like), one wonders how much its claim of "90 percent control" of the country reflected real popular support for Saigon. [83] But the shock of Tet did convince Thieu that he had better sport the trappings of democracy and at last undertake real reform. The Land to the Tiller law of 1970 restricted landlord holdings to a reasonable fifteen hectares (previous law allowed one-hundred-hectare holdings), which reduced the tenancy rate among farmers from 60 to 10 percent. [84] And with daily life in South Vietnam becoming more secure than at any time since 1958, one might even say that the United States succeeded in defeating the Southern insurgency — only to learn how little that difficult goal had to do with real victory when Hanoi launched its massive conventional assault across the demilitarized zone in 1972. As Norman Hannah aptly wrote, "The U.S. fought the war as a bull fights the toreador's cape, not the toreador himself." [85] To make matters worse, the same Tet Offensive that decimated the Vietcong also forced Johnson to cap, and Nixon to withdraw, the American forces that alone were capable of frustrating the real enemy in North Vietnam.

Above all, however one assesses rural pacification, Meliorist policies never came close to making South Vietnam a self-sufficient nation-state capable of defending itself and primed for economic takeoff. Consider that some 100,000 to 300,000 young men entered the labor force there each year in the late sixties and early seventies. Economists calculate that employing these workers "would have required an annual investment on the order of $400 million, or a net investment of about 15 percent of Vietnam's national income, *just in the manufacturing sector.*" Thanks to the United States, money was available, and if South Vietnam had been healthy, its bureaucrats and nouveaux riches would have reinvested their well- or ill-gotten gains and sparked a self-sustained growth. But the insecurity of war and the ease of living off Uncle Sam combined to depress South Vietnam's savings rate to an average of *zero* percent. (By contrast, Taiwan upped its savings rate from 6 to 30 percent between 1955 and 1975, and South Korea from zero to 22 percent.)[86]

So fragile, in fact, was South Vietnam's "prosperity" that as soon as the Americans left for good in 1973 the piaster dropped 25 percent in value against the dollar, inflation soared to 65 percent, a $750 million trade deficit devoured three-fourths of Saigon's foreign exchange reserve, and unemployment reached 20 percent. To be fair to Thieu, he had terrible luck: the rice crop failed in 1972 and the price of oil quadrupled after the 1973 Arab embargo. The point is that South Vietnam, absent the annual $400 million in aid, had no intrinsic strength to fall back on. Thieu scoured the world for capital (60 percent of his own country's budget went to the army) but came up empty. A "contagion of despair" swept the country, and officials great and petty succumbed to corruption that delegitimized the regime and mocked ten years of American effort.[87]

The Johnson administration's policies killed the potential of the industrious and resourceful Vietnamese, first because they failed on their own terms to spur economic development, and second because they took the place of sound military strategies that might have saved South Vietnam from the dead hand of Communism. No wonder Lucien Pye concluded that Vietnam displayed the "utter confusion of rationale" in U.S. foreign assistance, and erstwhile historian Newt

Gingrich reflected, "We designed a war we were going to lose, and we managed to lose it the way we designed it."[88]

Does that mean the anti-war protesters were right? It depends on which ones one means. The radical activists who defined the conflict as simply a civil war, and Ho Chi Minh as a benevolent nationalist rather than the Stalinist he was, were wrong. Those who shrugged that countries like Vietnam were better off under Communism anyway were wrong. And those who thought the war symptomatic of a fascistic "Amerika" were wrong: Vietnam was a liberal war. Rather, the anti-war critics who seem now to have gotten it right were those who hearkened to Senator J. William Fulbright (D., Ark.), George Kennan, Walter Lippmann, and other old-timers who spied in Global Meliorism a prideful and dangerous departure from Americans' earlier prudence. "The underlying assumption of these programs," wrote Fulbright, "is that the presence of some American aid officials is a blessing which no developing country, except for the benighted communist ones, should be denied. I think this view of aid is a manifestation of the arrogance of power."[89]

Frank Church (D., Idaho) of the Senate Foreign Relations Committee dramatized the traditionalist critique of the Vietnam War in a 1966 photo opportunity. Standing in front of a world map on which all but America was obscured, a beaming Church held up a portrait for the camera. Senators Fulbright and Wayne Morse (D., Ore.) gazed up at it with sober, admiring expressions. Mike Mansfield, perhaps caught by surprise, seemed not to know what to think.[90] The face on the portrait was William Borah's.

★

Vietnam dealt Global Meliorism a humbling blow, but did not suffice to kill it. Polls from 1972 showed that 68 percent of Americans continued to support foreign aid. One of them was President Nixon, who appealed to "humanitarian concerns" and "the creation of a peaceful world" on the assumption that *"political stability is unlikely to occur without sound economic development."*[91] But his new Foreign Assistance Act instructed USAID to eschew "export-oriented self-sustaining growth strategies" in favor of grants that stood a chance of improving living standards across the board.[92] Unfortunately, any chance of that was immediately wrecked when the OPEC surge in oil prices bankrupted poor countries and doomed even the United States to years of "stagflation."[93] More problematical were the billions of dollars in guaranteed loans and subsidized wheat conceded to the Soviet bloc in the name of détente. The Hooverian assumption behind such largesse was that provision of food, credits, and technology would open up the Communist system and give it a stake in good relations with the West. Historians may debate how effective those policies were, but it is clear their intent was Meliorist.

Jimmy Carter ran for president in 1976 on a platform repudiating what he considered the amoral realpolitik of his predecessors and pledging to trim military spending in favor of foreign aid. But with the U.S. economy in trouble, there was not much Carter could do: even after his increases, the United States spent just one-fifth the share of its gross national product on foreign aid that it had in 1960, while double-digit inflation ate up his increments. By the late 1970s, the same social scientists who had recently promised Third World miracles were reduced to arguing whether aid should be dispensed under a triage system (leaving "basket case" countries to their fate) or whether to jettison development programs altogether in favor of meeting "basic human needs."[94] The clearest proof of foreign aid's failure was that by 1981 the interest on the debt owed by poor countries exceeded the sum of new aid they received. They were going backward.

McNamara, now director of the World Bank, threw its resources behind "a new world economic order" on the premise that the rich "have a responsibility to assist the less developed nations. It is not a sentimental question of philanthropy. It is a straightforward issue of social justice."[95] Conservative critics had a field day with that. McNamara's scorn for the charitable impulse not only removed a big reason taxpayers supported foreign aid, but implied they had a duty to subsidize incompetent or corrupt regimes. Leftist critics, in turn, denounced foreign aid as a scam to make Cold War pawns of poor countries, prop up dictators, maintain Third World *dependencia,* or undermine non-Western cultures. To them, "foreign aid was imperialism."[96]

Carter displayed more confidence when he fired the Whiggish arrow in the Meliorist quiver: promotion of democracy and human rights. He rejoiced in his famous Notre Dame speech that "we are now free of that inordinate fear of Communism which once led us to embrace any dictator who joined us in that fear."[97] In so saying, he echoed the post-Watergate Congress, which in 1976 made it "a principal goal of the foreign policy of the United States to promote the increased observance of internationally recognized human rights by all countries" and required the State Department to report on the performance of all countries.[98] Foreigners deemed this latest sermon from Washington as cloying as the Nixonian policies it was meant to replace, but officials such as Patricia Derian, Carter's coordinator for human rights and later assistant secretary of state, escalated the Meliorist rhetoric. She denounced long-standing U.S. allies as "retrogressive fascists" who ruled by "torture," expanded the annual human rights reports from a hundred pages to over a thousand, and insisted that the United States "dissociate" (withhold aid) from twenty-eight countries even as Soviet influence grew in Asia, Africa, and Central America. U.N. Ambassador Andrew Young likewise blamed American Cold War policies for fostering "an apparatus of repression" and "imperialism, neo-colonialism, capitalism, or what-have-you." All presidents before Carter were racist, he said, and the British had "practically invented racism."[99]

Carter's policies failed to advance U.S. strategic or Meliorist interests. When the Sandinistas took over Nicaragua in July 1979, Carter asked Congress to give them $75 million in aid. Daniel Ortega showed his gratitude by allying with Cuba and the USSR, imposing one-party rule, and stoking another insurgency in El Salvador. Nor did Carter's removal of support for the shah of Iran win credit with the Ayatollah Khomeini, whose followers promptly took the American embassy hostage. That, plus the Soviet invasion of Afghanistan in 1979, sparked a showdown between National Security Adviser Zbigniew ("world politics is not a kindergarten") Brzezinski and the Meliorist secretary of state Cyrus Vance.[100] When Carter finally ordered the military to try to rescue the hostages, Vance became the first secretary of state since William Jennings Bryan to resign his office on principle.

By 1980, four out of five Americans polled gave Carter a thumbs-down on foreign policy. But the ultimate repudiation of his Meliorist stance came thirteen years later. The United Nations invited him, in light of his post-presidential career as a roving peacemaker, to be honorary chairperson of its June 1993 Vienna conference on human rights. When Carter was introduced, hundreds of Third World delegates mocked and heckled him until he abandoned the podium. To them he represented the worst sort of paternalistic American meddling.[101]

Carter's embarrassments also damaged Global Meliorism, but did not suffice to kill it. After a twelve-year hiatus, during which Reagan and Bush employed Wilsonian rhetoric but otherwise practiced Containment and rollback, President Bill Clinton's foreign policy team pronounced the purest Global Meliorist agenda to date, in the belief that the end of the Cold War meant that its time had come. How ironic that Senator Fulbright, Clinton's putative mentor and fellow Arkansan, had been the one to question most sharply "the ability of the United States or any other Western nation . . . to create stability where there is chaos, the will to fight where there is defeatism, democracy where there is no tradition of it, and honest government where corruption is almost a way of life."[102]

CONCLUSION
A Delightsome Spot

W. H. Auden once said of T. S. Eliot that he was not a man but "a household: a high church archdeacon, a wise and passionate old peasant grandmother, and a young boy given to slightly malicious practical jokes, all living somehow together." Nations, too, Walt Rostow surmised, reflect "discrete, fortuitous elements of heredity and environment, interacting, effectively coming to terms with problems (or failing to do so) in a recurrent fashion, building up over time relatively stable patterns of performance."[1]

I first began to see the recurrent patterns of U.S. foreign policy in 1987 while observing our debate over Central America. The Sandinistas seemed bent on spreading their revolution with the assistance of Cuba and the Soviet Union. How should the United States respond? The Reagan administration invoked Containment to justify its support for El Salvador and the Contras, and others echoed the Monroe Doctrine by suggesting that although the United States should not meddle in Asia or Africa, it did have a duty to police its own hemisphere. Other unabashed hawks took a page from Progressive Imperialism, hoping that Reagan would send in the marines, as he had done in Grenada. Some of the critics invoked American Exceptionalism and rebuked the Reaganites for disguising a bloody conflict as a crusade for democracy. Others voiced "neo-isolationist" sentiments, denying that Nicaragua threatened U.S. security and warning of another Vietnam. Still others wanted a Wilsonian policy based on multilateral negotiations through the U.N. or Organization of American States. Global Meliorists named poverty and oppression as the real sources of instability and called for economic and social aid to Central America.

No less a student of America than Soviet Ambassador Andrei Gromyko noticed how all our diplomatic traditions continued to inform and confuse our debates. The greatest flaw in our approach to world affairs, he said, was that we had "too many doctrines and concepts proclaimed at different times" and thus were unable to formulate "a solid, coherent, and consistent policy."[2] Of course, it was the comparatively coherent Soviet strategy that soon showed itself to be bankrupt. But after the end of the Cold War most American experts agreed that the time had come for a stocktaking of the lessons learned during our fifty years of emergency and an exercise of vision in the pursuit of new priorities, perhaps even a new world order.

Many bright people offered insights into how the world had changed and how U.S. policy ought to adjust. The trouble was that they all disagreed. Francis Fukuyama wrote of the final triumph of liberal market democracy over the ideologies that had plagued the world since the French Revolution. In a philosophical sense, he said, we had reached "the end of history."[3] No, said Henry Kissinger, not only would geopolitics continue to shape the international system, but the diffusion of economic and military power meant that the post-Cold War world was reverting to multipolarity. Hence the United States must learn to play the role of *primus inter pares* in a balance-of-power system.[4] No, said Samuel Huntington, neither the triumph of liberal democracy nor a classical balance of power would define the new era, but rather deepening cleavages between cultural zones — Muslim, Confucian, Hindu, Western — thus raising the risk of a "clash of civilizations."[5] No, said Edward Luttwak, geoeconomics would shape the global competition of the twenty-first century, so the United States had better get rid of its trade and budget deficits, boost savings and research, and restore productivity.[6] No, said Paul Kennedy, Jessica Tuchman Mathews, and Robert D. Kaplan, the greatest challenges of the coming century would include proliferation of weapons of mass destruction and demographic and environmental disasters resulting in widespread famines, mass migrations, and local genocides.[7]

These plausible futures inspired an array of policy options. Some experts urged the United States to exploit this rare "unipolar moment," in which it found itself the only superpower, "to extend American-style democracy world-wide" and serve "long-held American values, especially the ideas of perfectibility and continuous progress."[8] Nor were such sentiments confined to Wilsonian liberals, as demonstrated by the conservative intellectual William Kristol's candid call for an American "benevolent hegemony" over the whole world.[9] He thus defied such realists as Kissinger, Peter Rodman, Jeane Kirkpatrick, Fareed Zakaria, and Irving Kristol, all of whom argued that the United States must remain engaged overseas, but as a "normal nation" acting on the power-political precepts of Theodore Roosevelt rather than the "pompous, self-righteous moralizing" of Woodrow Wilson.[10] Still other new bedfellows drawn from the Left and Right promoted policies of nationalism and retreat. It was high time, they said, that Americans leave Europe and Japan to look to their own defense, address their own domestic needs, and even (in the case of Richard Gephardt, H. Ross Perot, and Patrick J. Buchanan) turn protectionist. By far the most sophisticated "neo-isolationist" was Eric Nordlinger. Not only did he argue that "going abroad to insure America's security is unnecessary" today, he even challenged the notion that U.S. security had been threatened by the fascists in 1941 and the Soviet Union after 1945. Nordlinger called for a sharply reduced defense budget, no foreign bases save for Diego Garcia in the Indian Ocean (to protect the maritime shipment of oil), no entangling alliances, and a "concurrent foreign policy" of "principled activism" on behalf of human rights.[11]

★

None of these trenchant suggestions seemed to have much impact in Washington. After the collapse of the Soviet bloc, George Bush spoke vaguely of a new world order, but lacked the time and apparently the inclination to rethink traditional approaches to foreign policy. Bill Clinton's foreign policy advisers were convinced that the end of the Cold War cleared the decks for a more militant Global Meliorism. Secretary of State Warren Christopher, National Security Adviser Anthony Lake, and Clinton himself had been harsh critics of the Vietnam War, but now they seemed eager to send U.S. forces abroad on state-building missions as ambitious as Lyndon Johnson's. First, U.N. Ambassador Madeleine Albright expanded Bush's relief project in Somalia into one aiming at "the restoration of an entire country as a proud, functioning and viable member of the community of nations." She coined the term "assertive multilateralism" to describe the administration's resolve to place U.S. power and money at the disposal of the United Nations. Next, Lake pronounced the doctrine of Enlargement, under which the United States would try to expand democracy and market economies around the world by "appropriate" multilateral or unilateral means. Clinton himself used phrases that might have been lifted verbatim from Truman, Kennedy, or LBJ when he declared before the U.N. General Assembly: "For the first time in history we have the chance to expand the reach of democracy and economic progress across the whole of Europe and to the far reaches of the world."[12]

Critics assailed Clinton's policies on a variety of grounds. Far from protecting American interests, they said, the administration seemed comfortable with foreign intervention only when vital U.S. interests were *not* at stake. It placed American policy and lives in the hands of a complicated, incompetent U.N. command structure that practiced the same incrementalism in the absence of clear goals that had characterized the Vietnam War. It focused on the quixotic goal of state-building in marginal, chaotic countries like Somalia, Haiti, and Bosnia, while allowing relations with Japan, China, and Europe to drift, and taking for granted a democratic Russia. In Michael Mandelbaum's cutting words, this "Mother Teresa foreign policy" seemed designed "to turn American foreign policy into a branch of social work."[13]

Liberals, for their part, chided the administration for not doing enough. Christopher might boast that nations were impressed to "see the most powerful nation on earth standing up for persecuted peoples everywhere," but Anthony Lewis and other journalists who criticized U.S. militarism in the past rebuked Clinton for hesitating so long to bomb and occupy Bosnia. Then, after the United States did intervene there, Jimmy Carter asked why we send twenty thousand troops to Bosnia but "don't pay any attention to Liberia and Rwanda and Burundi and Sudan." Because, he answered, those countries were populated by black people, hence Clinton's policy was "racist."[14]

Foreign critics were no less strident. Leaders of Pacific Rim countries from Japan and South Korea to China, Vietnam, and Singapore denounced Enlargement as a form of imperialism and claimed superiority for "Asian values." Europeans and Asians resented U.S. demands that they dismantle their barriers to trade. Hillary Rodham Clinton's lecture on reproductive issues at the Women's Conference in Beijing offended Muslims and Catholics.[15] Brazil and other developing nations resented the American environmental agenda. U.S. restrictions on the sale of nuclear and missile technology in the name of non-proliferation angered China, India, Iran, Pakistan, and other nations jealous of their right of self-defense. To all it seemed that a U.S. administration that extolled multiculturalism and diversity at home had no tolerance for them where other countries were concerned.

Neither Bush nor Clinton presided over a real reassessment of the old U.S. traditions. Instead, the Clintonites seized on our two most problematical ones — Wilsonianism and Global Meliorism — and made them the lodestones for policy in the post–Cold War era. Were they wrong to look to our past for models to follow today? Or were they right to look to the past, but mistook the folly they found there for wisdom? One last historical exercise — a sort of sketch for a national autobiography — may help us to answer those questions.

*

In the beginning, the American enterprise was born of two eighteenth-century impulses: Enlightenment rationalism, with its universal notions of natural law and human rights doctrine, and a Christian anthropology that stressed the flawed and unchangeable nature of man. The first impulse infused Americans with sublime aspiration, but also tempted them to imagine themselves a kind of gnostic elite possessed of a universal method for ordering human affairs. The framers of the Constitution were keenly aware of that utopian temptation, and so they established checks and balances to prevent any one faction from hijacking the federal government, and they shunned all "revolutionary" foreign policies.

The second, religious impulse infused Americans with humility and caution, but also tempted them to imagine themselves a spiritual elite possessed of a sort of monopoly of truth and called by Providence to right all wrongs. The framers were aware of that danger, too, so they drafted the Bill of Rights and prohibited established religion. Happily, the two impulses tended to check each other, allowing the United States to emerge as a secular and remarkably free republic whose cohesion and strength nonetheless derived in large part from an underlying social consensus that honored biblical mores.

Our first four foreign policy traditions — the Old Testament of American diplomacy — reflected that balance of reason and faith. Liberty at home, Unilateralism, the American System, and territorial and commercial Expansion not only reinforced one another but served the interests of an agricultural nation splendidly and at minimum risk. The authors of those traditions were not "isolationists," but neither did they seek to impose their values beyond the lands and waters staked out for them by Nature — or Nature's God. Moreover, none of them perceived any mortal conflict between morality and the national interest. Liberty, "no entangling alliances," and the Monroe Doctrine were moral because they were realistic expressions of the Promised Land's place in the world, and were realistic because they forbade the sort of self-righteous adventurism that might otherwise corrupt the Republic's moral foundation.

Of course, the mechanism that meshed Enlightenment reason and Christian faith was never perfectly efficient. To cite the most obvious examples, slavery and established churches in some of the states scandalized a nation founded on universal rights, and various religious and secular activists joined forces to correct these abuses over time. But as the nineteenth century wore on, Americans came gradually to reinterpret their original impulses in ways that eroded the ability of each to act as a check on the other. First, the assault on revealed religion propelled by "higher criticism" of the Bible, the growing prestige of science, and the power and promise of industrial technology encouraged secular thinkers to act as if their doctrine of progress constituted a veritable religion, complete with a teleology promising that through America the world itself would approach perfection. Walt Whitman only anticipated the future (which is what good poets do) when he wrote:[16]

> One thought ever at the fore —
> That in the Divine Ship, the World, breasting Time and Space,
> All peoples of the globe together sail, sail the same voyage,
> Are bound to the same destination.

As the twentieth century dawned and a newly urban, industrial America awoke to its power among nations, it became easier prey than before to apostles of progress who itched to reform the world. First McKinley and Theodore Roosevelt, then Wilson and FDR persuaded Americans to accept the growth of a central government able to mobilize power for the export of the nation's ideals.

Needless to say, that obliged Americans to set aside their Old Testament of foreign affairs. What became of the humble and cautious impulse that had formerly warned them that they too were flawed, that the willful accumulation of power corrupts, that one cannot force men to be free? The answer (it seems clear enough now) is that the twig of American Christianity was bent from the start, as measured by the yardstick of orthodoxy ("right reason"). The tendency of Protestant divines at the time of the Revolution to identify the New Israel with the United States rather than with the Church Universal was an appalling conceit, however much it encouraged a young nation risking its all for freedom. Then millenarianism, not only in marginal sects but in the preachments of mainstream denominations by the 1830s and

'40s, testified to the spread of a heresy: the presumption that man can prepare a place for the messiah (instead of the other way around) and so create heaven on earth. To be sure, their intolerance for injustice moved devout men and women to fight against slavery and promote social reform. But insofar as the churches demanded that government throw its power behind their causes, or subsumed their causes in those of the state, they could no longer function as a brake on the secular prophets of progress. William Appleman Williams thought this tendency could be traced all the way back to the Puritans. They had, he wrote, "a kink in their theology," hence

> . . . when they went wrong, they went very, very wrong. Devoted to the ideal of a corporate community guided by a strong moral sense, they developed a great talent for misinterpreting any opposition. From the outside, for example, they were prone to view the Indians as agents of the Devil. . . . The propensity to place Evil outside their system not only distorted the Puritans' own doctrine, it inclined them toward a solution which involved the extension of their own system over others.[17]

Some radical critics have made this fear and disdain for the Other the drivewheel of all American history. That is too pat, since our religious and secular perfectionists alike have been even more eager to reform their own countrymen than Indians or foreigners. But if the Puritans tended to judge the world according to their own notion of the perfect society, how much *more* likely were Americans to do so as rigorous Calvinism gave way to Unitarianism, Episcopal latitudinarianism, Methodism, and the Social Gospel, reinforced in the twentieth century by Reform Judaism, Dorothy Day's Catholic Worker movement, and liberation theology — all of which emphasized earthly good works or downplayed or denied original sin? In other words, the sort of humility that stayed the hand of John Quincy Adams and made Lincoln sweat over every assertion of presidential power ceased to restrain American statecraft, to the point that, by the twentieth century, politics came increasingly to function as a religion, and religion degenerated into politics. So while America the Promised Land had held that to try to change the world was stupid (and immoral), America the Crusader State held that to *refrain* from trying to change the world was immoral (and stupid).

But wait. Surely there was anything but a "moral consensus" in the years of this metamorphosis. Teddy Roosevelt and Woodrow Wilson, for instance, despised each other and advocated sharply differing foreign policies. Yes, they did, but they had far more in common with each other than either had with Grover Cleveland. And despite their differences, they both believed that their policies were moral and pragmatic responses to the world they knew in their times.

Fulbright sensed this great shift when he wrote, "The inconstancy of American foreign policy is not an accident but an expression of two distinct sides of the American character. Both are characterized by a kind of moralism, but one is the morality of decent instincts tempered by the knowledge of human imperfection and the other is the morality of absolute self-assurance fired by the crusading spirit."[18] Beginning in 1898, the first sort of moralism began to give way to the second, whereupon the prophets of the Crusader State canonized a new foreign policy testament. The role of John the Baptist was played by the Progressive Imperialists, who heralded the imminent gospel. Wilson played the savior and, as his hagiographers put it, was promptly crucified. The architects of Containment and Meliorism then wrote the epistles that taught Americans how to live out their new faith. And they, too, believed that their policies were moral and pragmatic responses to the world they knew in their times.

Now, Christians cannot set aside the real Old Testament for the simple reason that their New Testament is a derivative and fulfillment of the Old. To put it another way, if Judaism is false, then Christianity is, too. In like fashion, twentieth-century Americans have not forgotten their Old Testament of foreign relations. The Senate reservationists appealed to its precepts in 1919, as did the Unilateralists of the 1930s, the few holdouts against the Cold War, and the "neo-isolationists" of the post–Cold War era. The continued salience of our old foreign policy covenant is proven above all by the fact that believers in the new dispensation *also* pay homage to our Old Testament, on the grounds that it was valid at the time it was promulgated and was the source of such principles as liberty, self-determination, and the Open Door, which they believe twentieth-century America is called to share with the world.[19] And they are right to pay homage, for those first four traditions *were* valid for their time and *were* the source of our present ideals — except in one signal case. The Founding Fathers flatly denied that the United States ought to be in the business of changing the world, lest it only change itself — for the worse. Do I mean to say that the United States has done no good in the twentieth century? On the contrary, I believe that our fifty years' fight against fascism and

Communism may prove to have been our finest hour. But the Crusader State has also made many mistakes and done much that is bad and ugly, not least to itself.

Reinhold Niebuhr dissected the dilemmas of political moralism when he wrote that man can achieve a "progressively higher justice and more stable peace" only if he "does *not* attempt the impossible." What is more, governments had no moral right to ask their citizens to sacrifice for the interests of others. And yet, he concluded, "We cannot build our individual ladders to heaven and leave the total human enterprise unredeemed of its excesses and corruptions." Hence the idea that "the collective life of mankind can achieve perfect justice" is a "valuable illusion," albeit one that "encourages terrible fanaticisms. It must therefore be brought under the control of reason. One can only hope that reason will not destroy it before its work is done."[20]

Niebuhr was the favorite theologian of American statesmen of the 1930s and '40s, who had somehow to justify the New Deal and United Nations in terms of *realism,* and the atomic bomb and Containment in terms of *idealism.* For whatever the message they received from *vox Dei,* they had to answer, as Niebuhr implied, to *vox populi.* So the basic question in this realism-versus-idealism debate is this: what, in the aggregate, do Americans want? Do they really insist that their foreign policy reflect some "valuable illusion" perhaps even contrary to their national interest? Or do they still adhere to their Old Testament precept that a given policy is moral *because* it is in the national interest? I submit that the latter is true. If that doesn't sound right, turn the proposition around and ask what voters would say to a president who meant to pursue policies serving alien interests because U.S. interests were, in his view, immoral. That president would be lucky to serve out one term.

Jonathan Clarke, an English diplomat, sensed the falsity of the realist-versus-idealist dichotomy when he said the meaningful question was "Where do morality and practicality meet?"[21] So did Owen Harries, who observed, "Critics of realism claim that it is alien and inappropriate to the American tradition and temperament. It is neither."[22] Even Robert D. Kaplan, the poignant chronicler of Third World misery, argued that since the United States cannot save the whole world, it must intervene only where "moral, economic, and strategic interests intersect."[23] In fact, all American leaders, of whatever era, have claimed that their policies were both realistic and moral. And that means our real task is not to choose between the Old Testament and the New, or between TR and Wilson, but rather to examine all our past *identifications* of morality and self-interest, as embodied in our eight traditions, according to their principles, assumptions, and formulations in policy. Then we may discard what seems to us foolish or passé, reaffirm what is wise, and strive to make the philosophy and rhetoric of our foreign policy as lean and mean as they once were. I daresay, at the risk of raising the dead, that John Quincy Adams would approve.

★

Let us therefore command our eight traditions to do an about-face and parade back before us in reverse order.

On what principle is *Global Meliorism* based? It rests on the conviction that most of the phenomena that threaten us in this century — aggressor powers, "crazy" regimes, revolution, terrorism, and ethnic, racial, and religious hatred — are in great part the products of oppression and poverty. From that principle it follows that a wise foreign policy will attack the causes rather than symptoms of discord by promoting democracy, defending human rights, and fostering economic growth. Meliorism assumes that the United States alone possesses the power, prestige, technology, wealth, and altruism needed to reform whole nations. It assumes that the U.S. government, having tamed its frontier and helped its people achieve unprecedented wealth and freedom, having democratized Germany and Japan and rebuilt Europe, having led the free world to victory over fascism and Communism, *knows how* to deploy its assets to lift up the poor and oppressed. Finally, it assumes that Americans want their government to dedicate their lives, fortunes, and sacred honor to that purpose.

None of these postulates is proven; in fact, every one may be false. The causal connection between poverty and oppression on the one hand, and war and revolution on the other, seems plausible, but obviously not all poor or authoritarian countries threaten their neighbors, any more than all poor people become criminals. In addition, labels like "poor" and "oppressed," "rich" and "free" are so relative as to be practically meaningless. So is the label "democracy." If it just means elections, majority rule, or government by consent of the governed, there is nothing inherently decent about it. Dictators often command overwhelming support. Democracies can trample on human rights and the rule of law. Nor can we assume that all nations prefer democracy, however defined, or are moving toward the same destination.

Indeed, to diagnose and prescribe remedies for all other people on earth is nothing less than to mirror the Bolsheviks, who claimed to believe that scientific law was moving the world toward Communism, but acted as though history needed their "help."

Americans may well believe that their political and economic principles are universally valid. But to insist that everyone else in the world agree is to embrace the same solipsism that Wilson did when he said that his own depth of belief convinced him that he spoke for the American people. As a result, Global Meliorism can be woefully counterproductive. Far from persuading Chinese, Singaporeans, Iraqis, Libyans, or Russians to be "like us," our sermons about human rights, fair trade, the environment, and sexual and family issues only invite foreigners to remark on the poverty, crime, drugs, pornography, collapse of the family, inequality, and travesties of justice that characterize American society.

To assert that the U.S. government knows how to transplant democracy and kick-start economic development abroad is an even wilder leap of logic. Our half-century of experience with foreign aid has been almost a total loss, and the reason is not hard to find. It resides in the contradiction inherent in programs whose purpose is to demonstrate the superiority of the free market model but whose methods are entirely statist. This was true in the 1950s and 1960s, when USAID funneled American tax dollars through foreign government ministries, thereby subsidizing socialism at best and corruption at worst. It was true in the 1970s, when loans guaranteed by the U.S. Treasury subsidized Brezhnev's empire. It is even the case today, as we attempt to teach ex-Soviet peoples how to be good capitalists through the medium of government grants administered by government agencies for the benefit of our own and foreign bureaucracies.

What American of my generation never marveled, in some quiet moment in youth, at how phenomenally lucky he or she was to be born in twentieth-century America instead of in India or medieval Europe or a neolithic cave? And what American so blessed has never felt a twinge of guilt over the fact that "people are starving in China"? No wonder softhearted and hardheaded liberals alike leaped at the suggestion that bread was a mightier weapon than guns, and that American technology and development theory could trump the false doctrine of Communism. Yet however well meant, Global Meliorism is the least effective and in some ways the most arrogant of all our diplomatic traditions. Its great triumphs — the Marshall Plan and occupations of Germany and Japan — were arguably dubious and anyway no model for other parts of the world. Its great failures — Vietnam, our own inner cities — are a scandal. As for foreign aid, a recent and exhaustive study by the London School of Economics found that in ninety-two developing nations "no relationship exists between the levels of aid and rates of growth in recipient countries." Instead, foreign aid has tended to discourage the lowering of tax rates and other barriers to investment and growth in the target countries while "increasing the size of recipient governments and lining the pockets of elites."[24]

There is an alternative approach to foreign development derived from our own economic development (the most successful in history), our earlier foreign policy traditions, and our Enlightened and religious impulses alike. The alternative says that if Americans are moved to share their abundance with less fortunate peoples, let them do so through private charities and development funds like the estimable Soros Foundation. If stricken nations in Asia, Africa, or the ex-Communist world need capital, let their governments respect private property, establish the rule of law, enforce contracts and commercial conventions, and adjust tax rates so as to attract private investors. The principle on which this is based is just common sense: if other nations want our style of democracy and/or high rates of economic growth, they know what steps to take to achieve them. If they do not want to take those steps, the United States cannot force them or take those steps for them. It can only throw away American money and lives, reward the behavior it hopes to discourage, and receive in return the contempt that "charity cases" habitually show their benefactors.

The United States ought simply to close its Meliorist shop and abolish all its do-gooder agencies. If the president and Congress agree that transfers of money are needed to grease the skids for diplomacy (that is, to bribe foreign leaders) or perform a service of interest to the United States (for example, dismantle Soviet warheads), let the State or Defense Department dispense such funds from its own budget. Otherwise, the best way to promote our institutions and values abroad is to strengthen them at home. For other peoples, of whatever culture, will always be far more interested in what Americans are than in what they do — or, what is worse, promise to do but do not.

Containment, by contrast, was the most successful of our recent traditions. The principle on which it was based is that American prosperity and security require that no hegemonic behemoth dominate Europe or East Asia. Such an empire would force Americans to arm to the teeth, block American access to raw materials, markets, and sea lanes in much of the world, and, if it acquired sufficient naval and aerospace power, threaten America itself. Historians may argue about whether the Soviet Union posed such a threat or whether the Truman administration knowingly magnified the danger. But having just fought a two-ocean war to prevent a fascist hegemony, Americans after 1945 were in no mood to trust in Stalin's good will.

The Cold War had a hard ideological edge, but its origins can be traced back to the shifts in the distribution of power that occurred well before Lenin and Wilson made their appearances. Put simply, the inevitable diffusion of industrial technology from Britain to the European continent, America, and then Japan and Russia destroyed the nineteenth-century balance of power. Americans were slow to appreciate the dangers this posed, and Wilson only clouded their judgment by casting U.S. entry in World War I as a moral rather than a geopolitical act and by trying to replace rather than restore the balance of power. In the event, the failure of Wilsonianism after both world wars and the rise of another totalitarian empire with an apparently hearty appetite convinced Truman's people (who in turn convinced almost all Americans) that it was better to defend the balance of power *before* world wars broke out. That our cause was moral went without saying: one needed only compare life in France or Canada with that in East Germany or North Korea. That Containment was practical, despite its tensions and risks, was proven by the correctness of its architects' judgment that so long as the West remained strong and united, the Soviet empire would sooner or later collapse under its own contradictions.

But is Containment still relevant now that the Cold War is over? Why not? The United States still has a vital interest in preventing hegemonies in Europe and East Asia, which is why the dissolution of NATO or the U.S.-Japanese alliance would be shortsighted in the extreme. To be sure, the continuation of those engagements beyond the emergency for which they were made would appear to violate George Washington's Great Rule. I would answer that in Washington's day Britain and France were our most dangerous rivals. Today they are our best friends. In Washington's day the European powers could be trusted to maintain their own balance. Today U.S. power is a vital factor in the European and East Asian equations. In Washington's day the United States was inevitably the junior partner in any alliance. Today it is the senior partner in any combination it enters, and thus need not relinquish its freedom to act — or not to act — unilaterally and in the national interest. In effect, our core alliances today should be thought of less as violations of Unilateralism than as extensions of the American System to the opposite shores of the two American oceans.

Some say that NATO has lost its *raison d'être* and must go "out of area or out of business." But our European allies had trouble enough pulling together even while the Cold War was on; asking them to coordinate their policies toward all manner of non-European crises would place excessive stress on the alliance. Some ask why Americans continue to pay for Europe's defense. That is a sensible query. However dependent NATO remains on American sea power, airlift capacity, space systems, and certain high-tech weaponry, there is no reason why a division of U.S. ground troops occupies Bosnia while the Germans, for instance, stay home. But whatever adjustments need to be made in our alliances, we would be as foolish to throw them away as we were to throw away our magnificent Saturn/Apollo technology the moment we came home from the moon. Finally, Containment and deterrence remain our only tested techniques for blunting threats mounted by regional foes such as Iraq or Iran, especially once they acquire missiles and nuclear weapons.

That said, it cannot be denied that our Cold War experience was painfully mixed. Maintaining credible deterrence on the European and nuclear fronts was expensive and dangerous duty, while Containment in Asia landed us in two tortuous limited wars, one of which proved to be not at all vital to our security. What is more, the decision to resist Soviet, Maoist, and Castroist drives for influence in the Third World led us to attempt hothouse revolutions in some countries and consort with "friendly tyrants" in others. That is why we should not even whisper the word "Containment" with respect to China, for instance, lest we slip half aware into another protracted cold war. Instead, we should do three things by way of adjusting to China's potential. The first is to promote a regional security framework in hopes that Beijing will participate. The second is to identify how far and precisely where Chinese power would have to extend before our interests were truly threatened. The third, in case the first fails and the second occurs, is to maintain the alliances and military presence that we and the locals will need in case we must actively balance Chinese power. Nor dare we ever forget that the purpose of Containment is not to contest the rise of new powers, much less to carve out an empire of our own, but only to buttress the Eurasian balance that served us so well from 1776 to 1917.

That modest definition of Containment suggests why *Wilsonianism* has by contrast been an operational boondoggle. The principle on which it is based is that conflict is not inevitable in human affairs, but is a preventable byproduct of greed, hubris, militarism, suppression of self-determination, secret diplomacy, and the idolatrous worship of the balance of power. Wilson imagined a world purged of such sins and born again as a democratic league practicing disarmament, free trade, arbitration, and collective security through a "one for all and all for one" committee of the whole.

How seriously ought we to take Wilson's Fourteen Points today? Surely free trade and freedom of the seas are vital interests, and ones the United States ought to promote and, in the latter case, defend with grit because no other navy is up to the job. As for the others of Wilson's points, his new diplomacy based on "open covenants" did not survive even the first week of his own peace conference; the disarmament he preached was and is the quickest way for the United States to lose all its allies and invite the sort of mischief Wilson wanted to stop; democracy is a slippery concept unless it means "just like us"; and Wilson's principle of self-determination (as his own Secretary of State Lansing predicted) is a Pandora's box that spews forth new horrors to this day. As for Wilson's League of Nations, it certainly did require that member states abridge their sovereignty, and would have been a utopian project even if the Great Powers had not soon divided into liberal, fascist, and Communist blocs.

Today, as Kissinger observes, the dream of a Wilsonian order has even less chance of success, since the major powers will soon include such non-Western countries as Russia, China, India, Japan, Indonesia, Iran, and Nigeria, none of which has any historical affinity for Western liberal principles. Indeed, Wilsonianism increasingly appears in historical perspective to have been the product of one narrow and specific strain of turn-of-the-century, Anglo-American, Progressive, Protestant thought. Its broad appeal testifies to the power of its otherworldly vision, but in practical politics it has been at best an irrelevance, and at worst a distraction. After all, when, in regard to some crisis, the Great Powers and relevant local powers are in agreement, or at least don't dissent, the elaborate charades of the Security Council and General Assembly are unnecessary. When those powers do not agree, the U.N. is impotent. Nor does the United States need a U.N. stamp of approval on its actions. For either Americans still cherish their own standards of right and wrong, in which case they need only consult them, or they believe all morals are relative, in which case who cares what anyone thinks?

It is true that some U.N. agencies help to regulate international regimes for the oceans and seabed, outer space, and telecommunications, and do good works in fields like health. But do they perform those tasks more efficiently for being under the U.N. umbrella? The question is worth asking, for if U.S. foreign aid programs are often wasteful, top-heavy with management, stymied by bureaucratic rivalry, and skewed by domestic and foreign political agendas, how much more likely are U.N. programs to be?

The baby-boom generation — my generation — was spawned during Wilsonianism's post–World War II heyday, taught in school to revere the United Nations and blame its dysfunction on *nyet*-saying Russians, and invited to conclude that the only alternative to world peace was eventual nuclear holocaust. No wonder we made anthems of plaintive pop hymns such as "Blowin' in the Wind," "Imagine," and "We Are the World." In retrospect, that "Give Peace a Chance" response to the ubiquitous conflict in human affairs seems to have been less a protest against the American Crusader State than an expression of the same childlike innocence that inspired our Wilsonian crusades in this century. But whether hawks or doves, adults are meant to put away childish things.

Progressive Imperialism is a more complicated affair, because it arose on the cusp between our Old and New Testament eras. To the extent that turn-of-the-century imperialists justified their impositions abroad with rhetoric about an American mission, they anticipated the excesses of Wilsonianism and Global Meliorism. For all the good Americans did in their colonies in such matters as hygiene and epidemiology, their determination to expel the wicked Spaniards and to Americanize the politics, society, and even religion of their wards was an egregious violation of the Promised Land's "Thou shalt not" regarding ideological crusades. Moreover, the U.S. colonial record is a disgrace. Are the Philippines a model democracy, or model for anything, after a century of American influence? Is Cuba, Panama, Nicaragua, or Haiti? Puerto Rico remains a placid island, but it was that even under the Spaniards, and its subsidized economy is hardly a showplace for American social engineering.

The power-political principle of U.S. imperialism was sounder. By

1900, the American System was more endangered than at any time since the War of 1812. European imperialism was peaking, and British, Russian, French, Japanese, and soon German high-seas fleets steamed in uncomfortable proximity to waters Americans considered their own. Thus, if its hemisphere and trade were to remain secure in the coming technological century, the United States must assert more vigorously its spheres of influence in the Caribbean and Pacific, build a great fleet of its own with the requisite bases and coaling stations, guard the approaches to the Panama isthmus, and ensure that unstable local politics gave outside powers no pretext to meddle. What they did was not pretty, but McKinley, Roosevelt, and Taft had reason to wave the "big stick." And to judge by Clinton's defense of his occupation of Haiti and the Mexican bailout, the Roosevelt Corollary is valid today. Americans still have a keen interest in policing their neighborhood, not least because the most palpable challenges to our borders and laws now emanate *from our own hemisphere*. Irving Kristol has called Mexico our most important foreign problem, and one need only imagine illegal immigration and drug smuggling as attacks on our borders to get what he is driving at.[25]

Americans also have as much interest as ever in maintaining naval and air forces second to none and the foreign bases they need, for what we must never do is allow our ability to project power in defense of American lives, property, and commercial rights to shrink to the point where we are no longer feared and respected. The so-called isolationists of the nineteenth century never did, as proven by the fact that between 1801 (when Jefferson first chased the Barbary pirates) and 1904 (when TR said to Morocco, "We want either Perdicaris alive or Raisuli dead"), the United States dispatched its navy and marines to Asia, Africa, the Mediterranean, and Latin America no fewer than 110 times, to prevent or retaliate for molestation of American citizens and property.[26]

Of course, these days we do not go around annexing whatever islands look strategic. That sort of imperialism is taboo, and no vacant or unclaimed lands remain on the earth save for Antarctica and the odd ort like Wrangel Island north of Siberia. Therefore, since the continental and maritime growth the United States once practiced has no place in the twenty-first century, it would seem that our tradition of *Expansionism* is defunct. Not proven. One can imagine, for instance, that Puerto Rico will someday demand the full rights to which U.S. citizens are entitled and become the fifty-first state, or that several

Canadian provinces may, in the midst of a national crackup, seek to associate with the States. But even if the United States does not expand territorially (and admittedly the political and legal hurdles to new states would be daunting), the *principle* behind its Expansionism remains valid. It warns that unless opportunities continue to grow for a continually growing population, U.S. politics will degenerate into "beggar thy neighbor" battles over dividing the pie. In the nineteenth century that meant new farmlands had to be found. In the early twentieth century that meant markets had to be found, especially at home but also abroad, for our manufactures. After 1945 that meant a prosperous, open world economy had to rise on the wreckage of depression and war. In the post-industrial twenty-first century we cannot be certain what that will mean: perhaps "vertical expansion" made possible by cheaper, safe access to outer space; or "invisible expansion" made possible by more intensive exploitation of the electromagnetic spectrum, computer-driven fiber-optic communications networks, and the geosynchronous orbits plied by communications satellites; or even "submarine expansion" made possible by efficient techniques to mine and farm the seabed.

A more conventional form of economic expansion is the cultivation of new or more secure markets abroad. That is why the North American Free Trade Agreement (NAFTA), far from being unpatriotic, as its critics claim, is one of the greatest flights of the American eagle in this century. In the 1850s William Henry Seward dreamed of a single booming marketplace from the Arctic to Tierra del Fuego. That destiny was not manifest in his time, but today is within our reach.

So the Clinton administration was right to make expansion of economic opportunity a major goal of its foreign policy. It erred, however, in placing too much faith in the theory that geoeconomics had all but replaced geopolitics. On the contrary, all economic activity — from a corner store in the Bronx to a multinational enterprise based in Hong Kong — depends on a reasonably predictable security environment. We may hope to see economics dominate international affairs in more and more parts of the world, but the only way to realize and maintain that happy condition is through military prowess and shrewd diplomacy. What good would it do to jawbone Beijing into awarding U.S. firms a trillion dollars in contracts if East Asia was about to descend into war?

We must not forget, however, that the richest opportunities for Americans have always been in the United States itself. So even as we pursue foreign markets, we must never imagine that freedom to invest and sell abroad can make up for an abridgment of that freedom at home. Politicians can (and will) bicker forever over the tradeoffs, costs, and modalities of economic, fiscal, and social policy, but what they must bicker *about* is how best to release Americans' ingenuity, ambition, and eagerness to work. Those human qualities were what made our earlier forms of expansion possible and necessary in the first place.

NAFTA brings to mind *the American System,* another tradition that may at first glance seem dead and defiled. That is so only because the sorts of challenges the Monroe Doctrine was meant to deflect do not exist at present and may not again for a long while (knock on wood). But let a hostile China court friends and build bases in Central America, or a rearmed Japan cut loose from its U.S. alliance and meddle in South America, or a hostile Muslim state sponsor terrorism in the Americas, and speeches like Olney's "twenty inch gun" will be on the president's desk in a heartbeat. Suffice to say that the only major failure of the United States to enforce the Monroe Doctrine — Kennedy's 1962 promise never to molest even a pro-Soviet Cuba — caused more than three decades of grief. Indeed, the strongest retort the Reaganites had to the charge that they might make Nicaragua "another Vietnam" was that a failure to act there would make it "another Cuba."

The point is that the American System as John Quincy Adams conceived it was not about hemispheric politics at all. It was about Great Power politics as they ought *not* to apply to our hemisphere. And so long as the United States is itself a Great Power, the Monroe Doctrine (by whatever sanitized name it may go by) will rest lightly in the American holster against the day of a showdown.

Unilateralism has been under a heavy barrage because internationalists insist on branding anyone who sees some virtue in it as "isolationist." [27] Numerous commentators have nonetheless suggested that the United States pare back its transoceanic commitments in the wake of the Soviet collapse. Their recommendations may or may not be prudent, but they deserve to be debated on their merits and according to Washington's and Jefferson's unilateralist principle: that entangling alliances would impinge on U.S. sovereignty, harm its interests, or restrict its freedom of action. Since they both endorsed temporary alliances under certain conditions, the principle hangs on their word "entangling." Is NATO today an entangling alliance in that it restricts American sovereignty, or does it in fact help to secure it? Is the

U.S.-Japanese alliance entangling in that it harms our national interest, or does it in fact serve it? Does our partnership with Israel restrict our freedom of action, or are the president and Congress still free to choose when and how to act in the Middle East? If the answers to these questions are gloomy, as some unilateralists claim, then those associations should be abolished. If, on the other hand, those partnerships help to secure U.S. interests without compromising the constitutional powers of the Executive or Congress, then how do they violate Washington's rule?

Some American overseas commitments may even be justified by an appeal to the principle of national sovereignty. Immanuel Kant, ruminating on the prospects for perpetual peace (a favorite Enlightenment pastime), theorized that the only possible new world order would consist of a growing web of specific treaties to which likeminded nations adhered because their sovereignty would be more secure, their power enhanced, and their interests better served inside the cooperative system than outside it. Is that true of NAFTA, or NATO, or the U.N. and its various agencies, or the World Bank, or the World Trade Organization? If so, these engagements ought not to be cast away lightly. If not, the United States should cease underwriting them with taxpayers' dollars.

Whatever decisions we make about when to act unilaterally or multilaterally, we must never conceive of international organization as a substitute for national strength. Teddy Roosevelt and Senator Lodge were quite right about this. If the United States remains strong, it will attract allies and clients as a light attracts moths, whether or not some multilateral body is involved. If the United States becomes feeble, no amount of begging, bribing, or appeals to international norms will induce others to honor our interests or stand by us in danger.

Which brings us to the original tradition that all subsequent ones purported to serve: *Liberty at home.* We have learned that the leaders in our Old Testament era did not interpret Exceptionalism to mean that U.S. diplomacy ought to be pacifist, rigidly scrupulous, or devoted to the export of domestic ideals. Rather, they saw foreign policy as an instrument for the preservation and expansion of American freedom, and warned that crusades would belie our ideals, violate our true interests, and sully our freedom. At the same time, some of them fretted that a federal establishment mighty enough to defend America's interests against great foreign powers would *ipso facto* threaten the liberty of American citizens and states.

Those first dissenters, the Anti-Federalists, were right to worry. The price Americans have paid in life, liberty, and property for their career as a world power, however necessary and righteous their commitments may have been, includes levels of taxation shocking by turn-of-the-century standards, a far larger and more intrusive central government, a semi-militarized economy, military conscription, and domestic surveillance in the name of national security. Our need to prove the superiority of liberalism over Communism, especially to the peoples of the Third World, also helped to justify the expansion of a welfare state whose costs soon dwarfed even those of the "warfare" state. Our burdensome commitments abroad deprived our civilian economy of talent and capital, hastening our relative economic decline. And the American people — rich, poor, and middle class — behaved as people always do during protracted war: they slipped the moorings of traditional morality. So during the same decades that Americans sacrificed abroad as no people in history had done, they staged a debauch at home, as measured by their lust for public entitlements, corruption in government and business, drugs and crime, deterioration of education, loss of respect for all authority, sexual license, and the decline of the nuclear family.

No wonder that Americans, far from feeling puffed up by the collapse of the Soviet Union, looked instead at themselves and spoke of "the end of the American dream." That is why Confucians and Muslims laugh at the notion that our "decadent" country should be a model for them. That is why the beginning of wisdom is to remember that American Exceptionalism as originally conceived was to be a measure of all that we *are*, not what we *do* far away.

*

> On a delightsome spot,
> From other nations free,
> Lord thou hast fixed our lot.
> We owe, we owe, to thee
> The independence of our land.
> How happy does our nation stand.[28]

That was one of the most popular American hymns at the start of the nineteenth century. It might also serve as a fitting coda for the twentieth century. Never, perhaps, has the United States been more secure than it is today. But that only means that never before have

Americans been in more danger of creeping complacency. Are we secure because God takes care of the U.S.A.? Perhaps — but if we think that, we may decide not to take care of ourselves. Is it because of our virtuous struggles abroad in this century? Perhaps — but if we think that, we may ignore all that is not virtuous inside our country, displaying the pride that goeth before a fall. Is it because we are so mighty that no one dares cross us? Perhaps — but if we think that, we all but invite challenge, and risk forgetting that the United States is neither the largest nor most populous, nor most homogeneous, nor most disciplined of nations; that our economy is smaller than Europe's; and that our technology is only a few years ahead of some of our rivals. Instead, we must think that we are secure today because Americans have always been a determined, feisty, jealous, and fiercely loyal people whenever our independence and freedom were challenged: Don't tread on me! Absent that will, our material might would have been untapped or wasted. In other words, to the extent that we have been good citizens of the globe, it is because we have been good Americans.

At the Congress of Prague, staged in 1996 by the New Atlantic Initiative, former prime minister Margaret Thatcher told the delegates that if we had waited for the European Community, the United Nations, or the World Bank to drive the Soviet empire down, we would be waiting still. What made our Cold War victory possible, she said, was the North Atlantic alliance, organized to defend its members and their common Western values, including a "commitment to human rights, the rule of law, representative democracy, limited government, private property and tolerance." The strength of that alliance lay not in the fact that it transcended national sovereignty, but that it was based on mutual respect for the "old national identities."[29]

What Thatcher understood is that the only workable internationalism is one rooted in the same "healthy nationalism" postulated by Kant, defined and nurtured in America by Washington, Jefferson, and the Adamses, and espoused (in just those terms) by Theodore Roosevelt and Henry Cabot Lodge. For no international bureaucracy, much less a single nation, however powerful and idealistic, can substitute itself for the healthy nationalism of an alien people. Almost everyone agrees, for instance, that Saddam Hussein is bad for his country. But can Americans be better Iraqis than Iraqis themselves, or presume to tell the Chinese how to be better Chinese? If we try, we can only be poorer Americans.

Some may resent advice from Thatcher, given that so many of our political principles have already been imported from Britain: Liberty, Unilateralism, dependence on a European balance of power, commercial and territorial Expansion, the Monroe Doctrine, the Anglo-Saxon mission, the Protestant evangelical mission, Abolitionism, Navalism, Jingoism, the White Man's Burden, the Open Door, the League of Nations, even the Cold War (via Churchill's Iron Curtain speech) and Thatcher's own Cold War stance, followed by her embrace of Gorbachev. As Christopher Hitchens wryly observed, whenever the United States has been on the verge of a new diplomatic departure, "there has been a deceptively languid English adviser at the elbow, urging *yes* in tones that neither hector nor beseech but are always somehow beguiling."[30] But that is only to say that Britain and the United States have shared many cultural and political traits. So when Thatcher says do not junk NATO, and Jonathan Clarke whispers that "the age of the crusader has passed away," it behooves us to pay attention.[31]

If this book has been the least bit persuasive, however, readers will know that we need not defer to foreigners, nor suppress a crusading instinct — which we did not even have until the eve of this century — nor paralyze ourselves with false debates over morality and realism. We need only follow Kennan's commonsense policy founded, as it is,

> on recognition of the national interest, reasonably conceived, as the legitimate motivation for a large portion of the nation's behavior, and prepared to pursue that interest without either moral pretension or apology. It would be a policy that would seek the possibilities for service to morality primarily in our own behavior, not in our judgment of others. It would restrict our undertakings to the limits established by our own traditions and resources. It would see virtue in our minding our own business wherever there is not some overwhelming reason for minding the business of others.[32]

Kennan believed that the tenets of John Quincy Adams, "albeit with certain adjustments to meet our present circumstances and commitments," are "entirely suitable and indeed greatly needed as a guide for American policy in the coming period."[33] I leave it to people more expert than I to work out the details of those certain adjustments. For my part, this history leads me to conclude with a plea that as we approach the millennium, we lay aside millenarianism once and for

all. For that, I now see, is not a righteous and constructive mood, but
a petulant, ungrateful, and often destructive one. How much healthier
it is just to "do justice and walk humbly with your God," remember
that charity begins at home, husband the rare liberty and fragile unity
our ancestors won, give thanks that our recent enemies were put to
confusion, and hope that two centuries hence our descendants will be
as privileged as we to live on such "a delightsome spot."

NOTES

BIBLIOGRAPHY

INDEX

Notes

INTRODUCTION

1. See Kenneth C. Davis, "Ethnic Cleansing Didn't Start in Bosnia," *New York Times* (Sept. 3, 1995), sect. 4, p. 1: "The United States may not have written the book on ethnic cleansing, but it certainly provided several of its most stunning chapters — particularly in its treatment of the American Indian in the transcontinental drive for territory justified under the quasi-religious notion of 'manifest destiny.'"

2. *The Federalist: A Commentary on the Constitution of the United States* (New York: Modern Library, 1937), p. 3. For an extended argument, see Frederick W. Marks III, *Independence on Trial: Foreign Affairs and the Making of the Constitution* (Baton Rouge: Louisiana State University Press, 1973).

3. *The Federalist*, p. 9.

4. See Louis Hartz, *The Liberal Tradition in America* (New York: Harcourt, Brace, and World, 1955): "Surely, then, it is a remarkable force: this fixed, dogmatic liberalism of a liberal way of life. It is the secret root from which have sprung many of the most puzzling of American cultural phenomena" (p. 9). See also William Appleman Williams, *The Tragedy of American Diplomacy* (New York: Harper and Row, 1959): "Taken up by President Theodore Roosevelt and his successors, the philosophy and practice of secular empire that was embodied in the Open Door Notes became the central feature of American foreign policy in the twentieth century. . . . In essence, this twentieth-century Manifest Destiny was identical with the earlier phenomenon of the same name" (p. 59).

5. Thomas A. Bailey, *A Diplomatic History of the American People*, 8th ed. (New York: Appleton-Century-Crofts, 1969), p. 2.

6. Bradford Perkins, *The Cambridge History of American Foreign Relations*, vol. 1, *The Creation of a Republican Empire, 1776–1865* (Cambridge: Cambridge University Press, 1993), pp. 6–16.

7. Robert H. Ferrell, *Foundations of American Diplomacy, 1775–1872* (Columbia: University of South Carolina Press, 1968), pp. 9–15.

8. Cushing Strout, *The American Image of the Old World* (New York: Harper and Row, 1963), pp. ix–x, 14–18.

9. Paul Varg, *The Foreign Policies of the Founding Fathers* (East Lansing: Michigan State University Press, 1963), pp. 1–10, 304 (quote).

10. Felix Gilbert, *To the Farewell Address: Ideas of Early American Foreign Policy* (Princeton: Princeton University Press, 1961), pp. 4–6, 16–18.

11. Arthur M. Schlesinger, Jr., *The Cycles of American History* (Boston: Houghton Mifflin, 1986), p. 19.

12. Henry Kissinger, *Diplomacy* (New York: Simon and Schuster, 1994), pp. 29ff; Michael

Kammen, *People of Paradox: An Inquiry Concerning the Origins of American Civilization* (New York: Knopf, 1973), p. 298.

13. Edward Weisbrand, *The Ideology of American Foreign Policy: A Paradigm of Lockean Liberalism* (Beverly Hills: Sage Publications, 1973), p. 9. Weisbrand does not say that American policy makers practiced those norms punctiliously, only that they justify their policies on those hallowed grounds.

14. Michael H. Hunt, *Ideology and U.S. Foreign Policy* (New Haven: Yale University Press, 1987), pp. 17–18.

15. Eugene V. Rostow, *A Breakfast for Bonaparte: U.S. National Security Interests from the Heights of Abraham to the Nuclear Age* (Washington, D.C.: National Defense University Press, 1993), p. 22.

16. Walter A. McDougall in *Orbis: A Journal of World Affairs* 38, no. 3 (summer 1994): "So long as the U.S. government follows good principles, it can probably do without doctrine . . . at least in normal times. The principles of John Quincy Adams, for instance, or those of Adams plus Theodore Roosevelt, would suit our book fine for the time being" (p. 353).

17. George F. Kennan, "On American Principles," *Foreign Affairs* 74, no. 2 (March–April 1995): 116–26. Kennan erroneously placed the speech in 1823.

CHAPTER ONE

1. "America," lyrics by Samuel Francis Smith, in *The Hymnal of the Protestant Episcopal Church* (New York: Church Pension Fund, 1940), no. 141.

2. Lerner, *America as a Civilization* (New York: Simon and Schuster, 1957).

3. See, for instance, Paul Varg's *Foreign Policies of the Founding Fathers* (East Lansing: Michigan State University Press, 1963): "Jefferson and Madison gave expression to widely held views and their approach to foreign policy became the American approach that found its culmination in the moralizing of Woodrow Wilson at Versailles" (p. 147).

4. Felix Gilbert, *To the Farewell Address: Ideas of Early American Foreign Policy* (Princeton: Princeton University Press, 1961), pp. 4–6.

5. Thomas G. Paterson, ed., *Major Problems in American Foreign Policy*, vol. 1, *To 1914.* 3d ed. (Lexington, Mass.: D. C. Heath, 1989), p. 29.

6. Winthrop S. Hudson, ed., *Nationalism and Religion in America: Concepts of American Identity and Mission* (New York: Harper and Row, 1970), p. xxviii.

7. Philadelphia's George Duffield in 1873, cited by Hudson, *Nationalism and Religion*, p. 55.

8. Elhanan Winchester, *An Oration on the Discovery of America* (London, 1792), cited by Hudson, *Nationalism and Religion*, pp. 71–72.

9. Ezra Stiles, *The United States Elevated to Glory and Honor: A Sermon* (New Haven, 1783), in Paterson, *Major Problems*, pp. 38–41.

10. See Richard W. Van Alstyne, *Genesis of American Nationalism* (Waltham, Mass.: Blaisdell Publishing, 1970), p. 2.

11. See Stanley M. Burstein, "Greece, Rome, and the American Republic," *Laebertis: The Journal of the California Classical Association* 10, new series (1993–94): 1–24. Reading

Thucydides and Tacitus, wrote John Adams, was like "reading the History of my own Times and my own Life" (p. 13).

12. Van Alstyne, *Genesis*, p. 11.

13. Paine, "Common Sense" (1776), in Paterson, *Major Problems*, pp. 30–33.

14. Van Alstyne, *Genesis*, p. 63.

15. Bernard Bailyn, *The Ideological Origins of the American Revolution* (Cambridge: Harvard University Press, 1967), p. 1.

16. Gordon S. Wood, *The Radicalism of the American Revolution* (New York: Vintage, 1991), p. 179.

17. Samuel Flagg Bemis, *American Foreign Policy and the Blessings of Liberty, and Other Essays* (New Haven: Yale University Press, 1962): "We have not lacked a clear purpose as a nation. What we seem to have been lacking is a continued consciousness of that purpose, of these congenital Blessings of Liberty" (p. 2).

18. See Daniel J. Boorstin, *The Republic of Technology: Reflections on Our Future Community* (New York: Harper and Row, 1978), chap. 4.

19. Bernard Bailyn, ed., *Pamphlets of the American Revolution, 1750–1776* (Cambridge: Harvard University Press, 1965), 1:84.

20. Michael Kammen, *Empire and Interest: The American Colonies and the Politics of Mercantilism* (Philadelphia: Lippincott, 1970), pp. 126–27.

21. Gilbert, *To the Farewell Address*, p. 22.

22. Gilbert, *To the Farewell Address*, p. 28.

23. Gilbert, *To the Farewell Address*, pp. 11–12.

24. Gilbert, *To the Farewell Address*, p. 73.

25. Gilbert, *To the Farewell Address*, p. 67.

26. James H. Hutson, *John Adams and the Diplomacy of the American Revolution* (Lexington: University of Kentucky Press, 1980), pp. 1–10; Max Savelle, *The Origins of American Diplomacy: The International History of Angloamerica* (New York: Macmillan, 1967), pp. 446–51.

27. *The Works of John Adams*, ed. Charles Francis Adams, 10 vols. (Boston: Little, Brown, 1853–56), 10:269.

28. Lawrence S. Kaplan, *Colonies into Nation: American Diplomacy, 1763–1801* (New York: Macmillan, 1973), p. 143.

29. Richard B. Morris, *The Peacemakers: The Great Powers and American Independence* (New York: Harper and Row, 1965), p. 459.

30. Jerald A. Combs, *The Jay Treaty: Political Battleground of the Founding Fathers* (Berkeley: University of California Press, 1970), p. 24.

31. The object of the Constitutional Convention, said Madison to Jefferson, was "to unite a proper energy in the Executive and a proper stability in the Legislative departments, with the essential characters of Republican Government" (Gordon S. Wood, *The Creation of the American Republic, 1776–1787* [Chapel Hill: University of North Carolina Press, 1969], p. 551).

32. Wood writes that "what remains extraordinary about 1787–88 is not the weakness and disunity but the political strength of Antifederalism" (*Creation of the American Republic*, p. 498).

33. This, too, was an elaboration, or attempted perfecting, of England's system of "mixed" government and "self-balancing equilibrium" of institutions, with the radical difference (as Madison put it) that whereas in Europe "charters of liberty

have been granted by power," America would set the example of "charters of power granted by liberty." See Bailyn, *Ideological Origins*, chap. 3 (quotes from pp. 273, 55).

34. See Frederick W. Marks III, *Independence on Trial: Foreign Affairs and the Making of the Constitution* (Wilmington: Scholarly Resources, 1986), and Forrest McDonald, *Novus Ordo Seclorum: The Intellectual Origins of the Constitution* (Lawrence: University Press of Kansas, 1985), esp. pp. 247–52.

35. *The Federalist: A Commentary on the Constitution of the United States* (New York: Modern Library, 1937), pp. 13–17.

36. *The Federalist*, pp. 30–31 (*Federalist #6*). John Quincy Adams argued the same in a heated response to James Monroe, who was incautious enough to suggest that "free people seldom intrigue together." If Mr. Monroe had read his history, wrote Adams, "he would have found that the government of a Republic was as capable of intriguing with the leaders of a free people as neighboring monarchs" (*The Writings of John Quincy Adams*, ed. Worthington C. Ford, 7 vols. [New York: Macmillan, 1913–17], 2:323–24).

37. *The Federalist*, p. 69 (*Federalist #11*).

38. *Letters of Benjamin Rush*, ed. Lyman Henry Butterfield, 2 vols. (Princeton: Princeton University Press, 1951), p. 207.

39. Norman A. Graebner, *Foundations of American Foreign Policy: A Realist Appraisal from Franklin to McKinley* (Wilmington: Scholarly Resources, 1985), pp. 82–83.

40. Thomas A. Bailey, *A Diplomatic History of the American People*, 8th ed. (New York: Appleton-Century-Crofts, 1969), pp. 75–76.

41. Kaplan, *Colonies into Nation*, p. 243.

42. *The Writings of Thomas Jefferson*, ed. Andrew A. Lipscomb and Albert E. Bergh, 20 vols. (Washington, D.C.: Jefferson Memorial Assoc., 1903–4), 9:10.

43. Charles Warren, *Jacobin and Junto* (Cambridge: Harvard University Press, 1931), p. 90.

44. Joyce Appleby, *Capitalism and a New Social Order: The Republican Vision of the 1790s* (New York: New York University Press, 1984), p. 58.

45. Harry Ammon, *The Genêt Mission* (New York: W. W. Norton, 1973), p. 86.

46. The central government, wrote Jefferson, should "make us one nation as to foreign countries, and keep us distinct in domestic ones" (Marks, *Independence on Trial*, p. 206).

47. Washington's Farewell Address in Paterson, *Major Problems*, pp. 74–76.

48. Thomas G. Paterson, J. Garry Clifford, and Kenneth J. Hagan, *American Foreign Policy: A History*, vol. 1, *To 1914*, 3d ed. (Lexington, Mass.: D. C. Heath, 1988), p. 52.

49. "Were I to indulge my own theory, I should [wish the states] to practice neither commerce nor navigation, but to stand with respect to Europe precisely on the footing of China. We should thus avoid wars, and all our citizens would be husbandmen" (Van Alstyne, *Genesis*, p. 67).

50. Bradford Perkins, *The Cambridge History of American Foreign Relations*, vol. 1, *The Creation of a Republican Empire* (Cambridge: Cambridge University Press, 1993), p. 112.

51. Paterson et al., *American Foreign Policy*, p. 58.

52. Historian Paul A. Varg most clearly contrasted Jeffersonian idealism (unfavorably) with Hamiltonian realism in his *Foreign Policies of the Founding Fathers*. But Lawrence S. Kaplan argues from the same evidence (convincingly, in my opinion) that the Hamilton-Jefferson debates on foreign policy were more over tactics than ideology,

and that if Jefferson is to be labeled an idealist, he was a strikingly pragmatic one. See Kaplan, "Thomas Jefferson: The Idealist as Realist," in Frank Merli and Theodore A. Wilson, eds., *Makers of American Diplomacy* (New York: Scribner's, 1974).

53. In 1814 Federalists gathered at the Hartford Convention to protest the war. Some spoke of secession, but the convention contented itself with a recommendation that the Constitution be amended to make it harder for Congress to impose embargoes or declare war. Their campaign expired with the coming of peace.

54. Bradford Perkins, *Prologue to War, 1805–1812: England and the United States* (Berkeley: University of California Press, 1961), pp. 403–4.

55. Perkins, *Prologue to War,* pp. 393, 434–35.

56. Raymond Walters, Jr., *Albert Gallatin: Jeffersonian Financier and Diplomat* (New York: Macmillan, 1957), p. 288.

57. John Quincy Adams, *An Address Delivered at the Request of the Citizens of Washington; on the Occasion of Reading the Declaration of Independence, on the Fourth of July, 1821* (Washington, D.C.: Davis and Force, 1821).

58. See Hutson, *John Adams,* pp. 30–32.

59. John Winthrop's "City on a Hill," in Paterson, *Major Problems,* p. 29.

60. John A. Schutz and Douglas Adair, eds., *The Spur of Fame: Dialogues of John Adams and Benjamin Rush, 1805–1813* (San Marino, Calif.: Huntington Library, 1966), p. 76.

CHAPTER TWO

1. Isaiah 30:1–2 (*The Oxford Annotated Bible,* RSV [New York: Oxford University Press, 1962]).

2. George Washington's Farewell Address, 1796, in Thomas G. Paterson, ed., *Major Problems in American Foreign Policy,* vol. 1, *To 1914,* 3d ed. (Lexington, Mass.: D. C. Heath, 1989), p. 77.

3. Jerald A. Combs, *American Diplomatic History: Two Centuries of Changing Interpretations* (Berkeley: University of California Press, 1983), pp. 39–55.

4. *Washington Post* (June 2, 1898), cited by Thomas G. Paterson et al., *American Foreign Policy: A History,* vol. 1, *To 1914,* 3d ed. (Lexington, Mass.: D. C. Heath, 1988), p. 213.

5. Walpole to Lord Townshend (1723), and Pomfret in the House of Lords (Dec. 10, 1755), cited by Felix Gilbert, *To the Farewell Address: Ideas of Early American Foreign Policy* (Princeton: Princeton University Press, 1961), pp. 22, 27.

6. *The Works of John Adams,* ed. Charles Francis Adams, 10 vols. (Boston: Little, Brown, 1853–56), 8:35.

7. Gilbert, *To the Farewell Address,* p. 72.

8. Poetry of Timothy Dwight (1794), cited by Thomas A. Bailey, *The Man in the Street: The Impact of American Public Opinion on Foreign Policy* (New York: Macmillan, 1948), p. 244.

9. Thomas Pownall, *A Memorial most humbly addressed to the Sovereigns of Europe* (London, 1780), cited by Gilbert, *To the Farewell Address,* pp. 107–11.

10. Bailey, *Man in the Street,* p. 244.

11. *Journals of the Continental Congress,* ed. Worthington C. Ford, 34 vols. (Washington, D.C.: GPO, 1904–37), 24:394.

12. Samuel Flagg Bemis, "Washington's Farewell Address: A Foreign Policy of Inde-

pendence," *American Historical Review* 39, no. 2 (1934), reprinted in Bemis, *American Foreign Policy and the Blessings of Liberty* (New Haven: Yale University Press, 1962), pp. 240–58 (quote p. 251). See J. Fred Rippy and Angie Debo, "The Historical Background of the American Policy of Isolation," *Smith College Studies in History* 9 (spring 1914).

13. Letters of "Columbus" and "Marcellus," *The Writings of John Quincy Adams*, ed. Worthington C. Ford, 7 vols. (New York: Macmillan, 1913–17), 1:157–59, 140. Bemis, *American Foreign Policy*, pp. 272–75, compares John Quincy Adams's texts with the wording of Washington's Farewell Address.

14. On the evolution of the text, see Gilbert, *To the Farewell Address*, pp. 121–34.

15. Washington's Farewell Address, 1796, in Paterson, *Major Problems*, pp. 74–77.

16. Though it went down in history as Washington's Farewell Address, it was in fact published, not delivered as a speech.

17. Thomas Wentworth Higginson, *A Larger History of the United States of America to the Close of President Jackson's Administration* (New York: Harper and Bros., 1886), p. 332.

18. See Combs, *American Diplomatic History*, pp. 6–7; Harvey Wish, *The American Historian: A Social-Intellectual History of the Writing of the American Past* (New York: Oxford University Press, 1960), pp. 41–51; and especially Garry Wills, *Cincinnatus: George Washington and the Enlightenment* (Garden City, N.Y.: Doubleday, 1984).

19. *The Writings of Thomas Jefferson*, eds. Andrew A. Lipscomb and Albert E. Bergh, 20 vols. (Washington, D.C.: Jefferson Memorial Assoc., 1903–4), 9:405–6, in Albert Hall Bowman, *The Struggle for Neutrality: Franco-American Diplomacy during the Federalist Era* (Knoxville: University of Tennessee Press, 1974), pp. 268–69.

20. Bowman, *Struggle for Neutrality*, p. 415.

21. See Irving Brant, "James Madison and His Times," *American Historical Review* 57 (Nov. 1952): 853–70, reprinted in Nicholas Cords and Patrick Gerster, *Myth and the American Experience*, vol. 1, 3d ed. (New York: Harper Collins, 1991), pp. 191–203 (esp. p. 201).

22. Bailey, *Man in the Street*, p. 238.

23. George Tucker, *The History of the United States from Their Colonization to the End of the Twenty-sixth Congress, in 1841*, 4 vols. (Philadelphia, 1856), cited by Combs, *American Diplomatic History*, p. 15.

24. W. H. Trescot, *The Diplomatic History of the Administrations of Washington and Adams, 1789–1801* (Boston, 1857), p. 3; cited by Combs, *American Diplomatic History*, p. 13.

25. Paul A. Varg, *United States Foreign Relations, 1820–1860* (East Lansing: Michigan State University Press, 1979), pp. 20–42 (quote p. 39).

26. "Free security" advanced by C. Vann Woodward, "The Age of Reinterpretation," *American Historical Review* 66, no. 4 (1960), reprinted in Woodward, *The Future of the Past* (New York: Oxford University Press, 1989), pp. 75–84; the role of the British fleet elaborated in Lawrence S. Kaplan, *Entangling Alliances with None* (Kent, Ohio: Kent State University Press, 1987), p. xvii.

27. Alexis de Tocqueville, *Democracy in America* (New York: Vintage, 1945 [1834]), p. 446.

28. *The Collected Works of Abraham Lincoln*, ed. R. P. Basler (New Brunswick: Rutgers University Press, 1953), 1:109.

29. Between 1840 and 1870 the French navy attempted to make several quantum leaps in the adaptation of steam power and iron plating, prompting on each occasion parliamentary inquiries and public hand-wringing in Britain.

30. Bradford Perkins, *The Cambridge History of American Foreign Relations*, vol. 1, *The Creation of a Republican Empire* (Cambridge: Cambridge University Press, 1993), p. 205.

31. Thomas A. Bailey, *A Diplomatic History of the American People*, 8th ed. (New York: Appleton-Century-Crofts, 1969), p. 201.

32. Bailey, *Diplomatic History*, pp. 204–7.

33. Wilbur Devereux Jones, *The American Problem in British Diplomacy, 1841–1861* (New York: Macmillan, 1974), p. 6.

34. As it happened, Webster's misplaced trust in Harvard professor Jared Sparks cheated the United States of about 5,000 square miles of timber. Sparks thought he had seen a map drawn by Benjamin Franklin that confirmed the British claim, leading Webster to believe he had got the best of Ashburton through compromise. Meanwhile, Palmerston found a map in a British archive that confirmed the extreme American claim, so he knew he had got the best of Webster. On the other side of the ledger, Britain reaffirmed the 1818 boundary in what is now Minnesota, unwittingly conceding to the United States 6,500 square miles of the richest iron ore deposits in the world.

35. Tocqueville, *Democracy in America*, p. 446.

36. Perkins, *Creation of a Republican Empire*, p. 206.

37. Eugene V. Rostow, *A Breakfast for Bonaparte: U.S. National Security Interests from the Heights of Abraham to the Nuclear Age* (Washington, D.C.: National Defense University Press, 1993), p. 155.

38. The best expression of American ambivalence toward the British may be the observation that George MacDonald Fraser puts in the mouth of his fictional military raconteur Sir Harry Flashman, c. 1848: "By and large I'm partial to Americans. They make a great affectation of disliking the English and asserting their equality with us, but I've discovered that underneath they dearly love a lord, and if you're civil and cool and don't play it with too high a hand . . . they'll eat out of your hand and boast to their friends in Philadelphia that they know a man who's on terms with Queen Victoria and yet, by gosh, is as nice a fellow as they've ever struck" (*Flash for Freedom!* [New York: New American Library, 1985 (1981)], p. 112).

39. See Henry Adams, *The Degradation of the Democratic Dogma* (New York: Peter Smith, 1919), pp. 28–31 (quote p. 30).

40. Robert A. Divine, *The Illusion of Neutrality: Franklin D. Roosevelt and the Struggle over the Arms Embargo* (Chicago: University of Chicago Press, 1962), p. 44.

CHAPTER THREE

1. Bradford Perkins, *The Cambridge History of American Foreign Relations*, vol. 1, *The Creation of a Republican Empire, 1776–1865* (Cambridge: Cambridge University Press, 1993), p. 166.

2. Armin Rappaport, *A History of American Diplomacy* (New York: Macmillan, 1975), p. 92.

3. *L'Étoile* (Jan. 4, 1824), cited by Dexter Perkins, *The Monroe Doctrine, 1823–1826* (Gloucester, England: Peter Smith, 1965 [1927]), p. 30.

4. Thomas A. Bailey, *The Man in the Street: The Impact of American Public Opinion on Foreign Policy* (New York: Macmillan, 1948), p. 266.

5. C. K. Webster, ed., *Britain and the Independence of Latin America, 1812–1830*, 2 vols. (London: Oxford University Press, 1938), 2:508.

6. *New York Times* (Dec. 2, 1923).

7. Bailey, *Man in the Street*, p. 256.

8. See, for instance, Wayne S. Cole, "Myths Surrounding the Monroe Doctrine," in Nicholas Cords and Patrick Gerster, eds., *Myth and the American Experience*, vol. 1, 3d ed. (New York: Harper Collins, 1991), pp. 207–11.

9. On this last point, see Jerald A. Combs, *American Diplomatic History: Two Centuries of Changing Interpretations* (Berkeley: University of California Press, 1983), pp. 32–33, 67.

10. Howard I. Kushner, *Conflict on the Northwest Coast: American-Russian Rivalry in the Pacific Northwest, 1790–1867* (Westport, Conn.: Greenwood, 1975), p. 40.

11. *The Memoirs of John Quincy Adams*, ed. Charles Francis Adams, 12 vols. (Philadelphia: Lippincott, 1874–77), 5:252.

12. Samuel Flagg Bemis, *John Quincy Adams and the Foundations of American Foreign Policy* (New York: Knopf, 1965), p. 515 (italics in original).

13. *The Writings of James Monroe*, ed. Stanislaus Murray Hamilton, 7 vols. (New York: G. P. Putnam's Sons, 1898–1903), 7:361–65. Almost all the histories describe the scene. See Ernest R. May, *The Making of the Monroe Doctrine* (Cambridge: Harvard University Press, 1975), p. 3.

14. *Writings of James Monroe*, 7:365–66. For convenience, see May, *Making of the Monroe Doctrine*, pp. 5–6, or Thomas G. Paterson, ed., *Major Problems in American Foreign Policy*, vol. 1, *To 1914*, 3d ed. (Lexington, Mass.: D. C. Heath, 1989), pp. 181–82.

15. Parkman, *Pioneers of France in the New World* (1865), cited by Harvey Wish, *The American Historian: A Social-Intellectual History of the Writing of the American Past* (New York: Oxford University Press, 1960), p. 95.

16. Bemis, *John Quincy Adams*, p. 346.

17. Samuel Flagg Bemis, "Early Missions from Buenos Aires," in *American Foreign Policy and the Blessings of Liberty* (New Haven: Yale University Press, 1962), p. 309.

18. William Roderick Sherman, *The Diplomatic and Commercial Relations of the United States and Chile, 1820–1924* (New York: Russell and Russell, 1926), p. 12.

19. Arthur Preston Whitaker, *The United States and the Independence of Latin America, 1800–1830* (New York: W. W. Norton, 1964 [1941]), pp. 116–17.

20. Manuel Torres, "An Exposition of the Commerce of Spanish America," in Morrell Heald and Lawrence S. Kaplan, *Culture and Diplomacy: The American Experience* (Westport, Conn.: Greenwood, 1977), p. 82.

21. Heald and Kaplan, *Culture and Diplomacy*, p. 68.

22. Bemis, "Early Missions from Buenos Aires," in *Blessings of Liberty*, p. 320.

23. Heald and Kaplan, *Culture and Diplomacy*, pp. 74–75.

24. Heald and Kaplan, *Culture and Diplomacy*, p. 83.

25. Heald and Kaplan, *Culture and Diplomacy*, pp. 75–77.

26. John Quincy Adams, *An Address Delivered at the Request of the Citizens of Washington; on the Occasion of Reading the Declaration of Independence, on the Fourth of July, 1821* (Washington, D.C.: Davis and Force, 1821). For convenience, see the text in *John Quincy Adams and American Continental Empire*, ed. Walter LaFeber (Chicago: University of Chicago Press, 1965), pp. 42–46, and Adams's own explanation of his intentions in Whitaker, *The U.S. and the Independence of Latin America*, pp. 354–61.

27. *Memoirs of John Quincy Adams*, 5:324–25.

28. *Memoirs of John Quincy Adams*, 5:176.

29. Whitaker, *The U.S. and the Independence of Latin America*, pp. 210–11.

30. Bemis, *John Quincy Adams*, p. 353.

31. (Oct. 24, 1823), *Writings of Monroe*, 6:391–94, or *The Writings of Thomas Jefferson*, ed. Andrew A. Lipscomb and Albert E. Bergh, 20 vols. (Washington, D.C.: Jefferson Memorial Assoc., 1903–4), 15:477–80. See Norman A. Graebner, *Foundations of American Foreign Policy: A Realist Appraisal from Franklin to McKinley* (Wilmington: Scholarly Resources, 1985), pp. 169–70, or Paterson, *Major Problems*, pp. 182–83.

32. Adams wrote to the U.S. minister in Madrid in April 1823, "Cuba, forcibly disjoined from its own unnatural connection with Spain, and incapable of self-support, can gravitate only towards the North American Union." See *The Writings of John Quincy Adams*, ed. Worthington C. Ford, 7 vols. (New York: Macmillan, 1913–17), 7:372–73.

33. *Memoirs of John Quincy Adams*, 6:186.

34. *Memoirs of John Quincy Adams*, 6:179.

35. American citizens versed in' the classics were especially zealous for the Greek cause (taking their cue, as ever, from Britain, where societies of Philhellenes mushroomed). But when John Quincy Adams himself was asked to donate to a Greek relief fund, he refused: "We had objects of distress to relieve at home more than sufficient to absorb all my capacities of contribution." See *Memoirs of John Quincy Adams*, 6:324–25, or Walter LaFeber, *The American Age: United States Foreign Policy at Home and Abroad Since 1750* (New York: W. W. Norton, 1989), p. 82.

36. *Memoirs of John Quincy Adams*, 6:197–98.

37. Annual Message from the President (Dec. 2, 1823): *Writings of James Monroe*, 7:325–42. For convenience, see the excerpt in Paterson, *Major Problems*, pp. 184–85.

38. Though still the first nation to do so, the United States did not recognize Colombia and Mexico until 1822, Buenos Aires (Argentina) and Chile in 1823, Central America and Brazil in 1824, and Peru in 1826.

39. Perkins, *Monroe Doctrine, 1823–1826*, pp. 186–91.

40. See the discussion in Paul A. Varg, *United States Foreign Relations, 1820–1860* (East Lansing: Michigan State University Press, 1979), pp. 52–53.

41. Paul Schroeder, *The Transformation of European Politics, 1763–1848* (Oxford: Clarendon, 1994), p. 635.

42. Paterson, *Major Problems*, p. 180.

43. (Jan. 24, 1824), *Annals of Congress*, 18th Cong., 1st sess., cols. 1182–90. See Graebner, *Foundations of American Foreign Policy*, p. 178. According to Edith Hamilton (*Mythology* [New York: New American Library, 1940], p. 171), Nessus was a centaur slain by Hercules. Before expiring he bade Deianira to carry off some of his blood to use as a charm in case Hercules should ever love another woman. She anointed a robe with the blood, which then burned its wearer like fire but did not permit him to die.

CHAPTER FOUR

1. Frederick Jackson Turner, "The Significance of the Frontier in American History," a paper read at the meeting of the American Historical Association in Chicago, July 12, 1893, reprinted in Turner, *The Frontier in American History* (New York: Henry Holt, 1920), pp. 1–38 (quote p. 37).

2. "The Great Nation of Futurity," *The United States Magazine and Democratic Review* 6 (Nov. 1839). For convenience, see the excerpt in Thomas G. Paterson, ed., *Major Problems in American Foreign Policy*, vol. 1, *To 1914* (Lexington, Mass.: D. C. Heath, 1989), pp. 255–56.

3. Bradford Perkins, *The Cambridge History of American Foreign Relations*, vol. 1, *The Creation of a Republican Empire, 1776–1865* (Cambridge: Cambridge University Press, 1993), p. 170.

4. John Quincy Adams to John Adams (Aug. 31, 1811): *The Writings of John Quincy Adams*, ed. Worthington C. Ford, 7 vols. (New York: Macmillan, 1913–17), 4:209.

5. (1858) in Harry Jaffa, *Crisis of the House Divided* (Seattle: University of Washington Press, 1973), p. 406.

6. See Robert V. Remini, *Andrew Jackson and the Course of American Freedom, 1822–1832* (New York: Harper and Row, 1981), esp. pp. 109–15, 294–99, 382–92.

7. "Democracy Must Finally Reign," *Democratic Review* (March 1840), 215–29, reprinted in Norman Graebner, ed., *Manifest Destiny* (Indianapolis: Bobbs-Merrill, 1968), pp. 22–29 (quote p. 23).

8. See Michael Kammen, "Revolutionary Iconography in the National Tradition," in Kammen, *A Season of Youth: The American Revolution and the Historical Imagination* (New York: Knopf, 1978), pp. 76–109; and Stanley M. Burstein, "Greece, Rome, and the American Republic," *Laebertis: The Journal of the California Classical Association* 10, new series (1993–94): 1–24.

9. Robert H. Wiebe, *The Opening of American Society: From the Adoption of the Constitution to the Eve of Disunion* (New York: Knopf, 1984), p. 252.

10. Jackson Lears, "Playing with Money," *The Wilson Quarterly* (autumn 1995): 6–32 (quote p. 12).

11. W. J. Rorabaugh, *The Alcoholic Republic* (New York: Oxford University Press, 1979), esp. pp. 68–83.

12. Alexis de Tocqueville, *Democracy in America* (New York: Vintage, 1945 [1834]), p. 239. Another Philadelphian, E. C. Booz, marketed his whiskey in log-cabin-shaped bottles in 1840, the year of the "log cabin and hard cider" presidential campaign, and so inspired the slang word "booze" (Robert Gray Gunderson, *The Log Cabin Campaign* [Lexington: University of Kentucky Press, 1957], p. 129).

13. Rorabaugh, *Alcoholic Republic*, pp. 100–101. On the temperance movement see Robert Lacour-Gayet, *Everyday Life in the United States before the Civil War, 1830–1860* (New York: Frederick Ungar, 1969), pp. 42–43; and Alice Felt Tyler, *Freedom's Ferment* (Minneapolis: University of Minnesota Press, 1944), chap. 13.

14. Thomas A. Bailey, *The Man in the Street: The Impact of American Public Opinion on Foreign Policy* (New York: Macmillan, 1948), p. 58.

15. George Will, "The Fourth Awakening," summarizing a lecture by the University of Chicago's Robert Fogel, in *Newsweek* (Oct. 2, 1995).

16. See Timothy L. Smith, "Righteousness and Hope: Christian Holiness and the Millennial Vision in America, 1880–1900," *American Quarterly* 31, no. 1 (spring 1979): 21–45 (quotes pp. 38–39). On the varieties of American religion in this era, see Tyler, *Freedom's Ferment*. Mormonism, based on a fiercely American claim to new revelation, might be considered the extreme example of this trend in the Jacksonian era.

17. *New York Evening Post* (Jan. 28, 1803), in Albert K. Weinberg, *Manifest Destiny: A Study*

of Nationalist Expansionism in American History (Baltimore: Johns Hopkins University Press, 1935), p. 31.

18. Weinberg, *Manifest Destiny,* p. 41.

19. "Cuba and the Floridas," *Niles' Weekly Register* 17 (1820), in Weinberg, *Manifest Destiny,* p. 48.

20. *The Memoirs of John Quincy Adams,* ed. Charles Francis Adams, 12 vols. (Philadelphia: Lippincott, 1874–77), 4:438–39.

21. Weinberg, *Manifest Destiny,* pp. 194, 202.

22. Weinberg, *Manifest Destiny,* pp. 228–30.

23. John Winthrop, *Conclusions for the Plantation in New England* and *The History of New England from 1630 to 1649,* in Weinberg, *Manifest Destiny,* pp. 74–75.

24. Weinberg, *Manifest Destiny,* p. 79.

25. Emory Hollway, ed., *The Uncollected Poetry and Prose of Walt Whitman,* 2 vols. (Garden City, N.Y.: Doubleday, 1921), 1:159.

26. *New York Morning News* (Dec. 27, 1845), in Julius W. Pratt, *A History of United States Foreign Policy* (New York: Prentice-Hall, 1955), p. 216.

27. Frederick Merk, *Manifest Destiny and Mission in American History* (New York: Vintage, 1966 [1963]), p. 25.

28. "The Mexican War," *Democratic Review* 22 (1848), in Weinberg, *Manifest Destiny,* p. 178.

29. Weinberg, *Manifest Destiny,* pp. 104–5.

30. See, for example, Frederick Merk, *Albert Gallatin and the Oregon Problem* (Cambridge: Harvard University Press, 1950), p. 13. Benton was fond of the allusion: by way of protesting the Maine boundary settlement, he later proposed to "veil with black the statue of the god Terminus, degraded from the mountain which overlooked Quebec" (Jesse Reeves, *American Diplomacy under Tyler and Polk* [Baltimore: Johns Hopkins University Press, 1907], pp. 44–45). Terminus was in fact one of the Penates, or household gods. He guarded the boundaries of a family farm, not those of the Roman Republic or Empire.

31. See Thomas R. Hietala, *Manifest Design: Anxious Aggrandizement in Late Jacksonian America* (Ithaca: Cornell University Press, 1985).

32. Theodore Roosevelt, *The Winning of the West: An Account of the Exploration and Settlement of Our Country from the Alleghanies to the Pacific,* 6 vols. (New York: G. P. Putnam's Sons, 1889–96), 1:30.

33. The filibuster — a sort of civilian guerrilla operation carried out by Americans who occupied foreign soil, then demanded self-determination and forced their *own* government's hand — was a novel tactic. According to William H. Goetzmann (*When the Eagle Screamed: The Romantic Horizon in American Diplomacy, 1800–1860* [New York: John Wiley and Sons, 1966], p. xvi), it was "virtually the only original American contribution to the technique of worldwide imperialism."

34. See, respectively, Richard Drinnon, *Facing West: The Metaphysics of Indian-Hating and Empire-Building* (Minneapolis: University of Minnesota Press, 1980); Tom Engelhardt, *The End of Victory Culture* (New York: Basic Books, 1995); Alexander Saxton, *The Rise and Fall of the White Republic: Class Politics and Mass Culture in Nineteenth-Century America* (New York: Verso [New Left Books], 1990).

35. Reginald Horsman, *Race and Manifest Destiny: The Origins of American Racial Anglo-Saxonism* (Cambridge: Harvard University Press, 1981), pp. 107–8.

36. See Robert F. Berkhofer, *The White Man's Indian: Images of the American Indian from Columbus to the Present* (New York: Knopf, 1978).

37. *Cherokee Nation v. State of Georgia*, 1831, in Thomas G. Paterson, ed., *Major Problems in American Foreign Policy*, vol. 1, *To 1914* (Lexington, Mass.: D. C. Heath, 1989), pp. 216–20 (quote p. 219).

38. Remini, *Andrew Jackson and the Course of American Freedom*, pp. 257–79 (quote p. 265). Jackson's complicated mix of hostility and paternalism (he even adopted an orphaned Indian child) is well treated in Anthony F. C. Wallace, *The Long, Bitter Trail: Andrew Jackson and the Indians* (New York: Hill and Wang, 1993).

39. Thomas G. Paterson, J. Garry Clifford, and Kenneth J. Hagan, *American Foreign Policy: A History*, vol. 1, *To 1914*, 3d ed. (Lexington, Mass.: D. C. Heath, 1988), p. 87.

40. See Horsman, *Race and Manifest Destiny*, on Jefferson, the British roots of Anglo-Saxonism, and its growing influence in the United States.

41. Caldwell's 1830 book *Thoughts on the Original Unity of the Human Race* was highly influential. See Horsman, *Race and Manifest Destiny*, pp. 117–20.

42. Drew Gilpin Faust, "A Southern Stewardship: The Intellectual and the Pro-Slavery Argument," *American Quarterly* 31, no. 1 (spring 1979): 63–80 (Simms quote p. 73); Clay quote in Horsman, *Race and Manifest Destiny*, p. 198.

43. *The Emigrants' Guide to Oregon and California* (1845), in Horsman, *Race and Manifest Destiny*, p. 211; *Evening Post* in Walter LaFeber, *The American Age: United States Foreign Policy at Home and Abroad Since 1750* (New York: W. W. Norton, 1989), p. 97. It must be said that American bigotry was reinforced by the Mexican *hidalgos* themselves, who held their own peons in contempt and even directed racial slurs at the Yankee "rabble" in Texas who "scarcely had the look of men": Alexander DeConde, *Ethnicity, Race, and American Foreign Policy: A History* (Boston: Northeastern University Press, 1992), p. 33.

44. *Compilation of the Messages and Papers of the Presidents*, ed. James D. Richardson, 20 vols. (Washington, D.C.: GPO, 1897–1917), 3:1084.

45. Claude Milton Newlin, *The Life and Writings of Hugh Henry Brackenridge* (Princeton: Princeton University Press, 1932), in Horsman, *Race and Manifest Destiny*, pp. 113–14 (Tennessee quote p. 110).

46. Graebner, *Manifest Destiny*, p. 73.

47. Julius Pratt, *A History of United States Foreign Policy* (New York: Prentice-Hall, 1955), p. 244.

48. Norman A. Graebner, *Foundations of American Foreign Policy: A Realist Appraisal from Franklin to McKinley* (Wilmington: Scholarly Resources, 1985), p. 232.

49. *The Diary of James K. Polk*, ed. Milo Milton Quaife, 4 vols. (Chicago: McClung, 1910), 1:155.

50. Paul A. Varg, *United States Foreign Relations, 1820–1860* (East Lansing: Michigan State University Press, 1979), p. 150. On Buchanan's moderating influence, see Frederick Moore Binder, *James Buchanan and the American Empire* (Selinsgrove, Pa.: Susquehanna University Press, 1994).

51. Pletcher, *Diplomacy of Annexation*, pp. 334–45; "not an inch" in Thomas A. Bailey, *A Diplomatic History of the American People*, 8th ed. (New York: Appleton-Century-Crofts, 1969), p. 230.

52. (Feb. 16, 1846), in Bailey, *A Diplomatic History*, p. 230.

53. Charles Wilkes, *Narrative of the United States Exploring Expedition during the Years 1838, 1839, 1840, 1841, 1842*, 5 vols. (Philadelphia: Lee and Blanchard, 1845), 5:171–72.

54. Webster (March 11, 1845), in Graebner, *Foundations of American Foreign Policy*, pp. 212–14; "California," *The American Review: A Whig Journal of Politics, Literature, Art and Science* (Jan. 1846), in Graebner, *Manifest Destiny*, pp. 143–52 (quote p. 147).

55. *New York Herald* (Feb. 3, 1846) in Graebner, *Foundations of American Foreign Policy*, p. 216; "California in view" in *Diary of James K. Polk*, 1:71.

56. Pletcher, *Diplomacy of Annexation*, pp. 423–24.

57. Polk's War Message (May 9, 1846) in *Compilation of the Messages and Papers of the Presidents, 1789–1897*, ed. James D. Richardson, 9 vols. (Washington, D.C.: GPO, 1897–1900), 4:442. For convenience, see Paterson, *Major Problems*, pp. 258–62.

58. Pletcher, *Diplomacy of Annexation*, p. 459.

59. See Jerald A. Combs, *American Diplomatic History: Two Centuries of Changing Interpretations* (Berkeley: University of California Press, 1983), pp. 56–61.

60. Weinberg, *Manifest Destiny*, p. 179.

61. Perkins, *Creation of a Republican Empire*, p. 193.

62. Whitman in the *Brooklyn Daily Eagle* (Sept. 23, 1847) and Stockton, "Redeem Mexico from misrule and civil strife," *Niles' National Register* (Jan. 22, 1848), in Graebner, *Manifest Destiny*, pp. 207–9, 209–15.

63. Pratt, *History of U.S. Foreign Policy*, p. 279, says: "If the 1840s are labeled the decade of Manifest Destiny Triumphant, the succeeding ten years may well be called the era of Manifest Destiny Frustrated." Bailey, *Diplomatic History of the American People*, p. 297, speaks of "Manacled Manifest Destiny," and Paterson, *American Foreign Policy*, p. 124, of "Sputtering Expansion."

64. The lecturer John Fiske, cited by Bailey, *Man in the Street*, pp. 272–73.

CHAPTER FIVE

1. Foster Rhea Dulles, *The Imperial Years* (New York: Thomas Crowell, 1956), pp. 16–17.

2. Beveridge's Salute to Imperialism (1900) in Thomas G. Paterson, ed., *Major Problems in American Foreign Policy*, vol. 1, *To 1914* (Lexington, Mass.: D. C. Heath, 1989), pp. 389–91.

3. Richard H. Collin, *Theodore Roosevelt, Culture, Diplomacy, and Expansion: A New View of American Imperialism* (Baton Rouge: Louisiana State University Press, 1985), p. 30.

4. Walter LaFeber, *The American Age: United States Foreign Policy at Home and Abroad Since 1750* (New York: W. W. Norton, 1989), p. 160. On the varieties of responses to the perceived closing of the frontier, see David M. Wrobel, *The End of American Exceptionalism: Frontier Anxiety from the Old West to the New Deal* (Lawrence: University Press of Kansas, 1993).

5. James C. Bradford, ed., *Admirals of the New Steel Navy* (Annapolis: Naval Institute Press, 1990), p. 42.

6. Frederick W. Marks III, *Velvet on Iron: The Diplomacy of Theodore Roosevelt* (Lincoln: University of Nebraska Press, 1979), pp. 11–19.

7. Josiah Strong, *Our Country: Its Possible Future and Present Crisis* (1885), in Julius W.

Pratt, *Expansionists of 1898: The Acquisition of Hawaii and the Spanish Islands* (Baltimore: Johns Hopkins University Press, 1936), p. 6 (*Our Country* sold 175,000 copies); Strong, *The New Era, or The Coming Kingdom* (New York: Baker and Taylor, 1893), pp. 78–79.

8. David Healy, *U.S. Expansionism: The Imperialist Urge in the 1890s* (Madison: University of Wisconsin Press, 1970), p. 115.

9. See Pratt, *Expansionists of 1898;* Frederick Merk, *Manifest Destiny and Mission in American History* (New York: Vintage, 1966); Richard Hofstadter, *The Paranoid Style in American Politics and Other Essays* (New York: Knopf, 1966), pp. 145–87; Walter LaFeber, *The New Empire: An Interpretation of American Expansion, 1860–1898* (Ithaca: Cornell University Press, 1963); Ernest R. May, *American Imperialism: A Speculative Essay* (New York: Atheneum, 1968).

10. George Kennan, "The War with Spain," *American Diplomacy* (Chicago: University of Chicago Press, 1985 [1951]), p. 17.

11. William Appleman Williams, *The Tragedy of American Diplomacy,* rev. ed. (New York: Dell, 1962).

12. Ernest N. Paolino, *The Foundations of the American Empire: William Henry Seward and U.S. Foreign Policy* (Ithaca: Cornell University Press, 1973), quotations from pp. 26, 212. See also Walter A. McDougall, *Let the Sea Make a Noise: A History of the North Pacific from Magellan to MacArthur* (New York: Basic Books, 1993), pp. 269–70, 300–301.

13. LaFeber, *American Age,* p. 165.

14. David M. Pletcher, "Rhetoric and Results: A Pragmatic View of American Economic Expansion, 1865–1898," *Diplomatic History* 5 (spring 1981): 93–104. For a critique of the Open Door school, see Arthur M. Schlesinger, Jr., *The Cycles of American History* (Boston: Houghton Mifflin, 1986), pp. 128–52.

15. Frederick G. Drake, *The Empire of the Seas: A Biography of Rear-Admiral Robert N. Shufeldt* (Honolulu: University of Hawaii Press, 1984), p. 116.

16. See Charles Callan Tansill, *The Foreign Policy of Thomas Francis Bayard* (New York: Fordham University Press, 1940), chaps. 1–4, on Samoa. German quote from LaFeber, *The New Empire,* p. 55.

17. Dulles, *Imperial Years,* p. 10.

18. Pratt, *Expansionists of 1898,* p. 25.

19. David M. Pletcher, *The Awkward Years: American Foreign Policy under Garfield and Arthur* (Columbia: University of Missouri Press, 1962), p. 70.

20. Thomas G. Paterson et al., *American Foreign Policy: A History,* vol. 1, *To 1914* (Lexington, Mass.: D. C. Heath, 1988), p. 173.

21. Lodge in Marshall Bertram, *The Birth of Anglo-American Friendship: The Prime Facet of the Venezuelan Boundary Dispute* (Lanham, Md.: University Press of America, 1992), p. 14; Senator Collum in Dexter Perkins, *The Monroe Doctrine, 1867–1907* (Baltimore: Johns Hopkins University Press, 1937), p. 184.

22. Olney to Bayard (London), July 20, 1895: *Foreign Relations of the United States, 1895,* pp. 545–62. For convenience, see Paterson, *Major Problems,* pp. 350–53.

23. Bertram, *Anglo-American Friendship,* p. 118.

24. The German kaiser showed a brief flurry of interest, but when it became clear that Britain intended to give the United States a free hand in Cuba, the rest of Europe

left Spain to its fate. See Ernest R. May, *Imperial Democracy: The Emergence of America as a Great Power* (New York: Harcourt, Brace, and World, 1961), pp. 196–200.

25. Foster Rhea Dulles, *Prelude to World Power: American Diplomatic History, 1860–1900* (New York: Macmillan, 1965), p. 178.

26. Thomas J. Osborne, *"Empire Can Wait": American Opposition to Hawaiian Annexation, 1893–1898* (Kent, Ohio: Kent State University Press, 1981), pp. 132–33.

27. May, *Imperial Democracy*, p. 244.

28. Dewey in H. Wayne Morgan, *America's Road to Empire: The War with Spain and Overseas Expansion* (New York: Knopf, 1965), p. 94; John Foreman in *Contemporary Review* (July 1898): May, *Imperial Democracy*, p. 254.

29. Charles S. Olcott, *Life of William McKinley*, 2 vols. (Boston: Houghton Mifflin, 1916), 2:109–11.

30. Thomas A. Bailey, *The Man in the Street: The Impact of American Public Opinion on Foreign Policy* (New York: Macmillan, 1948), p. 204.

31. Pratt, *Expansionists of 1898*, p. 282.

32. May, *Imperial Democracy*, p. 248.

33. Foster Rhea Dulles, *America's Rise to World Power* (New York: Harper and Row, 1954), p. 48.

34. May, *Imperialism: A Speculative Essay*, pp. 188–89.

35. TR sent it on to Lodge with the note "Rather poor poetry, but good sense from the expansionist viewpoint": Christopher Hitchens, *Blood, Class, and Nostalgia: Anglo-American Ironies* (New York: Farrar, Straus, and Giroux, 1990), p. 66.

36. On the mugwump opposition (the term dated from the election of 1884), see Robert L. Beisner, *Twelve Against Empire: The Anti-Imperialists, 1898–1900* (New York: McGraw-Hill, 1968), pp. 5–17 (quote p. 10).

37. Hoar in Pratt, *Expansionists of 1898*, p. 347; Schurz and *World* in Beisner, *Twelve Against Empire*, pp. 34, 219–20.

38. Morrell Heald and Lawrence S. Kaplan, *Culture and Diplomacy: The American Experience* (Westport, Conn.: Greenwood, 1977), p. 146.

39. Akira Iriye, *From Nationalism to Internationalism: U.S. Foreign Policy to 1914* (London: Routledge and Kegan Paul, 1977), p. 337. On the American career in the Philippines, see Stanley Karnow, *In Our Image: America's Empire in the Philippines* (New York: Random House, 1989).

40. Walter LaFeber, *The Cambridge History of American Foreign Relations*, vol. 2, *The American Search for Opportunity, 1865–1913* (Cambridge: Cambridge University Press, 1993), p. 180.

41. Paterson, *Major Problems*, p. 461.

42. *The Letters of Theodore Roosevelt*, ed. Elting E. Morison, 8 vols. (Cambridge: Harvard University Press, 1951–54), 4:734. Secretary of State John Hay, alarmed by rumors of German interest in Denmark's Virgin Islands, did attempt to purchase the islands in 1902. The Danish parliament refused (until 1917), but the United States made clear it would not tolerate their transfer to any other power.

43. Speech at University of Pennsylvania (June 15, 1910): Walter V. and Marie V. Scholes, *The Foreign Policies of the Taft Administration* (Columbia: University of Missouri Press, 1970), p. 35.

44. Businessman H. B. LaRue complained in 1904, "To demand an open door in China

and maintain a closed door here is an outrage on common sense": Delber L. McKee, *Chinese Exclusion Versus the Open Door Policy, 1900–1906* (Detroit: Wayne State University Press, 1977), p. 112. Frederick Merk appears to have been the first historian to ask, "Is it not likely that racism prior to the war with Spain was a deterrent to imperialism rather than a stimulant of it?": *Manifest Destiny*, p. 247.

45. The movement for arbitration of international disputes provides a prime example of U.S. devotion to Unilateralism. At the first Hague Conference in 1899 the U.S. delegation affirmed a Permanent Court of Arbitration only on condition that it in no way require the United States to depart from its policy of non-entanglement or "traditional attitude toward purely American questions." In 1902 Roosevelt refused to submit the Venezuelan dispute to the Hague Court because it was "in my judgment better that I should arbitrate it myself . . . in such case there would be no possibility of the court rendering a decision which might be in conflict with the Monroe Doctrine." See Calvin DeArmond Davis, *The United States and the Second Hague Peace Conference: American Diplomacy and International Organization, 1899–1914* (Durham: Duke University Press, 1975), quotes on pp. 33, 83.

46. Guano was a major source of nitrates for fertilizer and, later, explosives, hence the object of brisk competition. See Jimmy M. Skaggs, *The Great Guano Rush: Entrepreneurs and American Overseas Expansion* (New York: St. Martin's, 1994).

47. Dulles, *Imperial Years*, p. 12.

48. Rubin Francis Weston, *Racism in U.S. Imperialism: The Influence of Racial Assumptions on American Foreign Policy, 1893–1946* (Columbia: University of South Carolina Press, 1972), p. 258.

49. See Glenn Anthony May, *Social Engineering in the Philippines: The Aims, Execution, and Impact of American Colonial Policy, 1900–1913* (Westport, Conn.: Greenwood, 1980).

50. Samuel Flagg Bemis, *Latin American Policy of the U.S.: A Historical Interpretation* (New York: Harcourt, Brace, 1943), p. 385.

51. *Speeches and Addresses of William McKinley* (New York: Doubleday and McClure, 1900), pp. 361–66, in Morgan, *Road to Empire*, p. 113.

52. Dulles, *Imperial Years*, p. viii.

53. Robert Dallek, *The American Style of Foreign Policy: Cultural Politics and Foreign Affairs* (New York: Knopf, 1983), pp. 8–10.

54. William Leuchtenberg first argued this case in "Progressivism and Imperialism: The Progressive Movement and American Foreign Policy, 1898–1916," *Mississippi Valley Historical Review* 39 (Dec. 1952): 483–504. See the summaries of the debate he provoked in Jerry Israel, *Progressivism and the Open Door* (Pittsburgh: University of Pittsburgh Press, 1971), xii–xxiv; and Jerald A. Combs, *American Diplomatic History: Two Centuries of Changing Interpretations* (Berkeley: University of California Press, 1983), pp. 269–71.

55. Combs, *American Diplomatic History*, pp. 84–97. Archibald Cary Coolidge, author of the influential *United States as a World Power* (1908), did fret about American expansion, but on the grounds that it was too *idealistic*: "vague moralistic passions" might lure the United States into overextension.

56. Robert V. Friedenberg, *Theodore Roosevelt and the Rhetoric of Militant Decency* (Westport, Conn.: Greenwood, 1990), p. 17.

57. Herbert Croly, *The Promise of American Life* (New York: Bobbs-Merrill, 1965 [1909]), pp. 289–314 (quote p. 309).

58. Dallek, *American Style*, p. 30.
59. Louis Hartz, *The Liberal Tradition in America* (New York: Harcourt, Brace, and World, 1955), p. 41.
60. Schlesinger, *Cycles of American History*, p. 17.
61. Norman A. Graebner, *Foundations of American Foreign Policy: A Realist Appraisal from Franklin to McKinley* (Wilmington: Scholarly Resources, 1985), p. 352.
62. Robert L. Beisner, *From the Old Diplomacy to the New, 1865–1900* (Arlington Heights, Ill.: AHM Publishing, 1975), p. 76.

CHAPTER SIX

1. Thomas J. Knock, *To End All Wars: Woodrow Wilson and the Quest for a New World Order* (New York: Oxford University Press, 1992), p. 76.
2. Knock, *To End All Wars*, pp. 76–78.
3. George D. Herron, *Woodrow Wilson and the World's Peace* (New York: Mitchell Kennerley, 1917), pp. 76–77; and Mitchell Pirie Briggs, *George D. Herron and the European Settlement* (Stanford: Stanford University Press, 1932), p. 249, cited by Lloyd E. Ambrosius, *Wilsonian Statecraft: Theory and Practice of Liberal Internationalism during World War I* (Wilmington: Scholarly Resources, 1991), pp. 11–13.
4. E. D. Morel, *The Morrow of the War* (1915), and Bertrand Russell, *The Foreign Policy of the Entente* (1914), in Michael Howard, *War and the Liberal Conscience* (New Brunswick: Rutgers University Press, 1978), pp. 75–77.
5. Wilson first used this phrase in reference to senators who filibustered his request to arm U.S. merchant ships in March 1917. See Ray Stannard Baker, *Woodrow Wilson: Life and Letters*, 8 vols. (Garden City, N.Y.: Doubleday Page, 1927–39), 6:481. It was later applied to those who blocked ratification of the Treaty of Versailles without reservations.
6. Just a sample of authors who dispute the influence of Wilson includes Walter Lippmann, *U.S. Foreign Policy: Shield of the Republic* (Boston: Little, Brown, 1943); George F. Kennan, *American Diplomacy, 1900–1950* (Chicago: University of Chicago Press, 1951); Hans J. Morgenthau, *In Defense of the National Interest: A Critical Examination of American Foreign Policy* (New York: Knopf, 1951); Robert E. Osgood, *Ideals and Self-Interest in America's Foreign Relations* (Chicago: University of Chicago Press, 1953); David F. Trask, *Victory Without Peace: American Foreign Relations in the Twentieth Century* (New York: John Wiley and Sons, 1968); Arthur S. Link, *The Higher Realism of Woodrow Wilson and Other Essays* (Nashville: Vanderbilt University Press, 1971); Ernest R. May, *The World War and American Isolation, 1914–1917* (Cambridge: Harvard University Press, 1959). For discussions of the historiographical debate, see Ambrosius, *Wilsonian Statecraft*, pp. ix–xvi, and Jerald A. Combs, *American Diplomatic History: Two Centuries of Changing Interpretations* (Berkeley: University of California Press, 1983), pp. 113–31, 259–68, 378–81.
7. Akira Iriye, *The Cambridge History of American Foreign Relations*, vol. 3, *The Globalizing of America, 1913–1945* (Cambridge: Cambridge University Press, 1993), p. 72.
8. "The only place" and "Presbyterian priest" in John Morton Blum, *Woodrow Wilson and the Politics of Morality* (Boston: Little, Brown, 1956), pp. 6–7.
9. "Very stupid indeed" and "ouija" in Henry Wilkinson Bragdon, *Woodrow Wilson:*

The Academic Years (Cambridge: Harvard University Press, 1967), pp. 23, 312. Wilson loved the fact that his name had thirteen letters (after he dropped his given first name, Thomas), that he was the thirteenth president of Princeton and took that office in his thirteenth year there. He would also become president of the United States in the year 1913.

10. Arthur S. Link, *Woodrow Wilson: Revolution, War, and Peace* (Arlington Heights, Ill.: Harlan Davidson, 1979), p. 6.

11. Blum, *Politics of Morality,* p. 15.

12. Thomas G. Paterson et al., *American Foreign Policy: A History,* vol. 3, *Since 1900,* 3d ed. (Lexington, Mass.: D. C. Heath, 1991), p. 263.

13. Bragdon, *Wilson: The Academic Years,* p. 113.

14. Bragdon, *Wilson: The Academic Years,* pp. 131–33.

15. Woodrow Wilson, "The Ideals of America," *Atlantic Monthly* (Dec. 26, 1901), in Niels Aage Thorsen, *The Political Thought of Woodrow Wilson, 1875–1910* (Princeton: Princeton University Press, 1988), p. 175.

16. Woodrow Wilson, *Congressional Government: A Study in American Politics,* 15th ed. (Boston: Houghton Mifflin, 1900), pp. xi–xii.

17. John Milton Cooper, Jr., *The Warrior and the Priest: Woodrow Wilson and Theodore Roosevelt* (Cambridge: Harvard University Press, 1983), pp. 106–7.

18. Blum, *Politics of Morality,* p. 31.

19. Thorsen, *Political Thought of Woodrow Wilson,* pp. 8, 16.

20. Ambrosius, *Wilsonian Statecraft,* p. 11.

21. See Ernest Lee Tuveson, *Redeemer Nation: The Idea of America's Millennial Role* (Chicago: University of Chicago Press, 1968), and Robert M. Crunden, *Ministers of Reform: The Progressives' Achievement in American Civilization, 1889–1920* (New York: Basic Books, 1982).

22. Link, *Revolution, War, and Peace,* p. 6.

23. Cooper, *Warrior and the Priest,* p. 195.

24. Blum, *Politics of Morality,* p. 40.

25. Baker, *Woodrow Wilson: Life and Letters,* 4:55.

26. Arthur S. Link, *Woodrow Wilson and the Progressive Era, 1910–1917* (New York: Harper and Bros., 1954), p. 83.

27. Circular note of Nov. 2, 1913, in Tony Smith, *America's Mission: The United States and the Worldwide Struggle for Democracy in the Twentieth Century* (Princeton: Princeton University Press, 1994), pp. 66–70.

28. Thomas A. Bailey, *A Diplomatic History of the American People,* 8th ed. (New York: Appleton-Century-Crofts, 1969), p. 556.

29. C. R. Conyne, *Woodrow Wilson: British Perspectives, 1912–21* (New York: St. Martin's, 1992), pp. 31, 37.

30. Tyrrell duly reported this to Sir Edward Grey, adding, "If some of the veteran diplomats could have heard us, they would have fallen in a faint." See Smith, *America's Mission,* p. 60.

31. *The Public Papers of Woodrow Wilson,* ed. Ray Stannard Baker and William E. Dodd, 6 vols. (New York: Harper and Bros., 1925–27), 3:127.

32. Knock, *To End All Wars,* p. 39.

33. Samuel Flagg Bemis, "Woodrow Wilson and Latin America," *American Foreign Policy*

and the Blessings of Liberty and Other Essays (New Haven: Yale University Press, 1962), pp. 379–95 (quotes p. 392).

34. Kurt Wimer, "Woodrow Wilson and World Order," in Arthur S. Link, ed., *Woodrow Wilson and a Revolutionary World, 1913–1921* (Chapel Hill: University of North Carolina Press, 1982), pp. 146–73 (quote p. 150).

35. Thomas A. Bailey and Paul B. Ryan, *The Lusitania Disaster* (New York: Free Press, 1975), p. 99.

36. *Public Papers of Woodrow Wilson*, 1:321.

37. Bailey, *A Diplomatic History*, p. 579.

38. *Public Papers of Woodrow Wilson*, 2:124.

39. *Public Papers of Woodrow Wilson*, 4:127–28. The biblical passage on love (or "charity") is in I Corinthians 13.

40. See S. D. Lovell, *The Presidential Campaign of 1916* (Carbondale: Southern Illinois University Press, 1980), esp. pp. 90–91.

41. Lloyd C. Gardner, *Safe for Democracy: The Anglo-American Response to Revolution, 1913–1923* (New York: Oxford University Press, 1987), p. 119.

42. *Public Papers of Woodrow Wilson*, 2:407–14.

43. Arthur S. Link, "President Wilson and His English Critics: An Inaugural Lecture" (Oxford: Clarendon, 1959), p. 15.

44. Paterson, *American Foreign Policy*, p. 271.

45. Cooper, *Warrior and the Priest*, p. 310.

46. What if the United States had constructed a navy "second to none" (Wilson's own phrase) and convoyed ships to Europe in the teeth of both blockades? Neither side would have dared interfere lest it push the Americans into the enemy camp. In that event, Wilson might have been able to pressure the Allies and the Germans into settling for "peace for victory." See John W. Coogan, *The End of Neutrality: The United States, Britain, and Maritime Rights, 1899–1915* (Ithaca: Cornell University Press, 1981), pp. 249–56.

47. *Public Papers of Woodrow Wilson*, 1:6–16.

48. Robert Dallek, *The American Style of Foreign Policy: Cultural Politics and Foreign Affairs* (New York: Knopf, 1983), pp. 64–65.

49. "War Message to Congress" (April 2, 1917): *Public Papers of Woodrow Wilson*, 1:6–16. For convenience, see Thomas G. Paterson, ed., *Major Problems in American Foreign Policy*, vol. 2, *Since 1914* (Lexington, Mass.: D. C. Heath, 1989), pp. 51–55.

50. Foster Rhea Dulles, *America's Rise to World Power, 1898–1954* (New York: Harper and Bros., 1954), p. 103.

51. *National Review* (Jan. 1913): 736–50; cited by Edward H. Buehrig, *Woodrow Wilson and the Balance of Power* (Bloomington: Indiana University Press, 1955), pp. 180–85.

52. Norman A. Graebner, *America as a World Power: A Realist Appraisal from Wilson to Reagan* (Wilmington: Scholarly Resources, 1984), p. 2. For a summary of the debate over U.S. entry into World War I, see Robert D. Schulzinger, *American Diplomacy in the Twentieth Century* (New York: Oxford University Press, 1984), pp. 79–81.

53. Link, *War, Revolution, and Peace*, p. 85.

54. Herbert Hoover, *The Ordeal of Woodrow Wilson* (Washington, D.C.: Woodrow Wilson Center Press, 1992 [1958]), pp. 24–25 (emphasis added).

55. Cooper, *Warrior and the Priest*, p. 331.

56. Hoover, *Ordeal of Woodrow Wilson*, pp. 14–15.

57. Wilson did name one Republican, the diplomat Henry White, but he was a non-entity. The other delegates were Secretary of State Lansing (whom Wilson distrusted), his personal crony Colonel House (whom he learned to distrust), and General Tasker Bliss, on whom he relied for military advice only.

58. "Weatherwise" and "the only thing" in Gardner, *Safe for Democracy*, p. 1. Wilson was alluding to Matthew 16:2–3: "When it is evening, you say, 'It will be fair weather; for the sky is red.' And in the morning, 'It will be stormy today, for the sky is red and threatening.' You know how to interpret the appearance of the sky, but you cannot interpret the signs of the times."

59. The Anglo-American battle over postwar shipping was at least as virulent as the one over naval power. See Jeffrey J. Safford, *Wilsonian Maritime Diplomacy, 1913–1921* (New Brunswick: Rutgers University Press, 1978).

60. The leftist *New Republic* wrote in March 1919 that since final justice was clearly not going to be done by the Peace Conference, "America should not be pledged to uphold injustices. . . . The result of Article Ten will be to guarantee the mistakes made at Paris": Knock, *To End All Wars*, pp. 252–53.

61. Hoover, *Ordeal of Woodrow Wilson*, p. 267.

62. Cooper, *Warrior and the Priest*, p. 333.

63. Lloyd E. Ambrosius, *Woodrow Wilson and the American Diplomatic Tradition: The Treaty Fight in Perspective* (Cambridge: Cambridge University Press, 1987), p. 155.

64. Lodge thought Wilson's duplicity "very characteristic": Ambrosius, *Wilson and the American Diplomatic Tradition*, p. 83.

65. Denna Frank Fleming, *The United States and the League of Nations, 1918–1920* (New York: Russell and Russell, 1968), p. 134.

66. Henry Cabot Lodge, *The Senate and the League of Nations* (New York: Scribner's, 1925), pp. 117–21.

67. Paterson, *American Foreign Policy*, p. 286.

68. Ambrosius, *Wilson and the American Diplomatic Tradition*, p. 165.

69. Beatrice Farnsworth, *William C. Bullitt and the Soviet Union* (Bloomington: Indiana University Press, 1967), pp. 61–62.

70. Ambrosius, *Wilson and the American Diplomatic Tradition*, p. 139.

71. The chairman of the Republican National Committee, Will H. Hays, spied in Borah's appeal to Americanism a theme that would "play in Peoria": "While we seek earnestly and prayerfully for methods lessening future wars, . . . we will accept no indefinite internationalism as a substitute for fervent American nationalism" (Borah and Hays in Ambrosius, *Wilson and the American Diplomatic Tradition*, pp. 89–90, 102).

72. Ambrosius, *Wilson and the American Diplomatic Tradition*, p. 149.

73. Armin Rappaport, *A History of American Diplomacy* (New York: Macmillan, 1975), p. 278.

74. Ambrosius, *Wilson and the American Diplomatic Tradition*, p. 250.

75. Knock, *To End All Wars*, pp. 270–71.

76. Rappaport, *History of American Diplomacy*, p. 275.

77. Ambrosius, *Wilson and the American Diplomatic Tradition*, p. 139. Characteristic of many Protestants, Sherman also feared Vatican influence over the League, since seventeen of the twenty-eight charter members were largely Catholic countries.

78. Link, *War, Revolution, and Peace*, p. 127.

79. Julius W. Pratt, *A History of United States Foreign Policy* (New York: Prentice-Hall, 1955), pp. 525–26.

80. As a Chicago paper wrote, "At the end of a long rope, the other end of which is held by the Senate, the United States enters the World Court provided with a bottle of disinfectant and a portable fire-escape": Thomas A. Bailey, *The Man in the Street: The Impact of American Public Opinion on Foreign Policy* (New York: Macmillan, 1948), p. 249. See Denna Frank Fleming, *The United States and the World Court* (Garden City, N.Y.: Doubleday, 1945).

81. "Think not that I am come to send peace on earth: I came not to send peace, but a sword": Matthew 10:34 KJV.

CHAPTER SEVEN

1. Roosevelt and Vandenberg in Foster Rhea Dulles, *America's Rise to World Power, 1898–1954* (New York: Harper and Bros., 1954), p. 207.

2. (March 1917) in Robert H. Ferrell, *Woodrow Wilson and World War I, 1917–1921* (New York: Harper and Row, 1985), p. 12.

3. Al Smith's 1928 campaign for president symbolized the new acceptance of Catholics, and one scholar named Jews "the most active single ethnic group in foreign policy questions in recent years" (Gabriel A. Almond, *The American People and Foreign Policy* [New York: Harcourt, Brace, 1950], p. 185).

4. Fredrick B. Pike, *FDR's Good Neighbor Policy: Sixty Years of Generally Gentle Chaos* (Austin: University of Texas Press, 1995), pp. 46–55 (quote p. 54).

5. Manfred Jonas, *Isolationism in America, 1935–1941* (Ithaca: Cornell University Press, 1966), p. 5.

6. Senators Borah and Johnson even opposed Nye's extreme legislation on the grounds that it surrendered America's rights on the high seas: C. David Tompkins, *Senator Arthur H. Vandenberg: The Evolution of a Modern Republican, 1884–1945* (East Lansing: Michigan State University Press, 1970), p. 127.

7. Senator Robert Taft (R., Ohio) in Jonas, *Isolationism in America*, p. 87.

8. Jonas, *Isolationism*, p. 81.

9. Herbert Johnson cartoon, *Saturday Evening Post* (Jan. 8, 1938).

10. FDR in 1932 in Robert A. Divine, *Roosevelt and World War II* (New York: Penguin, 1969), p. 55; speech at Chautauqua, New York (Aug. 14, 1936), in Thomas G. Paterson, ed., *Major Problems in American Foreign Policy*, vol. 2, *Since 1914*, 3d ed. (Lexington, Mass.: D. C. Heath, 1989), pp. 173–75.

11. Arsenal of Democracy fireside chat (Dec. 29, 1940), in Paterson, *Major Problems*, pp. 175–77.

12. Robert A. Divine, *The Illusion of Neutrality: Franklin D. Roosevelt and the Struggle over the Arms Embargo* (Chicago: University of Chicago Press, 1962), p. 301. For an excellent compilation of the documents of the America First Committee, see Justus D. Roenicke, ed., *In Danger Undaunted: The Anti-Interventionist Movement of 1940–1941 as Revealed in the Papers of the America First Committee* (Stanford: Hoover Institution Press, 1990).

13. Charles A. Lindbergh address in New York (April 22, 1941), in Richard D. Challener, ed., *From Isolation to Containment, 1921–1952* (New York: St. Martin's, 1970), p. 106.

The committee included, for a brief time, the young Gerald R. Ford. He resigned because he thought Yale University, where he was employed as an assistant football coach, might frown on his activism.

14. Wallace speech to the Foreign Policy Association (April 1941): Robert A. Divine, *Second Chance: The Triumph of Internationalism in America during World War II* (New York: Atheneum, 1971), p. 41.

15. R. E. Sherwood, *Roosevelt and Hopkins: An Intimate History* (New York: Harper and Bros., 1948), pp. 359–60.

16. Divine, *Second Chance,* p. 103.

17. Daniel Yergin, *Shattered Peace: The Origins of the Cold War and the National Security State* (Boston: Houghton Mifflin, 1978), p. 46.

18. Divine, *Second Chance,* pp. 152, 160.

19. Charles A. Beard, *The Republic* (1944); Carl Becker, *How Better Will the New World Be?* (1944); Nicholas J. Spykman, *America's Strategy in World Politics* (1942); Robert Strausz-Hupé, *Geopolitics* (1942); Reinhold Niebuhr, *The Children of Light and the Children of Darkness* (1944); Walter Lippmann, *U.S. War Aims* (1944), cited by Divine, *Second Chance,* pp. 174–76, 181.

20. Divine, *Second Chance,* p. 213. FDR died before the U.N. was up and running, but President Truman, at the close of the San Francisco Conference on June 26, 1945, called the U.N. Charter "a victory against war itself" which realized "the ideal of that great statesman of a generation ago — Woodrow Wilson. . . . Let us not fail to grasp this supreme chance to establish a world-wide rule of reason — to create enduring peace under the guidance of God."

21. Tompkins, *Senator Arthur H. Vandenberg,* p. 233.

22. William Roger Louis, *Imperialism at Bay: The United States and the Decolonization of the British Empire, 1941–1945* (Oxford: Clarendon, 1986 [1977]), p. 515.

23. Challener, *From Isolation to Containment,* pp. 118–19 (emphasis added).

24. Henrik Shipstead (R., Minn.) in Divine, *Second Chance,* p. 313.

25. Fireside chat after the Teheran Conference (Dec. 1943), in Divine, *Roosevelt and World War II,* p. 61, 64–65.

26. The American Federation of Labor, having observed the death of free unions in Russia and fought Communists in its own ranks, opposed any action "which could be construed as assistance to or approval of the Soviet government" (Morrell Heald and Lawrence S. Kaplan, *Culture and Diplomacy: The American Experience* [Westport, Conn.: Greenwood, 1977], p. 173).

27. Joseph E. Davies, *Mission to Moscow* (1941), and Wendell Willkie, *One World* (1943), cited by John Lewis Gaddis, *The United States and the Origins of the Cold War* (New York: Columbia University Press, 1972), pp. 34–42 (quotes pp. 36, 40, 41); Walter Duranty, *The Kremlin and the People* (1941), cited by Ralph B. Levering, *American Opinion and the Russian Alliance, 1939–1945* (Chapel Hill: University of North Carolina Press, 1976), p. 58.

28. Levering, *American Opinion and the Russian Alliance,* photo inserts.

29. Norman A. Graebner, *America as a World Power: A Realist Appraisal from Wilson to Reagan* (Wilmington: Scholarly Resources, 1984), p. 99.

30. Graebner, *America as a World Power,* p. 110.

31. Yergin, *Shattered Peace,* p. 68.

32. Readers curious about my views on this question may refer to my article "20th-

Century International Relations," *Encyclopaedia Britannica*, 15th ed. (1989), vol. 20, pp. 732–824 (esp. pp. 789–99), and the relevant chapters of Walter A. McDougall, . . . *the Heavens and the Earth: A Political History of the Space Age* (New York: Basic Books, 1985).

33. *The Forrestal Diaries*, ed. Walter Mills (New York: Viking, 1951), p. 127. See also Townsend Hoopes and Douglas Brinkley, *Driven Patriot: The Life and Times of James Forrestal* (New York: Knopf, 1992), pp. 262–63.

34. (April 1, 1945): Jean-Baptiste Duroselle, *From Wilson to Roosevelt: Foreign Policy of the United States, 1913–1945* (New York: Harper and Row, 1968 [1963]), p. 419.

35. Stephen T. Ambrose, *Rise to Globalism: American Foreign Policy Since 1938*, 4th ed. (New York: Penguin, 1985), p. 70.

36. Marc Trachtenberg, "The Myth of Potsdam" (Jan. 18, 1996), p. 13: unpublished conference paper based on the Potsdam series of the *Foreign Relations of the United States*.

37. Trachtenberg's interpretation of American thinking at Potsdam may seem provocative, but years ago Bruce Kuklick concluded, "The phraseology adopted . . . rejected dismemberment, but in fact the opposite was true. Ironically, when the Americans discarded partition in theory, they accomplished it in fact" (Kuklick, *American Policy and the Division of Germany: The Clash with Russia over Reparations* [Ithaca: Cornell University Press, 1972], p. 166).

38. "I've never been talked to like that," said Molotov after Truman chewed him out. "Carry out your agreements and you won't get talked to like that," bluff Harry replied: Harry S. Truman, *Memoirs: Year of Decisions* (Garden City, N.Y.: Doubleday, 1955), pp. 79–82.

39. Arthur M. Schlesinger, Jr., *The Cycles of American History* (Boston: Houghton Mifflin, 1986), p. 184.

40. Joseph C. Grew, *Turbulent Era: A Diplomatic Record of Forty Years, 1904–1945*, 2 vols. (Boston: Houghton Mifflin, 1952), 2:1445–46.

41. Michael A. Guhin, *John Foster Dulles: A Statesman and His Times* (New York: Columbia University Press, 1972), p. 135.

42. Fraser J. Harbutt, *The Iron Curtain: Churchill, America, and the Origins of the Cold War* (New York: Oxford University Press, 1986), p. 160.

43. Harbutt, *Iron Curtain*, p. 161.

44. George F. Kennan, *Memoirs, 1925–1950* (New York: Bantam, 1969 [1967]), pp. 260–64, 309 (quote).

45. "Telegraphic Message from Moscow of February 22, 1946": Kennan, *Memoirs*, pp. 583–98 (quotes pp. 586, 594–95).

46. *Times* in Harbutt, *Iron Curtain*, p. 156; Vandenberg in John Lewis Gaddis, *The United States and the Origins of the Cold War, 1941–1947* (New York: Columbia University Press, 1972), p. 295.

47. Harbutt, *Iron Curtain*, p. 172.

48. Winston S. Churchill's Iron Curtain speech (March 5, 1946), in Paterson, *Major Problems*, pp. 288–92.

49. Harbutt, *Iron Curtain*, p. 204.

50. Dulles, "Thoughts on Soviet Foreign Policy and What to Do About It," *Life* (June 3, 1946): 112–26, (June 10, 1946): 118–30; State Department memo in Henry Kissinger, *Diplomacy* (New York: Simon and Schuster, 1994), pp. 449–50; Clifford

memo in Walter Isaacson and Evan Thomas, *The Wise Men: Six Friends and the World They Made* (New York: Simon and Schuster, 1986), p. 376.

51. Ambrose, *Rise to Globalism*, p. 83.

52. Dean Acheson, *Present at the Creation: My Years in the State Department* (New York: W. W. Norton, 1969), p. 219.

53. Paterson, *Major Problems*, pp. 297–300.

54. Graebner, *America as a World Power*, p. 140. See also Henry A. Wallace, "The Path to Peace with Russia," *New Republic* (Sept. 30, 1946): 401–6.

55. Walter Lippmann, *The Cold War: A Study in U.S. Foreign Policy* (New York: Harper and Bros., 1947), p. 16.

56. James Warburg, *Faith, Purpose, and Power* (New York: Farrar, Straus, 1950), in David Steigerwald, *Wilsonian Idealism in America* (Ithaca: Cornell University Press, 1994), p. 163.

57. "The Sources of Soviet Conduct," *Foreign Affairs* (July 1947): 566–82, reprinted in George F. Kennan, *American Diplomacy: Expanded Edition* (Chicago: University of Chicago Press, 1984), pp. 107–28; John Lewis Gaddis, *Strategies of Containment: A Critical Appraisal of Postwar American National Security Policy* (New York: Oxford University Press, 1982), p. 28; Kennan, *Memoirs*, pp. 376–79.

58. John Gimbel, "The Origins of the Marshall Plan," in Charles S. Maier, ed., *The Origins of the Cold War and Contemporary Europe* (New York: Franklin Watts, 1978), p. 164.

59. Taft in Richard S. Kirkendall, *A Global Power: America Since the Age of Roosevelt*, 2d ed. (New York: Knopf, 1980), p. 26; other quotes in Divine, *Since 1945*, p. 15.

60. Armin Rappaport, *A History of American Diplomacy* (New York: Macmillan, 1975), p. 390.

61. Guhin, *John Foster Dulles*, p. 160.

62. Dulles, *America's Rise to World Power*, pp. 244–45. On the Euro-American origins of NATO, see Timothy P. Ireland, *Creating the Entangling Alliance: The Origins of the North Atlantic Treaty Organization* (Westport, Conn.: Greenwood, 1981).

63. See Yergin, *Shattered Peace*, pp. 196–200.

64. Truman said in May 1947, "The police state is a police state; I don't care what you call it": John Lewis Gaddis, *The Long Peace: Inquiries into the History of the Cold War* (New York: Oxford University Press, 1987), p. 36.

65. Divine, *Since 1945*, p. 35.

66. Walter LaFeber, *The American Age: United States Foreign Policy Since 1750* (New York: W. W. Norton, 1989), p. 490.

67. Robert Dallek, *The American Style of Foreign Policy: Cultural Politics and Foreign Affairs* (New York: Knopf, 1983), p. 183.

68. Thomas G. Paterson, J. Garry Clifford, and Kenneth J. Hagan, *American Foreign Policy: A History*, vol. 2, *Since 1900*, 3d ed. (Lexington, Mass.: D. C. Heath, 1991), p. 446.

69. Stanley Hoffmann, *Gulliver's Troubles, or the Setting of American Foreign Policy* (New York: McGraw-Hill, 1968), p. 96.

70. Melvyn P. Leffler, "The American Conception of National Security and the Beginnings of the Cold War, 1945–48," *American Historical Review* 89 (April 1984), p. 379. See also Leffler, *A Preponderance of Power: National Security, the Truman Administration, and the Cold War* (Stanford: Stanford University Press, 1992).

71. Europeans, Latins, and Japanese knew this from the start, which explains their growing resentment of American bossiness during the Cold War.

72. Tony Smith, *America's Mission: The United States and the Worldwide Struggle for Democracy in the Twentieth Century* (Princeton: Princeton University Press, 1994), p. 143.

73. "NSC 68: United States Objectives and Programs for National Security" (April 14, 1950), reprinted in Ernest R. May, ed., *American Cold War Strategy: Interpreting NSC 68* (Boston: Bedford Books, 1993), pp. 23–82.

74. "NSC 68" in May, *American Cold War Strategy*, p. 52.

75. *Public Papers of the Presidents: Harry S. Truman, 1951* (Washington, D.C.: GPO, 1966), pp. 548–49. Intellectual historian Bruce Kuklick, while granting the possible role of "hidden intentions" in U.S. Cold War policy, likewise sees in NSC 68 an expression of traditional "American ideals and even of their comparatively positive, not to say metaphysically benign, character" (May, *American Cold War Strategy*, p. 159).

76. "America and the Russian Future," *Foreign Affairs* 29, no. 3 (April 1951): 351–70, reprinted in Kennan, *American Diplomacy*, pp. 129–54 (quote p. 153).

77. Gaddis, *Strategies of Containment*, pp. 129, 135.

78. Raymond Moley in LaFeber, *American Age*, p. 380.

79. Townsend Hoopes, *The Devil and John Foster Dulles* (Boston: Little, Brown, 1973), p. 130.

CHAPTER EIGHT

1. Thomas G. Paterson, ed., *Major Problems in American Foreign Policy*, vol. 2, *Since 1914*, 3d ed. (Lexington, Mass.: D. C. Heath, 1989), pp. 572–76.

2. Stanley Karnow, *Vietnam: A History* (New York: Viking, 1983), p. 419.

3. Lloyd C. Gardner, *Pay Any Price: Lyndon Johnson and the Wars for Vietnam* (Chicago: Ivan R. Dee, 1995), pp. 185–91.

4. Luke 13:48 (*The Oxford Annotated Bible*, RSV [New York: Oxford University Press, 1962]).

5. *Memoirs of John Quincy Adams*, ed. Charles Francis Adams, 12 vols. (Philadelphia: Lippincott, 1874–77), 6:324–25, cited by Walter LaFeber, *The American Age: United States Foreign Policy at Home and Abroad Since 1750* (New York: W. W. Norton, 1989), p. 82.

6. Ralph S. Kuykendall, *The Hawaiian Kingdom*, 3 vols, vol. 1, *Foundation and Transformation, 1778–1854* (Honolulu: University of Hawaii Press, 1947), pp. 101–2.

7. See Walter A. McDougall, *Let the Sea Make a Noise: A History of the North Pacific from Magellan to MacArthur* (New York: Basic Books, 1993), esp. pp. 173–84.

8. Stephen Neill, *A History of Christian Missions* (New York: Penguin, 1977 [1964]), p. 179.

9. William R. Hutchison, *Errand to the World: American Protestant Thought and Foreign Missions* (Chicago: University of Chicago Press, 1987), pp. 77–84, 102–4. Quotes are from Anderson (p. 82) and William Newton Clarke (p. 104).

10. Rockefeller ("The Christian Church: What of Its Future?" [1918]), Buck, and R. Wayne Anderson in Hutchison, *Errand to the World*, pp. 148, 168, 203.

11. Joan Hoff Wilson, *Herbert Hoover: Forgotten Progressive* (Boston: Little, Brown, 1975),

pp. 5–7. Hoover's 1922 bestseller *American Individualism* specifically rejected "ruthless individualism."

12. David Burner, *Herbert Hoover: A Public Life* (New York: Atheneum, 1984), p. 115. Several of Hoover's ARA officials went on to distinguished careers. One of them, Eisenhower's secretary of state Christian Herter, said of Hoover, "He was the Chief, we were his boys, and we would have done anything in the world for him" (George H. Nash, *Herbert Hoover: The Humanitarian, 1914–1917* [New York: W. W. Norton, 1988], p. 376).

13. Benjamin M. Weissman, *Herbert Hoover and Famine Relief to Soviet Russia, 1921–1923* (Stanford: Hoover Institution Press, 1974), pp. 29–30.

14. Richard Norton Smith, *An Uncommon Man: The Triumph of Herbert Hoover* (New York: Simon and Schuster, 1984), p. 91.

15. Congressional opinion in Weissman, *Hoover and Famine Relief,* pp. 96–100; "battleships" quote in David Hinshaw, *Herbert Hoover: American Quaker* (New York: Farrar, Straus, 1950), p. 113; "helped to set the Soviet" quote in Wilson, *Forgotten Progressive,* p. 198.

16. See William J. Barber, *From New Era to New Deal: Herbert Hoover, the Economists, and American Economic Policy, 1921–1933* (New York: Cambridge University Press, 1985); Joan Hoff Wilson, *American Business and Foreign Policy, 1920–1933* (Lexington: University Press of Kentucky, 1971); Michael J. Hogan, *Informal Entente: The Private Structure of Cooperation in Anglo-American Economic Diplomacy, 1918–1928* (Columbia: University of Missouri Press, 1977).

17. One of Hoover's least-known projects was to prosper the American South, end black "peonage," and attract Negroes and "better white elements" to the Republican Party. See Donald J. Lisio, *Hoover, Blacks, and Lily-Whites: A Study of Southern Strategies* (Chapel Hill: University of North Carolina Press, 1985).

18. Walter Isaacson and Evan Thomas, *The Wise Men: Six Friends and the World They Made* (New York: Simon and Schuster, 1986), p. 220.

19. The remark was made by Louis Douglas, financial adviser to General Lucius D. Clay: Robert Murphy, *Diplomat among Warriors* (Garden City, N.Y.: Doubleday, 1950), p. 251.

20. David Culbert, "American Film Policy in the Re-Education of Germany," and other essays in Nicholas Pronay and Keith Wilson, eds., *The Political Re-Education of Germany and Her Allies* (Totowa, N.J.: Barnes and Noble, 1985).

21. Poll data in Richard L. Merritt, *Democracy Imposed: U.S. Occupation Policy and the German Public, 1945–1949* (New Haven: Yale University Press, 1995), pp. 97, 322. The swaggering U.S. official was chief of the military government in Bavaria: John Gimbel, *The American Occupation of Germany: Politics and the Military, 1945–1949* (Stanford: Stanford University Press, 1968), pp. 252, 257.

22. James F. Tent, *Mission on the Rhine: Re-education and Denazification in American-Occupied Germany* (Chicago: University of Chicago Press, 1982), p. 318; Edward N. Peterson, *The American Occupation of Germany: Retreat to Victory* (Detroit: Wayne State University Press, 1977), pp. 351–52.

23. Merritt, *Democracy Imposed,* p. 395.

24. Jean Edward Smith, *Lucius D. Clay: An American Life* (New York: Holt, 1990), p. 244.

25. Richard B. Finn, *Winners in Peace: MacArthur, Yoshida, and Postwar Japan* (Berkeley: University of California Press, 1992), p. 29.

NOTES

26. Joseph Grew, *Turbulent Era: A Diplomatic Record of Forty Years, 1904–1945*, 2 vols. (Boston: Houghton Mifflin, 1952), 2:1420.

27. See, for instance, the critical appraisal of MacArthur in Michael Schaller, *The American Occupation of Japan: The Origins of the Cold War in Asia* (New York: Oxford University Press, 1985); the favorable appraisals in Theodore Cohen, *Remaking Japan: The American Occupation as New Deal* (New York: Free Press, 1987), and Richard B. Finn, *Winners in Peace: MacArthur, Yoshida, and Postwar Japan* (Berkeley: University of California Press, 1972); and the problematical ones in Meirion and Susan Harries, *Sheathing the Sword: The Demilitarization of Japan* (New York: Macmillan, 1972), and John W. Dower, *Empire and Aftermath: Yoshida Shigeru and the Japanese Experience, 1878–1954* (Cambridge: Harvard University Press, 1979).

28. Yoshida Shigeru, *The Yoshida Memoirs: The Story of Japan in Crisis* (Westport, Conn.: Greenwood, 1973 [1961]), pp. 284–88.

29. On the origins and meaning of the Marshall Plan, contrast the interpretations of Hadley Arkes, *Bureaucracy, the Marshall Plan, and the National Interest* (Princeton: Princeton University Press, 1972); Michael J. Hogan, *The Marshall Plan: America, Britain, and the Reconstruction of Western Europe, 1947–1952* (New York: Cambridge University Press, 1987); and Charles L. Mee, Jr., *The Marshall Plan: The Launching of the Pax Americana* (New York: Simon and Schuster, 1984).

30. Harry Bayard Price, *The Marshall Plan and Its Meaning* (Ithaca: Cornell University Press, 1955), p. 398.

31. *U.S. News* suggested, "The real idea behind the program, thus, is that the United States, to prevent a depression at home, must put up the dollars that it will take to prevent a collapse abroad" (July 4, 1947): Robert E. Wood, *From Marshall Plan to Debt Crisis: Foreign Aid and Development Choices in the World Economy* (Berkeley: University of California Press, 1986), p. 36.

32. Charles S. Maier, "The Two Postwar Eras and the Conditions for Stability in Twentieth-Century Western Europe," *American Historical Review* 86 (April 1981): 327–52. On the variety of interpretations, see Hogan, *Marshall Plan*, 1–25, 430–32.

33. A British official groused, "The Americans want an integrated Europe looking like the United States of America — 'God's own country'": Hogan, *Marshall Plan*, p. 427. See also Alan S. Milward, *The Reconstruction of Western Europe, 1945–1951* (Berkeley: University of California Press, 1984), pp. 462–502.

34. McCloy in Isaacson and Thomas, *The Wise Men*, p. 732; Clayton in Wood, *From Marshall Plan to Debt Crisis*, p. 45.

35. Wallace in Peter W. Rodman, *More Precious Than Peace: The Cold War and the Struggle for the Third World* (New York: Scribner's, 1994), p. 62; State Department officer Joseph Marion Jones, *The Fifteen Weeks* (New York: Harcourt, Brace, and World, 1955), pp. 262–63.

36. Sallie Pisani, *The CIA and the Marshall Plan* (Lawrence: University Press of Kansas, 1991), p. 121.

37. Walter M. Daniels, ed., *The Point Four Program* (New York: H. W. Wilson, 1951), pp. 10–11.

38. Chester Bowles (May 13, 1951), *Far East Advertiser* (May 1951), and Galbraith in *Commentary* (Sept. 1950) in Daniels, *The Point Four Program*, pp. 34–38, 38–42, 47. See also Nelson A. Rockefeller et al., *Partners in Progress: A Report to President Tru-*

man by the International Development Advisory Board (New York: Simon and Schuster, 1951).

39. *The Herblock Book* (Boston: Beacon Press, 1952), in Robert S. Alley, *So Help Me God: Religion and the Presidency from Wilson to Nixon* (Richmond: John Knox Press, 1972), p. 74.

40. Morgenthau in Robert A. Goldwin, ed., *Why Foreign Aid?* (Chicago: Rand McNally, 1963), p. 82; Kissinger, *The Necessity for Choice: Prospects for American Foreign Policy* (New York: Harper and Bros., 1961), pp. 290–91.

41. Eisenhower's televised speech on foreign aid (May 21, 1957) in Rodman, *More Precious Than Peace*, p. 66.

42. Nicholas Eberstadt, *Foreign Aid and American Purpose* (Washington, D.C.: American Enterprise Institute, 1988), pp. 79–80.

43. John Lewis Gaddis, *Strategies of Containment: A Critical Appraisal of Postwar American National Security Policy* (New York: Oxford University Press, 1982), pp. 208–9.

44. Walt W. Rostow, *The Diffusion of Power: An Essay in Recent History* (New York: Macmillan, 1972), p. 89.

45. As early as 1960 he noted that the "instinctive effort to apply in the transitional areas the moral and institutional canons of American diplomatic practice yielded a series of frustrations and failure," most notably in China, thus challenging the "assumption that democracy in the American image was automatically and everywhere the wave of the future and morally right" (Walt W. Rostow, *The United States in the World Arena* [New York: Harper and Row, 1960], p. 479).

46. Walt W. Rostow, *The Stages of Economic Growth: A Non-Communist Manifesto* (New York: Cambridge University Press, 1960), p. 143.

47. David Halberstam, *The Best and the Brightest* (New York: Fawcett Crest, 1973), pp. 193–200 (quote p. 195).

48. Walt W. Rostow, *An American Policy in Asia* (Cambridge: MIT Press, 1955), p. 42.

49. Roger C. Riddell, *Foreign Aid Reconsidered* (Baltimore: Johns Hopkins University Press, 1987), p. 6.

50. "Special Message to the Congress on Urgent National Needs," May 25, 1961, *Public Papers of the Presidents: John F. Kennedy, 1961* (Washington, D.C.: GPO, 1962), pp. 396–406.

51. Walt W. Rostow, *Eisenhower, Kennedy, and Foreign Aid* (Austin: University of Texas Press, 1985), pp. 61–63.

52. Rostow, *Eisenhower, Kennedy, and Foreign Aid*, pp. 6–7.

53. Gaddis Smith, *The Last Years of the Monroe Doctrine, 1945–1993* (New York: Hill and Wang, 1994), p. 17. Latin elites jokingly said, "Gracias, Fidel" for this U.S. aid, but when the Americans asked in return for social reforms to benefit the poorest classes, authoritarian governments cried "*Yanqui* imperialism" and resisted interference in their internal affairs.

54. Rostow, *Eisenhower, Kennedy, and Foreign Aid*, pp. 170–71.

55. Rostow, *Diffusion of Power*, p. 185.

56. Rostow himself sat on the fence. He was the guru of developmental economics, but later stressed "that the most important pre-condition for take-off is often political" (*The Economics of Take-off into Sustained Growth* [New York: St. Martin's, 1968], p. xxvi).

57. Patrick Lloyd Hatcher, *The Suicide of an Elite: American Internationalists and Vietnam* (Stanford: Stanford University Press, 1990), pp. 19–20.

58. Hatcher, *Suicide of an Elite*, p. 66.

59. Rodman, *More Precious Than Peace*, p. 115.

60. Henry Kissinger, *Diplomacy* (New York: Simon and Schuster, 1994), p. 649.

61. Thomas G. Paterson et al., *American Foreign Policy: A History*, vol. 2, *Since 1900*, 3d ed. (Lexington, Mass.: D. C. Heath, 1991), p. 551.

62. Nitze in Larry Cable, *Unholy Grail: The U.S. and the Wars in Vietnam, 1965–1968* (London: Routledge, 1991), p. 4; Rostow in Lawrence S. Wittner, *Cold War America: From Hiroshima to Watergate* (New York: Praeger, 1974), p. 244.

63. NSAM 52 (May 11, 1961) in *The Pentagon Papers*, ed. Neil Sheehan et al. (New York: Quadrangle, 1971), p. 131.

64. British guerrilla war guru Sir Robert Grainger Ker Thompson in *Defeating Communist Insurgency* (1966), cited by Hatcher, *Suicide of an Elite*, p. 137.

65. LaFeber, *American Age*, p. 579.

66. George Ball, *The Past Has Another Pattern: Memoirs* (New York: W. W. Norton, 1982), p. 208. Ball was the sole Johnson administration official who questioned the deepening U.S. involvement and warned of disaster.

67. Seymour J. Deitchman, *The Best-Laid Scheme: A Tale of Social Research and Bureaucracy* (Cambridge: MIT Press, 1976), p. 4.

68. Quotes in Deitchman, *Best-Laid Scheme*, pp. 116, 7, 28. See also Irving Louis Horowitz, ed., *The Rise and Fall of Project Camelot* (Cambridge: MIT Press, 1967).

69. Harry G. Summers, Jr., *On Strategy: A Critical Analysis of the Vietnam War* (New York: Dell, 1984 [1982]), p. 229.

70. Cecil B. Currey, *Edward Lansdale: The Unquiet American* (Boston: Houghton Mifflin, 1988), p. 197. U.S. agronomists, doctors, and teachers in Vietnam did great good as individuals and, like missionaries, were often martyred. When Joseph Grainger was captured in 1964 the Vietcong held him up for ridicule, but villagers gave him food and water and said he was a good man. Realizing their error, the VC marched him to a province in which he was unknown for his ritual humiliation and torture. Grainger was "shot while trying to escape" in January 1965. See George K. Tanham, *War Without Guns: American Civilians in Rural Vietnam* (New York: Praeger, 1966), pp. 128–29.

71. "Footprints" in Paterson, *American Foreign Policy*, p. 553; "overriding rule" in Robert Dallek, *The American Style of Foreign Policy: Cultural Politics and Foreign Affairs* (New York: Knopf, 1983), p. 243; "had its origins" in Richard A. Hunt, *Pacification: The American Struggle for Vietnam's Hearts and Minds* (Boulder: Westview, 1995), p. 1.

72. William Conrad Gibbons, *The U.S. Government and the Vietnam War: Executive and Legislative Roles and Relationships*, part 4, *July 1965–January 1968* (Princeton: Princeton University Press, 1995), pp. 56–57, 61–62.

73. As one marine general growled about a pacification plan called Battle for Five Mountains: "It would be far easier to seize the high ground on five actual mountains than win over the people in these villages. This is a people's war. Terrain here doesn't mean a goddamn thing. If you have the people you don't need the terrain. And the only ones who can win back the people are the Vietnamese" (Richard Critchfield,

The Long Charade: Political Subversion in the Vietnam War [New York: Harcourt, Brace, and World, 1968], p. 279).

74. Hunt, *Pacification*, p. 71; Gardner, *Pay Any Price*, p. 284.

75. Frances FitzGerald, *Fire in the Lake: The Vietnamese and the Americans in Vietnam* (Boston: Little, Brown, 1972), pp. 232–35.

76. Hunt, *Pacification*, p. 80.

77. Gardner, *Pay Any Price*, p. 303. Based on U.S. spending of $135 billion from 1965 to 1972 and an estimated 400,000 enemy dead, the "price per enemy corpse" was really more like $337,500 (Hatcher, *Suicide of an Elite*, p. 270).

78. Maxwell D. Taylor, *Swords and Plowshares* (New York: W. W. Norton, 1972), p. 165.

79. Hunt, *Pacification*, pp. 25–30.

80. Hatcher, *Suicide of an Elite*, p. 107.

81. Interview with George Allen (May 3, 1996) in Cameron Pforr, "Pacification in Vietnam: America's Experiment in Nation-Building" (unpublished paper). As Pforr notes, Lodge's statement is especially fatuous given his complicity in the overthrow of Diem just three years before.

82. David M. Barrett, *Uncertain Warriors: Lyndon Johnson and His Vietnam Advisers* (Lawrence: University Press of Kansas, 1993), p. 90.

83. John Prados, *The Hidden History of the Vietnam War* (Chicago: Ivan R. Dee, 1995), pp. 209–19.

84. Thomas C. Thayer, *War Without Fronts: The American Experience in Vietnam* (Boulder: Westview, 1985), p. 237. Fifteen hectares equal about 37 acres; 100 hectares equal 247 acres.

85. Norman B. Hannah, *The Key to Failure: Laos and the Vietnam War* (Lanham, Md.: Madison Books, 1987), p. 306.

86. Douglas Dacy, *Foreign Aid, War, and Economic Development: South Vietnam, 1955–1975* (New York: Cambridge University Press, 1986), pp. 20–21, 259.

87. The data and "contagion of despair" in Samuel Lipsman and Stephen Weiss, *The False Peace, 1972–1974* (Boston: Boston Publishing, 1985), pp. 136–42.

88. Pye in Anthony Lake, ed., *The Vietnam Legacy* (New York: New York University Press, 1976), p. 380; Gingrich in George Donelson Moss, *Vietnam: An American Ordeal*, 2d ed. (Englewood Cliffs: Prentice-Hall, 1994), p. 311.

89. J. William Fulbright, *The Arrogance of Power* (New York: Random House, 1966), p. 236.

90. Paterson, *American Foreign Policy*, p. 562.

91. Poll data in Vernon W. Ruttan, *United States Development Assistance Policy: The Domestic Politics of Foreign Economic Aid* (Baltimore: Johns Hopkins University Press, 1996), p. 110; Nixon quoted in David Wall, *The Charity of Nations: The Political Economy of Foreign Aid* (New York: Basic Books, 1973), pp. 41–42.

92. Nicholas Eberstadt, *Foreign Aid and American Purpose* (Washington: American Enterprise Institute, 1988), pp. 37–38.

93. A thorough statistical survey of the foreign aid issue in the 1970s is Martin M. McLaughlin, *The United States and World Development: Agenda 1979* (New York: Praeger, 1979).

94. See Donald S. Spencer, *The Carter Implosion: Jimmy Carter and the Amateur Style of Diplomacy* (New York: Praeger, 1988), p. 127.

95. World Bank, *The McNamara Years, 1968–1981* (Baltimore: Johns Hopkins University Press, 1981), p. 120.

96. For a summary of rightist critiques, see P. T. Bauer, *Development Aid: End It or Mend It* (San Francisco: Institute for Contemporary Studies Press, 1993), and Desmond McNeill, *The Contradictions of Foreign Aid* (London: Croom Helm, 1981). A typical leftist critique is Teresa Hayter, *Aid as Imperialism* (Harmondsworth, England: Penguin, 1971).

97. *Public Papers of the Presidents: Jimmy Carter, 1977* (Washington, D.C.: GPO, 1978), 2:955–62.

98. Gaddis Smith, *Morality, Reason, and Power: American Diplomacy in the Carter Years* (New York: Hill and Wang, 1986), p. 50.

99. Spencer, *The Carter Implosion*, pp. 54–59.

100. Gaddis Smith, *Morality, Reason, and Power*, p. 37.

101. Timothy P. Maga, *The World of Jimmy Carter: U.S. Foreign Policy, 1977–1981* (West Haven: University of New Haven Press, 1995), pp. 24–25.

102. Spencer, *The Carter Implosion*, p. 5.

CONCLUSION

1. Walt W. Rostow, "The National Style," in Elting E. Morison, ed., *The American Style: Essays in Value and Performance* (New York: Harper and Bros., 1958), pp. 248–49.

2. Arkady N. Shevchenko, *Breaking With Moscow* (New York: Knopf, 1985), p. 279, cited by Peter W. Rodman, *More Precious Than Peace: The Cold War and the Struggle for the Third World* (New York: Scribner's, 1994), p. 541.

3. Francis Fukuyama, *The End of History and the Last Man* (New York: Free Press, 1992).

4. Henry Kissinger, *Diplomacy* (New York: Simon and Schuster, 1994).

5. Samuel P. Huntington, "A Clash of Civilizations?" *Foreign Affairs* 72 (summer 1993): 22–49. I anticipated this notion in my "Speculations on the Geopolitics of the Gorbachev Era," Alfred J. Rieber and Alvin Z. Rubinstein, eds., *Perestroika at the Crossroads* (Armonk, N.Y.: M. E. Sharpe, 1991), pp. 326–62.

6. Edward N. Luttwak, *The Endangered American Dream: How to Stop the United States from Becoming a Third World Country and How to Win the Geo-Economic Struggle for Industrial Supremacy* (New York: Simon and Schuster, 1993).

7. Paul Kennedy, *Preparing for the Twenty-first Century* (New York: Random House, 1993); Jessica Tuchman Mathews, "Redefining Security," *Foreign Affairs* 68 (spring 1989): 162–77; Robert D. Kaplan, "The Coming Anarchy and the Nation-State Under Siege" (Washington, D.C.: U.S. Institute of Peace, 1995). For a summary of contrasting theories, see Alexander Nacht, "U.S. Foreign Policy Strategies," *Washington Quarterly* 18, no. 3 (summer 1995): 195–210.

8. Norman J. Ornstein and Mark Schmitt, "Post–Cold War Politics," in Charles W. Kegley, Jr., and Eugene R. Wittkopf, eds., *The Future of American Foreign Policy* (New York: St. Martin's, 1992), p. 122. Proponents of aggressive American leadership with a bias toward international organization range from the Harvard political scientist Joseph P. Nye, *Bound to Lead: The Changing Nature of American Power* (New York: Basic Books, 1990), to American Enterprise Institute fellow Joshua Muravchik, *The Im-*

perative of American Leadership: A Challenge to Neo-Isolationism (Washington, D.C.: AEI Press, 1996).

9. William Kristol and Robert Kagan, "Toward a Neo-Reaganite Foreign Policy," *Foreign Affairs* 75, no. 4 (July–August 1996): 18–32.

10. Zakaria, "Back to a 'Big Stick' Foreign Policy," *Wall Street Journal* (July 31, 1995); Kristol, "America Dreaming," *Wall Street Journal* (Aug. 3, 1995); Kissinger, *Diplomacy*, chap. 31; and Rodman, *More Precious Than Peace*, chap. 18. The quote is from Kristol.

11. Eric A. Nordlinger, *Isolationism Reconfigured: American Foreign Policy for a New Century* (Princeton: Princeton University Press, 1995). Nordlinger died before the book appeared. For the argument about 1941, he relied on Bruce M. Russett's provocative *No Clear and Present Danger: A Skeptical View of U.S. Entry into World War II* (New York: Harper and Row, 1972), which asserts that the Nazis, having failed by December 7, 1941, to defeat the USSR, were bound to lose the war whether or not the United States became a belligerent.

12. Albright on U.N. Resolution 814 (March 26, 1993), *Facts on File*, April 1, 1993, p. 224; Lake, "From Containment to Enlargement," speech to the Paul H. Nitze School of Advanced International Studies, Johns Hopkins University (Sept. 21, 1993); Clinton, "Confronting the Challenges of a Broader World," *Department of State Dispatch* (Sept. 27, 1993): 650.

13. Michael Mandelbaum, "Foreign Policy as Social Work," *Foreign Affairs* 75, no. 1 (Jan.-Feb. 1996): 16–32 (quote p. 18). Anthony Lake himself said, "I think Mother Teresa and Ronald Reagan were both trying to do the same thing — one helping the helpless, one fighting the Evil Empire. One of the nice things about this job is you can do both at the same time and not see them as contradictory" ("The Man Inside Bill Clinton's Foreign Policy," *New York Times Magazine* [Aug. 20, 1995]: 35).

14. Warren Christopher, "Leadership for the Next American Century," speech at Harvard University (Jan. 18, 1996), *Department of State Dispatch;* "Jimmy Carter Says U.S. Foreign Policy Is Racist," *Philadelphia Inquirer* (Jan. 28, 1996). The phenomenon of Lewis and other former doves turning into post–Cold War hawks is treated at length in Alvin Z. Rubinstein, "The New Moralists on a Road to Hell," *Orbis* 40, no. 2 (spring 1996): 277–95.

15. See Camille Paglia, "A White Liberal Women's Conference," *New York Times* (Sept. 1, 1995).

16. Cited by Walt W. Rostow, *Essays on a Half-Century: Ideas, Policies, and Action* (Boulder: Westview, 1988), p. 30.

17. Williams, *The Contours of American History* (Cleveland: World Publishing, 1961), pp. 95–96. On Williams's thought and career, see Paul M. Buhle and Edward Rice-Maximin, *William Appleman Williams: The Tragedy of Empire* (New York: Routledge, 1995).

18. J. William Fulbright, *The Arrogance of Power* (New York: Random House, 1966), pp. 245–46.

19. As Michael Vlahos recently put it, the American mission has been made up of two opposing parts: "It must preserve itself from the world at the same time it proselytizes to that world," and both political parties, in all eras of our history, have had "to balance 'purifiers' and 'progressives.'" See "The End of America's Postwar Ethos," *Foreign Affairs* 66, no. 5 (summer 1988): 1091–1107 (quote p. 1093).

20. Reinhold Niebuhr, *Moral Man and Immoral Society* (New York: Scribner's, 1932), pp. 256, 266–67, 277.

21. Churchill cited by Clarke, "The Conceptual Poverty of U.S. Foreign Policy," *Atlantic Monthly* (Sept. 1993): 54–66 (quote p. 63).

22. Owen Harries, "My So-called Foreign Policy: The Case for Clinton's Diplomacy," *New Republic* (Oct. 10, 1994): 24–31 (quote p. 31).

23. Robert D. Kaplan, "Where America Stands amid the Mini-Holocausts," *Washington Post Weekly Edition* (April 25–May 1, 1994).

24. *Forbes* (March 11, 1996), p. 193. The study was directed by economist Peter Boone for the National Bureau of Economic Research.

25. Irving Kristol, "Who Now Cares About NATO," *Wall Street Journal* (Feb. 6, 1995).

26. Richard F. Grimmett, "Instances of Use of United States Armed Forces Abroad, 1798–1995" (Washington, D.C.: Congressional Research Service, 1996).

27. See, most recently, Joshua Muravchik, *The Imperative of American Leadership: A Challenge to Neo-Isolationism* (Washington, D.C.: AEI Press, 1996), which adds still another antinomy, or false dichotomy, to the discourse by dividing everyone up into "Washingtonians" and "Wilsonians."

28. From Isaac Watts's popular hymnal of the early nineteenth century, in William Gribbin, *The Churches Militant: The War of 1812 and American Religion* (New Haven: Yale University Press, 1973), p. 98.

29. Margaret Thatcher's address to the Congress of Prague, "The West after the Cold War," *Wall Street Journal* (May 14, 1996).

30. Christopher Hitchens, *Blood, Class, and Nostalgia: Anglo-American Ironies* (New York: Farrar, Straus, and Giroux, 1990), p. 360.

31. Clarke, "Conceptual Poverty," p. 65. At least the Brits are polite about it. In 1956 a choleric Gaullist fumed, "There would be less anti-Americanism in the world if America abandoned its philanthropic aspirations, its vocation of Santa Claus, its transcendental morality, all its missionary trappings, all its boy scout gear, and if, at last, it followed openly and intelligently the policy of its own self-interest" (Raymond Cartier in Rodman, *More Precious Than Peace*, p. 72).

32. George F. Kennan, *At a Century's Ending: Reflections, 1982–1995* (New York: W. W. Norton, 1996), p. 282. The article from which the quotation is drawn was written in 1985.

33. Kennan, "On American Principles," *Foreign Affairs* 74, no. 2 (March-April 1995): 116–26 (quote p. 125).

Bibliography

Acheson, Dean. *Present at the Creation: My Years in the State Department.* New York: W. W. Norton, 1969.

Adams, Henry. *The Education of Henry Adams: An Autobiography.* Cambridge, Mass.: Riverside, 1961 (1907).

———. *The Degradation of the Democratic Dogma.* New York: Macmillan, 1919.

Adams, John. *The Works of John Adams.* Edited by Charles Francis Adams. 10 vols. Boston: Little, Brown, 1853–56.

Adams, John Quincy. *The Memoirs of John Quincy Adams.* Edited by Charles Francis Adams. 12 vols. Philadelphia: Lippincott, 1874–77.

———. *The Writings of John Quincy Adams.* Edited by Worthington C. Ford. 7 vols. New York: Macmillan, 1913–17.

Alley, Robert S. *So Help Me God: Religion and the Presidency from Wilson to Nixon.* Richmond: John Knox, 1972.

Almond, Gabriel A. *The American People and Foreign Policy.* New York: Harcourt, Brace, 1950.

Ambrose, Stephen T. *Rise to Globalism: American Foreign Policy Since 1938.* 4th ed. New York: Penguin, 1985.

Ambrosius, Lloyd E. *Woodrow Wilson and the American Diplomatic Tradition: The Treaty Fight in Perspective.* Cambridge: Cambridge University Press, 1987.

———. *Wilsonian Statecraft: Theory and Practice of Liberal Internationalism During World War I.* Wilmington: Scholarly Resources, 1991.

Ammon, Harry. *The Genêt Mission.* New York: W. W. Norton, 1973.

Appleby, Joyce. *Capitalism and a New Social Order: The Republican Vision of the 1790s.* New York: New York University Press, 1984.

Arkes, Hadley. *Bureaucracy, the Marshall Plan, and the National Interest.* Princeton: Princeton University Press, 1972.

Bailey, Thomas A. *Wilson and the Peacemakers.* New York: Macmillan, 1947.

———. *The Man in the Street: The Impact of American Public Opinion on Foreign Policy.* New York: Macmillan, 1948.

———. *A Diplomatic History of the American People.* 8th ed. New York: Appleton-Century-Crofts, 1969.

Bailey, Thomas A., and Paul B. Ryan. *The Lusitania Disaster.* New York: Free Press, 1975.

Bailyn, Bernard. *The Ideological Origins of the American Revolution.* Cambridge: Harvard University Press, 1967.

Baker, Ray Stannard. *Woodrow Wilson: Life and Letters.* 8 vols. Garden City, N.Y.: Doubleday Page, 1927–39.

Ball, George. *The Past Has Another Pattern: Memoirs.* New York: W. W. Norton, 1982.

Bandow, Doug, and Ian Vásquez. *Perpetuating Poverty: The World Bank, the IMF, and the Developing World.* Washington, D.C.: Cato Institute, 1994.

Barber, William J. *From New Era to New Deal: Herbert Hoover, the Economists, and American Economic Policy, 1921–1933.* New York: Cambridge University Press, 1985.

Barrett, David M. *Uncertain Warriors: Lyndon Johnson and His Vietnam Advisers.* Lawrence: University of Kansas Press, 1993.

Bauer, Peter. *Development Aid: End It or Mend It.* San Francisco: Institute for Contemporary Studies, 1993.

Beard, Charles A. *The Republic.* New York: Viking, 1944.

Beisner, Robert L. *Twelve Against Empire: The Anti-Imperialists, 1898–1900.* New York: McGraw-Hill, 1968.

———. *From the Old Diplomacy to the New, 1865–1900.* Arlington Heights, Ill.: AHM Publishing, 1975.

Bemis, Samuel Flagg. *The Latin American Policy of the U.S.: A Historical Interpretation.* New York: Harcourt, Brace, 1943.

———. *American Foreign Policy and the Blessings of Liberty, and Other Essays.* New Haven: Yale University Press, 1962.

———. *John Quincy Adams and the Foundations of American Foreign Policy.* New York: Knopf, 1965.

———. *The Diplomacy of the American Revolution.* Bloomington: Indiana University Press, 1975 (1935).

Berkhofer, Robert F. *The White Man's Indian: Images of the American Indian from Columbus to the Present.* New York: Knopf, 1978.

Bertram, Marshall. *The Birth of Anglo-American Friendship: The Prime Facet of the Venezuelan Boundary Dispute.* Lanham, Md.: University Press of America, 1992.

Binder, Frederick Moore. *James Buchanan and the American Empire.* Selinsgrove, Pa.: Susquehanna University Press, 1994.

Blum, John Morton. *Woodrow Wilson and the Politics of Morality.* Boston: Little, Brown, 1956.

Boorstin, Daniel J. *The Republic of Technology: Reflections on Our Future Community.* New York: Harper and Row, 1978.

Bowman, Albert Hall. *The Struggle for Neutrality: Franco-American Diplomacy During the Federalist Era.* Knoxville: University of Tennessee Press, 1974.

Bradford, James C., ed. *Admirals of the New Steel Navy.* Annapolis: Naval Institute, 1990.

Bragdon, Henry Wilkinson. *Woodrow Wilson: The Academic Years.* Cambridge: Harvard University Press, 1967.

Buehrig, Edward H. *Woodrow Wilson and the Balance of Power.* Bloomington: Indiana University Press, 1955.

Burner, David. *Herbert Hoover: A Public Life.* New York: Atheneum, 1984.

Burstein, Stanley M. "Greece, Rome, and the American Republic." *Laebertis: The Journal of the California Classical Association* 10 (new series, 1993–94).

Cable, Larry E. *Conflict of Myths: The Development of American Counterinsurgency Doctrine and the Vietnam War.* New York: New York University Press, 1986.

———. *Unholy Grail: The U.S. and the Wars in Vietnam, 1965–1968.* London: Routledge, 1991.

Challener, Richard D. *Admirals, Generals, and American Foreign Policy, 1898–1914.* Princeton: Princeton University Press, 1973.

Challener, Richard D., ed. *From Isolation to Containment, 1921–1952*. New York: St. Martin's, 1970.

Clarfield, Gerard. *United States Diplomatic History*. 2 vols. Englewood Cliffs: Prentice-Hall, 1992.

Clarke, Jonathan. "The Conceptual Poverty of U.S. Foreign Policy." *Atlantic Monthly* 272, no. 3 (Sept. 1993).

Clarke, Jonathan, and James Clad. *After the Crusade: American Foreign Policy for the Post–Superpower Age*. Lanham, Md.: Madison Books, 1995.

Cohen, Theodore. *Remaking Japan: The American Occupation as New Deal*. New York: Free Press, 1987.

Cohen, Warren I. *The Cambridge History of American Foreign Relations*. Vol. 4, *America in the Age of Soviet Power, 1945–1991*. Cambridge: Cambridge University Press, 1993.

Cohen, Warren I., and Nancy Bernkopf Tucker, eds. *Lyndon Johnson Confronts the World: American Foreign Policy, 1963–1968*. Cambridge: Cambridge University Press, 1994.

Collin, Richard H. *Theodore Roosevelt, Culture, Diplomacy, and Expansion: A New View of American Imperialism*. Baton Rouge: Louisiana State University Press, 1985.

Combs, Jerald A. *The Jay Treaty: Political Battleground of the Founding Fathers*. Berkeley: University of California Press, 1970.

———. *American Diplomatic History: Two Centuries of Changing Interpretations*. Berkeley: University of California Press, 1983.

Compilation of the Messages and Papers of the Presidents. Edited by James D. Richardson. 20 vols. New York: Bureau of National Literature, 1897–1917.

Continental Congress. *Journals of the Continental Congress, 1774–1789*. Edited by Worthington C. Ford et al. 34 vols. Washington, D.C.: GPO, 1904–37.

Conyne, C. R. *Woodrow Wilson: British Perspectives, 1912–1921*. New York: St. Martin's, 1992.

Coogan, John W. *The End of Neutrality: The United States, Britain, and Maritime Rights, 1899–1915*. Ithaca: Cornell University Press, 1981.

Cook, Warren L. *Flood Tide of Empire: Spain and the Pacific Northwest, 1543–1819*. New Haven: Yale University Press, 1973.

Cooper, John Milton. *The Warrior and the Priest: Woodrow Wilson and Theodore Roosevelt*. Cambridge: Harvard University Press, 1983.

Cords, Nicholas, and Patrick Gerster. *Myth and the American Experience*. 2 vols. New York: Harper Collins, 1991.

Critchfield, Richard. *The Long Charade: Political Subversion in the Vietnam War*. New York: Harcourt, Brace, and World, 1968.

Croly, Herbert. *The Promise of American Life*. New York: Bobbs-Merrill, 1965 (1909).

Crunden, Robert M. *Ministers of Reform: The Progressives' Achievement in American Civilization, 1889–1920*. New York: Basic Books, 1982.

Currey, Cecil B. *Edward Lansdale: The Unquiet American*. Boston: Houghton Mifflin, 1988.

Dacy, Douglas. *Foreign Aid, War, and Economic Development: South Vietnam, 1955–1975*. New York: Cambridge University Press, 1986.

Dallek, Robert. *Franklin D. Roosevelt and American Foreign Policy, 1932–1945*. New York: Oxford University Press, 1979.

————. *The American Style of Foreign Policy: Cultural Politics and Foreign Affairs.* New York: Knopf, 1983.

Danaher, Kevin, ed. *Fifty Years Is Enough: The Case Against the World Bank and the International Monetary Fund.* Boston: South End Press, 1994.

Daniels, Walter M., ed. *The Point Four Program.* New York: H. W. Wilson, 1951.

Davies, Joseph E. *Mission to Moscow.* New York: Simon and Schuster, 1941.

Davis, Calvin DeArmond. *The United States and the Second Hague Peace Conference: American Diplomacy and International Organization, 1899–1914.* Durham: Duke University Press, 1975.

DeConde, Alexander. *This Affair of Louisiana.* New York: Scribner's, 1976.

————. *Ethnicity, Race, and American Foreign Policy: A History.* Boston: Northeastern University Press, 1992.

Deitchman, Seymour J. *The Best-Laid Scheme: A Tale of Social Research and Bureaucracy.* Cambridge: MIT Press, 1976.

Destler, I. M., Leslie Gelb, and Anthony Lake. *Our Own Worst Enemy: The Unmaking of American Foreign Policy.* New York: Simon and Schuster, 1984.

Divine, Robert A. *The Illusion of Neutrality: Franklin D. Roosevelt and the Struggle over the Arms Embargo.* Chicago: University of Chicago Press, 1962.

————. *Roosevelt and World War II.* New York: Penguin, 1969.

————. *Second Chance: The Triumph of Internationalism in America During World War II.* New York: Atheneum, 1971.

————. *The Reluctant Belligerent: American Entry into World War II.* 2d ed. New York: Knopf, 1979.

————. *Since 1945: Politics and Diplomacy in Recent American History.* 3d ed. New York: Knopf, 1985.

Doenecke, Justus D., ed. *In Danger Undaunted: The Anti-Interventionist Movement of 1940–1941 as Revealed in the Papers of the America First Committee.* Stanford: Hoover Institution, 1990.

Dower, John. *Empire and Aftermath: Yoshida Shigeru and the Japanese Experience, 1878–1954.* Cambridge: Harvard University Press, 1979.

Drake, Frederick G. *The Empire of the Seas: A Biography of Rear-Admiral Robert N. Shufeldt.* Honolulu: University of Hawaii Press, 1984.

Drinnon, Richard. *Facing West: The Metaphysics of Indian-Hating and Empire-Building.* Minneapolis: University of Minnesota Press, 1980.

Dull, Jonathan R. *A Diplomatic History of the American Revolution.* New Haven: Yale University Press, 1985.

Dulles, Foster Rhea. *America's Rise to World Power, 1898–1954.* New York: Harper and Row, 1954.

————. *The Imperial Years.* New York: Thomas Crowell, 1956.

————. *Prelude to World Power: American Diplomatic History, 1860–1900.* New York: Macmillan, 1965.

Duroselle, Jean-Baptiste. *From Wilson to Roosevelt: Foreign Policy of the United States, 1913–1945.* New York: Harper and Row, 1968.

Eberstadt, Nicholas. *Foreign Aid and American Purpose.* Washington, D.C.: American Enterprise Institute, 1988.

Eisenhower, John. *So Far from God: The U.S. War with Mexico, 1846–1848.* New York: Random House, 1989.

BIBLIOGRAPHY

————. *Intervention! The United States and the Mexican Revolution, 1913–1917.* New York: W. W. Norton, 1993.

Engelhardt, Tom. *The End of Victory Culture.* New York: Basic Books, 1995.

Farnsworth, Beatrice. *William C. Bullitt and the Soviet Union.* Bloomington: Indiana University Press, 1967.

Faust, Drew Gilpin. "A Southern Stewardship: The Intellectual and the Pro-Slavery Argument." *American Quarterly* 31, no. 1 (spring 1979).

Ferrell, Robert H. *Foundations of American Diplomacy, 1775–1872.* Columbia: University of South Carolina Press, 1968.

————. *Woodrow Wilson and World War I, 1917–1921.* New York: Harper and Row, 1985.

Finn, Richard B. *Winners in Peace: MacArthur, Yoshida, and Postwar Japan.* Berkeley: University of California Press, 1992.

FitzGerald, Frances. *Fire in the Lake: The Vietnamese and the Americans in Vietnam.* Boston: Little, Brown, 1972.

Fleming, Denna Frank. *The United States and the World Court.* Garden City, N.Y.: Doubleday, 1945.

————. *The United States and the League of Nations, 1918–1920.* New York: Russell and Russell, 1968.

Forrestal, James. *The Forrestal Diaries.* Edited by Walter Mills. New York: Viking, 1951.

Fossedal, Gregory A. *Our Finest Hour: Will Clayton, the Marshall Plan, and the Triumph of Democracy.* Stanford: Hoover Institution, 1993.

Friedenberg, Robert V. *Theodore Roosevelt and the Rhetoric of Militant Decency.* Westport, Conn.: Greenwood, 1990.

Fromkin, David. *In the Time of the Americans: The Generation That Changed America's Role in the World.* New York: Knopf, 1995.

Fulbright, J. William. *The Arrogance of Power.* New York: Random House, 1966.

Gaddis, John Lewis. *The United States and the Origins of the Cold War.* New York: Columbia University Press, 1972.

————. *Strategies of Containment: A Critical Appraisal of Postwar American National Security Policy.* New York: Oxford University Press, 1982.

————. *The Long Peace: Inquiries into the History of the Cold War.* New York: Oxford University Press, 1987.

Gardner, Lloyd C. *Safe for Democracy: The Anglo-American Response to Revolution, 1913–1923.* New York: Oxford University Press, 1987.

————. *Pay Any Price: Lyndon Johnson and the Wars for Vietnam.* Chicago: Ivan R. Dee, 1995.

Gelb, Leslie H., with Richard K. Betts. *The Irony of Vietnam: The System Worked.* Washington, D.C.: Brookings Institution, 1979.

Gibbons, William Conrad. *The U.S. Government and the Vietnam War: Executive and Legislative Roles and Relationships.* Princeton: Princeton University Press, 1995.

Gilbert, Felix. *To the Farewell Address: Ideas of Early American Foreign Policy.* Princeton: Princeton University Press, 1961.

Gimbel, John. *The American Occupation of Germany: Politics and the Military, 1945–1949.* Stanford: Stanford University Press, 1968.

Goetzmann, William H. *When the Eagle Screamed: The Romantic Horizon in American Diplomacy, 1800–1860.* New York: John Wiley and Sons, 1966.

Goldwin, Robert A., ed. *Why Foreign Aid?* Chicago: Rand McNally, 1963.

BIBLIOGRAPHY

Graebner, Norman A. *Manifest Destiny.* Indianapolis: Bobbs-Merrill, 1968.

————. *America as a World Power: A Realist Appraisal from Wilson to Reagan.* Wilmington, Del.: Scholarly Resources, 1984.

————. *Foundations of American Foreign Policy: A Realist Appraisal from Franklin to McKinley.* Wilmington, Del.: Scholarly Resources, 1985.

Graebner, Norman A., ed. *Traditions and Values: American Diplomacy, 1790–1865* and *1865–1945.* 2 vols. Lanham, Md.: University Press of America, 1985.

Grew, Joseph C. *Turbulent Era: A Diplomatic Record of Forty Years, 1904–1945.* 2 vols. Boston: Houghton Mifflin, 1952.

Gribbin, William. *The Churches Militant: The War of 1812 and American Religion.* New Haven: Yale University Press, 1973.

Guhin, Michael A. *John Foster Dulles: A Statesman and His Times.* New York: Columbia University Press, 1972.

Gunderson, Gray. *The Log Cabin Campaign.* Lexington: University of Kentucky Press, 1957.

Halberstam, David. *The Best and the Brightest.* New York: Random House, 1972.

Hamilton, Alexander, John Jay, and James Madison. *The Federalist: A Commentary on the Constitution of the United States.* New York: Modern Library, 1937.

Hamilton, Michael P., ed. *American Character and Foreign Policy.* Grand Rapids: Eerdmans, 1986.

Hammond, Paul Y. *Cold War and Détente: The American Foreign Policy Process Since 1945.* New York: Harcourt Brace Jovanovich, 1975.

Hannah, Norman B. *The Key to Failure: Laos and the Vietnam War.* Lanham, Md.: Madison Books, 1987.

Harbutt, Fraser. *The Iron Curtain: Churchill, America, and the Origins of the Cold War.* New York: Oxford University Press, 1986.

Harries, Meirion, and Susan Harries. *Sheathing the Sword: The Demilitarization of Japan.* New York: Macmillan, 1972.

Hartz, Louis. *The Liberal Tradition in America.* New York: Harcourt, Brace, and World, 1955.

Hatcher, Patrick Lloyd. *The Suicide of an Elite: American Internationalists and Vietnam.* Stanford: Stanford University Press, 1990.

Hayter, Teresa. *Aid as Imperialism.* Harmondsworth, England: Penguin, 1971.

Heald, Morrell, and Lawrence S. Kaplan. *Culture and Diplomacy: The American Experience.* Westport, Conn.: Greenwood, 1977.

Healy, David. *U.S. Expansionism: The Imperialist Urge in the 1890s.* Madison: University of Wisconsin Press, 1970.

Hickey, Donald R. *The War of 1812: A Forgotten Conflict.* Urbana: University of Illinois Press, 1989.

Hietala, Thomas R. *Manifest Design: Anxious Aggrandizement in Late Jacksonian America.* Ithaca: Cornell University Press, 1985.

Higginson, Thomas Wentworth. *A Larger History of the United States of America to the Close of President Jackson's Administration.* New York: Harper and Bros., 1886.

Hinshaw, David. *Herbert Hoover: American Quaker.* New York: Farrar, Straus, 1950.

Hitchens, Christopher. *Blood, Class, and Nostalgia: Anglo-American Ironies.* New York: Farrar, Straus, and Giroux, 1990.

Hoffmann, Stanley. *Gulliver's Troubles, or the Setting of American Foreign Policy.* New York: McGraw-Hill, 1968.

BIBLIOGRAPHY

Hofstadter, Richard. *The Paranoid Style in American Politics and Other Essays.* New York: Knopf, 1966.

Hogan, Michael J. *Informal Entente: The Private Structure of Cooperation in Anglo-American Economic Diplomacy, 1918–1928.* Columbia: University of Missouri Press, 1977.

——— . *The Marshall Plan: America, Britain, and the Reconstruction of Western Europe, 1947–1952.* New York: Cambridge University Press, 1987.

Hoopes, Townsend. *The Devil and John Foster Dulles.* Boston: Little, Brown, 1973.

Hoopes, Townsend, and Douglas Brinkley. *Driven Patriot: The Life and Times of James Forrestal.* New York: Knopf, 1992.

Hoover, Herbert. *The Ordeal of Woodrow Wilson.* Washington, D.C.: Woodrow Wilson Center Press, 1992 (1958).

Horowitz, Irving Louis, ed. *The Rise and Fall of Project Camelot.* Cambridge: MIT Press, 1967.

Horsman, Reginald. *Race and Manifest Destiny: The Origins of American Racial Anglo-Saxonism.* Cambridge: Harvard University Press, 1981.

Howard, Michael. *War and the Liberal Conscience.* New Brunswick: Rutgers University Press, 1978.

Hudson, Winthrop S., ed. *Nationalism and Religion in America: Concepts of American Identity and Mission.* New York: Harper and Row, 1970.

Hughes, Emmet John. *The Ordeal of Power: A Political Memoir of the Eisenhower Years.* New York: Dell, 1963.

Hunt, Michael H. *Ideology and U.S. Foreign Policy.* New Haven: Yale University Press, 1987.

Hunt, Richard A. *Pacification: The American Struggle for Vietnam's Hearts and Minds.* Boulder: Westview, 1995.

Hutchison, William R. *Errand to the World: American Protestant Thought and Foreign Missions.* Chicago: University of Chicago Press, 1987.

Hutson, James H. *John Adams and the Diplomacy of the American Revolution.* Lexington: University of Kentucky Press, 1980.

Ireland, Timothy P. *Creating the Entangling Alliance: The Origins of the North Atlantic Treaty Organization.* Westport, Conn.: Greenwood, 1981.

Iriye, Akira. *From Nationalism to Internationalism: U.S. Foreign Policy to 1914.* London: Routledge and Kegan Paul, 1977.

——— . *The Cambridge History of American Foreign Relations.* Vol. 3, *The Globalizing of America, 1913–1945.* Cambridge: Cambridge University Press, 1993.

Isaacson, Walter, and Evan Thomas. *The Wise Men: Six Friends and the World They Made.* New York: Simon and Schuster, 1986.

Israel, Jerry. *Progressivism and the Open Door.* Pittsburgh: University of Pittsburgh Press, 1971.

Jaffa, Harry. *Crisis of the House Divided.* Seattle: University of Washington Press, 1973.

Jefferson, Thomas. *The Writings of Thomas Jefferson.* Edited by Andrew A. Lipscomb and Albert E. Bergh. 20 vols. Washington, D.C.: Jefferson Memorial Association, 1903–4.

Jonas, Manfred. *Isolationism in America, 1935–1941.* Ithaca: Cornell University Press, 1966.

Jones, Joseph Marion. *The Fifteen Weeks.* New York: Harcourt, Brace, and World, 1955.

Jones, Wilbur Devereux. *The American Problem in British Diplomacy, 1841–1861.* New York: Macmillan, 1974.

Kammen, Michael. *Empire and Interest: The American Colonies and the Politics of Mercantilism.* Philadelphia: Lippincott, 1970.

————. *People of Paradox: An Inquiry into the Origins of American Civilization.* New York: Knopf, 1973.

————. *A Season of Youth: The American Revolution and the Historical Imagination.* New York: Knopf, 1978.

Kaplan, Lawrence S. *Colonies into Nation: American Diplomacy, 1763–1801.* New York: Macmillan, 1965.

————. *Entangling Alliances with None.* Kent, Ohio: Kent State University Press, 1987.

Karnow, Stanley. *Vietnam: A History.* New York: Viking, 1983.

————. *In Our Image: America's Empire in the Philippines.* New York: Random House, 1989.

Kegley, Charles W., and Eugene R. Wittkopf. *The Future of American Foreign Policy.* New York: St. Martin's, 1992.

Kennan, George F. *Russia and the West under Lenin and Stalin.* New York: Mentor, 1961.

————. *Memoirs, 1925–1950.* New York: Bantam Books, 1969.

————. *American Diplomacy, 1900–1950.* Expanded ed. Chicago: University of Chicago Press, 1984.

————. *At a Century's Ending: Reflections, 1982–1995.* New York: W. W. Norton, 1996.

————. "On American Principles." *Foreign Affairs* 74, no. 2 (March-April 1995).

Kirkendall, Richard S. *A Global Power: America Since the Age of Roosevelt.* 2d ed. New York: Knopf, 1980.

Kissinger, Henry. *The Necessity for Choice: Prospects for American Foreign Policy.* New York: Harper and Bros., 1961.

————. *American Foreign Policy: Three Essays.* New York: W. W. Norton, 1969.

————. *Diplomacy.* New York: Simon and Schuster, 1994.

Knock, Thomas J. *To End All Wars: Woodrow Wilson and the Quest for a New World Order.* New York: Oxford University Press, 1992.

Kolko, Gabriel. *The Politics of War: The World and United States Foreign Policy, 1943–1945.* New York: Vintage, 1968.

Komer, Robert W. *Bureaucracy at War.* Boulder: Westview, 1986.

Kraus, Michael. *A History of American History.* New York: Farrar and Rinehart, 1937.

Kuklick, Bruce. *American Policy and the Division of Germany: The Clash with Russia over Reparations.* Ithaca: Cornell University Press, 1972.

Kushner, Norman I. *Conflict on the Northwest Coast: American-Russian Rivalry in the Pacific Northwest, 1790–1867.* Westport, Conn.: Greenwood, 1975.

Kuykendall, Ralph S. *The Hawaiian Kingdom.* Vol. 1, Foundation and Transformation, 1778–1854. Honolulu: University of Hawaii Press, 1947.

Lacour-Gayet, Robert. *Everyday Life in the United States before the Civil War, 1830–1860.* New York: Frederick Ungar, 1969.

LaFeber, Walter. *The New Empire: An Interpretation of American Expansion, 1860–1898.* Ithaca: Cornell University Press, 1963.

————. *John Quincy Adams and American Continental Empire.* Chicago: University of Chicago Press, 1965.

————. *The American Age: United States Foreign Policy at Home and Abroad Since 1763.* New York: W. W. Norton, 1989.

————. *The Cambridge History of American Foreign Relations.* Vol. 2, The American Search for Opportunity, 1865–1913. Cambridge: Cambridge University Press, 1993.

Lake, Anthony. *Third World Radical Regimes: U.S. Policy under Carter and Reagan.* New York: Foreign Policy Association, 1985.

Lake, Anthony, ed. *The Vietnam Legacy.* New York: New York University Press, 1976.

Leffler, Melvyn. *The Elusive Quest: America's Pursuit of European Stability and French Security, 1919–1933.* Chapel Hill: University of North Carolina Press, 1979.

——— . *A Preponderance of Power: National Security, the Truman Administration, and the Cold War.* Stanford: Stanford University Press, 1992.

Lens, Sidney. *The Forging of the American Empire.* New York: Thomas Crowell, 1971.

Leuchtenberg, William. "Progressivism and Imperialism: The Progressive Movement and American Foreign Policy, 1898–1916." *Mississippi Valley Historical Review* 39, no. 4 (Dec. 1952).

Levering, Ralph B. *American Opinion and the Russian Alliance, 1939–1945.* Chapel Hill: University of North Carolina Press, 1976.

Levin, N. Gordon. *Woodrow Wilson and World Politics: America's Response to War and Revolution.* New York: Oxford University Press, 1968.

Lincoln, Abraham. *The Collected Works of Abraham Lincoln.* Edited by R. P. Basler. New Brunswick: Rutgers University Press, 1953.

Link, Arthur S. *Woodrow Wilson and the Progressive Era, 1910–1917.* New York: Harper and Bros., 1954.

——— . *President Wilson and His English Critics: An Inaugural Lecture.* Oxford: Clarendon, 1959.

——— . *The Higher Realism of Woodrow Wilson and Other Essays.* Nashville: Vanderbilt University Press, 1971.

——— . *Woodrow Wilson: Revolution, War, and Peace.* Arlington Heights, Ill.: Harlan Davidson, 1979.

Link, Arthur S., ed. *Woodrow Wilson and a Revolutionary World, 1913–1921.* Chapel Hill: University of North Carolina Press, 1982.

Lippmann, Walter. *U.S. Foreign Policy: Shield of the Republic.* Boston: Little, Brown, 1943.

——— . *U.S. War Aims.* Boston: Little, Brown, 1944.

——— . *The Cold War: A Study in U.S. Foreign Policy.* New York: Harper and Bros., 1947.

——— . *Isolationism and Alliances: An American Speaks to the British.* Boston: Little, Brown, 1952.

Lipsman, Samuel, and Stephen Weiss. *The False Peace, 1972–1974.* Boston: Boston Publishing, 1985.

Lisio, Donald J. *Hoover, Blacks, and Lily-Whites: A Study of Southern Strategies.* Chapel Hill: University of North Carolina Press, 1985.

Lodge, Henry Cabot. *The Senate and the League of Nations.* New York: Scribner's, 1925.

Louis, William Roger. *Imperialism at Bay: The United States and the Decolonization of the British Empire, 1941–1945.* Oxford: Clarendon, 1986.

Lovell, S. D. *The Presidential Campaign of 1916.* Carbondale: Southern Illinois University Press, 1980.

Lower, Richard Coke. *A Bloc of One: The Political Career of Hiram W. Johnson.* Stanford: Stanford University Press, 1993.

Maga, Timothy P. *The World of Jimmy Carter: U.S. Foreign Policy, 1977–1981.* West Haven: University of New Haven Press, 1995.

Maier, Charles S. "The Two Postwar Eras and the Conditions for Stability in Twentieth-Century Western Europe." *American Historical Review* 86, no. 2 (April 1981).

Maier, Charles S., ed. *The Origins of the Cold War and Contemporary Europe.* New York: Franklin Watts, 1978.

BIBLIOGRAPHY

Mandelbaum, Michael. "Foreign Policy as Social Work." *Foreign Affairs* 75, no. 1 (Jan.-Feb. 1996).

Marks, Frederick W., III. *Independence on Trial: Foreign Affairs and the Making of the Constitution*. Baton Rouge: Louisiana State University Press, 1973.

———. *Velvet on Iron: The Diplomacy of Theodore Roosevelt*. Lincoln: University of Nebraska Press, 1979.

May, Ernest R. *The World War and American Isolation, 1914–1917*. Cambridge: Harvard University Press, 1959.

———. *Imperial Democracy: The Emergence of America as a Great Power*. New York: Harcourt, Brace, and World, 1961.

———. *American Imperialism: A Speculative Essay*. New York: Atheneum, 1968.

———. *The Making of the Monroe Doctrine*. Cambridge: Harvard University Press, 1975.

May, Ernest R., ed. *American Cold War Strategy: Interpreting NSC 68*. Boston: Bedford Books, 1993.

May, Glenn Anthony. *Social Engineering in the Philippines: The Aims, Execution, and Impact of American Colonial Policy, 1900–1913*. Westport: Greenwood, 1980.

McCormick, Thomas J., and Walter LaFeber, eds. *Behind the Throne: Servants of Power to Imperial Presidents, 1898–1968*. Madison: University of Wisconsin Press, 1993.

McDonald, Forrest. *Novus Ordo Seclorum: The Intellectual Origins of the Constitution*. Lawrence: University Press of Kansas, 1985.

McDougall, Walter A. *. . . the Heavens and the Earth: A Political History of the Space Age*. New York: Basic Books, 1985.

———. *Let the Sea Make a Noise: A History of the North Pacific from Magellan to MacArthur*. New York: Basic Books, 1993.

———. "20th-Century International Relations." *Encyclopaedia Britannica*. 15th ed. (1989 et seq.).

McKee, Delber L. *Chinese Exclusion Versus the Open Door Policy, 1900–1906*. Detroit: Wayne State University Press, 1977.

McLaughlin, Martin M. *The United States and World Development: Agenda 1979*. New York: Praeger, 1979.

McNeill, Desmond. *The Contradictions of Foreign Aid*. London: Croom Helm, 1981.

McNeill, William H. *America, Britain, and Russia: Their Cooperation and Conflict, 1941–1946*. Oxford: Oxford University Press, 1953.

Mee, Charles L., Jr. *The Marshall Plan: The Launching of the Pax Americana*. New York: Simon and Schuster, 1984.

Merk, Frederick. *Albert Gallatin and the Oregon Problem*. Cambridge: Harvard University Press, 1950.

———. *Manifest Destiny and Mission in American History*. New York: Vintage, 1966 (1963).

Merli, Frank, and Theodore A. Wilson, eds. *Makers of American Diplomacy*. New York: Scribner's, 1974.

Merritt, Richard L. *Democracy Imposed: U.S. Occupation Policy and the German Public, 1945–1949*. New Haven: Yale University Press, 1995.

Middlekauff, Robert. *The Glorious Cause: The American Revolution, 1763–1789*. New York: Oxford University Press, 1982.

Milward, Alan S. *The Reconstruction of Western Europe, 1945–1951*. Berkeley: University of California Press, 1984.

BIBLIOGRAPHY

Monroe, James. *The Writings of James Monroe*. Edited by Stanislaus Murray Hamilton. 7 vols. New York: G. P. Putnam's Sons, 1893–1903.

Morgan, H. Wayne. *America's Road to Empire: The War with Spain and Overseas Expansion*. New York: Knopf, 1965.

Morgenthau, Hans J. *In Defense of the National Interest: A Critical Examination of American Foreign Policy*. New York: Knopf, 1951.

Morison, Elting E., ed. *The American Style: Essays in Value and Performance*. New York: Harper and Bros., 1958.

Morris, Richard. *The Peacemakers: The Great Powers and American Independence*. New York: Harper and Row, 1965.

Moss, George Donelson. *Vietnam: An American Ordeal*. 2d ed. Englewood Cliffs: Prentice-Hall, 1994.

Muravchik, Joshua. *Exporting Democracy: Fulfilling America's Destiny*. Washington, D.C.: American Enterprise Institute, 1991.

——— . *The Imperative of American Leadership: A Challenge to Neo-Isolationism*. Washington, D.C.: American Enterprise Institute, 1996.

Murphy, Robert. *Diplomat among Warriors*. Garden City, N.Y.: Doubleday, 1950.

Nacht, Alexander. "U.S. Foreign Policy Strategies." *Washington Quarterly* 18, no. 3 (summer 1995).

Nash, George H. *Herbert Hoover: The Humanitarian, 1914–1917*. New York: W. W. Norton, 1988.

Neill, Stephen. *A History of Christian Missions*. New York: Penguin, 1977 (1964).

Niebuhr, Reinhold. *The Children of Light and the Children of Darkness*. New York: Scribner's, 1944.

Nighswonger, William A. *Rural Pacification in Vietnam*. New York: Praeger, 1966.

Nordlinger, Eric A. *Isolationism Reconfigured: American Foreign Policy for a New Century*. Princeton: Princeton University Press, 1995.

Nye, Joseph F. *Bound to Lead: The Changing Nature of American Power*. New York: Basic Books, 1990.

O'Brien, Francis William, ed. *Two Peacemakers in Paris: The Hoover-Wilson Post-Armistice Letters, 1918–1920*. College Station: Texas A&M University Press, 1978.

Offner, Arnold A. *The Origins of the Second World War: American Foreign Policy and World Politics, 1917–1941*. New York: Praeger, 1975.

Olcott, Charles S. *Life of William McKinley*. 2 vols. Boston: Houghton Mifflin, 1916.

Osborne, Thomas J. *"Empire Can Wait": American Opposition to Hawaiian Annexation, 1893–1898*. Kent, Ohio: Kent State University Press, 1981.

Osgood, Robert E. *Ideals and Self-Interest in America's Foreign Relations*. Chicago: University of Chicago Press, 1953.

Paolino, Ernest N. *The Foundations of the American Empire: William Henry Seward and U.S. Foreign Policy*. Ithaca: Cornell University Press, 1973.

Paterson, Thomas G., ed. *Major Problems in American Foreign Policy*. Vol. 1, *To 1914*, and vol. 2, *Since 1900*. Lexington, Mass.: D. C. Heath, 1989.

Paterson, Thomas G., J. Garry Clifford, and Kenneth J. Hagan. *American Foreign Policy: A History*. Vol. 1, *To 1914*, and vol. 2, *Since 1900*. 3d ed. Lexington, Mass.: D. C. Heath, 1988.

Patterson, James T. *Mr. Republican: A Biography of Robert A. Taft*. Boston: Houghton Mifflin, 1972.

Pentagon Papers, The. Edited by Neil Sheehan et al. New York: Quadrangle Books, 1971.

Perkins, Bradford. *Prologue to War, 1805–1812: England and the United States.* Berkeley: University of California Press, 1961.

———. *The Cambridge History of American Foreign Relations.* Vol. 1, *The Creation of a Republican Empire, 1776–1865.* Cambridge: Cambridge University Press, 1993.

Perkins, Dexter. *The Monroe Doctrine, 1823–1826.* Baltimore: Johns Hopkins University Press, 1927.

———. *The Monroe Doctrine, 1826–1867.* Baltimore: Johns Hopkins University Press, 1933.

———. *The Monroe Doctrine, 1867–1907.* Baltimore: Johns Hopkins University Press, 1937.

Peterson, Edward N. *The American Occupation of Germany: Retreat to Victory.* Detroit: Wayne State University Press, 1977.

Pike, Fredrick B. *FDR's Good Neighbor Policy: Sixty Years of Generally Gentle Chaos.* Austin: University of Texas Press, 1995.

Pisani, Sallie. *The CIA and the Marshall Plan.* Lawrence: University of Kansas Press, 1991.

Pletcher, David M. *The Awkward Years: American Foreign Policy under Garfield and Arthur.* Columbia: University of Missouri Press, 1962.

———. *The Diplomacy of Annexation: Texas, Oregon, and the Mexican War.* Columbia: University of Missouri Press, 1973.

———. "Rhetoric and Results: A Pragmatic View of American Economic Expansion." *Diplomatic History* 5 (spring 1981).

Polk, James K. *The Diary of James K. Polk.* Edited by Milo Milton Quaife. 4 vols. Chicago: McClung, 1910.

Prados, John. *The Hidden History of the Vietnam War.* Chicago: Ivan R. Dee, 1995.

Pratt, Julius W. *Expansionists of 1898: The Acquisition of Hawaii and the Spanish Islands.* Baltimore: Johns Hopkins University Press, 1936.

———. *A History of United States Foreign Policy.* New York: Prentice-Hall, 1955.

Price, Harry Bayard. *The Marshall Plan and Its Meaning.* Ithaca: Cornell University Press, 1955.

Pronay, Nicholas, and Keith Wilson, eds. *The Political Re-Education of Germany and Her Allies.* Totowa, N.J.: Barnes and Noble, 1985.

Public Papers and Addresses of Franklin D. Roosevelt. Edited by Samuel I. Roseman. New York: Harper and Bros., 1938–50.

Public Papers of the Presidents. Washington, D.C.: GPO, 1957–.

Race, Jeffrey. *War Comes to Long An.* Berkeley: University of California Press, 1972.

Rappaport, Armin. *A History of American Diplomacy.* New York: Macmillan, 1975.

Reeves, Jesse. *American Diplomacy under Tyler and Polk.* Baltimore: Johns Hopkins University Press, 1907.

Remini, Robert V. *Andrew Jackson and the Course of American Empire, 1767–1821.* New York: Harper and Row, 1977.

———. *Andrew Jackson and the Course of American Freedom, 1822–1832.* New York: Harper and Row, 1981.

Riddell, Roger C. *Foreign Aid Reconsidered.* Baltimore: Johns Hopkins University Press, 1987.

Rockefeller, Nelson A., et al. *Partners in Progress: A Report to President Truman by the International Development Advisory Board.* New York: Simon and Schuster, 1951.

Rodman, Peter W. *More Precious Than Peace: The Cold War and the Struggle for the Third World.* New York: Scribner's, 1994.

Roosevelt, Theodore. *The Winning of the West: An Account of the Exploration and Settlement of Our Country from the Alleghanies to the Pacific.* 6 vols. New York: G. P. Putnam's Sons, 1889–96.

——— . *The Letters of Theodore Roosevelt.* Edited by Elting E. Morison. 8 vols. Cambridge: Harvard University Press, 1951–54.

Rorabaugh, W. J. *The Alcoholic Republic.* New York: Oxford University Press, 1979.

Rostow, Eugene V. *A Breakfast for Bonaparte: U.S. National Security Interests from the Heights of Abraham to the Nuclear Age.* Washington, D.C.: National Defense University Press, 1993.

Rostow, Walt W. *An American Policy in Asia.* Cambridge: MIT Press, 1955.

——— . *The Stages of Economic Growth: A Non-Communist Manifesto.* New York: Cambridge University Press, 1960.

——— . *The United States in the World Arena.* New York: Harper and Row, 1960.

——— . *The Diffusion of Power: An Essay in Recent History.* New York: Macmillan, 1972.

——— . *Eisenhower, Kennedy, and Foreign Aid.* Austin: University of Texas Press, 1985.

Rostow, Walt W., ed. *The Economics of Take-off into Sustained Growth.* New York: St. Martin's, 1968.

Rush, Benjamin. *Letters of Benjamin Rush.* Edited by Lyman Henry Butterfield. 2 vols. Princeton: Princeton University Press, 1951.

Russett, Bruce M. *No Clear and Present Danger: A Skeptical View of the United States' Entry into World War II.* New York: Harper and Row, 1972.

Ruttan, Vernon W. *United States Development Assistance Policy: The Domestic Politics of Foreign Economic Aid.* Baltimore: Johns Hopkins University Press, 1996.

Safford, Jeffrey J. *Wilsonian Maritime Diplomacy, 1913–1921.* New Brunswick: Rutgers University Press, 1978.

Savelle, Max. *The Origins of American Diplomacy: The International History of Angloamerica, 1492–1763.* New York: Macmillan, 1967.

Saxton, Alexander. *The Rise and Fall of the White Republic: Class Politics and Mass Culture in Nineteenth-Century America.* New York: Verso, 1990.

Schaller, Michael. *The American Occupation of Japan: The Origins of the Cold War in Asia.* New York: Oxford University Press, 1985.

Schlesinger, Arthur M., Jr. *The Cycles of American History.* Boston: Houghton Mifflin, 1986.

Scholes, Marie V. *The Foreign Policies of the Taft Administration.* Columbia: University of Missouri Press, 1970.

Schroeder, Paul. *The Transformation of European Politics, 1763–1848.* Oxford: Clarendon, 1994.

Schulzinger, Robert D. *American Diplomacy in the Twentieth Century.* New York: Oxford University Press, 1984.

Schurmann, Franz. *The Logic of World Power.* New York: Random House, 1974.

Schutz, John A., and Douglas Adair, eds. *The Spur of Fame: Dialogues of John Adams and Benjamin Rush, 1805–1813.* San Marino, Calif.: Huntington Library, 1966.

Seymour, Charles, ed. *The Intimate Papers of Colonel House.* 2 vols. Boston: Houghton Mifflin, 1926.

Shapley, Deborah. *Promise and Power: The Life and Times of Robert McNamara.* Boston: Little, Brown, 1993.

Sherman, William Roderick. *The Diplomatic and Commercial Relations of the United States and Chile, 1820–1924*. New York: Russell and Russell, 1973 (1926).

Sherwood, R. E. *Roosevelt and Hopkins: An Intimate History*. New York: Harper and Bros., 1948.

Skaggs, Jimmy M. *The Great Guano Rush: Entrepreneurs and American Overseas Expansion*. New York: St. Martin's, 1994.

Smith, Daniel M. *The American Diplomatic Experience*. Boston: Houghton Mifflin, 1972.

Smith, Gaddis. *American Diplomacy during the Second World War*. 2d ed. New York: Knopf, 1985.

———. *Morality, Reason, and Power: American Diplomacy in the Carter Years*. New York: Hill and Wang, 1986.

———. *The Last Years of the Monroe Doctrine, 1945–1993*. New York: Hill and Wang, 1994.

Smith, Jean Edward. *Lucius D. Clay: An American Life*. New York: Holt, 1990.

Smith, Richard Norton. *An Uncommon Man: The Triumph of Herbert Hoover*. New York: Simon and Schuster, 1984.

Smith, Timothy L. "Righteousness and Hope: Christian Holiness and the Millennial Vision in America, 1880–1900." *American Quarterly* 31, no. 1 (spring 1979).

Smith, Tony. *America's Mission: The United States and the Worldwide Struggle for Democracy in the Twentieth Century*. Princeton: Princeton University Press, 1994.

Spencer, Donald S. *The Carter Implosion: Jimmy Carter and the Amateur Style of Diplomacy*. New York: Praeger, 1988.

Steigerwald, David. *Wilsonian Idealism in America*. Ithaca: Cornell University Press, 1994.

Strausz-Hupé, Robert. *Geopolitics*. New York: G. P. Putnam's Sons, 1942.

Strout, Cushing. *The American Image of the Old World*. New York: Harper and Row, 1963.

———. *The New Heavens and New Earth: Political Religion in America*. New York: Harper and Row, 1973.

Summers, Harry G., Jr. *On Strategy: A Critical Analysis of the Vietnam War*. New York: Dell, 1984.

Tanham, George K. *War Without Guns: American Civilians in Rural Vietnam*. New York: Praeger, 1966.

Tansill, Charles Callan. *The Foreign Policy of Thomas Francis Bayard, 1885–1897*. New York: Fordham University Press, 1940.

Taylor, Maxwell D. *Swords and Plowshares*. New York: W. W. Norton, 1972.

Tent, James F. *Mission on the Rhine: Re-education and Denazification in American-Occupied Germany*. Chicago: University of Chicago Press, 1982.

Thayer, Thomas C. *War Without Fronts: The American Experience in Vietnam*. Boulder: Westview, 1985.

Thies, Wallace J. *When Governments Collide: Coercion and Diplomacy in the Vietnam Conflict, 1964–1968*. Berkeley: University of California Press, 1980.

Thorsen, Niels Aage. *The Political Thought of Woodrow Wilson, 1875–1910*. Princeton: Princeton University Press, 1988.

Tocqueville, Alexis de. *Democracy in America*. New York: Vintage Books, 1945 (1834).

Tompkins, C. David. *Senator Arthur H. Vandenberg: The Evolution of a Modern Republican*. East Lansing: Michigan State University Press, 1970.

Trachtenberg, Marc. *History and Strategy*. Princeton: Princeton University Press, 1991.

Trask, David F. *Victory Without Peace: American Foreign Relations in the Twentieth Century*. New York: John Wiley and Sons, 1968.

Truman, Harry S. *Memoirs: Year of Decisions*. Garden City, N.Y.: Doubleday, 1955.

Turner, Frederick Jackson. *The Frontier in American History*. New York: Henry Holt, 1920.

Tuveson, Ernest Lee. *Redeemer Nation: The Idea of America's Millennial Role*. Chicago: University of Chicago Press, 1968.

Tyler, Alice Felt. *Freedom's Ferment*. Minneapolis: University of Minnesota Press, 1944.

Valentine, Douglas. *The Phoenix Program*. New York: William Morrow, 1990.

Van Alstyne, Richard W. *Genesis of American Nationalism*. Waltham, Mass.: Blaisdell, 1970.

Varg, Paul A. *Foreign Policies of the Founding Fathers*. East Lansing: Michigan State University Press, 1963.

—————. *United States Foreign Relations, 1820–1860*. East Lansing: Michigan State University Press, 1979.

—————. *America: From Client State to World Power*. Norman: University of Oklahoma Press, 1990.

Vlahos, Michael. "The End of America's Postwar Ethos." *Foreign Affairs* 66, no. 5 (summer 1988).

Wall, David. *The Charity of Nations: The Political Economy of Foreign Aid*. New York: Basic Books, 1973.

Wallace, Anthony F. C. *The Long, Bitter Trail: Andrew Jackson and the Indians*. New York: Hill and Wang, 1993.

Walters, Raymond, Jr. *Albert Gallatin: Jeffersonian Financier and Diplomat*. New York: Macmillan, 1957.

Warren, Charles. *Jacobin and Junto*. Cambridge: Harvard University Press, 1931.

Webster, C. K., ed. *Britain and the Independence of Latin America, 1812–1830*. 2 vols. London: Oxford University Press, 1938.

Weinberg, Albert K. *Manifest Destiny: A Study of Nationalist Expansionism in American History*. Baltimore: Johns Hopkins University Press, 1935.

Weisbrand, Edward. *The Ideology of American Foreign Policy: A Paradigm of Lockean Liberalism*. Beverly Hills: Sage Publications, 1973.

Weissman, Benjamin D. *Herbert Hoover and Famine Relief to Soviet Russia, 1921–1923*. Stanford: Hoover Institution Press, 1974.

Weston, Rubin Francis. *Racism in U.S. Imperialism: The Influence of Racial Assumptions on American Foreign Policy, 1893–1946*. Columbia: University of South Carolina Press, 1972.

Whitaker, Arthur Preston. *The United States and the Independence of Latin America, 1800–1830*. New York: W. W. Norton, 1964 (1941).

Wiebe, Robert H. *The Opening of American Society: From the Adoption of the Constitution to the Eve of Disunion*. New York: Knopf, 1984.

Wilkes, Charles. *Narrative of the United States Exploring Expedition during the Years 1838, 1839, 1840, 1841, 1842*. 5 vols. Philadelphia: Lee and Blanchard, 1845.

Wilkins, Mira. *The Emergence of Multinational Enterprise, 1776–1914*. Cambridge: Harvard University Press, 1970.

—————. *The Maturing of Multinational Enterprise, 1914–1970*. Cambridge: Harvard University Press, 1974.

Williams, William Appleman. *The Tragedy of American Diplomacy*. New York: Harper and Row, 1959.

Willkie, Wendell. *One World*. New York: Simon and Schuster, 1943.

Wills, Garry. *Cincinnatus: George Washington and the Enlightenment*. Garden City, N.Y.: Doubleday, 1984.

BIBLIOGRAPHY

Wilson, Joan Hoff. *American Business and Foreign Policy, 1920–1933.* Lexington: University of Kentucky Press, 1971.

———. *Herbert Hoover: Forgotten Progressive.* Boston: Little, Brown, 1975.

Wilson, T. Woodrow. *Congressional Government: A Study in American Politics.* 15th ed. Boston: Houghton Mifflin, 1900.

———. *The Public Papers of Woodrow Wilson.* Edited by Ray Stannard Baker and William E. Dodd. 6 vols. New York: Harper and Bros., 1925–27.

Wish, Harvey. *The American Historian: A Social-Intellectual History of the Writing of the American Past.* New York: Oxford University Press, 1960.

Wittner, Lawrence S. *Cold War America: From Hiroshima to Watergate.* New York: Praeger, 1974.

Wood, Gordon S. *The Creation of the American Republic, 1776–1787.* New York: W. W. Norton, 1972 (1969).

———. *The Radicalism of the American Revolution.* New York: Vintage, 1993.

Wood, Robert E. *From Marshall Plan to Debt Crisis: Foreign Aid and Development Choices in the World Economy.* Berkeley: University of California Press, 1986.

Woodward, C. Vann. *The Future of the Past.* New York: Oxford University Press, 1989.

World Bank. *The McNamara Years, 1968–1981.* Baltimore: Johns Hopkins University Press, 1981.

Wrobel, David M. *The End of American Exceptionalism: Frontier Anxiety from the Old West to the New Deal.* Lawrence: University Press of Kansas, 1993.

Yergin, Daniel. *Shattered Peace: The Origins of the Cold War and the National Security State.* Boston: Houghton Mifflin, 1978.

Yoshida Shigeru. *The Yoshida Memoirs: The Story of Japan in Crisis.* Westport, Conn.: Greenwood, 1973 (1961).

Index

INDEX

Chile, 65, 68, 73, 131, 231*n*38

China
Boxer Rebellion, 116
Communism in, 184
Japan vs., 104, 140, 145
Opium War, 79
as postwar power, 154, 156, 159
-U.S. relations, 96, 118, 120, 202, 220, 250*n*45
change in position, 8
containment, 171, 212
immigration restricted, 107, 116
"missionary diplomacy," 129
Open Door policy, 116, 145
trade treaties, 51, 107, 112
Chinese Exclusion Act (1882), 107
Choiseul, Étienne, 24
Christopher, Warren, 201, 202
Church, Frank, 195
Churchill, Winston, 151, 155, 156
"iron curtain" speech, 159, 160–61, 221
Churchman, The (journal), 112
Civil Operations and Revolutionary Development Support (CORDS), 191, 192, 193
Civil War, U.S., 1, 89, 97, 108
Clarke, Jonathan, 207, 221
Clarke, William, 24
Clay, Henry, 63, 64, 68, 69, 88, 95
Clay, General Lucius D., 164, 178, 248*n*19
Clayton, Will, 181
Clayton-Bulwer agreement (1850), 114
Clemenceau, Georges, 135, 140
Cleveland, Grover, 51, 101, 110, 206
refuses Hawaii, 108, 109, 111, 117
Clifford, Clark, 162, 180, 181
Clinton, Bill, 198, 201–2, 215, 216
Clinton, Hillary Rodham, 202
Colby, William, 192–93
Cold War, 2, 125, 146, 156, 169, 178, 183, 206, 212, 221, 247*n*71
begins, 161–66
containment of, see Containment
end of, 3–4, 170, 198, 200, 201, 211, 220
and global meliorism, 174, 179, 180, 197
militarizing of, 165, 170
Collin, Richard, 103
Colombia, 68, 72, 108, 114, 231*n*38
Columbian Exposition (1893), 103
Combs, Jerald, 40
Commission to Study the Organization of Peace (1941), 151

Committee of Secret Correspondence (1776), 24
Common Sense (Paine), 19, 24, 41, 45
Communism, 138, 183, 219
containment of, 148, 157–58, 168–69
in Europe and Third World, 160, 162–65 passim, 212, 219
fight against, 174–78 passim, 182–87 passim, 207, 208
and "isolationism," 149
U.S. and British distrust/fears of, 154, 155, 157, 158–61, 167, 196
and Vietnam, 184–87 passim, 192–96 passim
Conant, Charles, 116
Confucians, 219
Congress, U.S.
Communism as viewed by, 160
created, 27
globalism of, 125, 147
House of Representatives, 27, 111, 164
and Marshall Plan, 164
and neutrality, 133
post-Watergate, 196
Republicans control, 139, 146, 161
Senate, 18, 27, 125, 127, 137, 164
Foreign Relations Committee, 109, 141, 142, 152, 195
and Fourteen Points/League of Nations, 124, 125, 139–44 passim
Congressional Government (Wilson), 127, 128
Congress of Europe, 65
Congress of Prague, 220
Congress of Troppau, 60
Congress of Vienna, 60
Connolly, Tom, 152
Constitution, U.S., 5, 28
and foreign policy, 27, 37, 119
Wilson and, 127, 144
Constitutional Convention, 26, 225*n*31
Containment, 10, 147–71, 198, 199, 206, 207
bipartisan support of, 148
birth of, 166–69
Cold War and post-Cold War, 10–11, 148, 166–71 passim, 212
of Communism, 148, 157–58, 168–69
extended to Asia, 186
vs. global meliorism, 174
success of, 210–13
as U.S. tradition, 5, 167–68
Yalta and, 157–58

276

INDEX